OXFORD ENGLISH MONOGRAPHS

General Editors

CHRISTOPHER BUTLER   VINCENT GILLESPIE
DOUGLAS GRAY   EMRYS JONES
ROGER LONSDALE   FIONA STAFFORD

LATE SHAKESPEARE

A NEW WORLD OF WORDS

SIMON PALFREY

CLARENDON PRESS · OXFORD

OXFORD

UNIVERSITY PRESS

Great Clarendon Street, Oxford OX2 6DP

Oxford University Press is a department of the University of Oxford.
It furthers the University's objective of excellence in research, scholarship,
and education by publishing worldwide in

Oxford New York

Athens Auckland Bangkok Bogotá Buenos Aires Calcutta
Cape Town Chennai Dar es Salaam Delhi Florence Hong Kong Istanbul
Karachi Kuala Lumpur Madrid Melbourne Mexico City Mumbai
Nairobi Paris São Paulo Singapore Taipei Tokyo Toronto Warsaw

with associated companies in Berlin Ibadan

Oxford is a registered trade mark of Oxford University Press
in the UK and in certain other countries

Published in the United States
by Oxford University Press Inc., New York

© Simon Palfrey 1997

First published in paperback 1999

British Library Cataloguing in Publication Data

Data available

Library of Congress Cataloging in Publication Data

Palfrey, Simon.
Late Shakespeare : a new world of words / Simon Palfrey.
—(Oxford English monographs)
Includes bibliographical references (p.   ).
1. Shakespeare, William, 1564–1616—Tragicomedies.
2. Shakespeare, William, 1564–1616—Political and social views.
3. Politics and literature—Great Britain—History—17th century.
4. Political plays, English—History and criticism. 5. Shakespeare,
William, 1564–1616—Style. 6. Violence in literature.
7. Tragicomedy. 8. Metaphor. I. Title. II. Series.
PR2981.5.P34 1997 822.3'3—dc21 97-10036

ISBN 0-19-818619-3 (hbk)
ISBN 0-19-818689-4 (hbk)

1 3 5 7 9 10 8 6 4 2

Printed in Great Britain
on acid-free paper by
Bookcraft Ltd,
Midsomer Norton, Somerset

For my parents
BRIAN AND EILEEN

Preface

The title of this book is borrowed from a Jacobean Italian–English dictionary, called *Queen Anna's New World of Words*. Compiled by Montaigne's translator into English, John Florio, the dictionary was published in 1611, the same year as *The Tempest* was first acted. Florio's trumpet of a title points to the particular promise-crammed vigour of his historical moment: a moment whose plenty and potential Shakespeare's late plays seek to tap. The title attests to a growing philological pride and excitement, and a kind of custom-buttressed openness to innovation. Linguistic and civic self-consciousness were harnessing and invigorating one another. The spoken tongue, both intimate and exotic, was beginning to find artistic and printed canonization. Florio's dictionary, like the King James Bible and the works of Shakespeare, points to a self-defining, indeed 'patriotic', discourse in equal measure learned and vulgar. As Florio's bilingual work suggests, it was a time when the renaissance love of learning and discovery, having travelled north and west, was being filtered and transmuted in vernacular currency. An intertextual, cross-cultural, folk humanism began to spread, epitomized in the Elizabethan and Jacobean popular theatre.

At the same time, a 'New World of Words' evokes not only the travel of words, texts, ideas, but the recent opening and annexing of distant hemispheres. So, the new worlds in Shakespeare's late plays will certainly include *The Tempest*'s famously unlocatable island, with its teasing glances at imperial ambition and unillusioned responsiveness to colonial desire. But Florio's title, perhaps as wry or ironical as celebratory, intimates how it is language that is as much a missionary and expropriative force as guns, gold, or god. Consequently, the new worlds of my title will include each of the plays' fascination with the genetics of speech and writing, and with the political mutations of each. Furthermore, it invokes the romance genre's preoccupation with transformation, and with the desire as it were to alchemize freshness and justice out of malaise.

Such a basically *political* imperative suggests how the 'new world of words' is not, as it might literally imply, some hermetically sealed textual construct, abjuring clear historical accountability: far from it. None the less, there is in Shakespeare's late work a type of nominalism, in so far as he invests in his language a genuinely new constructive power; one might almost understand it as speech's 'self-accountability'. Characters are built out of metaphoric patterns: unlike the appropriative masteries of a Mercutio, Rosalind, Falstaff, of a Hamlet or Iago, speech is now manipulated in the service of Shakespeare's supra-characterological ambitions. There is a movement away from verisimilitude, into a kind of exploratory mode of discourse which is at base level responsible to Shakespeare's 'generic task'. And this task, conceived of in figurative terms, is one of replacing a more traditional genre's pre-Copernican 'meta-*body*' with a proleptically modern generic *brain*: a seat of stimulus, response, organization, complementarily crowded and individual, single- and multi-tracked, centrifugal and centripetal; where meaning is at once honed into present articulation, and banked up, latent but dynamic, in flowing currents of memory and desire. One must recover this sense of a tremendous over-determination, both sensuous and linguistic, which lends the plays their peculiarly cerebral density and energy. For the romance 'world of words' proffers its own contingent, inherently contrapuntal, laws of physics: within or around the hopeful verities of order and *telos*, it is an edgy universe of occluded origin and abrupt ellipses, of warps and falls and asymmetries, and of endings unresolved whatever the nostalgic pleadings.

Furthermore, and as the metaphor of a 'romance brain' will imply, this new liberty with language links to a novel use of the period's analogical architecture, and more particularly its instinct for microcosm. Shakespeare transforms the classic metaphors of a putatively harmonious 'world picture'. For instance, he is as likely to give a slave as a king the privilege of representing the social and ideological environment. Furthermore, any symbolizing burden is usually shared, or interpenetrating, among various characters; together they both 'are', and negotiate, the 'new world of words' that in turn creates them. So, not only in terms of genre, but of metaphor, politics, and character, the plays seek out and test new decorums. Hence their abstention from allegory. Allegory usually finds source in either traditional morality figures or contemporary repute: both are more static and grounded than suits these radically projective plays. For Shakespeare's characters are simply not discrete enough, and their language is too allusive, to peel off into straitened allegorical referents. And this almost amoeboid quality in turn suggests Shakespeare's faithfulness to his generic task of scrutiny, wanderlust, revivification. Late Shakespeare, then: a new world of words.

Acknowledgements

I owe thanks to many. For scholarly and creative help, encouragement, and advice, pre-eminently David Norbrook, but also John Pitcher, Graham Holderness, Nick Jacobs, Paul McNamara, and numerous students in Oxford and Melbourne; for financial aid, the Rhodes Trust and Jesus College, Oxford; for time off and other kind concessions, Denis White of the Trinity Education Centre, University of Melbourne; for permission to reproduce his ceramic 'Two-Ended Figure With Horns', Arthur Boyd; for ballast and whimsicality, the Renshaw and Palfrey families respectively; for much else, friends who know their credit; and for the rest, before and beyond all, Jo.

Contents

Abbreviations

All quotations from plays in Shakespeare's First Folio are taken from *The Norton Facsimile: The First Folio of Shakespeare*, prepared by Charlton Hinman (London, 1968).

I have used as my copy of *Pericles* the Malone copy of the 1609 quarto in the Bodleian, edited by W. W. Greg (London, 1940).

For ease of reference I have taken act, scene, and line numbers from the most recent Arden edition of each of Shakespeare's plays. For the four plays mainly studied this means: *Pericles*, ed. F. D. Hoeniger (London, 1963); *Cymbeline*, ed. J. M. Nosworthy (London, 1955); *The Winter's Tale*, ed. J. H. P. Pafford (London, 1963); *The Tempest*, ed. Frank Kermode (London, 1954). As there is no Arden edition of *The Two Noble Kinsmen*, references are taken from Eugene M. Waith's Oxford edition (1989).

Introduction

SHAKESPEARE's last romances have a reputation as courtly works, composed and performed within the ambit of state power, and complimentary to ruling decorums. Vast myths have been discovered at their core: they are redemptive journeys of nature and grace, the basic ethics those of aristocratic fortitude beneath a careless but ultimately beneficent destiny. They thus contribute to a milieu, typified by the masque, in which entertainment works as a flattering mirror of authority. Poesy, for Philip Sidney, had the honour not only of repairing nature and history, but of being the 'first nurse' of national and linguistic nobility.[1] Shakespearian romance, it is often thought, is mainly an amplification of some such idealism, with a vision not simply patriotic, but dream-sewn, hierophantic, celestial. So, whereas history is a tale of irony—of hopes misconceived, gaps between intent and end, of massive hyperbole and *sotto voce* subversion—romance is history's impossible, itinerant, escapist corrective.

To Ben Jonson, the Jacobean period's unofficial poet laureate, the romances' subsequently hallowed reputation would have seemed a remote and risible proposition. Jonson's edgy policing records a 'nest of *Antiques*', a 'Seruant-monster', a 'concupiscence of *Iigges* and *Dances*'.[2] Shakespeare's plays are remarkable for their confusion of manners and men, and for the promiscuity and buoyancy of their transgressions. Jonson's phrases suggest a dangerous fecundity, Shakespeare's 'nest' a copulating hive, his jigs a cover for May Day embraces. If things masque-like are invoked by Jonson's reference to '*Dances*', then their 'concupiscence' suggests that Jonson, the state's premier composer of masques, understood Shakespeare's vanities as an impertinently persistent antimasque. He speaks of a head mixed with 'other mens heeles', suggesting how organicist metaphors of an ordered body politic are inverted and chaotic in

---

[1] *A Defence of Poetry*, ed. J. A. Van Dorsten (Oxford, 1966), 18–19, 23–4.

[2] *Bartholomew Fayre*, Induction, 127–32, in *Ben Jonson*, ed. C. H. Herford and Percy and Evelyn Simpson, 11 vols. (Oxford, 1925–63), vol. vi.

Shakespeare's cartwheeling inventions.[3] Rather than solemn poems of mystery, they are '*Drolleries*', full of buffoonery and jests, facetious caricature, the sly waggishness of a puppet-show. One needn't share Jonson's defensive punctiliousness to recognize how the modern academic tradition has lost access to something of the plays' keenness and vim.

The more incisive nineteenth-century engagements with the plays—for instance those of Shelley, Hazlitt, and Coleridge—show themselves aware, if also at times afraid, of the plays' potent mixture of symbolism and politics.[4] More characteristic of romantic critics, however, is a celebration of Shakespeare's sublime creative imagination, and more particularly of *The Tempest* as the crowning epitome of such genius ('Here nothing takes us back to the real world').[5] And it has been such intimations of sublimity, mixed with a Jonsonian-cum-Johnsonian moral prescriptiveness, which have since dominated the plays' critical fortunes. This has been evident in the priority given to pre-emptive master-cribs over polysemous or performative liberties; in the disdaining of popular investment in either form or meaning; and in a willingness to construct meta-narratives about the function of great art which prefer evasion or euphemism before allowing significance unpropitious to established proprieties. This is I think mistaken. Shakespeare's late works are partly about the hunt for deliverance; but they are neither blandly neo-Christian nor serviceably courtly. They need to be looked at with more probing eyes. It is important not to allow a too stately or static sense of the generic term—itself conferred upon these works well after their initial provenance—to restrict one's points of reference. The hermeneutic predict-ability of the conventional romance model has proved unable to accommodate the plays' magically insinuative tangents and essays.

Nosworthy's Arden edition for instance, has to ignore

---

[3] Compare lines 9–10 of Jonson's *Horace: His Art of Poetrie*: 'Whose shapes, like sick-mens dreames, are fain'd so vaine, As neither head, nor foot, one forme retaine': *Ben Jonson*, ed. Herford and Simpson, viii. 303-55.

[4] See Jonathan Bate, *Shakespeare and the English Romantic Imagination* (Oxford, 1989), and *The Romantics on Shakespeare* (Oxford, 1992).

[5] Ludwig Tieck, *Kritische Schriften*, 4 vols. (Leipzig, 1948–52), i. 44 ff; reference in G. F. Parker, *Johnson's Shakespeare* (Oxford, 1989), 125.

or forgive—'cheerfully'—vast tracts of *Cymbeline* which undermine his apprehension of Elysian fields. Noting that 'lapses into realism' are 'detrimental' to the 'romantic tone', he argues that 'they do nothing to impair the final impression, and it would be merely pedantic to emphasize them'.[6] Nosworthy writes as if he is doing the play a favour, like a vigilant but kindly headmaster; really he is protecting the security of his 'impression', pretending generosity while in fact sophistical and exclusive. Philip Edwards offers what is in many ways a subtle and inclusive sense of *Pericles* in his New Penguin edition. He is sensitive to the play's artful mixing of genres, and not too blithely facile in locating providential patterns. But still his idea of what 'romance' is will prejudice his criticism with silent preferences and elisions: it is the 'simple and clear-cut' genre of 'lost innocence', 'readily charged with universal or spiritual meanings'; if bound in finite space it concerns itself with 'chastity', 'nobility', 'courage'; it revolves, fairy-tale fashion, around impermeable oppositions, of 'good and evil', 'misery and happiness', 'bereavement and affection', and so on.[7] The problem with such a definition is not that the elements are wrong, but that their efficient teleology is already inscribed: we know who must win and what always matters. There is little room for local detail, still less for subversion or surprise; the *material* qualities in history and language are effaced by a binarism which is never a mirror, never conflation or confusion, but at best a stark contrast framing unswerving loyalties and necessities.

It has been a common ruse to complain that *Pericles'* comic scenes are somehow 'not the right sort of comedy for such a play'.[9] Shakespeare's indecorousness is an affront to the critics' propriety, which is then by sleight-of-hand projected back onto the playwright who, as if unknowingly, has fouled his own turf: so Boult in the brothel asks 'an awkward

---

[6] Introduction, pp. xlviii–lxxxiii.
[7] *Pericles*, ed. Philip Edwards (Harmondsworth, 1976), 15–31.
[8] Ibid. 29–31.
[9] *Pericles*, ed. J. C. Maxwell (Cambridge, 1956; repr. 1969), p. xxix. Although compare Edwards, *Pericles*, 20, who sees a 'purposeful and important mingling' of genres, so that idealism can be tested against knowledge.

question that cannot be answered out of the Arcadian book
and for the moment it seems as if Shakespeare has broken
his own wicket'.[10] Danby's metaphor rather seals the politics of
such criticism: pastoral romance is a gentleman's game, and
Shakespeare's profanities are simply not cricket. An odd blindness to the theatre's mischief canonizes, as irrefutable orthodoxy, an almost imperial politics of criticism. Edwards is less
squeamish than some in granting that the fishermen and brothel
belong in the play, but they do so only to counterpoint the
romance's genuine subject-matter, which is of course those
platonic monuments (nobility, virginity, divinity) which dress
the hallway to redemption. The apparent apoliticism of such
criticism is of course nothing of the kind; more than one kind
of stasis—indeed more than one kind of status—is thereby
ensured.

All three critics identify important cruxes. All three, however,
have as a point of interpretive refuge a conviction that the plays'
basic earth and air is a celestial kind of idealism. Thus, however
probing the criticism, it still operates within a kind of moral
cocoon, legitimized by a too-sanguine sense of Shakespeare's
inherited and euphonious genre. The critic will tend to exculpate
or evade rather than explore. For it may be in disjunction
itself that one identifies Shakespeare's dialectical ambition
and political preoccupations. It is important to recognize
'difficult' moments, and to see how romance might incorporate purposefully clashing tropes and traditions. But one
must go a little further, and renounce expectations that
all generic doubling-up will imply a pre-established moral
and rhetorical hierarchy. It may be more fruitful to think in
terms of a kinetic dialectic, unresolved and combative, between
co-existing yet antinomic ideologies. And the only way to
'get at' such dialogues is to attend, as much as possible
without prejudice, to all the play's voices with an equal will to
listen.

Of course the influence of solemnly conservative approaches
has waned. Nevertheless, an orthodoxy has remained, reaffirming a basic pattern of ruling class redemption, ultimately on and

---

[10] John F. Danby, *Poet's on Fortune's Hill: Studies in Sidney, Shakespeare,
Beaumont & Fletcher* (London, 1952), 101.

in that class's own terms.[11] The plays already give an oddly
antinomic appearance—at once awkward and obvious—which
may be why they have not encouraged many general attempts to
'get at' their substance. Instead, the critical approach to these
plays in recent years has remained basically allegorical, only
now with the ambition of discovering specific, local, topical
sources. But what is most noteworthy about the attraction of
allegory is that the methodology almost requires the pre-
acceptance of received teleologies: the aim is to give new or
alternative 'names' to relationships already ineffably established. Almost by definition allegorism cannot consider the medium, the occasion of language and gesture, in much detail.

The absence between 1608 and 1612 of 'chatter of each
post' issues further lessens the appropriateness of topical
allegories. Contemporary debates included much to prompt
Shakespeare's creative mind—absolutism, Scottish union, conjugal diplomacy, colonialism, beggars, taxation—but none
during the period is as pressing or ubiquitous as were or would
be the Spanish match, the Overbury murder, the Gunpowder
Plot, the Armada, or perhaps even the fears over the succession
in the dying days of Elizabeth. Other than the Julich-Cleves
crisis and the assassination of Henri IV, politics tended to be of
an endemic rather than sensational variety: impositions, enclo-
sures, monopolies and projects, liberties of the subject, and
inviolability of private property; the early Jacobean Church, in
a sense, was deceptively settled.[12] Consequently, the plays will
tend to evoke matters of state that are lingering and long
evolved.

Nevertheless, allegorists such as Wickham, Bergeron, Yates,
Marcus, and Hamilton identify in the travails of King James VI
& I a clear topical framework for one or more of the

[11] Even those critics who are scornful of the providential or Christian readings
of, for example, S. L. Bethell, *The Winter's Tale: A Study* (London, 1954) or
Derek Traversi, *Shakespeare: The Last Phase* (New York, 1954), still tend to depend
upon a watered-down version of 'destiny' as the chief narrative and moral authority.
Thus, Ernest Schanzer, in his edition of *Pericles* (New York, 1965), p. xxxix, sees the
'power of accident in human affairs' as sovereign in *Pericles*, using words like
'translucent', 'melodious', 'remote', and 'dreamlike'. The stubbornness of this orthodoxy is partly due to the long sway held since the 1950s by similarly orientated,
vaguely 'neo-Christian' critical editions.

[12] See Patrick Collinson, *The Religion of Protestants: The Church in English
Society 1559–1625* (1982; repr. Oxford, 1985).

romances.[13] Sometimes they will recognize the contentiousness of prevalent symbols; too often, though, it is assumed that a universal 'court' line was dutifully followed, as if the King's Men really were simply and always the king's men. Privileging the court over the more popular and populous franchise, allegorical practice invariably robs theatre of its bustle and complexity. For the romances play so many tricks with place and chronology, conflate so many moments and characters, shadow so many scenes with the warp of burlesque or double-take of irony, that it is naïve to understand every contemporary echo as either singular or deferential. Too often allegorical readings denude historical pressures of internal variety, of the capacity to argue or alter within themselves.[14] And they lead to inert, accidental, almost absent-minded explanations of motive or character: rigidity of framework here creates facile, expedient, superficial criticism.[15]

One might take the example of Cloten in *Cymbeline*. He has been identified with the parliamentary xenophobes, his anti-tribute patriotism suggesting hostility to James's plans for English union with Scotland. Alternatively, he has been identified with the papal Antichrist of Protestant demonology, and so with those subjects hostile to James's oath of allegiance.[16] The papists were, like Cloten, tirelessly reconstructed in terms of a litany of scatological epithets and rotten humours. Revelation prescribed that the Antichrist had multiple horns and heads, was a martyr to voluptuous abomination. But the language was hardly owned by any one group: while the Protestant militants would have the satanic hydra-head cut off, so too would the Jesuits decapitate the presumptuous 'head' of the English Church; a call, as James knew so well, to regicide. The point is that the rhetoric of abuse surrounding Cloten is so familiar as to elude clear contemporary

---

[13] Glynne Wickham, 'Shakespeare's Investiture Play: The Occasion and Subject of *The Winter's Tale*', *TLS* (18 Dec. 1969), 1456; David M. Bergeron, *Shakespeare's Romances and the Royal Family* (Lawrence, Kan., 1985); Donna B. Hamilton, *Virgil and The Tempest: The Politics of Imitation* (Columbus, Oh., 1990).

[14] Hamilton, *Politics of Imitation*, 147.

[15] e.g. Hamilton, '*The Winter's Tale* and the Language of Union, 1604–1610', *Sh. Studies*, 21 (1993), 228–50, where Bohemia, a land of aliens, is Scotland, and Autolicus, a beggar and rogue who plays a bagpipe, a Scot.

[16] Donna B. Hamilton, *Shakespeare and the Politics of Protestant England* (London, 1992), 139–45.

referents. For example, the anti-Puritan theatrical revenge upon Martin Marprelate, shown in both public and private theatres, portrayed Martin with 'a cocks combe, an apes face, a wolfs bellie', having his blood spilt upon the stage in a mock letting of humours.[17] Certain of the organizers of these Elizabethan satires came to the king's attention around 1605; they were prominent among the noncomformist presbyterians who, James feared, held both monarchy and bishops in poor respect.[18] Does this justify seeing such fears of 'distraction' in Cloten? It seems doubtful, even if the terms of the mockery are identical. Historicism here confers various rough coincidences, perhaps, but anything more is selective conjecture. Just as the buffoon lives in the hero, so too might the same similitude give a home to violently opposed political energies. Cloten's topicality might be as darting and immanent as Ariel.

Seeing *Cymbeline* as a text loyal to James's desire for the union of England and Scotland, Marcus has produced the most theoretically informed allegorical reading of one of the romances. Marcus recognizes linear allegory's proclivity for predeterminate surface patterns, and the methodology's necessary indifference toward textual ambiguity and disjunction.[19] But still her 'local' interpretation reproduces familiar problems. The overriding problem is that hermeneutic preconceptions are distant from the play's reception, whether off stage or page. The method is academic, not only transposing the need for a scholarly 'thesis' onto the play, but understanding such need as the originating cause of the play. Marcus recognizes the paradox— that the play's *raison d'être* is all but invisible to those who are not scholars of the union debate—but responds mainly with a factitious separation of the play as allegory from the play as theatre. That is, *Cymbeline*'s 'Stuart text', apparently friendly to Jacobean absolutism, can be forgotten or evaded through the

---

[17] See John Lyly, 'Pappe with an Hatchet', *The Complete Works of John Lyly*, ed. P. Warwick Bond, 3 vols. (1902; repr. Oxford, 1967), iii. 393–414. Janet Clare, *'Art made tongue-tied by authority': Elizabethan and Jacobean Dramatic Censorship* (Manchester, 1990), 25.

[18] Roger Lockyer, *The Early Stuarts: A Political History of England 1603–1642* (London, 1989), 109.

[19] 'Localization depends on an odd breed of temporary, provisional positivism': Leah S. Marcus, *Puzzling Shakespeare: Local Reading and Its Discontents* (Berkeley, 1988), 214.

untold variety of theatrical performance. Different per-
formances will bring out different things: for example Jupiter,
if represented at court with masque-like splendour, may evoke
a sacramental, irresistible power which seems quite absurd
at the public theatre, where a familiar player 'descends' on
a hobby-horse eagle. Elsewhere, the play's 'subtle critique of
ideas about textual authority' is the register of how 'Shakespeare gave the play back to the institution of the theater,
created a potential for multiplicity and diversity in performance
that the Stuart *Cymbeline* did not—by definition, could not—
have'. But why take the play away from the 'institution of
the theater' in the first place? One wonders whether allegory's
emperor is left with any clothes. Interpretive priority here
depends mainly upon the exclusive crib with which the task
began.[20]

That literary and 'non-literary' texts, and their tropes, circu-
late inseparably within cultural exchange systems is a basic tenet
of the 'new historicism', a movement which has been of particular importance in stressing the material embeddedness of expres-
sive acts, including literary criticism, and so helping to correct
the temptation to understand canonical works as unique chan-
nels to impermeable human truths.[21] This reluctance to distinguish 'literary' foreground from 'historical' background has
questioned the validity of the specific allegory, and even of
allusion: each text is an anxious, unknowing network of such
cultural influence. However, this concentration upon the impossibility of textual autonomy has necessarily precluded a close
and sustained attention either to a text's language or to the
priority of its sources and analogies. The influence of a
Foucauldian sense of the saturating immanence of 'power' has,
in turn, further contributed to a rather immobile concept of a
panoptically manipulative state. In this model, the state acts as
a kind of fake 'other'; any act or thought of subjective difference
is in fact recuperated as one of socialized conformity. Similarly,
hostile 'others' are used or invented to promote the beauty and
necessity of conventional virtues; they too, like any notion of
resistance, become folded into and indistinguishable from the

[20] Ibid. 14.
[21] See H. Aram Veeser, ed., *The New Historicism* (New York, 1989), 'Introduction', pp. xi–xii.

governing hegemony.[22] Textualizing and aestheticizing political and semantic agency, the movement's predetermining paradigms rob both self and language of suppleness, surprise, and liberty.

And indeed, the pessimistic determinisms of new historicism's 'paradigm of containment' have come under pressure from less static, more interstitial models of social representation and reproduction, countenancing complexity and contradiction not absorbed into some insatiable state sponge.[23] The monolithic model of the 1980s has had to incorporate aspects of British cultural materialist practice, which shares new historicism's accent upon a culturally produced medium, but with less tendency to hypostasize the state and more willingness to identify textual disjunction, resistance, and the possibility of effective agency.[24] In a move similar to Derrida's 'pharmakon-pharmakos' linguistics of absent presence, they recover the silenced and marginalized and unravel the history a play 'contains yet does not represent': 'What is socially peripheral is often symbolically central.'[25] While my approach stays aloof from Marxist teleological commitments, it has been helped by this and other such politically committed work. And it has some affinities with recent 'materialist' criticism that, often from a feminist perspective, has repaired a tendency in some earlier work of similar theoretical persuasion to organize textual and cultural practice according to somewhat schematic preceptive dichotomies: patriarchy, hegemony, humanist essentialism, and their

[22] Frank Lentricchia, 'Foucault's Legacy: A New Historicism?', in Veeser, *The New Historicism*, 231–42, particularly criticizes Stephen Greenblatt's seminal *Renaissance Self-Fashioning: From More to Shakespeare* (Chicago, 1980).

[23] Greenblatt himself sounded the death-knell for new historicism 'mark one' in an apology for his 'totalizing' practice and 'monolithic entities' which, ironically, serves as an introduction to a collection of essays largely illustrating the methods he now finds suspect: *Shakespearean Negotiations: The Circulation of Social Energy in Renaissance England* (1988; repr. Oxford, 1990), 1–3 ff.

[24] See for example Alan Sinfield, *Faultlines: Cultural Materialism and the Politics of Dissident Reading* (Oxford, 1992).

[25] Jonathan Dollimore, *Radical Tragedy: Religion, Ideology and Power in the Drama of Shakespeare and his Contemporaries* (1984; 2nd edn., New York, 1989), p. xxvi; 'Transgression and Surveillance in *Measure for Measure*', in Jonathan Dollimore and Alan Sinfield, eds., *Political Shakespeare: New Essays in Cultural Materialism* (Manchester, 1985), 73 ff.; Barbara Badcock, *The Reversible World: Symbolic Inversion in Art and Society* (Ithaca, NY, 1978); Frank Lentricchia, *Criticism and Social Change* (Chicago, 1983), 15.

complementary subversions. There is instead a growing recognition that unitary, univocal, or ideologically pre-emptive meta-narratives cannot do justice to the heterogeneity of either the dramatic text or its cultural functioning.[26] Any evolving social body must harness both 'subversion' and 'containment'; but to build all interpretation around these concepts has the effect of denuding both of real meaning. It is more interesting and important to identify, within these general rubrics, types of desire, violence, resistance, and fear, and the way such energies, inscribed textually, evoke their political moment.

Furthermore, I think it important to break away, at least to some degree, from the language of recent criticism, with its array of ideological-cum-linguistic master-codes, and their respective pre-framing strategies. The critic's language begins to control the enterprise, with interpretation led like a bear by the sense-stilled nose. Whereas recent critical frameworks routinely acknowledge textual indeterminacy and materiality, their broad-brushed, panoptical methods rarely tease out the politics of a particular phrase or character, or how the language operates 'in and around' its unique spoken moment. So I have tried to write about the plays in a way that is supple and nuanced, alive to sun and shade, stream and counter-stream; this means perhaps a slightly more figurative language than has been conventional in recent criticism. The plays resist easy paraphrase, a resistance which, in the interests of critical sensitivity, must at times apply to my own analyses.

Much recent criticism has tended to see material practices as 'destabilizing' and dramatic scripts as mostly not.[27] This emerg-

---

[26] For example see Patricia Parker, *Shakespeare from the Margins* (Chicago, 1996); Catherine Belsey, 'Towards Cultural History—in Theory and Practice', *Textual Practice*, 3 (1989), 159–77; and Belsey, 'Afterword: A Future for Materialist Feminist Criticism', in Valerie Wayne, ed., *The Matter of Difference: Materialist Feminist Criticism of Shakespeare* (New York, 1991), 257–70. See also Graham Holderness, Nick Potter, and John Turner, *Shakespeare: The Play of History* (Iowa City, 1987); and *Out of Court: Dramatizations of Court Society* (Basingstoke, 1990); Annabel Patterson, *Shakespeare and the Popular Voice* (Oxford, 1989).

[27] e.g. Jean Howard, 'Scripts and/versus Playhouses: Ideological Production and the Renaissance Public Stage', in Wayne, *The Matter of Difference*, 221–36. Graham Holderness, *Shakespeare Recycled: The Making of Historical Drama* (Hemel Hempstead, 1992), 126: 'As *drama* the play holds an enormously greater potential for "iterability", for the production of plurality of meaning, than the written or printed text.' Compare Harry Berger Jr., '*Richard II*, 3. 2: An Exercise in Imaginary Audition', *ELH* 55 (1988), 755–96.

ing orthodoxy needs qualification. A particular occasion of a performance can have a unique excitement, an electricity linked to the moment in time, the thronging crowds, the sheer physicality and shared freedom of the moment. Indeed, Shakespeare's public theatre was a potent commodity, a civic event offering an exchange both sensuous and hermeneutic, aesthetic and ideological. And yet textual exploration remains crucial: a thrilling performance suggests, as much as anything, a company culture of fearless reading. Contrarywise, an actor can virtually dictate a script's interpretive reception in a way the mute printed word cannot; however sense-stealing the performance, however evocative to memory and desire, Shakespeare's texts hold in reserve all kinds of potential. And, while the idea of the audience possesses an enigmatic, irrefutable kind of perfection, it is an irrecoverable plenty which only repeated reading can hope to approximate.[28] One must attend to 'representation *qua* representation' as well as to the material practices and conventions of the stage and theatre-going. The timid predictability of reading has more to do with deadening educational practice than to the limitations of the printed word. And one should not forget here the somewhat differently tuned interpretive 'ears' of Shakespeare's age: language was not merely an instrument, but a *subject*, an agile, almost supra-notional, metaphor of evolving self-presence. Everyone was alive to analogy and proverb, and, if the drama's own reflexivity is any guide, excited by the growing swagger and surprises of the vernacular; furthermore, anyone of grammar school standard enjoyed a rhetorical training highly sophisticated by modern standards.[29] Many in Shakespeare's first audiences could pick up subtly etched links and parallels which, today, are left mainly to the careful reader.

Shakespeare's own thoughts about the printed word are notoriously opaque. One can speak in negatives: not dealing in dedicatory epistles, commendatory verses, prefaces, his plays are

---

[28] William Empson, *Some Versions of Pastoral* (1935; repr. London, 1986), 67–8, writes of the audience as a macrocosm of the reader, the reader a microcosm of the audience, and of 'a sort of sensibility held in common . . . wider, more sensible, than that of any of its members'.

[29] Emrys Jones, *The Origins of Shakespeare* (Oxford, 1977), 66 et al.; James Daly, 'Cosmic Harmony and Political Thinking in Early Stuart England', *Transactions of the American Philosophical Society*, 69, part 7 (1979), 9 ff.; also see Ben Jonson's explanation of his emblems in the Herford and Simpson edn., vii. 90–1.

without the literary trappings enjoyed by Jonson, Marston,
Heywood, and Dekker. Shakespeare didn't oversee a meticulous
collection of his own works, as Jonson did. Nevertheless, his
friends in the company had received from him his drafts, and
they imply in the Folio that they merely perform what their
author would have done had circumstances permitted.[30]
Heminge and Condell do not prioritize speech over print or
print over speech: they acknowledge how each supplements the
other. It is the success of Shakespeare's plays on the stage which
justifies their collection in print; but then, as Heminge and
Condell insist in their message 'To The Great variety of Readers': 'Reade him, therefore; and againe, and againe: And if then
you doe not like him, surely you are in some manifest danger,
not to understand him.' They seem here to acknowledge the
difficulty and surprise of Shakespeare's work: not only his freedom with discrete words, but the liberties he takes scenically,
and with convention or decorum. Shakespeare's work is always
semantically more tolerant than Jonson's, whose pedantic classicism would find a kind of vindication in the printed text, fixed
for all time, and his ammunition against careless or ignorant
reception. Heminge and Condell, however, suggest a printed
text which always withholds a final layer to be peeled, a text
which defers and dilates the pleasures of understanding. They
also countenance a 'Variety of Readers', perhaps no two ever
quite alike: in such circumstances the printed word should be
assumed no more fixed than the spoken word, even if the sturdy
Folio book-form was designed to assert print's constancy over
and against quarto counterfeits. Of course they are advertising
their collection, and are anxious that browsers should become
buyers. But if the Folio commodifies language, it does not do so
by simplifying the product for ease of exchange.

Indeed there is much in these plays which seems to anticipate
the intensely tricky textuality of post-structuralism, and particularly deconstructionism: the dilation or problematizing of the
'centre'; the destabilizing of convenient 'oppositions'; the under-

---

[30] A collection of ten Shakespeare plays in quarto was contemplated in 1619 by
Thomas Pavier, who was forced to abandon it after the Lord Chamberlain granted
the King's Men an injunction protecting their interests. See W. W. Greg, *The
Shakespeare First Folio: Its Bibliographical and Textual History* (Oxford, 1955), 9–
16; E. K. Chambers, *The Elizabethan Stage*, 4 vols. (Oxford, 1923), iii. 181.

cutting of teleological linearity; a persistent, sceptical sensitivity to the tropes and techniques justifying 'natural' hegemony; the desire for an origin which endlessly recedes; and of course a wariness and enjoyment of linguistic lability. However, my project imposes necessary limits to the applicability of a deconstructionist critique. Derrida's early work assumes as its bogey a classical logocentrism which might be thought an inappropriate or unrealized 'metaphysic' for Shakespeare's unstable and inwardly shifting 'episteme' (to haul in Foucault's own inexact and contentious term). Shakespeare is at once proleptic and of his age; as Terry Eagleton wryly notes, he seems to have anticipated Marx, Freud, Nietzsche, Derrida, and sundry other modern giants;[31] and while there are 'Cartesian' speculations galore in Shakespeare, still his work remains in important senses free from the dichotomizing epistemologies which, from Descartes 'cogito' on, have characterized the modern metaphysical tradition. It is indeed partly Shakespeare's very 'primitivism'—for instance his unsentimental willingness to find root for both language and temperament in the desiring body—which makes him seem so 'modern', so imminent. And this openness to novelty, in turn, suggests Shakespeare's scrupulous intimacy to his own historical moment. Consequently, an awareness of philological, or indeed ideological, 'différance' is useful mainly in so far as it might help to tap the strains and nuances within the political discourse of Shakespeare's time and place. The referents are there, the signs signify; it is just that they are neither straightforward nor univocal: differing constructions of civic beginnings, various strategies of legitimation; conceptions of citizenship and subjectivity, and of the state's coherence as ruler, model, or educator; the thrills and threats of a widening franchise or burgeoning public voice; the pressures for change or urges for destruction. The important point is that so-called 'theory', with its suspicion of 'phallogocentric' assumptions and its alertness to discursive violence, can help refine and sensitize putatively 'empirical' philology and historicism. No doubt my methodology is somewhat bastardized, lacking theoretical 'purity'; but so too is life and language. The critical challenge is how best to reconstruct renaissance discourse, engaged as it is

---

[31] *William Shakespeare* (Oxford, 1986), pp. ix–x.

with recovering, revamping, and at times challenging ancient models: in order to thus build up, however, one's readings must first break things down a little. Shakespeare's intellectual world is kinetic, disjunctive, swiftly alive to contradictory possibilities. Above all, it is this fact of a world in process, unfinished, clamorous and turbulent, which must be respected and, through rigorous attention to the plays' mnemonic and metaphoric multiplicity, retrieved.

ROMANCE AND DECORUM

The very capaciousness of 'romance' hinders attempts to pigeon-hole the genre's politics: it is this bagginess which makes the term useful to suggest, if not to explain, Shakespeare's puzzling last works. For instance, though it is true that the genre's rambling inelegance was at times thought antipathetic to terse humanist disciplines, pastoral romance was never actually beneath learned appropriation. Sidney's *Defence*, for instance, likens Pindar's 'gorgeous eloquence' to the 'blind crowder' singing with rough voice and 'rude style' the 'old song of Percy and Douglas', while both Spenser and Sidney used the world of romance as a nursery of the epic.[32] Indeed, distinctions between the two can become rather specious: both romance and humanism raided and renovated the past; both sought transformation through varieties of fantasy, lyricism, engagement, critique; if either are 'escapist', then they are so in a peculiarly *rhetorical* fashion, designed to persuade and challenge as much as delight.

Political discourse in Shakespeare's period was almost always umbilical: constructs of legitimacy drew shape and sustenance from some putatively moulding source. The desire for such origin was competitive, its formulations often highly imaginative. Translated into romance's always creative engagement with beginnings, one finds myth interlacing with history, fantasy transforming allegorical satire. The point is to expect miscegenation, and to prepare for dialectics which overlay differing times and places, which gain strength and surprise from contra-

---

[32] Sidney, *A Defence of Poetry*, 46.

ries, anachronism, and impossibility. Accordingly, Shakespeare enjoys the mode's sometimes extravagant liberties, but always ballasts any flightiness with classical or contemporary contextualization. In *Pericles*, ancient Athens and Jacobean London underlie the story's oceanic itinerance; *Cymbeline* filters Roman and British mythographies; *The Winter's Tale* reworks Ovid and secular analogy; while *The Tempest*'s multiple utopias juggle Virgilian, Ovidian, and various topical New World discourses. Similarly, each play's exile to wild places is a means less of escape than of historical distillation, allowing a kind of liberated critique of what was, is, and might be. Shakespeare fully exploits the paradox of wilderness, as an environment equally of purification, punishment, and recapitulation. Romance's poetic geography is therefore not prelapsarian. Each evocation of origin is highly contested, shadowed by intimations both of ending and perhaps delusion, and counterpointed always with its symbiotic cause and consequence: the court-cum-city, never truly left behind. Shakespearian romance doesn't batten upon some ignorant moor, lost to either cultural relativity or rhetorical seriousness.[33]

To get a closer measurement of the political and dialogical ambition of these plays, one must consider Shakespeare's particular vivification of decorum. The modern connotations of 'decorum' might suggest a rather stiff regard for seemliness and propriety: a concentration on good manners, regard for one's betters, a lightly oiled cog in the cultural machine. And certainly, then as now, the elegancies of decorum would not, indeed definitively could not, facilitate upheaval. For many humanists, however, a 'properly' employed respect for decorum implied anything but the empty reiteration of authority. It was the measure of an interrogative mind, politically engaged. Cicero defines decorum in the political realm as 'prudence'. While prudence was inherently and ineffably connected to virtue, to an ethical standard innate or intuitive in the 'good man', it was equally a practice contingent upon the needs and

---

[33] Teskey, 'Introduction', to George M. Logan and Gordon Teskey, eds., *Unfolded Tales: Essays on Renaissance Romance* (Ithaca, NY, 1989), 7, notes how romance's caprice was used in epic, comedy, and tragedy as a 'staging area where new ideas can be experimented with and introduced as innovations into the classical forms'.

permissions of the occasion.[34] Words should be opportune, appropriate to the moment, person, and place. Contextual sensitivity will demand that discursive manners be flexible and various: for Cicero, it is the compelling orator who is exemplar. Decorum becomes the rhetorical expression of opinion, identified not 'with the static representation of transcendental ideas, but rather with the dynamic activity of persuasion'.[35] However, with its 'truth' claims being so contingent, and its techniques so much an 'art', decorum itself represents opportunity. One text might prefer seamless iterations of order, almost Platonic in their faith that the best in man shadows the ideal. Another might exploit the incongruence or incompatibility in decorum's figurative employments: 'truth' is rhetorical, a suit for the occasion, patchy or glamorous as perception allows.

Here one comes close to the art of Shakespeare's late plays. For it is his use of analogy which epitomizes Shakespeare's marriage of rhetorical humanism to wider questions of the decorum (personal, linguistic, political) of a given situation. The possibility of analogy—whether a relation of cause and effect or of likeness—presupposes a divine or a natural standard of order from which the analogy derives legitimacy. But faith in the efficacy of analogy was under pressure, and its status as truth-bearer still more so. It remained a popular and effective technique to buttress an argument with analogical padding, but it was routinely acknowledged among rhetoricians that, whilst to argue from similitude could be useful, it could not compel the listener's assent. Nature, so various and capricious, furnishes nothing more nor less than an immense storehouse of ideologically neutral material, awaiting rhetorical appropriation.[36] Importantly, there re-

---

[34] Cicero's *De Officiis*, I. xxxvii–xxxviii; see *Cicero on Moral Obligation: A New Translation of Cicero's 'De Officiis'*, by John Higginbotham (Berkeley and Los Angeles, 1967), 72–4.

[35] See Victoria Kahn, *Rhetoric, Prudence, and Skepticism in the Renaissance* (Ithaca, NY, 1985), 32–3.

[36] See David Norbrook, 'Rhetoric, Ideology and the Elizabethan World Picture', in Peter Mack, ed., *Renaissance Rhetoric* (Basingstoke, 1994), 140–64. Geoffrey Miles, *Shakespeare and the Constant Romans* (Oxford, 1996), sees the essence of Ciceronian decorum as a 'self-consistency' which can lead to 'ethical relativism' (p. 33); Cicero's influential sense of decorum has been taken to mean both 'proper behaviour' and a more unbridled 'individualism', potentially amoral or antisocial: 'At the same time, decorum could tip over in the opposite direction into

mained certain putatively authoritative tropes, truisms of rule couched in metaphoric or metonymic convention; it is these that a more sceptical discourse might play upon, recalling so as to challenge the tendentious or factitious status of 'naturally' buttressed authority.

Similarly, the notion of 'genre' is one which proffers certain conventions and expectations whose effect is found as much in the breach as the observance: a reader or audience knows the basic model, often depends upon it, but will be equally attuned to shifts and variations which play off or even out of the basic frame. Furthermore, the late Elizabethan theatre was quickly revolutionizing itself, exhausting old and stiff dramatic rituals, or burnishing them up by transporting them into new secular settings; consider *Doctor Faustus* and its scuttling of conventions. Of course many dramatists stuck to more disciplined generic settings; Shakespeare himself did, albeit occasionally. But the fact is that if drama is to be adequate to one's sensuous and historical occasion, putatively discrete genres will often mix. And indeed, coming to Shakespeare's late plays, there was ample precedent for the opportunistic incorporation of epic, lyric, classical myth, miracle and mummers' plays, chronicle history, slapstick, tragedy, comedy, and pastoral. Indeed the cipher we call 'romance' is almost a symbol of the inadequacy of 'classic' generic classifications: so, a 'popular romance' like *Locrine* depends for its evocation of both homely partisans and noble warriors upon a slap-happy juxtaposition of comic demotic and stately expostulation.[37] And yet a basic decorum remains a touchstone: nobility speak in verse, the vulgar in prose, within which framework bawdiness, scatology, insurrection, might all retain the propriety accorded to proper place. The popular tradition of pastoral romance or comic epic is lively and mischievous, mocking the turgid ineffectualities of authority. However, both metaphoric and generic organization—and

mere public role-playing. There is clearly a tension between the ideal of truth to oneself and Cicero's metaphor of the *persona*, of wearing a mask or playing a role.' (p. 36).

[37] Rosalie Colie, *The Resources of Kind: Genre-Theory in the Renaissance*, ed. Barbara Kiefer Lewalski (Berkeley, 1973), and Claudio Guillen *Literature as System: Essays toward the Theory of Literary History* (Princeton, 19; t), emphasize the generic inclusionism and experimentation of Renaissance t eory and practice.

therefore the hierarchies of station and person—remain in a fundamentally assured place. There is no 'new world of words' here, but rather a kind of sentimental image of shared nostalgias, based in the airing of familar language (proverbs, puns, aphorisms, stock jokes, and metaphors) and generic situations that are at once liberating and comforting. It is not so much that theatre here offers by and large a social narcotic—it may well invariably do so, but who should expect more from their pleasures?—but rather that the vision as it were 'in' the language is pre-scripted, expected, and therefore vaguely flattering of its audience in the fashion of most conventionally decorous art: it lacks the ambition of wonder and surprise, the fearful questions of a truly rigorous 'mirror'. Shakespeare, famously, is different.

For his romances both observe and subvert conventional distinctions. And crucial here is the traditionally hierarchical separation of verse and prose. In Shakespeare's late work, both are constructed out of the same peculiar intensity and, one might say, sleeplessness, of metaphor; 'noble' and 'popular' are forever interpenetrating and reorganizing one another. Aristocratic verse is laced with rude puns; the monster speaks in lilting iambic pentameters; folly endlessly recapitulates the acts of state. *Cymbeline*, for instance, offers as its most memorable moment a triumph of gauche inelegance: Imogen crawls over the dead Cloten, propounding the absurdity of her circumstance with desperate, mistaken garrulity. The princess, babbling like Caliban should do but never does, is hurled down to a linguistic and physical register which cannot fail to embarrass tidy notions of propriety. The mongrel formed as the princess envelops her would-be rapist can suggest, at the very least, a new audacity, even recklessness, in Shakespeare's habitual freedom with conflations and chiasmata. A new 'genre'—represented in newly concatenating, almost atomically concordant metaphors and characters—is here emerging amid the wreckage of old distinctions.[38]

Shakespeare's is a medium interwoven with homologies: often, as here, somewhat violent and surprising. This principle of connectedness gives the texts their liberty to test, to tease, and to reformulate inherited or enforced assumptions of power. The

---

[38] Cf. T. A. McAlindon, *Shakespeare and Decorum* (London, 1973), for argument that Shakespeare basically observes conventional decorous hierarchies.

consequent analogies work between scenes, between discrete images, and between characters. The often highly intricate internal analogies, sometimes inventing their own tropes and sometimes manipulating popular organicist metaphors, allow basically three reorientations of voice and motion. First, they can facilitate the diffusion of narrative authority among a number of characters. Shakespeare of course invariably employs multi-perspectives; the radical quality of the romances emerges, paradoxically, from their appearance of being determined by one or another form of 'divine' authority. Second, the analogic technique fosters the creation, through multiple displacements and parallels, of shared bodies, wherein one body can take on the burden of various others, or each fill the place of the other. Third, and an extension and sophistication of the two, one figure can take upon in its own body and/or voice the words and desires of the whole community. These 'characters' become cumulative embodiments of 'unwilled', lime-like language, the plastic semiotics of the particular crises at hand. Such effects draw upon the plays' basic forward-and-backward structures, certain subjects thereby becoming textual 'screens' onto whom can be projected surrounding desire. Through disguise, surrogacy, victim-hood, they are shape-shifters, or shape-shifted. Character, whether understood as flesh or mind, enjoys the lability of words: it is amoeboid. This does not deny these figures all 'say' in what they do or desire, any more than it denies the dialectical importance of audience empathy. It does, though, make the figures represent much more than they, as subjective agents, can realize. In a crucial sense, the romances' pivotal characters—not only the strange chameleons like Caliban and Autolicus, but the 'noble' paragons like Guiderius, Marina, Imogen, Pericles—are 'written' by that which surrounds them: that is, the supra-characterological metaphoric energy which is Shakespeare's 'take' on his times.

For Ben Jonson, this novel 'decorum' of Shakespeare's was an affronting mix of popular impertinence and sophisticated mendacity. The 'true Artificer will not run away from nature, as hee were afraid of her'.[39] In 1610 Shakespeare is accused, like an arrant child, of just such fearful escape from nature; by 1614,

[39] *Timber, Or Discoveries*, in *Ben Jonson*, ed. Herford and Simpson, viii. 772–3.

his impudence assumes more monstrous shape: he 'make[s] Nature afraid', as if proffering some desacralizing rival ontology. Shakespeare's example is both untutored and dangerous. In *The Alchemist*, Jonson's words 'To the Reader' offer what seems to be an arch pun upon his too facile friend's name—perhaps recalling the obsessive paronomastic manners of Shakespeare's own sonnets 135 and 136—where, after criticizing those poets who run rudely from nature's rule, Jonson claims not to 'speak this out of a hope to do good on any man against his *will*; for I know, if it were put to the question of theirs and mine, the worse should find more suffrages because the most favour common errors' (my italics)'.[40] Jonson's complaints, sustained over decades, don't always name Shakespeare. But his consistent targets—the wild and woolly exuberance, the factitious resort to impossibilities, the casual jewel sparkling all the more for the dross that surrounds it—suggest that, at best, Jonson saw Shakespeare as the ill-disciplined pattern and justification for a tribe of less talented public panderers.[41] Shakespeare is thus the ache in Jonson's aesthetic, nagging like a migraine through twenty years of doggedly Horatian literary theory. And Shakespeare's transgressions, as understood by Jonson, point unfailingly to issues which this book probes: characters who violate possibility; metaphors that are 'writhd and tortur'd', 'scatter'd' and 'rude';[42] the unwillingness to rest with official proprieties as the foundation of cultural analyses and, consequently, a casting about for alternative sources of order; the plays' dialogue with 'vulgar' judgements; and an ensuing politics

[40] *Alchemist*, 'To the Reader', 6–7; *Bartholomew Fayre*, Induction, 129.

[41] In 'To the memory of my beloued, The AVTHOR MR. WILLIAM SHAKESPEARE', Jonson praises Shakespeare for his 'Art', though still having a dig at his limited classicism. E. A. J. Honigmann, *Shakespeare's Impact on His Contemporaries* (London, 1982), 36–8, suggests that Jonson's mind was changed radically about his rival upon seeing the whole of Shakespeare's work in print. Certainly sections of *Discoveries* date from at least as early as *The Alchemist*; and it is interesting that in *The New Inn* and *A Tale of a Tub* Jonson himself turned to romance, in tribute perhaps to Shakespeare as well as to the Elizabethan romances to which Shakespeare also alludes. See Anne Barton, *Ben Jonson, Dramatist* (Cambridge, 1984).

[42] *Timber, Or Discoveries*, ll. 578, 641–2, in Herford and Simpson, viii. 555–649.

which, as if 'alwayes grudging', refuses to be 'rein'd with one bridle'.[43]

Jonson refers partly to Shakespeare's resort to types of supernaturalism, by turns primitive, untrustworthy or blackly ambiguous, so as to drive his plots to conclusion. And his moral unease dwells equally upon the 'nest of *Antiques*' who, as if multiplying out of some liminal hedge, confuse the sometime courtliness of these plays. But Jonson's target is not simply the representation of moral licentiousness. The point is one of decorum, and of the paradigmatic assumptions which can frame the action within certain ethical 'givens'. Jonson will dramatize a gallery of rogues on the understanding that he is doing just that. He gives to them an environment, station, and language which accords with mundane experience. As Hazlitt wrote, the 'sense of reality exercised a despotic sway over his mind, and equally weighed down and clogged his perception of the beautiful or ridiculous'.[44] The consonance of place and voice is invariably satisfied: but Jonson's work cannot surprise the world into new forms. Shakespeare, by contrast, as often as not denies verisimilitude or, when using a self-evidently unrealistic genre—such as pastoral—confuses it with abrupt accountabilities or anti-bucolic shadows. The ethical scheme has to be constructed from within the world of the play, as it goes along; neither introductory *sententiae* nor local knowledge—the staples of the Jonsonian world-picture—will provide much guidance.

For example, Autolicus in *The Winter's Tale* endlessly resists classification. Always more than any single epithet, he rather takes on, as a kind of microcosm, the liberties of the play he is in. This point can be neatly emphasized by considering Jonson's *Bartholomew Fayre*, which at one level seems to be a translation of as well as response to Shakespeare's '*Tales, Tempests,* and

[43] Significantly, Jonson's *Discoveries* uses 'bridle' as the restraint necessary for both high and swelling wit (678–80) and a grudging and ill-natured multitude (972–6). Nancy Klein Maguire, *Renaissance Tragicomedy: Explorations in Genre and Politics* (New York, 1987), 4, suspects 'that the vigorous dispute over Aristotle's generic canons . . . mirrored the political upheaval over absolute and limited sovereignty. In both the generic and the political realms, the individual was beginning to assert himself over authority.'

[44] 'On Shakespeare and Ben Jonson', *Lectures on the English Comic Writers, and Fugitive Writings*, ed. Arthur Johnston (1910; repr. London, 1967), 41.

such like *Drolleries*'.[45] Jonson's litany of rogues, merchants, wayfarers, and fair-dwellers can be understood as discovering a collective source in Shakespeare's own theatrically economical fairground: Autolicus. The functional and verbal echoes take in the cutpurse Edgworth, the ballad-monger Nightingale, and the hobby-horse and 'motion' seller Leatherhead. They embrace the 'rogue's eye view of the law' disguise of Justice Over-doo, the mercenary holiness of Dame Purecraft, and the 'warrantable' obsession of the 'ragged prophet', Trouble-All. If Jonson orchestrates a sense of popular comprehensiveness, so too does Shakespeare, collecting all in one shape-shifter whose most meaningful discourse is, as one might expect, with himself. Where Jonson's world is fastidiously localized, Shakespeare takes similar materials and dumps them next to a chimerical sea-shore; the density and economy of Shakespeare's method both escapes and refutes Jonson's complaints about prolixity and carelessness. A definitively indecorous figure—Autolicus the ventriloquial chameleon, the ape of authority—epitomizes a romance world, utopian or dystopian, based meticulously in both semantic and cultural displacement.

So, the liberty to explore and question is not conferred blithely by topological strangeness; such strangeness, or novelty, is more accurately an effect of Shakespeare's particular manipulation of metaphor. And indeed, Jonson's strictures against his rival seem as much as anything to focus upon the minutiae of Shakespeare's language. 'Would he had blotted a thousand', opined Jonson, infamously, of Shakespeare's promiscuous pen, going on to ridicule a line which, if Jonson's memory is correct, was indeed 'blotted' from *Caesar*: 'Caesar did neuer wrong, but with just cause'.[46] What is most apparent here is not Shakespeare's illogic but Jonson's obtuseness, the restrictively literal quality of his thought. One might speak here of Shakespeare's grasp of the duplicity of political language and motive, the contingent morality of praxis, the necessary ambivalence of a Machiavellian *virtu*. Shakespeare's rhetorical sensitivity, then, both spawns and feeds upon political and dialogical violence. This is Shakespeare's 'decorum'. He builds both function and

---

[45] 'Induction', l. 130.
[46] *Discoveries*, 650–66.

character out of paradox: and paradox here invokes what to Jonson must seem both linguistically and behaviourally solecistic. This non-existent line evidently encapsulates how Shakespeare lacks a 'bridle' of propriety: Jonson's rigidity suggests how inadequate his theoretical framework is to explain Shakespeare's devices.[47]

Shakespeare may offer veiled responses to Jonson's criticisms in his own plays. The manifold examples of 'art' in *The Winter's Tale*—ballads, bear, sculptor, oracle, feast, disguise, flowers, and so on—evoke Shakespeare's thrilling embrace of theatrical heteroglossia, his pleasure in identifying analogues, noble or otherwise, of his own lying arts, and his recognition, ironically through audacious manipulation of textual material, that neither writer, king, nor god can truly possess a prescriptive sovereignty. More archly, *The Tempest* might frame a response to the high-brow scorn of Jonson's preface to *The Alchemist*. It has often been noted how, quite unwontedly, Shakespeare observes in *The Tempest* the unities so beloved of Jonson. Of course in many ways this works like a joke: plays 'shall not fly from humanity',[48] declares Jonson as the kernel of his Aristotelian faith, but *The Tempest* is premissed upon a radical, impossible transmogrification of Jonson's own play's inaugurative power matrix. Thus, *The Alchemist* begins with a furious fight for power between Subtle and Face, each claiming to have set free, indeed created from nothing, the other. The stakes at issue are basically the right to possess and be praised for ill-gotten gains, the environment a vigorously evoked Jacobean London: '*Face*: You most notorious whelpe, you insolent slaue . . . Doe but collect, sir, where I met you first.' *Subtle*: 'No, you *scarabe*, I'll thunder you, in peeces. I will teach you How to beware to tempt a *furie* againe That carries tempest in his hand and voice . . . Thou vermine, haue I tane thee, out of dung, So poore, so wretched . . . And haue I this for thanke? Doe you rebell? Do

---

[47] Jonson's unease seems also to find focus in Shakespeare's licentious willingness to 'quote', and perhaps derogate, absolutism, a scepticism or irony which after *Sejanus* Jonson gradually disdained. It is interesting how the examples of proper speech or writing given in Jonson's *The English Grammar*, in Herford and Simpson, viii. 453–553, almost without exception, warn against ignorance or malice, or uphold moral and political propriety of the '*Feare God. Honour the King*' variety (Jonson's illustration of the '*future*', ch. V. 30, p. 541).

[48] *Discoveries*, 776.

you flie out, i'the *proiection*? . . . Slave, thou hadst no name'.[49]
Anticipations of *The Tempest* are unmistakable. *The Alchemist*
derides presumptions of individual power over origin, just as its
recurrent celebration of the whore Doll as the *'Queene of Fairie'*
or *'Dousabell'* invokes a romance wonder already and irretriev-
ably bastardized. Jonson's Sir Epicure Mammon enters Subtle's
house of alchemy as if setting 'foot on shore In *novo orbe'*, the
New World; he imagines translating parts of England to a
'perfect Indies'.[50] Shakespeare, however, takes Jonson's exposé
of extravagantly mendacious metaphor and, impossibly, makes
it come true: Prospero carries a tempest in his hand, Caliban
rises out of mud, Ariel flies away; there is indeed a state at issue,
a language learnt from nothing, a genuine rebellion. By making
language keep its promises, Shakespeare inaugurates a marvellously 'unnatural' kind of 'decorum'. Of course one's vocabulary here is inadequate: but that is the point.

It is also, I think, a point to which Shakespeare returns.
Jonson's Induction to *Bartholomew Fayre* takes part of its cue
from a specific moment in *The Tempest*: 'if there be neuer a
Seruant-monster i'the fair, who can help it?', is Jonson's rhetorical question, alluding to the drunken confederates' party: *'Ste.*
Seruant Monster, drinke to me. *Trin.* Seruant Monster? the folly
of this Island' (III. ii. 3–4). It is Trinculo who repeats and
savours the strange sobriquet: and who in doing so might be
thought equally to echo the prescriptive mockery of Ben Jonson.
For Shakespeare invests in Trinculo a persistent desire to com-
ment, jealously, disbelievingly, stingily, upon the increasingly
extravagant action. He apostrophizes the spirituous coalition
of Caliban and Stephano with a sequence of pejorative adjectives for 'Monster': 'shallow', 'weake', 'creadulous', drunken',
'puppi-headed', 'scuruie', 'poore', 'abhominable', 'howling' (II.
ii. 144–79). Partly he panders to any ethnological superiority
felt in an audience; at the same time, by speaking the obvious
judgement so volubly and unsympathetically, Trinculo releases
the audience from any such obligation. Sometimes Trinculo can
be played so as to possess a complicitous intimacy with an
audience; equally, he can be played to seem envious, resentful,

---

[49] *Alchemist*, I. i. 11–81.
[50] See II. i. 1–2, 35–6; III. iii. 41, 78; III. v. 6.

and somehow irrelevant, his desire for collusion spluttering into an ignominious and anachronistic chorus. It has often been noted how Caliban, despite his drunkenness, gathers in whatever dignity is available; Trinculo's censoriousness contributes to this relative, paradoxical humanizing of the beast. For like the cynical aristocrats earlier, Trinculo here objects to the very genus of the island and its play: it and its amphibian are *sui generis*, and Trinculo is unable to accept the novelty. Instead he is anxious to domesticize its oddness by importing English fairs, like Jonson's, as its context: 'were I in *England* now . . . and had but this fish painted; not a holiday-foole there but would giue a peece of siluer' (II. ii. 28–30). Trinculo rests his dignity upon a type of literalizing hermeneutic which, throughout these works, and whoever the observer, is invariably and joylessly reductive: 'Thou liest most ignorant Monster . . . wilt thou tell a monstrous lie, being but halfe a Fish, and halfe a Monster?' Caliban, at times as linguistically precise as Holofernes, is sensitive to the insult: 'Loe, how he mockes me, wilt thou let him my Lord?', to which Trinculo provides the consummate Jonsonian riposte: 'Lord, quoth he? that a Monster should be such a naturall?' (III. ii. 26–31). Shakespeare may or may not have had Jonson in his sights here.[51] But certainly Trinculo's punning indignation chimes with Jonson's disdain for similar insults to 'nature'. Thus, by 'naturall' he jokes upon Caliban's pretence at fine speech, a presumptuousness which makes of him another kind of 'naturall', a fool. Jonson plays frequently upon the same critical chord: 'But how out of purpose, and place, doe I name Art? when the Professors are growne so obstinate contemners of it, and presumers on their owne Naturalls, as they are deriders of all diligence that way'.[52] Caliban, presuming on his own 'naturals', here merges into momentary conflation with carelessly flippant playwrights. At the same time, Trinculo's contempt points to the contrast between Jonson's mirror of nature and Shakespeare's strangely packed, distorting, distending specular figurations. As Jonson says of *The Alchemist*'s parade of gulls and rogues both on stage and off: 'They are so naturall

---

[51] Harry Levin, 'Two Magian Comedies: *The Tempest* and *The Alchemist*', *Sh. S.* 22 (1969), 48, sees Stephano as 'more of a Jonsonian type, with his petty airs and ill-supported pretensions'.

[52] *Alchemist*, 'To the Readers', 6–11; *Discoveries*, 735–50.

follies, but so showne, As euen the doers may see, and yet not owne'.[53] Where Jonson offers an accelerated realism, each person discrete and verifiable, Shakespeare supplies metaphor-in-process.

Shakespeare's revivification of decorum, then, is equally and symbiotically linguistic, characterological, generic: each is a kind of metonym of the other. For example, Stephano circles the strange hybrid beneath the gaberdine, evoking its wonder in much the same terms as, in *Bartholomew Fayre*, Ben Jonson rebuked his rival's latest fangled inventions: 'What's the matter? Haue we diuils here? Doe you put trickes vpon's with Saluages, and Men of Inde? ha?' (II. ii. 58–9). The butler identifies lucrative public entertainment in the hybrid's strangeness. The moment might oddly evoke an impresario's discovery of tragi-comic pastoral, the ugly generic mule ready to be dusted off and sold to a half-mocking, half-enthralled public: 'if I can recouer him, and keepe him tame, I will not take too much for him; hee shall pay for him that hath him, and that soundly' (II. ii. 78–80).[54] Stephano's registering of two confutacious voices further suggests the antinomic medium upon which he has stumbled and in which he partakes: 'his forward voyce now is to speake well of his friend; his backward voice, is to vtter foule speeches, and to detract' (I. ii. 92–4). The two mouths can embody, successively or simultaneously, dissonance, rebuttal, confusion, competition; they invoke dialogue without harmony.

Still more specifically, Stephano puns upon the immemorial scatological sources of comedy: the 'backward voice' and its 'foule speeches' evoke the activity of cacology, of carnivalesque inversion and faeces. But the comic here is also a fundamental source of wonder: 'how cam'st thou to be the siege of this Moone-calfe? Can he vent *Trinculo's*?' (II. ii. 106–8). Shakespeare sustains the excremental metaphors, as though enveloping the whole scene of burlesque recapitulation and rebirth within a symphony of farts: 'I tooke him to be kil'd with a thunder-strok', replies Trinculo (II. ii. 109), identifying Prospero's 'foule bumbard' with the 'foule speeches' of the

---

[53] *Alchemist*, Prologue, 23–4.
[54] Compare Sidney's disparaging reference to 'mongrel tragi-comedy', *The Defence of Poetry*, 67.

hybrid. The analogies continue multiplying with bewildering abandon; the whole scene, for instance, is continuing the play's pivotal interest in the genetics of language. One sees, then, how the 'forward' and 'backward' voices cohere and engage despite the absence, or dispersal, or chimerical quality, of the speaking body. The hybrid is never 'real', and it quickly breaks up into its constituent parts, a jester and a moon-calf. Romance wonder is here readied for sarcasm, incongruity, for ironical forms of duality: the two heads incarnate how the plays amplify the double-voice of the pun, splicing meaning and splitting degree. But more than this, the scene's strange beast both collapses and animates a kind of gothic mirror. Decorous fantasy sustains the cosmetic, flattering separation of opposing images: Shakespeare's analogies, however, repeatedly draw out the paradox of specularity, how the mirror-image is both likeness and opposite, faithful and inverting, real and illusionary. When Trinculo and Caliban become, according to Stephano's fantastic report, one body, they exemplify the way metaphorical dialogue in these plays undresses and reorganizes the assumptions, indeed the very assumption, of both conventional place and verisimilitudinous character. For this moment also describes the way these plays build character: 'literally', out of language, from the joining, splitting, and rejoining of often outlandish—even outlawish—metaphor. So, the 'delicate monster' in a sense re-prophesies Caliban himself: Trinculo is separated from the 'islander', but the descriptions of the four-legged thing still apply perfectly to the exotic beast. Caliban is augmented, made the sum of his surroundings, whether or not his flesh is 'really' joined with another's. Hence Caliban's continuing, nameless, perfectly meta-dramatic elusiveness: 'romance', in this formulation, coheres in the 'Monster'. The genre, like the magic island, stays defined, or undefined, in characters and moments such as these.

AUDIENCE AND RECEPTION

Assumptions that Shakespeare's last plays must be courtly are often buttressed by reference to the works' contemporary audiences. For while there is no record of either *Pericles* or

Cymbeline being performed at court, both *The Winter's Tale* and *The Tempest* contributed to the wedding celebrations of Elizabeth and Frederick in 1612–13. Both plays had already been performed before the king in the holidays of 1611–12. Yet, while state surveillance and patronage may help explain the political prudence of much Jacobean drama, they do not appear to have exercised paralysing limitations. The plays presented at court suggest nothing so much as a distillation of those produced at the more affluent London playhouses. The 1611–13 period saw, among others, *Macbeth*, *The Tempest*, *Philaster*, *The Winter's Tale*, *Julius Caesar*, *Othello*, *1 Henry IV*, and *The Maid's Tragedy*, too complex and various a collection to support any theory about courtly mollification. When James was present, as Dudley Carleton wrote to John Chamberlain, 'he liked or disliked as he saw cause; but it seems he takes no extraordinary pleasure in them'.[55] Indeed, the court as playhouse seems to have been surprisingly tolerant. Thus, even *Eastward Ho!* —whose jokes against Scottish favourites and 'thirty pound knights' initially caused its authors' arraignment—was played before James at court in 1614. The players may or may not have suppressed the offending passages; the play was by then almost ten years old. What they could hardly have elided is the play's repeated mockery of court lightness and dishonesty. As Jonson suggests in *Bartholomew Fayre*, and no doubt as the cloistered king assumed, not every play was a '*Seller* of *Mouse-trappes*'.[56]

Still, even if the royal influence itself was oblique, it has been a common assumption that Shakespeare's last works were written specifically for the indoors theatre at Blackfriars, and so for a rich and privileged audience who attended to the players as they might their private glass: for preening self-correction and grateful applause. Richard Burbage took the Blackfriars lease in August 1608, but plague meant that the King's Men could not really use it until late 1609 or early 1610. It is highly likely that, once they could, Shakespeare's romances were among those put

[55] Reference in Chambers, *Elizabethan Stage*, i. 7 n. 'The Queen and Prince were more the players frends, for on other nights they had them privatly, and hath since taken them to theyr protection': dated 15 Jan. 1604.
[56] 'The Indvction on the Stage', 145.

on.[57] The major advantage of the indoor theatre, perhaps, was financial: Blackfriars was roofed and warm, allowing not only more expensive prices but—excepting plague—entertainment all year round. Thus a King's Men's play need not be a commercial failure because of the vagaries of the seasons. It is difficult to see why the acquisition of Blackfriars should have prompted, in itself, the production of a more courtly drama. *Pericles*, of course, pre-dates the purchase.[58] A slowing down of the acting, a quietening of the voices, a more attentive and less restless audience may have facilitated less bombast, more gentle and insinuative moral dialogues. However, the more considering and thoughtful environment—if such it was, with the gallants crowding like peacocks on the stage—will equally have encouraged finesse, intellectuality, the expectation that small details will be picked up and remembered. Consequently, even if the plays were written with the new theatre in mind, this enhances the likelihood that they encode subtle political dialogues.[59] A stately, star-gazing theatre is hardly more likely indoors than at the rowdier amphitheatres. Of course, Shakespeare's work was never like this; the closest it gets is probably *Henry VIII*, which, nevertheless, contains in its first half an hour language as turbid and figurative as anything in the canon.[60]

Nor should one be simplistic about the political prescriptiveness necessary to a 'well-to-do' audience. To be 'courtly' might mean various things. On the one hand there are the gallants, prepared for sparring wits and mockery of the gauche; on the other is something more careful of the privilege of rank and the dignity of government. Blackfriars may have been a haunt of the wealthy, but the proximity of the Inns of Court made it a young man's theatre, conducive to satire and iconoclasm, its patrons anxious to seem both clever and fashionable; railing

[57] Andrew Gurr, '*The Tempest*'s Tempest at Blackfriars', *Sh. S.* 41 (1989), 91–102, sees the musicality and costume changes of *The Tempest* as evidence that it was the first unquestionably Blackfriars play; however, he also sees it as a 'play which consistently arouses, challenges, and disappoints courtier expectations' (102).

[58] *Pericles* was entered on the stationers' register on 20 May, 1608. For evidence regarding first performance see J. Leeds Barroll, *Politics, Plague, and Shakespeare's Theater: The Stuart Years* (Ithaca, NY, 1991), pp. 192–8.

[59] Compare G. E. Bentley, 'Shakespeare and the Blackfriars Theatre', *Sh. S.* 1 (1948), 38–50.

[60] It was a Globe performance of *Henry VIII* which caused the theatre to burn down.

against the court was known to 'choke the theatres' with patrons. Jonson's critique of popular taste might here help to
suggest the manners to which both he and Shakespeare played:
'they commend Writers, as they doe Fencers, or Wrastlers; who
if they come in robustuously, and put for it with a great deale of
violence, are receiu'd for the brauer fellowes'.[61] Jonson may
seem to envisage a more 'sordid' auditorium than Blackfriars
(for which *The Alchemist* was evidently intended). But he was
equally dismissive of 'the neater sort of our *Gallants*: for all are
the multitude; only they differ in cloaths, not in judgement, or
understanding'.[62] Thus, his scorn for public opinion might easily
embrace the supposed sophistication of Blackfriars, as it evidently does the more vulgar assemblies at the Hope or the
Globe. That Shakespeare was not the captive hand of courtly
dictation is reinforced by the fact that, throughout the 'romance
years', the Globe remained the King's Men's major source of
fame and revenue. Indeed to Jonson the sweet swan of Avon
appears to have been royal, or courtly, mainly in the waste and
excess of his fantastical bounty: he assesses Shakespeare, not as
a rival for the king's grace, but as a man of the theatre, playing
to a vast and vulgar crowd. That his plays were also seen at
court suggests, if anything, that one should be wary of facileness
in identifying deterministic links between anticipated audiences
and political dialogues: neither is monolithic or univocal. Even
Jonson's court masques draw upon the material of his plays,
while *Bartholomew Fayre* had its first performance at the 'stink-
ing' Hope and its second, the very next night, before the king at
Whitehall.[63] Shakespeare's suffrages, I think, remained 'general'.[64]

---

[61] *The Alchemist*, 'To the Reader', 16–18, in *Ben Jonson*, ed. Herford and
Simpson, v. 273–407.

[62] *Discoveries*, 643–5.

[63] *Bartholomew Fayre*, Induction, 160; *Alchemist*, 'To the Reader', 30.

[64] Consider the anonymous verses, *Pimlyco, or Runne Red-Cap* (London, 1609):
'(As at a *New-play*) all the Roomes | Did swarme with *Gentiles* mix'd with *Groomes*,
| So that I truly thought all these | Came to see *Shore* or *Pericles*.' Quoted by P. Z.
Round, introduction to *Pericles: The First Quarto, 1609, A Facsimile from the
British Museum Copy*, ed. Charles Praetorius (London, 1886), p. iv. The Globe had
a higher proportion of the 'privileged' in its audiences than the other public theatres.
For arguments about the ratio, see Ann Jennalie Cook, *The Privileged Playgoers of
Shakespeare's London 1576–1642* (Princeton, 1981); Andrew Gurr, *Playgoing in
Shakespeare's London* (Cambridge, 1987); Martin Butler, *Theatre and Crisis 1632–
1642* (Cambridge, 1984), Appendix 2.

POLICY OF INCLUSION

Working within a critical tradition which has canonized the 'four romances' as a discrete group, culminating in *The Tempest*'s valedictory perfection, I have chosen not to look in detail at *The Two Noble Kinsmen* and *Henry VIII*. The critical conventions surrounding the four earlier works require, I think, sustained challenge; sticking to the traditional group has helped define my work's scope. Furthermore, the nature of my task has made necessary extensive explications of each of the plays. Simple restrictions of time and space have contributed to my policy of exclusion. And indeed, if there is a generic link between *The Tempest* and *The Two Noble Kinsmen*—and on most counts the two appear fairly remote—then, as my first chapter suggests, there is equally a link between the civic debates of *Pericles* and *Coriolanus*. Similarly, romantic myths of origin are a crucial subject in *King Lear* and *Macbeth*. And *Henry VIII* is tied to historical fact in ways that the others, superficially luxuriating in romance's fabled 'anonymity', are not. To go 'forward' in time, then, was no more tempting than to go 'backward': such a project is there to be done, but not quite here.

Still more, there is a sense in which *The Tempest*, particularly in its construction of Caliban, brings to a consummation the romances' magnetic, amoeboid heteroglossia: both *Kinsmen* and *Henry VIII* lack that shape-shifting figure onto whom so much of the earlier plays' political dialogue is loaded. This is not to say that the later plays are without all kinds of fascinating conflations; and it may well be that Shakespeare's work was moving into still newer experimentation with apparently linear, processional, chronicle form, complicating stateliness with strangely reticent scenic jokes. But there is enough missing from the two post-*Tempest* plays to suggest that Shakespeare knew that a certain mastery had been achieved. Perhaps further associable to a certain feeling of completion, Shakespeare's final three works (if one includes the lost *Cardenio*) are all collaborations. Of course *Pericles* almost certainly is as well, but the way in which its preoccupations so evidently feed into Shakespeare's next three plays argues strongly for inclusion. While this book understands Shakespeare in the context of surrounding theatrical policies and agitations, it remains interested in how Shakespeare's own peculiar structures and language revivify and transform conventional cultural preoccupations. Consequently, my policy has been that I will not include lengthy material about either *Henry VIII* or *Kinsmen* unless the later play seems indispensably to illuminate the texts that precede it.

My hope is that, by concentrating in detail upon a few chosen works, something of the potential and orientation not only of Shakespeare but of the theatre in his day and age can be illuminated. The cultural and historical 'breadth' of this study, then, should emerge in its detail; the implications of such detail might then easily be perspectivized in terms of any number of contemporary works or discourses. There has been much scholarship in recent years which has preferred to apply a critical or anthropological idea, or to cover a vast field with the aim of identifying a medium's or period's ideological diachronics. My approach, in turn, might work to test the sustainability of some of the 'meta-texts' often thought able to apprehend the media within which Shakespeare worked.

TEXTS

I have used as my basic text the earliest. This means facsimiles of the First Folio versions of *The Tempest*, *The Winter's Tale*, and *Cymbeline*, and of the corrupt first quarto of *Pericles*.[65] As regards *Pericles*, I accept the emerging consensus that Wilkins was probably Shakespeare's collaborator, and that his *Painful Adventures*, purporting to be a 'true' prose account of the successful stage performance, can be accounted a second imperfect reported text of a performed play.[66] Wilkins's 'novel' some-

---

[65] *The Norton Facsimile: The First Folio of Shakespeare*, prepared by Charlton Hinman (London, 1968), is an attempt to represent an 'ideal', fully corrected copy, using thirty copies, the best two of which provided about 180 pages each (pp. xxii–xxvii). No copy of 'The Folio' is satisfactory, and Hinman's choices are inevitably arbitrary, but in the absence of an authorially sanctioned edition the Norton is probably a better option than fixing upon a particular copy, with its own idiosyncratic, equally arbitrary, foibles.

[66] See Macdonald P. Jackson, '*Pericles*, Acts I and II: New Evidence for George Wilkins', *Notes and Queries* (1990), 192–6.

times conforms to the quarto play text, sometimes borrows from Twine's prose version of the story of Apollonius, and sometimes appears to fill in gaps which make good stage sense yet which are absent from all other versions. Why Wilkins so plagiarizes Twine (reprinted in 1607, either as a spur to the play's composition or to cash in on its successs) is difficult to explain unless one hypothesizes that this roguish character was for some reason retrenched or excluded from the production and so was not privy to the papers or the processes through which Shakespeare finished the job.[67] I use Wilkins to help recover the basic action of the play, but I don't attempt to piece together the 'actual' words of the popular Globe performance.

Q1 has priority, but nothing like infallibility. Three quarto versions were produced before the First Folio's publication in 1623, each based on the preceding edition; a further three editions appeared by 1635. One might assume, in such circumstances, that the 1609 quarto at least approximates to the way the piece was performed. But the text remains manifestly 'corrupt', with its first two acts in particular hobbled by lacunae, inconsistencies, and lameness. Shakespeare could not have written much of the opening two acts as they stand; this seems a safe if unprovable assumption. However, it cannot explain why they begin a play which manifestly is by Shakespeare after (and perhaps at times during) the scenes at Pentapolis. He may have found an old play and finished it; he may have had an inferior collaborator; he may have written an entire play whose transmission has suffered from imperfect memorial reconstruction, perhaps with one actor considerably worse at recalling parts than the other[s]; or the answer may rest in a combination of such elements, for instance a collaborative, immensely popular play, duly pirated

---

[67] Stanley Wells, Gary Taylor, John Jowett, and William Montgomery, eds., *William Shakespeare: A Textual Companion* (Oxford, 1986), 557–8, argue that a collaborator need not possess a personal copy of the manuscript, and that the foul papers would probably have passed out of Wilkins's hands well before performance. They speculate that the King's Men didn't trust the unscrupulous petty criminal Wilkins. It is intriguing, in the light of *Pericles* and its textual history, that Wilkins soon left the literary world for a life as a tavern, or perhaps brothel, keeper. See Stanley Wells, introd., *William Shakespeare: The Complete Works: Original Spelling Edition*, ed. Wells *et al.* (Oxford, 1986), p. xxi.

in a text cobbled together by unemployed players or other opportunistic auditors.[68]

Significant emendation is obviously often necessary with *Pericles*, and occasionally with *Cymbeline*. However, I have preferred the earliest editions so as to escape the often silent preferences and partialities of modern editorial practice. I have consulted many such modern editions: but avoiding reliance upon any single one has I think often permitted a fresher, less unconsciously predetermined response. For if a phrase appears to be 'defined' by an editor, this will invariably prevent any further investigation; sometimes it is just such investigation which untaps discourse that modern scholarly apparatus has, no doubt invariably against its will, repressed. Annotation can of course rarely be comprehensive, and one wouldn't particularly wish it to be so; but it is remarkable the extent to which editorial annotation distorts or abbreviates possible meanings.

I also think that to read the texts in their 'original' print, spelling, and punctuation allows the words to 'breathe', and to give one some sense, however imperfect, of the accents and rhythms of the period.[69]. Of course any sense of 'naked' communion is deceptive. The three Folio plays are among those edited by Ralph Crane who, although an accurate copyist, habitually brought his own fussy and erratic practices to bear upon the texts.[70] Crane was heavy with hyphens, capitals, inverted commas, brackets, and commas; some guide to syntax and semantics might still be gleamed, but one should renounce illusions abut Shakespeare's fastidious guiding hand.[71] None the

---

[68] For varying hypotheses see: Sidney Thomas, 'The Problem of *Pericles*', *SQ* 34 (1983), 448–50; F. D. Hoeniger's, 'Gower and Shakespeare in *Pericles*', *SQ* 33 (1982), 461–80; S. Musgrove, 'The First Quarto of *Pericles* Reconsidered', *SQ* 29 (1978), 389–406; Philip Edwards, 'An Approach to the Problem of *Pericles*', *Sh. S* (1952), 25–49; Gary Taylor, 'The Transmission of *Pericles*', *Papers of the Bibliographical Society of America* (1986), 193–217; Wells et al., *Textual Companion*, 556–7.

[69] See Vivian Salmon's essay on spelling in Wells et al., *Original Spelling Edition*, pp. xxxvi–liii.

[70] See T. H. Howard-Hill, *Ralph Crane and Some Shakespeare First Folio Comedies* (1972); Wells et al., *Textual Companion*, 20–2.

[71] Margreta De Grazia, *Shakespeare Verbatim: The Reproduction of Authenticity and the 1790 Apparatus* (Oxford, 1991), 16–18, notes the typographic irregularity of the First Folio, its 600 different typefaces, erratic spelling, scene-divisions, punctuation, inconsistent 'proofing', and so on.

less, the texts do emerge from the King's Men, and theatre remains a fundamentally collaborative art. The Folio plays are all of fairly good copy, with no quarto edition to quarrel with or over; and modern editors use little else themselves.[72]

---

[72] I have not altered character names from the 'original', even where such practice disagrees with convention (Autolicus–Autolycus) or with evidence which might refute the authority of the Folio (Imogen–Innogen); in this latter case the Folio preference may reflect company practice altering Shakespeare's initial choice of 'Innogen' (evidence for which is quite persuasive, see Wells et al., *Textual Companion*, 604, for summary) perhaps simply because it sounded better and flowed more easily. Where a name is spelt in various different ways I choose the one used most 'authoritatively' (where possible: cf. Ariel–Ariell).

I

Romance, Irony, and Humanism

By Shakespeare's time there had developed two broad traditions of 'romance', treating of its heroic subject-matter in fairly
distinct ways. There was the tradition represented most famously by Spenser's *Faerie Queene* and Sidney's *Arcadias*, highly
wrought, esoteric imitatios of classical, medieval, and continen-
tal epic-pastoral. And there was the cheery demotic trade in
ballads, penny chap-books, and open-air plays. Where Sidney
and Spenser attempted intricate *entrelacement* and allegoric
counsel, the popular media offered gauche, episodic bast-
ardizings of archetypal heroic exemplars. Long after aristocratic
audiences had come to disdain them, fictional knights and
crusading zeal remained the staple fare of majority desire. The
facile inelegancies of popular plagiarism were thought to express 'the irregular impulses of the unlearned'.[1] The old
tales of Dido, Aeneas, Arthur, and Griseld would filter down,
transformed by the empathetic imperatives of an extemporiz-
ing crowd: Guy of Warwick discovers plebeian parents, the
disguised king is pilloried by unsuspecting commoners, rags-
to-riches becomes the daily festive theme.[2] Neither mode of
appropriation, humanist or vulgar, was a meek or deferential
one. And Shakespearian romance—distinct from both, drawing
from each—offers a further generic vivification: a new word in
old worlds.

So, whereas the 'romance' genre is often thought of in terms
of privilege and hierarchy, even in the hands of its most noble
exponents it was anything but politically apologetic. Sidney and
Spenser, politicians both, engage in sustained appraisals of
Elizabethan policies and ideology. Shakespeare enjoyed less intimacy with the ruling classes, and had less investment in the

[1] Northrop Frye, *The Secular Scripture: A Study of Romance* (Cambridge, Mass.,
1976), 23.
[2] See Bernard Capp, 'Popular Literature', in Barry Reay, ed., *Popular Culture in
Seventeenth-Century England* (London, 1985), 198–243.

personages and orientation of government; but he emulates his illustrious predecessors in presuming the liberty to analyse matters of state. However, he does so from within and for a quite distinct franchise. Sidney and Spenser, however critical of contemporary arrangements, observe aristocratic decorums which assume themselves and their heroes ineffably beyond the common ruck. Such assumptions feed into a disdain for popular taste. In his *Arcadia*, for instance, Sidney derides the 'low' Mopsa's literary tastes, foreshadowing how seventeenth-century prose romance would often publish militantly anti-populist sentiments.[3] Things 'classic', and so worthy of serious emulation, become defined by an aloofness from proletarian appetites. Shakespeare, by contrast, worked in a popular medium with its own self-respecting and correspondingly more irreverent traditions. His plays remain humanist, at times scholarly, and always engaged with the questions of liberty, apostasy, and virtue which so move Sidney and Spenser. But still there are matters of tone, perspective, and priority which will distinguish the literary epic from the urban dramatic event. As Gower says in his introduction to *Pericles*: 'It hath been sung at Feastiuals, On Ember eues and Holy-dayes', quite as often as it has been 'red' by 'Lords and Ladyes' (I Chorus, 5–7). The old tale is brushed off as a genuine popular entertainment, a song as much as a book, prone to all the dilations and mutations which the oral tradition confers.

So, in turning to the romance mode Shakespeare not only invokes the *Arcadia*, but pays a type of homage to popular Elizabethan plays such as *The Rare Triumphs of Love and Fortune*, *Sir Clyomon and Sir Clamydes*, *Mucedorus*, *The Thracian Wonder*, and *Locrine*. These works tirelessly invoke chivalrous motif and sentiment but, as if faithful to their demotic franchise, remain strangely disobedient beasts. They share audience and orientation with old tales and ballads, possessing a tabloid topicality, a capacity to satirize, and an instinct toward allegory; they draw similarly upon fables, a genre rooted in the self-preservation and emotional democratizing of 'proletarian'

---

[3] See Paul Salzman, *English Prose Fiction 1558–1700: A Critical History* (Oxford, 1985), 112, 156–63, *et al.*

communities.[4] Improbable tales are not always the mollifying slave either of escapism or hegemony.

And, indeed, so-called 'escapism' can be inherently political. As Pocock has written, there was in Renaissance England an 'excess of civic consciousness', more than the 'available institutional and conceptual schemes could contain'.[5] Frustrated public aspiration may be displaced onto those figures or arenas, like the theatre, in which appetite can notionally be met. Burgeoning desire will be inscribed in the violent over-production of metaphor, or anticipated in the waiting promise symbolized by audience empathy. Public theatre fills in for the belatedness of political institutions: playing in the gap between desire and achievement, it can be the auditorium of disappointment, but equally of legitimate expectation.

An environment like this will develop an unfussy sense of 'class', and of the self-projections surrounding rank and achievement. Public theatre-goers rarely sought, or saw, images of their own mundanities. Instead, plays would feature the over-vaulting *virtu* of an unusually ascendant 'every-man' (or -woman); or, of course, the dashing and noble aristocrat. Either way, those who watch would not do so as at church, with hats off, heads bowed, lips sealed. The 'entertainment' is both vicarious and projective, a dialogue of desire. Escapism, flattery, and empathy here join in self-vindicating circle. The more ingenuous style of Elizabethan dramatic romance invariably discovers the roots of chivalrous discourse in a romantic alliance of noble and peasant.[6]

Some such idealized partnership can be seen exemplified, for example, in *The Thracian Wonder*. Various nobles and commoners unite in a crusade against perceived corruption at court. The rebellious 'Rabble' seek to win back the shepherd-princess, Ariadne, from the clutches of the king who abducts her. The

---

[4] See Annabel Patterson, *Fables of Power: Aesopian Writing and Political History* (Durham, 1991).

[5] J. G. A. Pocock, *The Machiavellian Moment: Florentine Political Thought and the Atlantic Republican Tradition* (Princeton, 1975), 348.

[6] Richard C. McCoy, *The Rites of Knighthood: The Literature and Politics of Elizabethan Chivalry* (Berkeley, 1989), 158–9, *et al.*; Perez Zagorin, *The Court and the Country: The Beginning of the English Revolution* (London, 1969), 75, 83, *et al.* Aristocratic peers would often stand upon their ancient privileges; wary of giving too much prerogative to the monarch, they thought themselves on the one hand the protector of the rights and liberties of the people, and on the other the monarch's bulwark against the 'insolency of the multitude'.

king offers the leader of the rebels—the disguised but noble
Radogan—a private conference. Radogan refuses: 'I better understand the Name and Honor of a General, Than to disgrace it
'gainst the Law of Arms'.[7] Asked later whether he accepts peace,
Radogan replies that 'Were it in me To give an answer, you
should soon prevail, But 'tis a General voice': there is a consonance between honourable leadership and popular equity.[8] Public speech and accountability are a measure and satisfaction of
chivalrous idealism: 'If you have ought to say, speak publickly,
No private Protestations, Bribes, nor Fears, Have power to
convert our Resolutions'.[9]

While a polarization in taste was in its early stages, such
material hadn't entirely disappeared from the minds and entertainments of the better-off; it has been argued, for instance, that
James's daughter Elizabeth liked to recast her own travails in
terms of the romances of which she was so fond.[10] However,
there had developed a fashion for parodying the mode's more
foolish and hackneyed pretensions. This was already evident in
some of the stirring 'romances' of the 1590s, the sceptical bent
of which has led to suggestions that some may have been coterie
rather than popular plays.[11] Amid much pomp and chivalry, one
identifies in Elizabethan dramatic romance a repeated openness
to irony and travesty. The plays are populated strategically with
lowly characters who profane what is noble with colloquial
humour or clumsy mistake. Like any clowns, they presume
intimacy with their audience. Satire is discernible even in very
early works. The knave Shift is a sardonic choric presence in
Clyomon and Clamydes, while in *Love and Fortune* Lentulo
responds bullishly to the hero's father's esoteric pastoralism:
'Hee'le do nothing all day long but sit on his arse, as my mother
did when she made poutes', just as he mocks the hero's love-lorn

---

[7] *The Thracian Wonder: A Comical History* (London, 1661), 'by John Webster
and William Rowley', sig. G^v.

[8] Ibid. G2^v.

[9] Ibid. G2^r.

[10] Barbara Kiefer Lewalski, *Writing Women in Jacobean England* (Cambridge,
Mass., 1993), 45–6.

[11] For example, *The Lamentable Tragedy of Locrine: A Critical Edition*, ed. Jane
Lytton Gooch (New York, 1981), 20, 32–4; Fredson Bowers, *Elizabethan Revenge
Tragedy 1587–1642* (Gloucester, Mass., 1959); Brian Vickers, *The Artistry of
Shakespeare's Prose* (London, 1968), 16, 24, 43.

cry against Venus and Fortune: 'Love, my maisters, is a parlous matter! How it runnes out of my nose!'[12]

The japes of Mouse in *Mucedorus*—a work whose numerous revisions and revivals offer an almost tangible bridge between the Elizabethan and Jacobean popular romance—are similar.[13] Running around drinking and eating, indulging in curiously aimless lechery, he smirks at all that surrounds him. Mouse's register is one of indifference, of political and generic atheism. He derides the assiduity of loyal servants, using a wilful deafness to explain disobedience and to pressure tired commands into exhausted puns. His master is the ostensible heir to the throne, but also a usurous coward; yet Mouse shows no more respect for the romantic chevalier, and revels in the furtive sensuality of the heroine. The play's choric motions may be formulaic, but the market which they serve is one of popular insouciance and iconoclasm. The commercial success of *Mucedorus* suggests that it wasn't only the fashionable and privileged who enjoyed teasing chivalry's neoplatonic certainties. Indeed the public theatre's manners themselves depend upon a casually blithe kind of erudition. The name of the hero is taken from Sidney's *Arcadia*; that he is treated less than reverentially suggests the popular theatre's power of affectionate mockery, and its habit of taking a cultural 'brand-name' and making of it something which both counterpoints and transforms the 'original'. Shakespeare of course does it, in immensely more complex ways, both with famous stage-figures (Hamlet, Lear-Leir) and notorious history-makers (Caesar, Cleopatra, Oldcastle-Falstaff). It is interesting, in the light of *Mucedorus*, that the name of Sidney's other hero is 'Pyrocles'. The talismanic name can itself establish the new romance's up-to-the-moment brief: invoking, teasing, and reappraising the manners of heroic pastoral romance.

In *Locrine*, still less naïve and more reflexive, the comedian Strumbo's first scene has him seduce a young woman, Dorothea, through a self-flattering show of 'new coined words'. A stage direction then reads 'Turning to the people', whereupon Strumbo advises 'us' to copy his tricks if we too seek sexual

---

[12] *An Edition of The Rare Triumphs of Love and Fortune*, ed. John Isaac Owen (New York, 1979), ii. 646, 1000.

[13] *A most pleasant Comedie of Mucedorus*, 'sometimes ascribed to Robert Greene' (London, 1598; repr. Amersham, 1913), ed. John S. Farmer.

success (I. iii). It is both endearing and transparent; one sides with him, while remaining quite able to see that his 'learning' is in fact a familiar malapropizing simplicity. Annotated all the while by his own unblushing candour, Strumbo's character is a kind of compendium of low-life appetite. Benign and invincible, he is more akin to a puppeteer's Punch than to a 'subjective' stage artisan. He is constantly the butt of satire—for instance for being ruled first by lust and then by the woman—but in his demotic significance undiminished because he is his own mocker and so his own audience. Strumbo's orchestrations make him a type of ringmaster, or even playwright, who at the same time incorporates the audience, anticipating and in a sense forestalling their own potentially sarcastic judgements.

This multi-reflexivity is an important guide to the manners of such ironized romance: even where, as in *Pericles*, the master of ceremonies is neither impudent nor ironical, the generic attitude of the work will itself impute just such a presence. Gower is from a distant time, and never pretends that his hobbling commentary can do justice to, let alone complete, the story. He ends most of his framing narratives with a humble deferral to the arts of the theatre. He sees his job as a bridging one, filling in the gaps, and begging the audience's patience and acceptance toward the story's patent violations of the unities. This in itself may be an unnecessary posture of apology, one that draws attention less to the play's sweeping freeness with time and place—think of any of Shakespeare's tragedies—than to Gower's own outmoded conservatism. In other words, Gower is an old style master of ceremonies who implies, and indeed invites, the presence of a more modern counterpart, one who hasn't slept through recent theatrical history. Such recent precedent forms part of the audience's hermeneutic equipment: they are in there, nudging things along.

At another moment in *Locrine* the great warrior Albanact, bereft following defeat, kills himself after one final imprecation against 'Dame Fortune'. We then see Strumbo lying on the ground feigning death. His apprentice Trompart enters and tells a joke about the dead prince: 'O what hath he don, his nose bleeds?' Then, seeing Strumbo, he begins a ditty-cum-elegy which, in celebrating 'the fine mery cobler of Cathnes towne', quite swamps all thoughts of the fallen leader (II. vi. 91–112).

Service and loyalty are shown to be local and provincial, as
Trompart's monody spreads out to evoke the commonwealth's
multifarious franchise: 'O you cockatrices and you bablatrices,
that in the woods dwell: You briers and brambles, you cookes
shoppes and shambles, come howle and yell. With howling and
screeking, with wailing and weeping, come you to lament, O
colliers of Croyden, and rusticks of Royden, and fishers of Kent'
(II. vi. 101–8). Of course, Strumbo is not dead; but this doesn't
undercut the requiem's priorities even if it makes its occasion
absurd. Again, after the Scythians have burnt to cinders
Strumbo's house and his wife, Albanact promises to repair the
loss by rebuilding his lodging by 'our pallace gate'. Strumbo
takes it as a condescending and somehow ignorant insult: 'O
pettie treason to my person, no where else but by your
backside . . . you must build our houses by the Tauerne' (II. iv.
82–8). The insult is threefold: to assume for himself the prerogative of arraignment, to dismiss the prince's reparations as
'petty', and, relishing his moment as carnival king, to identify
proximity to the palace with the arsehole of a prince. Strumbo
here represents a whole community, encapsulated in 'the
Taverne'. On behalf of them he looks at Albanact and, as if into
an impudent mirror, sees himself dressed in and deriding the
arrogance of dominium. To the extent that Strumbo still speaks
here as Albanact's subject he affirms the duty of government to
provide for the people in ways the people want; 'you must', he
says, and the imperative tone might well provoke a similar
horrified indignation as the tribune's peremptory 'shall' did in
Coriolanus (III. i. 87–94). Such moments suggest the effective
'heteroglossia' of popular media, and also an inherent scepticism toward the more pious, self-regarding morals of romance.
'Decorum' is usually thought of as imposed from above, serving
the proprietorial interests of degree. But it might equally protect
the humble and, in the sense that they 'own' certain tropes
and topographies, give to the multitude a narrative and
hermeneutic sovereignty. Furthermore, a certain larcenous,
cocksure energy in Strumbo might remind one just how
unimmutable and factitious supposed hierarchies can seem.
If Strumbo speaks for the 'base', it is less some undistin-
guished mass than a clever, rather 'modern' force which can
be at once 'upwardly mobile' and proudly nostalgic. There is

a form of class consciousness, defined against monolithic but powerful folly; but it is not the sort of collectivity interested in stopping one of its number from peeling off and becoming, as it were, a player.

Moreover, as the plays of Marston, Day, Chapman, and Beaumont attest, there were plenty of contemporary examples, particularly among the boy companies' repertoires, of drama returning to the hoary genre so as to mock its platitudes and impossibilities. Romance's mercantile derivatives—for instance Thomas Heywood's 'prodigal plays'—had enjoyed their own flowering on the London stage from the turn of the century to around 1607, and were themselves now the objects of burlesque. These derivatives were invariably 'citizen' plays, celebrating the assiduous morality of the city's new Dick Whittington-style heroes, itinerant xenophobes fighting beneath the banner of majesty, divinity, and a kind of all-in guildhall solidarity. *Eastward Ho!* is a marvellous parody of these ventures, at once scathing and forgiving of figures like its Sir Petronel Flash, a 'knight adventurer' speculating abroad, while callous, feckless, and scheming at home. Beaumont's *The Knight of the Burning Pestle* has a similar ironical programme while making more explicit both its targets-cum-models—fanciful romance and citizen moralities—and the theatrical context of these battles. By making the Blackfriars' stage part of the play's setting, and then populating it with an aesthetically naïve and tendentious 'citizen' audience—made to turn up, as it were, at the wrong theatre—Beaumont dramatizes contrasting notions of imitative decorum. The basic distinction is between a drama which praises its audience through the naïve representation of triumphant bonhomie and virtue, and that which praises its audience by teasing such hearty sincerities: each is the property of a basic social rank.[14] *The Knight*'s reflexiveness, like its initial unpopularity, points to a genre under strain, one battling to accommodate confusing cultural mobility. A further generic transmutation was necessary. Sophisticated romance's mythopoeic, transformatory, but essentially unillusioned political aesthetic was the perfect vehicle for political critique; the trick

---

[14] *The Knight*'s initial failure was, according to Burre the Stationer, because its 'privy mark of irony' was not understood ('Dedicatory Epistle', line 6, p. 51). Blackfriars was not without its quota of 'naïve' spectators.

necessary for success was to tap prevailing energies, but without divisive or condescending ridicule.

It is Shakespeare's last plays which achieve such a feat, but he was undoubtedly influenced by his colleagues' recent history. Of course, it is almost certainly misguided to presume a continuity of policy between the theatre's boy company and the King's Men. Heywood's *Apology for Actors* criticizes the children's plays for 'inueighing against the State, the Court, the Law, the Citty and their gouernements, with the particularizing of priuate mens humors (yet aliue) Noble-men, & others',[15] and contrasts the licentiousness of the boys with the more mature and reticent men's companies. But there was a certain amount of crossing-over both of writers and plays between companies: Marston's *Malcontent*, for instance, was written for the boys and later performed by the King's Men with only minor alterations, while Jonson and Beaumont and Fletcher produced major works for each. The careers of Beaumont and Fletcher in particular testify to the continuance of a sceptical, mischievous temper within the most courtly of milieux. Their work was seen more often at court than anybody's, yet a similar quick, jocular, proverbial satire is discernible in *Philaster*—written for the King's Men—as permeates *The Knight of the Burning Pestle*—produced for and by the children.

The Knight anticipates Shakespeare's romances in various ways. Rafe, the apprentice who becomes the chameleon of all subjects' desires, is a kind of carnival figure: dressed in a veritable parade of impersonated liberties, he is given monarchy's capacity to embody the city. Such fluid interchangeability anticipates particular roles like Autolicus', who similarly spends part of his act as mannequin for a nation's dreams. But the ultimate 'burlesque' of the romance hero is found in Merrythought. Throughout the play he is as negligent as Quixote is of financial imperatives, and yet mutates at the play's end into an all-powerful fount of forgiveness. Merrythought's role involves a consistent travesty of pastoral and romance tropes—the parent who has lost his children, the simple man without means, the mendicant philosopher, base matter transmuting into gold—none of which he believes in but all of which 'pay off'. The

---

[15] Thomas Heywood, *An Apology for Actors* (1612), ed. Richard H. Perkinson (New York, 1941), G3ᵛ.

'Thankes Fortune' of Pericles when his father's armour comes floating into the fisher's net is, in the light of such neighbouring parodies, made a thoroughly dubious encomium to providence (II. i. 120). It is unlikely that Shakespeare, even if he had wanted to, could have returned to pastoral romance without at least accepting—as if part of the contract—such a manipulative scepticism toward its myths.

Similarly, in *Philaster* Beaumont and Fletcher invoke a golden age of damsels and warriors which every turn confirms as a kind of otiose joke. But to treat heroic romance ironically doesn't necessitate a politics of exquisite separation. Political comedy must often tread a subtle line between mockery and conviction; parody will rarely imply civic indifference. So, the play's reflexivity doesn't prevent it from dramatizing, with stirring colloquial good humour, a populace galvanized by insult to the brink of insurrection. *Philaster* teases courtly duplicity, conceited politicians and feckless sovereignty; its rioting citizens are intelligent, individuated, and witty, even if their legitimacy depends finally upon the imprimatur of the hero. And, crucially, it is the urban rebellion which, with characteristic suddenness, draws down the romance ending. The *deus ex machina* is both multiple and popular: comparisons might be made with *Cymbeline*, a play probably influenced by *Philaster*, and one in which the bewildering sequence of events which lead to the closing reconciliations—including the murder of a prince and the swamping of Roman gentry by a raggedly liminal army— suggest that a similarly aggressive, popular heroism, unafraid of mocking the mighty, contributes to any romance transformation. Shakespeare's works are more elusive than those of his fellow King's Men; but they too seek to root out the popular sources which give to chivalrous fantasy its power to project desire.

And yet neither sophistication nor popularity implies the complete adulteration of 'once upon a time' idealism. One might consider *Don Quixote*. Immensely influential, not least in its monumentalization of romance parody, Cervantes' work made it more difficult to play chivalry straight. But undercutting here gives new life to old dreams. Its secularizing of fantasy, its dignifying of mistake, re-endorse the wonder of transcendent self-fashioning. But 'romance' will now, invariably, celebrate or pander to different 'subjects' than medieval knights. It is in such cases that nostalgia—in the sense of challenging contemporary structures through appeal to old forms—can become politically engaged.

That James's son, Prince Henry, was helping to bring a traditional aristocratic chivalry back in vogue is the counter necessary to balance such popular, sceptical appropriations, and so to arrive at a more nuanced sense of the influences which were available to inform the late plays.[16] But such chivalrous ambition was again hardly the stuff of blind obedience: romance here might remain broadly monarchical, but its chivalry became a lightning rod for pan-European political grievances. For chivalry can be 'oppositional', evoking as it so easily does a period of bastard feudalism and private armies. Much of the insult of Essex was in his claim to represent a purer chivalry, a more blue-blooded honour, than could any others crowding around Queen Elizabeth for preferment. Indeed, in seeking to maximize the privileges attaching to his high feudal offices of Constable, Steward, and Earl Marshal, the earl disputed the priority of majesty's prerogative, effectively arguing for the superiority of mixed government. Many 'well-bred' Jacobean malcontents were survivors of Essex's party; they miscegenated humanist scholarship and sceptical sympathies with a thoroughgoing faith in ancient stock and noble honour.[17] Hegemony, in such a context, is racked with sharply contrary priorities. Monarchy can become isolated, or factionalized; the point is that 'romance' was an apposite form in which to portray, with respectful economy, the fact of discord and perhaps the hopes for change.

One recognizes here the folding of the chivalrous knight into the courtly counsellor. For the chivalric revival was itself an expression of humanism's restorative classicism; it was thought that the ancient Romans were the founders of chivalry. Erasmian humanism encouraged a move away from vainglorious heroism toward an emphasis on public service: the honour and fortune of a people, as well as the individual, became the cause. But it was still essentially chivalric virtues—'humanitas', 'virtus'—which fed into the humanist ideal of service to the

---

[16] Philip J. Finkelpearl, *Court and Country Politics in the Plays of Beaumont and Fletcher* (Princeton, 1990), 90–1.
[17] McCoy, *The Rites of Knighthood*, 88–95 ff.

mother- or fatherland. Humanistic training in the liberal arts and military aptitude found specific antecedents in curiality and courtesy.[18]

The chivalrous figure therefore had an inbuilt doubleness. It was open to abuse or mockery, certainly; but the 'best in men' could still be located in the romance quest for perfection. Consequently, while the secularizing trend might doubt the dignity of all things chivalrous, it will also multiply the numbers who may become blessed with a worth once felt attainable only by knights. In other words, if questions about the national future and patriotic definition are to be pursued with seriousness, and are not to be fobbed off with easy scapegoats or anachronistic saviours, then there must prevail a conviction in the genuine worth of 'romance' hope. The resurrection of rusty armour might be part of this, but the sources of such dispensations will now be analysed rather than left as the gift of providence. This doesn't dispense with aristocratic saviours: it implies that their source and responsibilities rest in more than a tiny class of courtiers.

Dramatic romance, then, although a popular form with a popular franchise, does not exclude humanist or sceptical ambitions. The irony with which romance could be treated, coming from various sources—'public', academic, courtly—allowed it to be a particularly appropriate genre for social and political criticism. However, the fact that it is a mode with roots in idealism and transformation allows the criticism to include or lead to projections both constructive and, at times, utopian.

USES OF HISTORY AND HUMANISM

In resurrecting the fourteenth-century poet John Gower, *Pericles* asks the Globe audience to look backward so as to cast ahead: '*Et bonum quo Antiquius eo melius*' (a good thing is better for being older, I Chorus, 10). And old his story is: it is derived from the ancient Greek romance of Apollonius of Tyre. The play is an uncertain palimpsest, the discourse of one age half-obscuring another: ancient odyssey, medieval homily,

---

[18] See Aldo Scaglione, *Knights at Court: Courtliness, Chivalry, and Courtesy from Ottoman Germany to the Italian Renaissance* (Berkeley, 1991), 219–41.

Elizabethan pastoral, Jacobean city comedy. However, the play's apparently nebulous 'medievalism' has invariably fore-stalled real engagement with its particular form of precedent-hunting, its own interrogative humanism. For it is unlikely that the classical sources behind *Coriolanus*, *Timon of Athens*, and *Anthony and Cleopatra*—all written around the same time as *Pericles*—would be relinquished in Shakespeare's return to romance. Each of these plays uses as a major source Plutarch's *Lives of the Noble Grecians and Romanes*. And while it may be true that Plutarch is regularly Shakespeare's channel to the 'Greek tragic spirit',[19] *Coriolanus* in particular does not rest with the dramatization of a heroic or destructive soul. Shakespeare's subject is in part that of humanist political theory in its republican form: how to define civic virtue and create a sustainable balanced state. The great historian of such affairs is Livy, his subject the plebeians and patricians of Rome, and their struggle over centuries to establish not only empire, but social, political, and economic equilibrium. Shakespeare drew upon Livy's *Ab Urbe Condita* for Menenius' belly fable;[20] one can presume that he read more of Livy than this, and it may well be that the remarkable eloquence and individuation of *Coriolanus'* mobs is influenced by the creative, if often capricious, energy of Livy's multitude. *Coriolanus* is not in any simple sense democratic, any more than it is martialistic: it would be surprising if any Jacobean public discourse advocated a system notorious for being as intemperate and irrational as tyranny. But it is, among other things, an analysis of competing civic institutions, of their principles, suffrages, and origin.

Shakespeare's royal patron, however, offered at best ambiguous encouragement to such thought. Whereas James pursued and sponsored various humanist projects, his philosophy of government was providential. While acknowledging as axiomatic the need for good counsel, James had little use or love for civic historicism. He regretted, and attempted to counter, the growing attraction at court of the works of Tacitus. These elegantly clipped accounts of the early Roman emperies were popular not only with the malcontented inheritors of Sidney and Essex's Protestant impatience, but with the young Prince

---

[19] See *Coriolanus*, ed. Philip Brockbank (London, 1976), 29–33.
[20] 'Englished' in the translation by Philemon Holland, published in 1600.

Henry's household, and with intellects as diverse as Francis Bacon, Fulke Greville, William Camden, and his fellow antiquarian Robert Cotton. Likewise popular throughout the continent's Catholic monarchies, Tacitus' *Histories* and *Annals* were an emerging focus for a sceptical, resistant political temperament which Shakespeare at least partly shared.[21] Astringent and unillusioned, they identify the seamy, factitious quality of public life, exposing self-interest and subterfuge where the monarch, perhaps, would prefer to draw a veil of providence and inscrutability. The king's distrust of Tacitus fed into his disbanding of Camden and Cotton's Society of Antiquaries: analysing institutions, demystifying crown sovereignty, confirming the historic rights of the subject, the tendency of the Society was intolerable.

For to publish the origins and methods of monarchy is to advertise its violability. James's convictions here were as well attested as contentious: because 'Kings are not only GODS Lieutenants Vpon earth, and sit Vpon GODS throne, but euen by GOD himselfe they are called Gods', it is 'sedition in Subiects, to dispute what a King may do in the height of his power'.[22] Only a tyrant, James was willing to concede, will choose to live outside the law, or to stay silent on his reasons and doings. But the choice, like the law, is the king's to make. James acknowledged the popular sources of monarchy, but understood such evolution as preparing for the subsequently revealed truth of monarchical prerogative: 'then did kings set down their minds by laws, which are properly made by the King only, but at the rogation of the people'.[23] By 'rogation' James means a formal request, like a supplication for alms, his people accorded the status of grateful beggars. James enjoys the faintly saintly aura the term grants him, while silently correcting the ancient Roman application wherein 'rogation' means the act of submitting a proposed law to the people for their acceptance.

Two basic theories of the commonwealth can be seen here tussling for priority: the first sees unity and order proceeding from the divinely ordained prerogative, the second identifies the

---

[21] See J. H. M. Salmon, 'Stoicism and the Roman Example: Seneca and Tacitus in Jacobean England', *Journal of the History of Ideas*, 50 (1989), 220 ff.

[22] Speech to Lords and Commons at Whitehall, Mar., 1609: *The Political Works of James I*, ed. C. H. McIlwain (Cambridge, Mass. 1918), 307.

[23] Ibid. 309.

inherited rights and liberties of every free-born member of
the realm. 'Liberty' and 'franchise' here begin to take on modern connotations, distinct from the exclusive privileges and
immunities—usually the possession of organized collectivities—
characteristic of the Middle Ages. The identity here emerging—
between subjectivity and 'citizenship'—suggests important
parallels between the early seventeenth-century English commonweal and the general dynamics of republican humanism.
Justice, like good fortune, rests upon human virtue and mutual
enterprise. A sustainable community requires the political virtue
of its inhabitants.

None the less, mainstream English thought was hostile to
innovation, and in its subservience to hierarchical order barely
compatible with the balanced estates of republicanism. Even
where literal faith in a 'God's Lieutenant' was strained, powerful arguments of custom, rhetoric, patriotism, and security
might tie one, not perhaps without irony but yet without undue
ideological violence, to conventional obediences. There were
heterodox traditions, particularly among Jesuit and Huguenot
thinkers, which put obedience to God before all secular duty.
And Scottish historiography, represented most eloquently by
George Buchanan, had developed a tradition unafraid of finding
in their land's bloody history examples of justifiable regicide.
However, orthodox Tudor and Stuart political theory accounted all rebellion both treasonous and sacrilegious. Prayers
and tears, claimed King James, were the subject's only weapon
against their king: Caesar should be left alone for God.[24]

Aversion to rebellion, however, does not translate into
unreflective Pauline obedience. Felix Raab has noted the 'curious dualism' in some Elizabethan responses to Machiavelli,
where the spheres of politics and theology would find tenuous
separation. The Florentine's terse secularism, divorcing political
authority from theology, would find frequent citation while
its wider implications remained studiously ignored.[25] Though
Shakespeare seems undoubtedly to have had knowledge of
Machiavelli's writings, he was no simple disciple of the Italian

---

[24] James warned his fractious 1610 parliament in these terms. See J. P.
Sommerville, *Politics and Ideology in England 1603–1640* (London, 1986), 26–9.
[25] Felix Raab, *The English Face of Machiavelli: A Changing Interpretation 1500–
1700* (London, 1964), 51–2, 71–6 ff.; Pocock, *Machiavellian Moment*, 355–7.

republican. Machiavelli, discovering virtue in dissension, praising the dynamism of a militarized citizenship, identifying the refreshing virtue in innovation, was more theoretically radical than the Englishman. To the Florentine, 'la moltitudine', possessed of wisdom superior to any knightly class, were the best electors and judges of public officials.[26] Shakespeare is certainly sceptical about aristocratic authority, but his distrust of nobility in government is hardly as comprehensive as Machiavelli's. Or again, Shakespeare takes the less harsh view of Coriolanus' anti-democratic, anti-pluralistic convictions.[27] None the less, an influence can be identified.

Shakespeare's late works appear ideologically closer to the more prudential approach of Machiavelli's fellow Florentine, Guicciardini, an English translation of whose history was published in 1579.[28] Like Livy, and again distinct from Plutarch's concentration upon the personality of great men, Guicciardini understood liberty as the ascendancy of public laws and decisions over private appetites. Rejecting any formally closed oligarchy, Guicciardini was at the same time a consistent advocate of aristocratic predominance. The challenge, however, was to. reconcile such an élite with the principle of 'vivere civile'.[29] An imbalance on either side might provoke chaos and disorder. Guicciardini's writings conduct a nuanced, sometimes ironical, often ambivalent enquiry into the need for personal ambition and, as its necessary bridle, public scrutiny; similarly, the danger of corruption requires a principle of prudence. The people are not a sleeping irrelevance or monstrous obstacle to good government: they are its cause, purpose, and surety. It is just such issues which pulse throughout *Pericles* itinerant tale of estates under pressure.

As the influence of Livy, Tacitus, Machiavelli, and Guicciardini will suggest, Shakespeare was typical of Renaissance England in looking to Italy before Greece for inspiration. Nevertheless, certain influential thinkers known to

[26] *Machiavels Discourses, upon the first Decade of T. Livius*, trans. Edward Dacres (London, 1636), I. lviii. 231–3 et al.

[27] Ibid. I. vii. 38–9; III. xxiii. 559.

[28] *The Historie of Guicciardin*, trans. Geoffrey Fenton (London, 1579). This was the source for Barnabe Barnes's *The Divil's Charter* (1607), which uses 'Guicciardine' as a presenter and interpreter like Gower.

[29] See Pocock, *Machiavellian Moment*, 122–53; 270, et al.

Shakespeare—More, Machiavelli, Montaigne—would draw
upon Athens or Sparta as cultural models.[30] The 1620s marked
the real awakening of interest in Greece, but there are earlier
traces in the wind; Shakespeare of course was an avid reader of
Plutarch's lives of the Greeks. And certainly, the odd Greek
name rose beyond the general indifference into a grammar-
school familiarity: above all, the name of Pericles. For to the
educated Renaissance individual, the name meant only one
thing: it meant the great Athenian demagogue, his 'Age' his
own, the golden period of Hellenism. Certainly, it is as the
'prince of Tyre', and so another child of the Apollonius legend,
that Shakespeare's hero should primarily be known. But still the
question stands: why 'Pericles'? Might the choice have more
political resonance than has customarily been allowed?

In his *Parallel Lives* Plutarch devotes a whole 'life' to Pericles,
coupled with that of Fabius Maximus.[31] Shakespeare would
have known the Athenian's biography; it immediately precedes
that of Coriolanus. Plutarch got much of his information from
the great historian of the Peloponnesian War, Pericles' Greek
contemporary, Thucydides. Thucydides formed a powerful
model for 'civil' historians unsatisfied by providentialist teleologies. He is a crucial founder of history as irony, as the record
of the mistaken and unintended. Shakespeare didn't need to
read Greek to be familiar with Thucydides. It had long been
available in French, and was translated into English, from the
French, in the time of Edward VI.[32] Thomas Hobbes's first
published work, in 1628, was a translation of Thucydides into
English. Hobbes's choice suggests not only the fame and reputation of the work in the century's early decades, but its status as
political epitome, as humanist exemplar.

[30] See K. J. Dover, *Perceptions of the Ancient Greeks* (Oxford, 1992), esp. ch. 6,
Peter Burke, 'The Renaissance', 128–46.

[31] J. M. S. Tompkins, 'Why Pericles?', *RES* 3 (1952), 315–24, argues that Shakespeare 'skipped over' Plutarch's politics.

[32] By Thomas Nicolls in 1550. A further translation dating from the early years
of James's English reign is held in manuscript at Christ Church, Oxford. Arthur F.
Kinney, 'Sir Philip Sidney and the Uses of History', in Heather Dubrow and Richard
Strier, eds., *The Historical Renaissance: New Essays on Tudor and Stuart Literature
and Culture* (Chicago, 1988), 294, notes that Thucydides' work was taught at both
Shrewsbury and Christ Church, where Sidney was educated, and that the revised
Arcadia attempts a humanist *imitatio* of Thucydides' history. The name of Shake-
speare's hero is most usually thought to suggest *Arcadia*'s Pyrocles.

At various points Thucydides' hero anticipates the milieu of the play. The Athenian left his first wife for a 'courtesan', Aspasia, and stayed in a kind of thrall to her all his life. She taught rhetoric and philosophy to a band of admiring men, but was notorious for less esoteric entertainments. Numerous comedies called her 'naughty whore', 'past all kynde of shame'.[33] Pericles was accused by the comic writers of having a bastard by her, and worse, of her being his procurer, his common bawd.[34] 'Satyres' pictured the 'Olympus' giving peacocks to his prized lady lovers. Further calumny 'durst falsely accuse Pericles of detestable incest, and of abusing his own son's wife'.[35] Pericles seems to have responded by sponsoring the 'law against comedy' of 439–436, banning stage raillery, a short-lived but unprecedented censorship of Athens's famous 'wits'.[36] A trace of each can be found, if not in Shakespeare's prince, then in the responsibilities discovered through his travels. Furthermore, the knights at Pentapolis are of Corinth, Sparta, Athens, and Macedon, while Pericles' wife stays at Ephesus, his daughter at Mytilene. Neither Twine nor Gower offer any such specificity; these are all Thucydides' locations (as well as Sidney's in *Arcadia*).[37]

Such matters, however, are incidental to that which remains the kernel of Pericles' historical reputation: his great public speeches about patriotism and the civic life. And the particular pregnancy of these for the seventeenth century may well have been the poised, polyvalent quality of his civic position. Pericles was nominally a demagogue, drawing his pre-eminence from the voice of the Assembly. At the same time, however, this ancient noble's temperament was haughty, arrogant, diffident toward the common people: 'It was in the name a state Democraticall, but in fact, A gouernement of the principall Man'.[38] He was at once of and above the citizens. The sternly absolutist Hobbes

---

[33] *Plutarch's Lives of the Noble Grecians and Romanes*, trans. Sir Thomas North, 6 vols. (1579; repr. London, 1895), ii. 31.

[34] Ibid. ii. 40.   [35] Ibid. ii. 20.

[36] Rex Warner, *Pericles the Athenian* (London, 1963), 193.

[37] Wilkins fills in details here omitted in Q. George Wilkins, 'The Painfull Adventures of Pericles Prince of Tyre', in Geoffrey Bullough, ed., *Narrative and Dramatic Sources of Shakespeare*, 8 vols. (1966; repr. London, 1977), vi. 509.

[38] Thucydides, *The Peloponnesian War: The Complete Hobbes Translation*, ed. David Grene (1959; repr. Chicago, 1989), 116–17.

appears to have interpreted the institutional ambiguity of Pericles in blankly contemptuous terms; Hobbes's marginalia to Pericles' famous 'Funeral Oration' suggest the philosopher's mordant disdain for Athens's open polity, understanding Pericles' performance as a hyperbolical, hypocritical pandering to the multitude's appetite for flattery. Thus, he accuses Pericles of 'Carping secretly' at the Spartans more astringent and exclusive manners, and of envying them 'because they euer looked sowrely on soft and loose behauiour'. Hobbes glosses Pericles' praise of informed political participation with an aloof reductiveness: 'All the Athenians spend their time in nothing but hearing and telling of news. The true character of politicians without employment.'[39] But whatever Hobbes's derision, and however much 'Democracie' was anathema to conventional English thinking, the stirring rhythms and patriotic sentiment of Pericles' oration inevitably retained a power to impress. The speech's classic articulation of civic duty and pride in an imperial democracy was a 'chestnut' in Tudor grammar-schools, cribbed for its noble message of selflessness.[40] In Shakespeare's England, then, Pericles' reputation was highly contentious: his name could act as a lightning rod for debates about popular participation in government.

Pericles' oration goes to the heart of the identity of subject and state. Here is an excerpt from the version Shakespeare might have read:

Also our gouernment ys called Democracie, which ys not conuenie[n]t for a fewe people, but for many. By reasonne wherof, euery of us, of what qualitie that he be, (prouyded that he haue some qualitie of vertue) hathe asmuch righte to come to honnors of the cytie, as the other. And it is not regarded of what house, nother of what parte of Citezeins, he is, but onely what vertue he hath. For what poore man it may be, . . . howe vyle or unknowen that it be, so that he maye proffytte the common wealthe, he is not impesched to haue charge and publique office.[41]

[39] *Eight Books of the Peloponnesian Warre*, by Thucydides, Interpreted with Faith and Diligence Immediately out of the Greek by Thomas Hobbes (London, 1629), 102–3.

[40] Kinney, 'Sir Philip Sidney and the Uses of History', in Dubrow and Strier, *Historical Renaissance*, 295.

[41] *The Hystory Writtone by Thucidides*, trans. Thomas Nicolls (London, 1550), liiii^{r–v}.

Those who refuse admission to the political processes by avoiding the Assembly, or otherwise show contempt for the people and their constitution, are held to be worthless; Athenian man was indeed a political animal:

[T]hose, which be occupied in their pryuate busynes, haue not therfore lesse knowlaige of the estate of the comon wealthe. For we haue that for synguler, that he, whyche hath no knowlaige of the comon wealthe, we repute him not onely to be slouthful and necligent, but also we take him not, for a cytezein.[42]

Thucydides' Pericles gives a second speech (reaffirming the sacrifices demanded by imperial might) in the wake of the ravening plague which threatens not only individual lives but the moral and political fabric of the commonwealth. The plague is a framing symbol of the corruption and contagion which threatens the Periclean sentiments, and against which civic duty must define itself.

The twin terrors of plague and foreign invasion recur in *Pericles*; that Shakespeare may have been influenced by Thucydides becomes still more plausible once it is recalled that one of the Athenian Pericles' greatest foes when alive, and the most powerful man in Athens after Pericles' death, was one Cleon. Cleon's lasting claim to fame was his leadership of that group who would have had every single man of Mytilene put 'presently to death', and 'to make slaves of the women and children'. The consequent debates formed another ancient 'gobbet' popular in English schools.[43] The Mytileneans had 'revolted' against Athens, an 'insolence' anathema to the bellicose Cleon, 'who in the former assembly had won to have them killed, being of all the citizens most violent and with the people at that time far the most powerful'. Cleon's position is simple: clever conceits have too much sway in a democracy: 'I maintain that you ought not to alter your former decree nor to offend in any of these three most disadvantageous things to empire, pity, delight in plausible speeches, and lenity.' He decries 'combats of eloquence and wit' that reduce politics to showy semiotics and the commonwealth to a theatre:

---

[42] Ibid. lv^r.
[43] Following quotations from the debate all from Hobbes's translation of *The Peloponnesian War*, ed. Grene, pp. 175–9.

And to speak plainly, overcome with the delight of the ear, you are rather like unto spectators sitting to hear the contentions of sophisters than to men that deliberate of the state of the commonwealth.

Cleon is rebutted by Diodotus, who returns the debate to a more hopeful humanistic register:

And whosoever maintaineth that words are not instructors to deeds, either he is not wise or doth it upon some private interest of his own. . . . For a good statesman should not go about to terrify those that contradict him but rather to make good his counsel upon liberty of speech. And a wise state ought not either to add unto, or, on the other side, to derogate from, the honour of him that giveth good advice.

The debates upon Mytilene's destiny offer a kind of meta-argument about the truth and virtue inhering in public discussion: what is the place of oratory, persuasion, and indeed theatre, in good government? Eloquently championing the justice inherent in talking to the people, Diodotus narrowly won the day: the people of Mytilene were spared. But Cleon's voice echoes ringingly of the untrustworthiness of orators, the dangers to the state in promiscuous debate, and the gullibility of a popular audience.

So, at those points where *Pericles* appears most notably to intercept Thucydides—and three of these ancient gems in particular, the funeral oration, the plague, and the debate over Mytilene, were favourites for extraction and study in Elizabethan classrooms—one can identify the fundamental cruces of humanist political enquiry. What virtue might reside in active and resilient citizenship so as to counter and alter fortune? What should be the role of the people in political institutions? How are order and justice best secured and served? And how vital to liberty and decorum is the place of free speech, the public forum, the opened book of law? Thucydides' Cleon prefers the certainty of bad laws to the 'dexterity' of good ones.[44] He would sanction one will, one law, 'immoveable'. And this, exactly, is the situation with which Shakespearian romance begins, as Pericles arrives in Antioch to seek his bride.

[44] Ibid. 176.

2

Pericles and the Idea of the Hero

TRADITIONAL romance is built around the hero who leads, cultivates, and somehow consummates the ruling ideas of his place: he has the force of symbol, his deeds a blazon of legitimate power. But what happens when noble heroism is under pressure, subject to the ironies and attritions of cultural change and generic conflict? How does one construct a romantic paragon who, as it were bypassing tragic sacrifice, is neither ineffectual cipher, reedy genre-joke, nor turgid pastiche from superannuated pastoral? In the light of the popular romance tradition outlined in the previous chapter, what are the possibilities and responsibilities of the hero? In a sense, it is only *Pericles* of Shakespeare's romances which presents anything like a familiar heroic protagonist. That the subsequent plays eschew such a figure says much about both their dialogical techniques and their politics. The peculiar, almost tentative quality of Pericles is a kind of step on the way toward this erasing of unilateral salvational agency.

For he is a vapid sort of figure. Where 'subjective' motive appears to be provided, its reasonings seem oddly bewildered, inconsistent, or detached from desire. It may well be that this faintness, the sense that one is straining to hear through leaded walls, is entirely due to the shattered, almost senile quality of the first two acts, rendering any 'original' drama as inscrutable as its eponym. Yet it still seems unlikely that the play at any time represented in its hero a deeply interiorized individual, or that his motives and desires were ever the decisive engine of the action. For the figure of Pericles can fruitfully be approached not only as the sharded remnant of a lacunal text, but as a metaphor and epitome of his own dramatic mode, at times similarly faint, contested, at cross-purposes: he is in and of a genre whose precedents, parents, and contemporary orientation are at once half-otiose and acceleratingly over-determined.

Pericles' trials begin when he encounters the classic tragic evil: the incest of king and daughter at Antioch. Politically, royal

incest's connotations are predictably dire. At its core is a denial
of history in the sense that, in 1608, it could mean anything:
legitimacy required a nourishing origin, but here all source—
maternal, paternal, or communal—is consumed. It is the ultimate anti-romance, killing all futures, neutering hopes for
transformation. To thus feed on one's likeness invokes civil war,
a prospect coyly flaunted by the daughter's Aesopian analogue.[1]
Equally, it suggests the danger of investing all claims of and for
originality in a single royal family. At the same time, their
actions undermine Pericles' own discourse of courtly praise ('See
where she comes, appareled like the Spring . . . Her face the
booke of prayses', I. i. 13–16). Such language seems merely to
decorate the thriving authority of vice; the prince's epideictics
become a mirror, an inert, self-inverting reflection of gorgeous
tyranny. Antiochus himself has the same myths and metaphors
at his disposal, but he warns repeatedly of the serpent within
their allure ('Before thee standes this faire *Hesperides*, With
golden fruite, but dangerous to be toucht', I. i. 28–9). The terror
at Antioch is thereby characterized not only by obvious
criminality—its clammy aura of incest and assassination—but
by the proscription of persuasive speech. In its place, the available lessons of state are the province of spectacle.[2] The dead
suitors persuade with 'speachlesse tongues, and semblance pale':
they are death masks, frozen in eloquent testament to the unspeakable. Counsel here is mirthless, ironic, and mute: 'with
dead cheekes [they] advise thee to desist' (I. i. 37–40).

Later on at Tharsus, Dionyza's project of a marmoreal Marina, a blackly comic mockery of 'golden' courtly 'prayse', is
likewise an ironic baal of a tyranny beyond question or account
(IV. iii. 31–46). In Antioch's princess, too, persuasiveness is
silent, the possession of sight alone. Pericles is 'emboldned With
the glory of her prayse' (I. i. 4), his words adorning, almost
creating, the 'booke of prayses' which is her visage: 'where is

---

[1] The young Henry VI invokes the platitude of the viper as state dissension: *1
Henry VI*, III. i. 71–3.

[2] David Norbrook, '*Macbeth* and the Politics of Historiography', in Kevin Sharpe
and Stephen N. Zwicker, eds., *Politics of Discourse: The Literature and History of
Seventeenth Century England* (Berkeley, 1987), 112, notes humanist suspicion of
popular theatre's appeal to the emotions rather than the intellect, based partly upon
knowledge of how Roman emperors used spectacle to distract the people from their
loss of liberty.

read, Nothing but curious pleasures' (I. i. 16–17). And it is this
'Nothing' here, this absence of appropriate language, which the
play and its hero must attempt to amend. Antiochus' welcoming
speeches to Pericles are thus a kind of shorthand for the wide-
spread manipulation of the tropes and myths of idealism. In
such circumstances silence—Pericles' frequent refuge throughout the play—is a kind of collusion. At Antioch's hermetic
court, the 'breath is gone' (I. i. 100): it is a theatre of narcissism,
paralysis, and, if not silence, then verbal atrophy.

The opening scene thereby suggests the inadequacy of
Pericles' courtliness: 'Like a bold Champion I assume the Listes',
he pronounces, but Antiochus notes mainly his similarity to
previous victims ('like thyself', I. i. 35). The lesson of Antioch,
therefore, might seem to be the impotence of tourneying when
faced with tyranny. But, having heard the challenge, Pericles
takes a less politicized tack: '*Antiochus*, I thanke thee, who hath
taught, My frayle mortalitie to know it selfe . . . life's but breath,
to trust it errour' (I. i. 42–7). However grave and wise his tone,
Pericles' point is really one of how amatory idealism is all the
more virtuous for being reckless. He thus enjoys the armour of
both youth and genre: not so much self- as mode-fashioned,
Pericles is a vacant if frisky chivalrous archetype. But if the text
were happily settled in a romantic discourse, the morality here
would be entirely personal and, accordingly, civically forgetful.
That is, the dead wights would attest Antiochus' harshness, but
also the veracity of the challenge facing Pericles. He becomes
heroic through surpassing his predecessors. However, while
these satisfactions are briefly allowed, more profound is the
inability of Pericles' mores or accomplishments to cope with the
challenge.

Antiochus presents a rich, sensual, over-roasted fairy-tale
scene. The horror once deciphered, one might expect the deft
slash of Pericles' sabre, hearty vengeance, and improbable escape. Instead, he concludes that 'least my life be cropt, to keepe
you cleare, By flight, Ile shun the danger which I feare' (I. i. 142–
3). Somehow the code of adventure has been terminated, or is
out of style. In a text pock-marked with lacunae, Pericles here
hurries off into an ideological absence, into a sort of fog. It's as
if he's been concussed, and the convictions that led to the
collision can never quite bear retrieval. The play refuses the

extravagant coherence of old-fashioned fantasy. Instead of
vaulting heroism, it presents a form of ignominy. Pericles is no
better than knighthood's previous decapitated failures: after
all, perhaps they too were condemned for solving the riddle.
Whereas Sidney's Arcadian princes lead or encourage rebellious
activities against all kinds of governments (other than a fair and
just monarchy), Pericles, though confronted by the shame of
warped majesty, is unable to respond with anything but wan-
ness and fear. His situation trembles with the inadequacy of
current princely models. These models, political, rhetorical, and
generic, are out of date, hollowed by latent mockeries.

So, Pericles is a figure marooned in more than one way. His
historical situation renders him strangely, though unavoidably,
abandoned by those fictions which might once—perhaps in the
world after which Gower hearkens—have formed and directed
him. He begins as a kind of book of courtesy, befitting the
courtly chivalry he tries to embody; as has been seen, however,
such a text has been corrupted, mocked into anachronism.
Running from both tyranny and his own generic bewilderment,
Pericles must in a sense be built from nothing. He retreats from
Antioch, and finds himself in a sequence of wildernesses: first a
mental alienation, then geographical homelessness, and finally
the wild hinterland, quite alarming in a prince, of unkempt
silence. This trope of the inner and outer desert returns in all of
the romances: it represents both loss and opportunity. And what
is significant about *Pericles*, and a pointer to the subsequent
works, is the sources of the necessary rebuilding. They are not
discovered 'in' the hero, who remains fundamentally bereft.
They are found, rather, in his audiences: that is, both those
whom he meets on his travels and, equally importantly, those
who watch or read the play, whose expectations are often
'ahead' of the hero, but which in turn effectively pre-script him.
As the protagonist, Pericles remains the vessel of any audience's
desires, courtly or popular. So, seeking the hand of a princess, he
is a model of possible kingship; but, faced with the riddling
'Law' as his only path toward satisfaction or enfranchisement,
he doubles as the archetypal subject beneath tyranny. However,
the very helplessness with which he is so suggests the lack, the
gap in consciousness, which the action must supply. Each place
Pericles visits is a projection, a consequence, or a metaphor of

his authority. And yet his role as the unfinished or inadequate hero imbues Pericles with the expectation that he will redress whatever failing in such authority is suggested by the condition of the place he visits. *Pericles* overlays one place and period with another, dramatizing various analogous city-states; these models contextualize and so inform the 'authority' of Pericles. His 'character' is less a personal thing than a text of civic potential.

This approach might help manage the problem of Pericles' guilt. Pericles desires a beautiful princess, but as soon as he discovers her crime his desire turns to repugnance, and he runs away. But his travels are then haunted by echoes of incest: the vicious filial possessiveness of Cleon and Dionyza would send Marina to her death; Simonides pretends an executioner's fury when his daughter falls for a 'Traytor' (II. v. 35–85); Lysimachus seeks to bed Pericles' child with words which cruelly profane the only satisfaction liable to release Pericles from his pain: 'Faith, she would serue after a long voyage at Sea' (IV. vi. 42). Furthermore, the play keeps pushing conflations between Antiochus and Pericles. For instance, his counsellor Hellicanus identifies Pericles' 'pyning sorrow' as the likely precipitant of a 'disorder' which Pericles, meanwhile, fears will come in the form of Antioch's army (I. ii. 25–6): Pericles' delinquence obscurely colludes with Antiochus' despotism. Fearful that the multitude will suffer for his knowledge, Pericles seems to admit, half-wryly, that the transgression is somehow his own: 'When all for mine, if I may calle offence, Must feel wars blow, who spares not innocence' (I. ii. 92–3). The hesitation here is partly to let in a wan joke, in that Antiochus imagines or invents 'offence' where there is none; but, however unjustly, Pericles feels obtusely stained. Antiochus' crime—considered as civic transgression, political censorship, and so on—is passed into Pericles as his personal burden. It is not that Pericles is genuinely self-destructive or irresponsible, but that the crime is somehow both kingly and communal, and not so much borne by him as his responsibility, inadequately recognized, to purge. The threatened 'innocence' is both his own, a rueful acknowledgement of his introduction to knowledge, and, proleptically, his subjects'. Pericles is strung between oppressor and oppressed, painfully responsible for both. The continuing

presence of incest—it is catalytic, immanent, and perhaps imminent—is a measure of the hero's generic dilemma. For this great
archetypal transgression is equally the stuff of fairy-tale as it is
of tragedy. In fairy-tale, incestuous guilt is transcended or ab-
solved; in tragedy, it stays to pay its promise. *Pericles* appears to
disown the Sophoclean-cum-Senecan destructiveness, but the
hero's exile from fairy-tale clarities and closures raises spectres
which only a new genre, fully accountable, un-amnesiac, can
allay. Pericles' meta-task is to quest for some such responsible
irenic discourse.

The speech which Pericles makes to Antiochus, hinting that he
knows the secret and pleading for his life, offers a fuller sense of
the dilemmas he faces:

> Great King,
> Few loue to hear the sinnes they loue to act,
> T'would brayde your selfe too neare for me to tell it:
> Who has a booke of all that Monarches doe,
> Hee's more secure to keepe it shut, then showne.
> For Vice repeated, is like the wandring Wind,
> Blowes dust in others eyes to spread it selfe;
> And yet the end of all is bought thus deare,
> The breath is gone, and the sore eyes see cleare:
> To stop the Ayre would hurt them, the blind Mole castes
> Copt hilles towards heauen, to tell the earth is throng'd
> By mans oppression, and the poore Worme doth die for't.

> (I. i. 92–103)

Pericles makes it clear to Antiochus that he has deciphered the
riddle: to pretend ignorance would be to bring instant execution. But he hopes to persuade the despot that he will never
speak his knowledge, and therefore be allowed safely to leave
Antioch. Pericles' situation is invidious, and offers him few
options. However, the question is not only whether Pericles'
actions are prudent or pusillanimous, but whether he helps to
harbour crime. The basic message is that to publish the crimes of
kings is dangerous to both speaker and audience. But it is of
crucial importance here that, in the act of disavowing public
speech, Pericles not only gives forceful expression to the particular crime, but generalizes its significance: there are many bad
kings (a point soon doubly reinforced by Thaliard's wry reiteration of the wise-saw that it is safest to stay ignorant of a king's

secrets: I. iii. 3–6). As with Marina's chastising of Lysimachus, to rebuke a ruler is itself to engage in political resistance (IV. vi. 78–101). In opening the vice of kings to the popular ear, Pericles does exactly what he disclaims. This is a measure of how his heroic role, as constituted by the audience, needs to be matched by his role within the world of the play.[3] The auditorium is as it were already imbued with a Thucydidean conviction of the value of a popular forum in which the virtues of government can be debated and defined.

Pericles, though, remains split and paralysed, bereft of confident clarities. His analogy of the mole and the worm emphasizes how he is 'in' both oppressor and oppressed. The text here may suffer from corruption, but as it stands the metaphor's referents are self-cancellingly multiple. Pericles appears to sympathize with the 'poore worme' who, unable to defend itself against the reprisals of authority, may represent equally himself or 'the people'. However, whether he also identifies with the mole is ambiguous. If worm and mole are identical, then the mole too will represent the humble, burrowing hopelessly to escape injustice; or the mole's hills may be a simple topographic equivalent of the 'book' of a monarch's crimes, a martyr's protest against corruption. But the contemporary reputation of the mole was hardly one which any prince, chivalrous or empathetic, should take comfort in appropriating. Often the mole was disdained as an unworthy grasper after others' titles, degrading the nobility of rank and power.[4] The mole's hills and chambers could evoke ambition, presumption, the arrogance of the expropriative, killing the little 'worms'—here not the same as the 'mole'—who like peasant tenants hinder the encloser. The mole thereby echoes and anticipates the cannibalistic terrorism of Pericles' two other anthropomorphic cousins, the adder of Antiochan incest, and the rich miser whale of Pentapolis. Equally, the mole could be seen as vermin, a worthless parasite like the 'drones' of the fishermen's contempt. Contemporary references are invariably

---

[3] Maurice Hunt, *Shakespeare's Romance of the Word* (Lewisburg, Pa., 1990), 25–6, sees four early scenes as identifying the benefits of redemptive speech—I. ii, I. iv, II. i. II. V—and two others where, although Pericles is absent, a declaration proves reparative, I. iii, IV. vi. 'The audience, rather than the hero, primarily appreciates the virtue of the idea repeatedly staged.' (p. 151).

[4] Although cf. Marlowe, *Tamburlaine Part One*, II. vi. 1–3.

disdainful: the mole was used to evoke levelling malice and literary envy, a mock-familiar devil, Gunpowder Plot under-miners, popish Spanish mendacity, inept and dreamy kingship, or the evil king 'Mouldwarp' in Merlin's prophecy.[5] Each, in one way or another, suggests an agency of inversion or cor-ruption: if not simply confused, Pericles' metaphor is either subversive or brutally antinomian. As the straining against 'op-pression' ensures, there remain powerful populist connotations in the mole, and so a sense of Pericles' painful identity with his people. But the poignant fatalism of his words is undermined by suspicions about their self-protective speciousness: is he justify-ing a timid nod beneath despotism? Or does Pericles—himself a prince—identify with the erring king, expressing a concern for monarchy's reputation which then leads to a cynical affirmation of the power of censorship and the sense in silent obedience? The doubleness, indignity, even self-annihilatory qualities in his analogy epitomize a broader denotative and generic instabil-ity, an insecurity further encapsulated in Pericles' decision to keep the book of rule 'shut'. The prince inhabits a discursive wasteland.

The image of a wasteland can suggest the antinomies in both the historical moment and its representative genre. It is at once a graveyard, a site of ideological husk and rubble, and a pres-sured nativity, the place from which futures must be born. Furthermore, there is in the topos a danger of morbidity, of luxuriating in the fact of loss or decay. When Pericles scents the worm in Antioch's rose, and senses the fall of a whole manner of being, he is tempted by just such a death languor, by the ennui of defeat and bereavement. It is a reflex that, significantly for the play's political manners, returns later to overwhelm him. Hu-manism's commitment to the active life, to the superiority of praxis over contemplation, condemned the recluse, like the mis-anthrope, to political marginality. In *Pericles* the hero becomes a misanthropic hermit: in this tale of buffeted rectitude, human-

---

[5] Jonson, *Sejanus*, 'To the Readers', 25–8; *Hamlet*, I. v. 170–1; J. King, Serm., Nov. 1605, 'Romish pioners, Anti-christian molewarps', *OED* 'Mouldwarp': 1; Thomas Middleton, *A Game at Chess*, ed. J. W. Harper (London, 1966), IV. iv. 83–100; 'King of a molehill' was the sarcastic proverb, *3 Henry VI*, I. iv. 67, II. v. 14; Leviticus 11: 30; Keith Thomas, *Religion and the Decline of Magic* (1971; repr. Harmondsworth, 1984), ch. 13, cf. *1 Henry IV*, III. i. 140–4.

ist *virtu* is as much under pressure as any other ideal. In the face of civic intemperance and majestic occlusions, a certain type of humanism—that which seeks to mould a clear-eyed, virtuous, educated governing class—might have emerged as the sanguine corrective to tyranny. Faithful to the legitimacy of true monarchy, a class of noble courtiers could yet be the prince's exemplary mirror. *Pericles* appears to sketch in something like such a princely education: Hellicanus tutors him about flattery, he practises magnanimity in Tharsus, music and martialism in Pentapolis. Indeed the whole narrative is partly impelled by the idea that the prince is learning from, or being incorporated into, the reflections that revolve around him. But the play is not remotely satisfied with the decorous accretions appropriate to a prince's 'Christian education'. Its ambit is much wilder, the hero's 'mirrors' being often alarming and unsettling and, importantly, rarely confined to things courtly. Just as he is made to feel for, even feel with, the degenerate Antiochus, he is positioned empathetically in relation to all he sees and meets: famines, fires, and storms, pirates and pimps, one corrupt ruler after another. The fact is that the manifold expressions of wilderness in the play suggest a certain 'academic' quality in aristocratic humanism: the play enacts a debate, for example, between a 'mixed estate' and absolutist monarchy, but romance's engagement with history is too much taken with things primal and irrational to be contained by either the ends or the eloquence, however admirable, of a 'vir civilis'. Shakespeare makes violence part of his subject, as both a precursor of and threat to whatever political and linguistic orders might be at stake. When Pericles himself figuratively ditches the 'speculum principum', grows hair and beard to wildness and cuts off tongue and ears to all-comers, he is expressing not only grief but his inextricable connectedness to the wildness and turbulence that surrounds him. He grows out of it, is shrunk or silenced by it; he is part of it, and in a sense responsible for it. In this way the prince himself is a site of wilderness, a waxing and waning wasteland.

What must be stressed, then, is the violence, the savagery, inhering in each of the cities Pericles visits. Each place presents not only a black rebuke to monarchical negligence or complicity, but an overwhelming challenge to present strategies of repair. Here is Tharsus:

> These mouthes who but of late, earth, sea, and ayre,
> Were all too little to content and please,
> Although they gaue their creatures in abundance,
> As houses are defil'de for want of vse,
> They are now staru'de for want of exercise,
> Those pallats who, not yet two sauers younger,
> Must have inuentions to delight the tast,
> Would now be glad of bread and beg for it.
> . . . So sharpe are hungers teeth, that man and wife,
> Drawe lots who first shall die, to lengthen life.
> Here stands a Lord, and there a Ladie weeping:
> Heere manie sincke, yet those which see them fall,
> Haue scarce strength left to giue them buryall.

> (I. iv. 34–49)

Tharsus' dearth and degradation find a suggestive analogue in the sudden plague which descended on the crowds of Athens, described in wrenching detail by Thucydides. This plague too, like Tharsus', suggests the precariousness of political ethics. Not only is there physical devastation, but a coterminous collapse of values. Athenian 'liberty', so proud and cherished, becomes lawless:

For through the violence of the sickenes, they knewe not what they dydde, and hadde loste the knowlaige and reuerence of religion of the hollynes of places. And the righte of the graves, whiche they used in tyme paste, were all troubled and co[n]fused. For every man buryed his, there, as he might.[6]

Athens's topography is tumbled into humiliation, all solidarity separating into private, dissolving, ignominy:

[M]en had presently tha[n] no shame to do things openly, whiche in tymes paste were wylled not to be done in secret. By this, that they were kepte and restrayned from wantonnes and voluptuosnes. . . . The poore people to whome the goodes or ryches came, cared not, but for to spende it shortely in all thynges of pleasure and voluptuousnes, and they thought that they could not do better, hauing no hope to enioye it longe . . . But all that, which for the time, they founde playsant and delectable for mans appetyte, they reputed profytable and honneste, wythoute any feare of Goddes or of lawes. For that, that they thought

---

[6] *The Hystory Writtone by Thucidides*, trans. Nicolls, lvii[v].

it to be all one to do yll, or good, consydered & aswell dyed the good, as the euyll.[7]

The plague works as a framing challenge to the Athenian Pericles' great enunciation of civic pride and communal duty. Physical corruption and contagion suggest the tenuousness of even the finest political institutions, and recall one to the basic questions which must underpin any humanist faith. Can the self-organizing public resist a fall into licentious anarchy? When public idealism is threatened, how binding and persuasive can be an idea of liberty, community, consensualism? Or must one prefer authoritarianism—*noblesse oblige* at best, tyrannous silencing at worst—as order's only protection? It is in the perspective of the need for such reflexive public discourse that the situation at Tharsus needs to be assessed.

The misery of Tharsus works structurally as a displacement of Pericles' own;[8] and indeed the Tharsian royal couple are introduced through a conversation which seems like a meta-theatrical analysis of the very decorum of such projection, and its relation or otherwise to a humanist textual politics:

> My *Dyoniza*, shall wee rest vs heere
> And by relating tales of others griefes
> See if t'will teach vs to forget our owne?

> (I. iv. 1–3)

The romances tend to distrust discursive amnesia; and so it is here. For Cleon invokes the play's pass-the-parcel style of narrative, but would quite invert its cumulative potency to teach and amend. Rather than a panacea, the royals' escapist narrative confirms the contagiousness, the familiarity, of Tharsus' illness. For the famine is merely the signature to a long tale of decadent insouciance: 'riches strew'de her selfe euen in her streetes, Whose towers bore heads so high they kist the clowds, And strangers nere beheld, but wondred at' (I. iv. 23–5). The motifs are of pride before a fall, of promiscuous, prostitutive materialism; of heads both smug and phallic, and of civic self-congratulation

---

[7] Ibid. lviii[v–r].

[8] Tharsus' misery is a parallel to that of Tyre in Twine and Gower, which falls into catastrophic heaviness, penance, and abandonment once their Prince leaves. See Geoffrey Bullough, *Narrative and Dramatic Sources of Shakespeare*, 8 vols. (1966; repr. London, 1977), xi. 381, 429–30.

sold as if at a Turkish bazaar. 'Civilization' has become lurid, the over-rich entrée to collapse. Elements of suicide and disease are embedded analogically: first, through recollections of the severed clot-poles of the slain princes; and second, through anticipations of Mytilene's trade in maidenheads and scattered crowns. If old Tharsus evokes the destructiveness of narcissism, its present decline is measured by cannibalism:

> Those mothers who to nouzell vp their babes,
> Thought nought too curious, are readie now
> To eat those little darlings whom they lou'de,
> So sharpe are hungers teeth, that man and wife,
> Drawe lots who first shall die, to lengthen life.
>
> (I. iv. 42–6)

If this suggests Athens's plague, then Thucydides' awful exemplar finds further dilations in the similar cannibalism of Antioch's court, Mytilene's brothel, and Pentapolis' rich men. The repeated lack of robust governmental resistance to corruption feeds the familiar aestheticization of both aspiration and discourse, manifested principally in adorning spectacle. In the pre-famine Tharsus, for instance, routine is stage-managed into endless sights of self-praise: 'men and dames' are 'jetted and adorn'de', each the other's 'glasse to trim them by' (I. iv. 26–7); riches are 'strew'de' in the street like a glutted courtesan; food is arranged and consumed as an accoutrement for the eyes, 'to glad the sight, And not so much to feede on as delight' (I. iv. 23–31). One might compare the way Stephano and Trinculo are waylaid by the 'glistering apparel' (IV. i. 222–56), or the 'fierce vanities' of *Henry VIII*'s Field of the Cloth of Gold (I. i. 1–40): the romance sense of history seems to seek a more articulative, less gluttonous politics. Correspondingly, Cleon suffers from the same kind of induced inertia as does Pericles; again, the blame is less personal than civic. He repeats Pericles' fear of being overrun by a greater power: 'One sorrowe neuer comes but brings an heire, That may succeede as his inheritor; And so in ours, some neighboring nation, Taking aduantage of our miserie . . .' (I. iv. 63–6). The play's recapitulative tableaux suggest the haplessness of political virtue before fortune: 'wee are vnable to resist' (I. iv. 84).

Such homologies are the basic architecture of Pericles' 'education'; the circumstances of Tharsus can express Pericles' civic problems while keeping himself free to enter and repair. Thus, Pericles returns politics to what hitherto has been lacking: a dialogue between needs and capabilities, franchise and responsibility:

> We haue heard your miseries as farre as *Tyre*,
> And seene the desolation of your streets,
> Nor come we to adde sorrow to your teares,
> But to relieue them of their heauy loade;
> And these our Ships you happily may thinke,
> Are like the Troian Horse, was stuft within
> With bloody veines expecting ouerthrow,
> Are stor'd with Corne to make your needie bread.
>
> (I. iv. 88–95)

In alluding to the Homeric or Virgilian tale of the Trojan horse, Pericles offers an apt metaphor of his own responsibilities and, correspondingly, of the romances' box-within-box figures: the discrete body can house a multitude of surprises, quite opposite to appearance, expectation, and perhaps desire. At the same time, the putative monolith—the ship, the giant wooden horse, the microcosm that is the prince—can be multiple, housing a combative array of influences and messages. Here, the surprise is for the common good, as Pericles corrects the cruelties of both classical source and Tharsian context. The terms in which Pericles responds to the needs of the people might be understood as *noblesse oblige*, the magic of generous valour, revokable and unique, rendering no rights and admitting no obligations.[9] However, Pericles' action is responsive not only to perceived desolation, but to a state in which the enemy of a sustainable polity is now identified as 'superfluous riots', the extravagance and waste of élitist opulence. Consequently, one might wish to consider the food and enclosure riots of 1607 to which *Coriolanus*, more famously, seems a response. A lateral logic may find easy cause for the dearth, as one state of 'superfluous riots' prompts another: pitchfork rebellion. As the citizens say

---

[9] Stephen Mullaney compares *Pericles* to the sources, and sees the play as effacing the prince's mercantile preoccupations, proffering an alternative symbolic economy, less tainted by the market, more attuned to 'princely decorum': *The Place of the Stage: License, Play, and Power in Renaisance England* (Chicago, 1988), 138 ff.

in *Coriolanus*: 'what Authority surfets one, would releeue vs . . . our sufferance is a gaine to them. Let vs reuenge this with our Pikes, ere we become Rakes' (I. i. 15, 21–2). The Roman nobility's perceived crime was to ignore that 'moral economy' which dictated the subjects' inalienable right, in time of dearth, to the fair price and communal distribution of bread. Paternalistic action can come nominally from authority, but find effective cause in the people's legitimate expectation of satisfaction.[10]

The ensuing context reinforces the argument that Pericles' action is that of a populist monarch within a tacitly consensual polity. For the statue which the people of Tharsus subsequently build to 'remember' all that Pericles has done for them signifies both their repair from decadence and a necessary 'consideration'—one might indeed think here in contractual terms—in Pericles' treatment of this populace. When Pericles leaves the baby Marina with the Tharsian royal couple, the memory of such mutuality in government suggests how the princess is both a surety and symbol of symbiotically responsive public estates:

> Feare not (my Lord) but thinke Your Grace,
> That fed my Countrie with your Corn; for which,
> The peoples prayers still fall vpon you, must in your child
> Be thought on, if neglection should therein make me vile,
> The common body by you relieu'd,
> Would force me to my duety.

> (III. iii. 17–22)

The people construct a statue to make Pericles, in Gower's word, 'glorious' (II. Chorus. 14). Gower uses the same adjective when describing the purpose of the play: 'The purchase is to make men glorious' (I. Chorus. 9). The two artworks conflate: the audience and Pericles are each made 'glorious' by respectful art and grateful industry. The statue might not quite be a metaphor of public theatre, but their purposes contextualize one another. The king's patronage notwithstanding, theatre is not a duping spectacle, orchestrating anxious obedience to the state.

[10] E. P. Thompson, 'The Moral Economy of the English Crowd in the Eighteenth Century', *P&P* 50 (1971), 76–136. Annabel Patterson, *Shakespeare and the Popular Voice*, suggests how such an 'economy' operates in her chapter on *Coriolanus*.

And, as Cleon's recognition of the 'force' of the 'common body' suggests, the statue is less an inert testament to majesty than a vital symbol of the commonalty's interests and potency. This statue therefore corrects the aestheticizing lies of Antioch's grim suitors and, later, the monument to Marina. It frames rather than mocks public discourse; neither mendacious nor censorious, it is freely given like the corn it thanks. The question at issue with spectacle is what kind of labour or longing it illustrates; one should think less in terms of inert civic decoration, than a form of present public art, maintained and respected for as long as the power which creates it. So, 'the people's prayers still fall upon' Pericles, two years after his gift of the corn (III. iii. 19). At the same time as the statue is supremely deferential, a measure of thankfulness beneath good monarchy, the voice which creates and sustains it is popular. And Cleon's fears are indeed founded: 'For wicked *Cleon* and his wife, when Fame Had spred his cursed deede, [to] the honor'd name Of *Pericles*, to rage the Cittie turne, That him and his they in his Pallace burne' (Epilogue, 11–14). The populace is not to be despised, a message which, in the mirroring fashion of *Pericles*, is reiterated throughout the 'litigous peace' and mutinies of Tyre. In the play it is Tyrian peers who are restless; in Wilkins it is the people who are 'uncivil and giddy'; in both texts Hellicanus has a 'mutanie' to 'oppresse' or 'appease'. Hellicanus has to listen to the 'clamours of the multitude' before calling the peers together and undertaking to seek their absent prince.[11] Every site in the story repeats this imperative: the people have a role in sustaining order and defining government.

The scene at Pentapolis in which Pericles listens and speaks to the fishermen is a further important set piece in the story's analysis of popular expectation, monarchical responsibility, and so the 'construction-cum-deconstruction' of the romantic hero. The piscatorial mode—that is, a kind of georgic-pastoral but with fish instead of sheep and sea rather than farm—here evokes a conventional allegory of the state. The 'watry empire' tells the 'infirmities of men' (II. i. 49–50): 'the great ones eat vp the little ones', just as the rich consume both city and citizens (II. i. 26–46). The fishermen-labourers would rebel, they think

---

[11] See Bullough, *Narrative and Dramatic Sources*, vi. 395, 502, 512.

legitimately: the expropriated parish was originally their own. However, they can only fantasize about a gift-laden gorge in which 'Belles, Steeple, Church and Parish' are 'cast' up again (II. i. 36–43). But then, as if by robust incantation, and as though in partial, perhaps mocking answer, out of the brine pops the bedraggled stranger: 'What a drunken Knaue was the sea, To cast thee in our way?' (II. i. 57–8). The identification of the vomiting whale with the sottish sea suggests how the fate of the common goods and franchise joins with that of the castaway: he might contain the returning 'parish'.

But the stranger also evokes the biblical tale of Jonah trapped inside the belly of a whale, in which the leviathan is both an agent of God and a prolepsis of hell. *Pericles* here reinforces its interest in open speech and, more precisely, public revelation. For both Jonah and Pericles are boxed up and spewed out because of the need to remedy corruption. The casting of Jonah upon dry land implies a clear direction to cry out, as his prophetic honour demands, against vice. Whereas Jonah's task is set by God, Pericles' is defined by the causes which lead him to be washed ashore at Pentapolis, and by the consequent expectations of the fishermen who feed and clothe him. The analogic roots effect an implicit transference—if not of power, then of the expectation of satisfaction—from the Old Testament God to a loosely conceived amalgam of honest labour.

It is important here to see how familiar and archetypal a moment this is in the world of Shakespearian romance. Nameless and naked, available to be dressed by a common expectation, Pericles could be anyone:

> What I haue been, I haue forgot to know;
> But what I am, want teaches me to thinke on:
> A man throng'd vp with cold.

> (II. i. 71–3)

One might think of other 'nameless' types who drop in, as it were from sea or sky, to offer visions of novel dispensations: Perdita and Autolicus in *The Winter's Tale*, Prospero and Stephano in *The Tempest*. As these chalk and cheese analogues might suggest, Pericles is here both more and less than a prince. Bereft of clothes and title, his very body evokes the promise-laden fragility of silence; he presents an absence which takes things back to beginnings. What can be built? What shall be spoken? What discourse or symbol is adequate to the moment's needs? The 'romance' genre, here undressed into a type of piscatorial nativity scene, must quickly work out an appropriate decorum.

Pericles, however, only acknowledges the responsibilities of his anonymity once a conventional aristocratic discourse has been tried and failed. As the stately rhythms of his confession suggest, Pericles stands upon a periphrastic dignity which the fishermen repeatedly undermine. Retrieving the mocking liberties of a Mouse or Strumbo, the fishermen arrest Pericles' courtly flow, or in profane fashion literalize his conceits:

> *Per.* Peace be at your labor, honest Fisher-men.
> *Second fish.* Honest good fellow what's that. . . .
> *Per.* May see the Sea hath cast vpon your coast—
> *Second Fish.* What a drunken Knaue was the Sea,
>   To cast thee in our way?

> (II. i. 52–8)

Pericles seems somehow a refugee not only from Tyre, but from a foreign genre. His words attempt a rigid propriety which, in the context, is rendered hapless: for he has lost property of that (name, place, robes) which might make the old discourse appropriate. His decorums are indecorous, and the fishermen are allowed to make merry with his rhetorical discomfort:

> A man whom both the Waters and the Winde,
> In that vast Tennis-court, hath made the Ball
> For them to play vpon, intreates you pittie him:
> Hee askes of you, that neuer us'd to begge.
> *First Fish.* No friend, cannot you begge?
> Heer's them in our countrey of *Greece*,
> Gets more with begging, then we can doe with working.
> *Second Fish.* Canst thou catch any Fishes, then?
> *Pericles.* I never practizde it.
> *Second Fish.* Nay then thou wilt starue sure: for heer's
> nothing to be got now-adayes, vnlesse thou canst
> fish for 't.

> (II. i. 59–70)

Pericles' courtesy is given a sharp lesson in economics by the fishermen's amused, abrasive inversions. So, his poetry having met with mockery or bewilderment, Pericles moves to a more direct register:

> [M]y Veines are chill,
> And haue no more of life then may suffize
> To give my tongue that heat to ask your helpe.

(II. i. 73–5)

The clashing discourses are then quickly sublimated within a co-operative romanticism. Offering food, merriment, and clothing (II. i. 79–83), the fishermen provide Pericles with the car-nivalesque generosity which—their earlier fable implied—might have been expected to emerge from the regurgitated figure of the stranger. The expectation implied by Pericles' casting forth—that he is the potential answer to the fishermen's prayer for repair—is rendered less unilateral. The powerful gift of the fishermen here politicizes the moment in terms of mutual trust and implied contract; one might compare Pericles' own gift of corn to the needy Tharsians.

However, the tensions and options within such mutuality do not vanish within some sublime feast. So, while there is a momentary satisfaction of the necessary populist-aristocratic orientation of romance—as it were retrieved from a sea of rust and inequity—the play continues to analyse the teleology of romance. Who determines its utopian compulsion? Might fortune, providence, or secular virtue best possess narrative priority? For just as the play resists a facile humanism, so does it question the sustainability of romantic, nostalgic, utopian *rapprochements*. The play undertakes a new kind of romance quest, a highly reflexive one concerning its own status as politi-cal agent and metaphor. The sea, as always, offers death and birth, debris and instauration, and in doing so metaphorizes the world of the theatre itself as much as that of politics. Hence the armour that next emerges from the sea. A rival birth from the amneotic? a corroded husk awaiting burial?—the rusty me-dieval metal *is* the genre, its use newly negotiable.

Correspondingly, the tone of this moment is far from assured. Pericles' armour might easily appear the target of a reflexive literariness; compare Cervantes:

And first of all he caused certaine old rusty armes to be scoured, that belonged to his great Grand-father, and lay many ages neglected, and forgotten in a by-corner of his home . . . to make tryall whether his pasted Beaver was strong enough, and might abide the adventure of a blow, he out with his sword, and gave it a blow or two, and with the very first did quite undoe his whole weekes labour . . .[12]

The boys' plays at Blackfriars had further contributed to a fashion for scepticism when 'nature' seemed abused; the tropes of providential magic had begun to seem 'super-annuated'. But, as Jonson's criticism attests, to thus 'run from Nature' remained popular. Of course, magic and coincidence can have a similar attraction to rhyme, offering a warm sense of supra-rational order: but such a sense needn't preclude gentle irony, or awareness of things factitious, any more than it need serve a conservative teleology. One can here distinguish between a debunking, superior ridicule (Jonson's), and a more questing kind of scepticism (Shakespeare's). *The Alchemist* undresses 'magic' and derides gullibility, leaves precious little wonder left standing, and returns us, unillusioned, to the familiar; Shakespeare, by contrast, protects the currency of magic, of happy accident or strange beneficence, while causing us to question its sources and possibility. Wonder may well be apprehendable in temporal terms, but it is still surprising, perhaps wistful, often whimsical; it is not scoffed out of the picture. Above all, if hedged with an un-murderous irony, wonder is opened out to doubleness, to tension, to history.

So, to the nameless prince the armour represents a return to source so wonderful as to quite outdo the fishermen's dreams of a restoration of their 'original' parish:

> Thankes Fortune, yeat that after all crosses,
> Thou giuest me somewhat to repaire my selfe:
> And though it was mine owne part of my heritage,
> Which my dead father did bequeath to me.

> (II. i. 120–3)

Joining Pericles' future glory with his origin, the armour satisfies the basic trope of restorative romance. 'Keepe it my *Perycles*', he recalls his father commanding: the inherited 'Coate of worth' (II. i. 135), now retrieved by a loving divinity, seems to confirm

---

[12] Cervantes, *Don Quixote*, i. 26.

an equally inherited, equally blessed sovereignty.[13] However, the scene's broader context might invoke a simple and indignant opposition to any historical transcendentalism. For the armour doesn't simply appear, a gift of providence; it is drawn in by hard labour:

> Helpe Maister helpe; heere's a Fish hanges in the Net,
> Like a poore mans right in the law: t'will hardly come out.
> Ha bots on't, tis come at last; & tis turnd to a rusty Armour.

(II. i. 115–18)

Pericles' purportedly inherited performance is resumed only through rustic co-operation; furthermore in the process of rejoining the knight with 'destiny' the fishermen charge the moment's symbol with a political resonance which works as magically and magnetically as any romantic talisman. Pericles' armour is indeed 'a poore mans right in the law': not exclusively or finally, but in such a fashion as to endow he who wears it with the cause which the metaphor ropes in.[14] That is, a law more felicitous to the many who aren't wealthy. Like the armour dragged from the sea, the law should be dragged from the rich miser's clutches. The fishermen thus stubbornly resist the stranger's feudal interpretation, and his attempted annexation of enfranchising origin:

I but harke you my friend, t'was wee that made vp this Garment through the rough seames of the Waters: there are certain Condolements, certain Vailes: I hope sir, if you thriue, you'le remember from whence you had them. (II. i. 147–51)

He claims not only to have fished the thing from the brine, but to have 'made' it. Fortune's armour is correspondent not to monarchical inheritance, but to their trade. The sea's 'rough seames' transmute contiguously into the fishermen's patched fishing net and breeched labour. Consequently, if Pericles is to

---

[13] Cf. Thomas Nashe, *Christs Teares over Ierusalem* (1593): 'The frayle flesh wherein thou art inuested is nothing but a sin-battred Armour, with many strokes of temptations assaulted and brused, to breake in to thee & surpryse thee.' In *The Works of Thomas Nashe*, ed. Ronald B. McKerrow, 5 vols. (1958; repr. with corrections by F. P. Wilson, Oxford, 1966), ii. 143.

[14] Cf. Nashe, *Christs Teares*, 155: 'As when a poore mans cause hangs so long in Court ere it can be decided, that through the Iudges sloth hee is vndone with following of it'.

go off tourneying and courting, it is because the fishermen facilitate it: he has to 'begge' of them his coat of worth. For the fisherman points out that Pericles has received 'Vailes' and 'Condolements'—sympathy, charity, some patched-up cloth— and they expect the same generosity in return. When the Second Fisherman gives Pericles his 'best Gowne' for him to make a pair of braces, the knight truly is clothed in community attire (II. i. 161–2). Of course, Pericles' greatest fervour remains his own glory. Mounted delightfully on a 'Courser', pursuing his 'Will', he continues to imagine himself in terms of chivalrous prec- edents (II. i. 156–65). However, the scene with the fishermen both popularizes and problematizes the origin of any regained dignity.

Accordingly, the armoured Pericles' courting of Thaisa is an early step in the fishermen's hopes for reparation. His scruffiness at Simonides' court ('by his rustie outside, he appeares, To haue practis'd more the Whipstocke, then the Launce', II. ii. 49–50) lends him not only that air of mystery and power which attracts the princess, but suggests an uncertain origin, a potentially demotic valency. Furthermore, Pericles' eventual marriage to Thaisa chimes doubly with the fishermen's ambitions. First in that the union produces a daughter whose very name and gen- esis suggest her investment in and definition through their 'wat'ry empire'; and second in the way Thaisa is sent overboard to join 'the belching Whale' (III. i. 62) before being 'belche[d]' back up by the 'Seas stomacke' (III. ii. 54–6). The figurative connections suggest the political pattern: Thaisa becomes part of the 'parish' engrossed by the whale, so that to retrieve her is to offer some kind of answer to the fishermen's nostalgic radi- calism. Their voices—echoing, unappeased, expectant—remain in the play's collective mind, contributing to the play's poly- phonic search for repair. And they do so through their almost procreative role in the reconstruction, the re-dressing, of the hero.

The romance hero is thus made and unmade by those he meets. For one sees in this process a preparation for the hero's redundancy, even annihilation. There are no real heroes from now on in the romances. Various 'others' precede, and shall succeed, Pericles' privilege. He soon goes from his beached namelessness and nakedness, alleviated only by the fishers, into a still wilder, more regressive condition of languageless hairiness, alleviated only by his daughter. Pericles spends much of the play, in one sense or another, stateless, estranged, savage. Intimating a kind of post-heroism, this pre-civility anticipates a new political dispensation. But what will it consist in? Beset by threats and temptations, humanist faith and aptitudes are shown to be in equal measure necessary and uncertain. The plays seek new faiths, forms, instruments, but lack a clear, precedent-buttressed identification of effective and legitimate agency. Hence the increasing diffusion of narrative authority, and increasing authority of metaphorical diffusion. Conventional generic tropes are split: the technique is one of fission, new cells emerging from the cleaving of the old. Coterminously, 'straight' genre-roles like the noble hero, accustomed to a tidiness of function, cannot accommodate the messy turbulence of the age. Different 'characters' are needed to take up the unrecuperable energies of a language which, in its metaphorical plenty, registers desire beyond strict precedent and decorum. Pericles is as lacunal a 'hero' as Shakespeare ever set forth. His gaps and absences, and his repeated reliance upon an 'other' for his own being, prepare for Shakespeare's increasingly decentred, analogy-driven, supra-naturalistic characterizations.

3

Body Language at Court

SHAKESPEARE'S romances play off conventional uses of political analogy, twisting and dilating them into surprising forms.
This metaphoric audacity in turn challenges and reformulates
the political assumptions which inform the stock analogies. This
is not to say that popular metaphors were chained down to
irrevocable denotations. On the contrary, it was quite usual
to exploit the slippery proteanism of metaphor. Humanist
rhetoric's very reliance upon argument from analogy implies an
awareness of the discourse's tricks, its politic opportunism.
Nonetheless, one can identify 'master tropes', weighty analogues which invoke certain presumptions about order and
authority. A well-known speech of James to his parliament,
for example, suggests how pastoral conceits were used to assert
controlling unities, here centred in the person of the shepherd-
king:

I am the Husband, and all the whole Isle is my lawful Wife; I am the
Head, and it is my Body: I am the Shepherd, and it is my Flocke: I hope
therefore no man will be so unreasonable as to thinke that I that am a
Christian king under the Gospel, should be a Polygamist and husband
to two wives; that I being the Head, should haue a deuided and
monstrous Body; or that being the shepherd to so fair a flock (whose
fold hath no wall to hedge it but the four seas) should have my flock
parted in two.[1]

Speaking here in stubborn pursuit of union beween England and
Scotland, James lists various analogues of an absolute monarch
and then fastidiously unpacks the logic of each simile. His intent
is to evoke absurdity or monstrosity so as to publish its impossibility. But the effect is to draw attention to how easily the
king's paternal conceits can be wrenched into profanity or
illegality. James's dissevering linguistic concentration thereby
anticipates that of Shakespeare's romances. One need not

---

[1] Speech to Lords, Mar. 1603: *The Political Works of James I*, ed. McIlwain, 272.

suggest that James's desire for union is the prime context for the plays; the same metaphors were used in all kinds of contexts. However, James anticipates his political failure in tropes of indecorum which, equally, are the subject-matter of the romances. For Shakespeare's disjunctive pastorals seem to ensue from just such a failure of authority, such a collapse of linguistic and conceptual wholeness. The grotesque spectres James raises are all brought tumbling forth: the beastly flesh, the severed head, the polygamous lust and banished wives; endangered flocks, 'preposterous' shepherds, bodies monstrous and mutating. At another moment James speaks of England and Scotland as 'two twins, they would have grown up together':[2] his rhetoric farms its tropes from the kind of fairy-story shattered in Leontes' Sicilia, or fractured with the alarming twinnings of *Cymbeline*. James's necessary opposites become unsettlingly conjoined. The plays endlessly work at this impasse between totalizing ideologies and their unruly media.

Contemporary satire often concentrates specifically upon the court's 'politic' language. To give but one of numerous examples: in *Antonio and Mellida* Marston repeatedly mocks the delaying rhetoric of aposiopesis and periphrasis, pleonasm and occupatio: 'Will squeeze out tears from out his spongy cheeks, The rocks even groan, and—Prithee, prithee, sing, Or I shall ne'er ha' done, when I am in, 'Tis harder for me end than begin'.[3] Marston ridicules the detachment of affect from effect; the tyranny of fashion over communication; and the sense that the self-regarding analogues, conceits, and parentheses within courtly discourse render the whole farrago finally and purely self-referential, a medium of exquisite paralysis. Shakespeare's late plays, too, use the pressures within political discourse as both subject and medium. But when the epideictic language fails it does not do so to isolate the absurdity of the display or for a quick and pleasing 'hit'. Caliban's recourse during the assassination plot to an exaggerated self-abasement is a rare example of something close to conventional satire; but one's permissible responses remain various, poised disarmingly between amusement, condescension, complicity, and disgust: 'Wilt thou be

[2] Speech of 31 Mar. 1607 on adjournment of the Houses. The whole speech is full of such analogues: see *Political Works*, ed. McIlwain, 290–305.

[3] *Antonio and Mellida*, ed. W. Reavley Gair (Manchester, 1991), IV. i. 150–4.

pleas'd to hearken once againe to the suite I made to thee?' (III.
ii. 36–7); 'How does thy honour? Let me licke thy shooe' (III. ii.
22–3). One may laugh because his routines are so hackneyed, or
for such a pitiable 'sot'; or because, having been taught by
Prospero to play the courtier, Caliban now lays it on thick for
his new god. But whatever the focus of one's amusement, an
important source of the irony is a shared awareness of how
courtly language is derisively manipulated, its periphrases revealed as mendacious and violent. As much as the state is
suffering an assault from the effluence of carnival, it is threatened by a parody of the very discourses which would canonize
the élite's supremacy.

The lesson is salutary: as often as the plays seem to celebrate
a beautiful neoplatonism, they dramatize an oxymoronic version where the formal etiquette of place, voice, and person is in
disarray. Civility's adversary, the physically disordered Caliban,
practises a rare hobgoblin lyricism; the courtly and fine-bodied
Cloten speaks in 'snatches' and 'burst[s]' of inelegant staccato
(IV. ii. 105–6); both Miranda and Marina curse with a vim too
splenetic for generations of gentlemanly editors to credit. Speech
in these plays is more restless, surprising, and inverting than if it
sought only to represent the assumptions of achieved or perceived station. And the body is no more fixed: when the 'beautiful' prince, Florizel, invokes as his models of courtship
rapacious gods who take on the form of bleating ram or bellowing bull (*The Winter's Tale*, IV. iv. 25–34), he suggests not only
the romance world's impatience with stolid decorums, but the
possible beastliness of authoritative discourse, the seductiveness,
for both object and subject, of physical mutation, and the persuasive surprises of rhetorical *imitatio*. For the genetic links
between language and body enjoy an almost Ovidian capacity
for partition, division, accretion, transmutation; for wickedly
punning literalisms where an airy wish or word takes on physical form; and for the half-laughing denial of 'common-sense' as
much as neoplatonic certitudes. In a culture for whom the 'body
politic' metaphor was perhaps the pre-eminent trope of public
constitutional discourse,[4] an unstable choreography of the body

---

[4] See Mervyn James, 'Ritual, Drama, and Social Body in the Late Medieval
English Town', in *Society, Politics, and Culture: Studies in Early Modern England*
(Cambridge, 1986); James Daly, 'Cosmic Harmony and Political Thinking in Early

will imply a sustained analysis of political circumstances and necessities. Released into new freedoms and surprising servitudes, the body's history is correlative to that of language.

An alternative view has been argued by Terry Eagleton, who proposes two basic homologies: the theatrical body, organic and contained, is feudal, while its voices, multiplying and transgressive, are capitalistic.[5] Theatre becomes a medium which threatens the order Shakespeare would champion, and language an ambiguously rebellious servant. Words undertake a constant battle to reconcile their fluidity with the unified, unitary social body. Such multiplicity cannot be contained and ordered in the idealized heroic body: hence the tragedy of organicist logos. The tragic plays as it were mourn this; the villains are invariably those individualists who exploit and fracture the communal verities of organicism. Shakespeare's romances, meanwhile, occlude or euphemize historical contradiction through devices of magical romance surplus. Figures who, through correlative linguistic and physical fluidity, deny the intrinsic ideological violence, do so either factitiously or criminally: *Macbeth*'s witches must be ostracized if the organic order is to assert itself, while only through magic can Ariel effect a wistfully reconciliatory utopianism.

However, the romances complicate the neatness of any such antithetical dialectic. Their radically distending sense of both language and body represents the shifting conflicts between received and nascent sociological forms with considerably less disingenuousness or nostalgia than Eagleton allows.[6] The plays do indeed attempt some kind of fruitful alliance between 'capitalism and feudalism', between reciprocity and profit, service and liberty. Concomitantly, body and language are at times united in the romances: but not quite as simply or serviceably as Eagleton reckons. Metaphor creates bodies without perceivable

---

Stuart England', *Transactions of the American Philosophical Society*, 69, part 7 (1979), 15–18; Patterson, *Fables of Power*, ch. 4, 'Body Fables'; Thomas Sorge, 'The Failure of Orthodoxy in *Coriolanus*', in Jean E. Howard and Marion F. O'Connor, eds., *Shakespeare Reproduced: The Text in History and Ideology* (New York, 1987), 225–39; Mikhail Bakhtin, *Rabelais and His World*, trans. Hélène Iswolsky (Bloomington, Ind., 1984), 22–3.

[5] Terry Eagleton, *William Shakespeare* (Oxford, 1986), 94–5 ff.

[6] Eagleton, ibid. 100, understands the last plays to idealize the 'feudal surplus' as the 'largesse or superabundance of nature'.

flesh, or supplements discrete existing bodies with signs which belong to no particular tongue or agency at all. This process takes the promiscuous body of carnival—Cloten, Autolicus, and Caliban are each both grotesque and mutating—and reinvests it, reorganizes it, through a dialectical surplus which one can identify with an unstable social and economic order. Eagleton understands this process, whereby 'signs come to surpass the body' and to 'escape its sensuous control', in the Marxist sense of the 'fetishism of commodities', wherein the producers lose control of their products, which start to establish and determine their own social relations.[7] Certainly Shakespeare's interlacing dialogues do just this. Shakespeare's transsubjective liberty with metaphor, consequently, is an application rather than evasion of the transformatory cultural and economic environment. Caliban is not a symbol of pure body for whom language is merely a means to renewed enslavement. His apparently heavy tread, his sloth and sludge, belie the restless physics of his body; these physics, in turn, are constituted as much by language as by Caliban's torturous engagement with nature and nurture. Through Caliban the play engages with history in ways that are not escapist, which push themselves as a kind of 'reality principle' more and more to the 'centre', and remain as the condition which must be faced even as it appears to be left behind. Autolicus, too, is constructed in such a way that 'body' becomes something cerebral, something as split, manipulable, and shifting as language. First, though, I want to look at the creative relationship of body and metaphor in *Cymbeline*, so as to get a sense of the type of being which the play uses to represent both the court and the emerging British polity.

CYMBELINE

The lords at Cymbeline's court seem intent on expressing definitive judgements. There appear to be two discursive registers— praise or blame—and the courtiers want to establish the respective sides as if sealing the court's ethical direction. But repeatedly they fail, uncovering indistinction instead of platonic

---

[7] Ibid. 97–8.

distillations. The problem seems to be that nobody spoken of
is quite as clearly right or wrong as the available linguistic
options invite them to publish. They try to state their judgements accurately but, restricted to professional diction, any
caveats must be as absolute as the thing qualified. Clarity is
confused amid the exchange of opposites. Hence the inaugural
praise of Posthumus, palpably ambiguous:

> He that hath miss'd the Princesse, is a thing
> Too bad, for bad report: and he that hath her
> (I meane, that married her, alacke good man,
> And therefore banish'd) is a Creature, such,
> As to seek through the Regions of the Earth
> For one, his like; there would be something failing
> In him, that should compare. I do not thinke,
> So faire an Outward, and such stuffe Within
> Endowes a man, but hee.
>
> (I. i. 16–24)

The very fact of having to clarify ('I meane . . .') suggests the
temptations toward a blurring of identity. The praise seems to
construct a kind of straw-man, half-scarecrow, half-mannequin
('So fair an Outward, and such stuff Within'). His namelessness
makes of him both anyone and no one. This nullifying conven-
tionality is twice used as if to deny that such a thing could exist;
he is a 'Creature', still impersonal, without hope of 'one his like'.
The strange sense that the praise lacks a centre has the effect of
inverting a precise direction to idolize the hero. Instead of romantic hagiography, there emerges a portentous synonymity of
what is 'good' with what is 'bad'. The later scene in Rome, when
the assorted Europeans discuss Posthumus' reputation, reinforces this definitive ambiguity: doubting his virtues, they speak
of him as though 'he' indeed is the reports of him, a constructed
text or 'Catalogue' that one can table and 'peruse . . . by Items',
and which alters according to how one 'words him' (I. v. 4–5,
14). Posthumus' very being is bartered and renegotiated, literally engendered with every passing judgement: 'You speake of
him when he was lesse furnish'd, then now hee is, with
that which makes him both without, and within' (I. v. 7–9).
The whole of *Cymbeline* is built around such pointedly insufficient figures: it presents straw-men without centres, oddly

interchangeable, defined like shop-models by their shifting shirts. 'I cannot delue him to the roote', says a gentlemen of Posthumus (I. i. 28): as with his fellow young men, we cannot quite be sure where we start from, or what we start with. Desire is detached from source, and all the more turbulent for the fact.

Hence the unstable currency of courtly discourse. By turns opaque, oxymoronic, and otiose, the courtiers' analogies draw from a figurative body no longer capable of the burden:

> I do extend him (Sir) within himselfe,
> Crush him together, rather then vnfold
> His measure duly.

> (I. i. 25–7)

The courtier's boast of diffidence is, taken literally, a coy paean to cruelty. A certain decadent affectlessness suggests how a self-aggrandizing language, loosened from the accountabilities of precise referentiality, becomes a screen or charter for injustice. For the fact is that there is no one at court willing to 'speak up' for the subject; the courtier plays the bored hostage-holder, in mindless iteration of some invisible authority's bidding. The subject's worth becomes strangely by-the-way, a nostalgic essentialism in an age of political paralysis and nominalism. There is, of course, 'another' world at the door, hence the tearing, repressive strain here placed upon courtly tropes. But in the blithe refusals and contradictions of the courtier one can see the resistance of an old ruling caste, and the smug, careless viciousness of an '*ancien régime*' in which sovereign language occludes the violence of accustomed self-interest. For it is not far from here to the taciturn censorships of Antioch's court. *Cymbeline*'s courtier may seem to speak for the virtuous up-and-coming, or if not, as a type of classic courtly time-server, hedging his bets as to the succession; more pertinently, his is the language of complaisant and ultimately merciless reaction.

A further, crucial, point to notice is the way this turbid world finds source and effect in Shakespeare's experimental, de-centred, figurative process of character construction. Consider the courtier's use of 'him'. The first 'him' is, most obviously, the product of language alone, the spoken word building its denotative castles; at the same time, the thought that courtly praise 'extend[s] him' is itself a wry intimation of hyperbole.

The 'him' is then double: first, that Posthumus who, in his own person, small and poor, a kind of stubbornly present overleaper who as the princess' consort cannot be ignored, is puffed up by the exigencies of the diplomatic moment; and second, a 'subjectivity' reconstructed out of words, its truth-value absolutely 'on parole'. The next use of 'him', however (in 'himselfe'), is different. The courtier motions toward some kind of Platonic 'reality' that 'is' Posthumus—'himselfe'—and within which capacious truth the courtier's words can only seek and then shrink into unfitness. Rhetoric's art is impoverished next to the ungraspable substance of achieved virtue. But the next moment this ideal is almost gloatingly besmirched. The speaker's artful undisclosing implies that sovereign courtly language has its own ungilded prestige, a kind of puissance that must abide beyond the ins and outs, ebbs and flows of such caterpillars-cum-butterflies as Posthumus. In this way, the 'him' of 'crush him together' seems to conflate and then destroy the three referents juggled in the opening line (man, description, ideal). The speaker acknowledges an idea of 'measure' that evokes the very decorum and justice which his language emerges out of, is putatively grounded in, but which is here an impossible or undesirable standard. And it is made thus impossible by the socio-economic pressures which the speaker resists and, in his violence, records. The only 'measure' then left standing is the courtier's would-be transcendent faith in his language's power, a faith founded—unsteadily enough—upon sureness of rank and its linguistic correspondents. Consequently, the thing that possesses some tenuous power of 'the real' is almost the language itself. It controls the body, and constructs a 'virtual' world that has more potency and centrality than a 'real' world which, more than describing, it subdues. At the same time, and to reiterate, this near-nominalism serves a particular, deeply ideological, political dispensation. 'Posthumus', then, is the effect of the 'crush[ed]', 'extend[ed]', and *folded* senses of each 'him' in the courtier's appraisal: discretely, in aggregate, and in almost-mindless kinetic competition.

This inhospitable 'new world' in turn correlates to a confusion of genre, a scrappy hiatus of things lingeringly dying and labouringly new born. It is a state for which Posthumus more or less consciously bleeds. The sun and plenty of traditional pastoral romance assume an economic surplus, effortlessly beyond commerce and fluctuation; such leisure of place accordingly implies an assured ethical and political order where debts are of honour and credit means fame. It is not so here: reputation is in the red, striving for capital, always on the edge of shame. Even when he is in gaol, contritely aware that his own wrong out-weighs Imogen's, Posthumus still personifies himself fiscally, his life a bad debt and dwindling principal (V. iv. 15–28). Earlier, he could hardly have pronounced this ethos more baldly: 'that most venerable man, which I cauld my father, was, I know not where when I was stampt. Some Coyner with his Tooles Made me a counterfeit' (II. iv. 155–8). The 'Tooles' of parenthood evoke either a mint—the valorizing power of government—or a penis—the fetishized dismembered organ. Personality is less 'natural', a magical gift uniquely one's own, than a product of barter or function. It is as if romantic sufficiency, a freedom from factitious self-strivings, depends upon a 'legitimate' par-entage which, in this play of the absent origin, is quite lost from view. Even when Posthumus' dream seems to reunite him into a kind of Lacanian pre-natal wholeness (V. iv. 30–151), the image is not only hedged by incredulity and impending violence, but split by the news of his 'unnatural' birth. Ripped from the womb through instrument of the knife, he is as parentless as Macbeth. Posthumus not only bewails, but personifies, what the Scottish tyrant effects: the disintegration of organicist secu-rities.

Hence Cloten's and Posthumus' mix of violence and bewilderment, the sense that proof of courage, generosity, and virtue, the old chivalrous blazon of true being, can find expression only in endless 'oppositions' or empty heroic ges-tures. Posthumus' wager with Iachimo over Imogen's virtue is a perfect example of the play's 'all and nothing' attitude to gov-erning ideals. The wager expects, indeed almost wills, a kind of profane apocalypse, a judgement day when the angel becomes the harlot and Iachimo, the beauty-besotted time-server, offers the pattern of the age. The 'single oppositions' which, as Cloten boasts, are the pure measure of chivalrous manhood (IV. i. 15), are mocked by the 'opposition' of Imogen's hymen: the effect is like a pun, making of romance a denuded memory. Indeed Posthumus' misogynist rant, as he moves from one pornographic snap-shot to its sequel, invokes a vicious parody of chivalrous combat. Imogen is imagined as both horse and opposer: 'Perchance he spoke not, but Like a full Acorn'd Boare, a Iarmen on[e], Cry'de oh, and mounted; found no opposition But what he look'd for, should oppose, and she Should from encounter guard' (II. iv. 167–71).[8] The ferocity of his vision is stoked by memories of Imogen's resistance to his own 'lawfull pleasure'. On the one hand this over-careful chasteness might confirm the survival of a kind of hierophantic romance, transcending ownership and appetite; on the other hand, it seems to niggle at Posthumus as if proof of his own unworthiness in this game of high birth and sharp practice. There's a touch of Groucho Marx in Posthumus: that the princess chose him says little for her taste; her whims are fickle and undiscriminating. Whether making absurd wagers, grotesque assassination plans, or suicidal abdications, Posthumus is confused into violence—against himself, his wife, his rivals, his country—because he measures everything, all morality and purpose, against an ideal which his own ostensible exemplification of 'proves' has done its dash. Like Imogen with the headless trunk (IV. ii. 306–22), Posthumus is, throughout the play, a strangely embarrassed figure, left isolated and hysteric, pumping hot air into a memory shafted by mistake and corruption.

To claim such a representative role for Posthumus in a sense sets him up as an oddly misdirected hero, as if the exemplar of the wrong play in an unwelcome genre. However, if he is some such comically mistaken paragon, he is not so alone. He shares the status with his 'brothers': not only Cloten, but the lost princes. For it is crucial to an understanding of *Cymbeline* to recognize how Shakespeare's metaphorical and situational rhymes construct a shared body. This textually figured body doesn't have a perfect or original owner; nor is it necessarily represented by an identifiable human shape. It may be carried through metonyms or other tropes of the body. This at times

---

[8] Patricia Parker, *Shakespeare from the Margins*, 127–33, notes how Germans had a contemporary reputation as imitators and copyists, both 'faithful' and cheating translators, and also Shakespeare's frequent punning upon the word's closeness to 'Gemmen', meaning twin/duplicate, cousins/cozeners. All of this is very appropriate for *Cymbeline*'s mirroring-cum-plagiarizing young men.

will mutate beyond the strictly human into contiguous or analogous figures. At times, as in the scene when the mountain-men meet the court dolt (IV. ii), the burden will be shared or multiplied so that, myth defying mathematics, both each separate figure and the various characters conceived of *en bloc* carry the weight of the whole. Sometimes, as if the play's metaphors meet, clash, and metamorphose into groaning life—as, pre-eminently, in the battle scene (V. iii)—individual bodies are barely distinguished, as the totality of public desire congeals into suitably composite plastic form. The important point is that this mutating mannequin can be at once complete and captured in one being, and shared throughout all the present members. Just as the king as head, or the artisans as arms, can embody both the whole commonwealth—for better or worse—and themselves as a part to add to or subtract from the sum, so too can each moment, each character, encapsulate the realm or a creaking limb within it.

To understand exactly how this works, it will be useful to think more carefully about the exact status of Cloten, apparently so foolish, venal, and expendable. The play invites a constant disdain of Cloten, which asks one to find out reasons for his indecorousness. The answer as it were waiting to be discovered is that Cloten is foreign, like the Spanish prince Pharamond in *Philaster*, or a usurer's son like Segusto in *Mucedorus*. But no such answer is provided, and the play is the more probing and unsettling for it. Cloten's background remains mysterious. There are hints at intervals throughout the play that Cloten is base born, son to a tailor or, as the paronomasia might hint, a 'Squires Cloth' like his rival (II. iii. 122; compare 'Clot-pole' at IV. ii. 184). His fury when faced with the upward mobility of others might conform to what has been called the 'instability of the class aspirant's own position', its oscillations further 'articulated within misogynistic discourse'.[9] This of course serves to characterize Posthumus as much as Cloten. Each gains his status through being a kind of consort, Posthumus as husband to a princess ('By her electió may be truly read, What

---

[9] Peter Stallybrass, 'Patriarchal Territories: The Body Enclosed', in Margaret W. Ferguson, Maureen Quilligan, and Nancy J. Vickers, eds., *Rewriting the Renaissance: The Discourses of Sexual Difference in Early Modern Europe* (Chicago, 1986), 133–4.

kind of man he is', I. i. 53–4) and Cloten as son to a queen by second marriage.

Cloten is routinely embarrassed by ineptitude and slaughtered with a perfunctory disdain. But certain signs point to something less despicable. He is anything but a coward—he is not even a bully—and his trumpetings of native worth are both witty and orthodox. Cloten is the play's most strident advocate of order and degree (II. iii. 112–24), a doctrine which, his shrillness aside, echoes the warnings of Ulysses or Laertes and, if it is immoderate, finds a 'too noble' fellow in the thundering denunciations of Coriolanus. But he works at disparate ideological registers. It is Cloten who is given the clowning lecher's franchise as, sniggering confidentially on his way to rape the heroine, his salacious puns induce a kind of complicity in the eavesdropping audience (IV. i. 1–27).

Such intimacy is unusual but not unique; Cloten's figure permits surprisingly contradictory responses. Clearly in some ways Cloten is a caricature, but he is a caricature who both represents and challenges existing notions of authority: hence in his own right he can be both hegemonic and subversive. There can be both contempt and a kind of licentious joy in beholding his haplessness in office. If the play exploits the ludicrousness of such folly holding power, any amusement is partly licensed by the comic certainty that the villain shall come to grief—if not quite murder, then at least humiliation. One might react against Cloten with a 'noble' disdain, because he is crass and gauche; equally one might see in him a kind of inferior peer, inviting emulation from the ranks. Cloten may seem merely satirical, a parody of the fops and fools hanging around court; less conventionally, he can represent the fecklessness of primogenitive institutions. Yet, from the opposite side, he might connote the regrettable triumph of indecorous commercial energies. There is no sure 'class' franchise upon his buffoonery. He might be one of the Blackfriars' stage-peacocks, astonishing in his ignorance; or he might be, like Bohemia's clown, an obscure dolt raised through accident to the dizzy heights of court. The eminence of his 'empty purse' suggests how tremendous social mobility is much more at the centre of things than it is, say, in *Twelfth Night*, where comic elegance keeps it marginal and risible. Tropes of the grotesque help further to determine Cloten's significance. Cloten's philosophy is doggedly hostile to the 'lower Messes', but the climate of his body declares his sources within it (see below). Discovered initially in his sweat and his arse (I. iii), the locus of Cloten's body later moves to his 'Clotpole', a figure not only of the phallic head but of the 'empty purse' (IV. ii. 113–16; 184–6). Shakespeare conflates the popular with the mercantile and the courtly: to be exiled or liminal—ideologically and cerebrally as Cloten is, physically as are Posthumus and Guiderius—becomes a kind of *non sequitur*, depending upon a vanished centre.

The only sure thing is that Cloten's mixed genre includes categories which, in their sum, contain much of the social tensions of the period. Middleton in *The Phoenix* suggests, in the relationship between father and son, the kind of generational and cultural differences which Cloten straddles: 'What a fortunate elder brother is he, whose father being a rammish ploughman, himself a perfumed gentleman spending the labouring reek from his father's nostrils in tobacco, the sweat of his father's body in monthly physic for his pretty queasy harlot! he sows apace i'th' country; the tailor o'ertakes him i'th' city.'[10] Cloten's carcass and his cloth—the properties which, as will be shown, define him—seem equally appropriate to both father or son: he stages historical transformation. Similarly, his dicing and gambling might take its copy from various Jacobean entrepreneurs. The nation's economy was floated on the exchange of gambles, public lotteries, and joint-stock speculations. Cloten, then, caricatures an abundant turbulence of historical energies. Linear realism is not the measurement for such a 'man'.

It follows that an understanding of Cloten's role must take into account the play's peculiarly intense metaphorical networks, and its consequent patterns of parallelism and proxying. And pivotal here is the relationship between Cloten and Posthumus. The two never appear on stage together, but their relationship is introduced through report of a duel which, in establishing the terms of their rivalry, also prepares for the ensuing working-out of their conflict-cum-identity during the play. Either can fill in for the other; when together, they animate the conflicts which exist 'independently' within each and which the story goes on to dramatize. Shakespeare's dense

---

[10] *The Phoenix* (1607), played by the Children of St Paul's, and presented before the king: *The Works of Thomas Middleton*, ed. A. H. Bullen, 8 vols. (London, 1885), i, I. ii. 57–6.

patterns of metaphor, textually both proleptic and mnemonic, not only help to 'figure' the various characters, but they possess a power of prediction, indeed of impulsion. Consider the puns which dress Cloten's first entrance:

Sir, I would advise you to shift a Shirt; the Violence of Action hath made you reek as a Sacrifice: where ayre comes out, ayre comes in: There's none abroad so wholesome as that you vent. (I. iii. 1–4)

The lord flatters Cloten in language which lays the ground for a series of subsequent themes. Recoiling from Cloten's bestial smell, the courtier manipulates his aversion into praise both exorbitant and cynical. He is saying that Cloten's foul perfume comes from the court air outside of him which, now that his shirt has been ripped, can invade his tailored defences and give itself off in the guise of his own smell. Cloten, then, is imagined as somehow the sum, and in a sense the oblivious victim, of his surrounding environment. The courtier's puns identify the subjects with whom Cloten shares his body. Most immediately, this means simply everybody: 'there's none abroad . . . '. But the person who has been sent 'abroad' is Posthumus. So, the lord praises Cloten by decrying his rival. However, the grotesque imagery suggests a power to cause and possess as well as to metaphorize: analogy supplies political, physical, or psychological motivation. Posthumus is therefore a 'vent' of Cloten: his exile is Cloten's physical discharge, his moral quality Cloten's putrescence. Just as in the opening scene the encomiums of Posthumus fail to identify the proper subjects of 'good' and 'bad', rendering the inhospitable somehow exchangeable, so too here Posthumus, as the one 'abroad', can equally be either as 'wholesome' as Cloten (being vented by him) or not as 'wholesome' as Cloten (being 'abroad'). Putative opposition collapses into identity. Posthumus is not only Cloten's foe, but his child, his turd, his air, his consequence. If the faecal metaphor evokes thoughts of carnivalesque inversion or regeneration, there is no clear sense here as to which way up any due order is in the first place, let alone which of the two, if either, is the object of demotic hope or popular derision.

The duel between Cloten and Posthumus is an early example of a situation repeated time and again throughout the play: one figure seeks to defeat, kill, possess, buy, or rape another. Frequently the language of one—for instance, to buy or to win of—will mutate into another—to have sex with. In Cloten's second scene (II. i), for instance, he talks of having 'kist the Iacke': the jack is the small ball called the 'mistress', and to kiss it is to touch and lay beside it. The erotic imputations neatly encapsulate the play's clashing and synonymizing agencies. The subject of most of the play's duels and games, of course, is the 'mistress' Imogen; the surrounding context of this brief scene is Iachimo's attempt upon her chastity. It is possible, therefore, to identify the 'Iacke' from which Cloten is 'hit away' with both Imogen and Iachimo. The Italian then doubles as the one who, standing by, either inflicts or witnesses Cloten's defeat. Iachimo merges into the 'whoreson Iackanapes' who criticizes Cloten's language: character is disembodied, figured linguistically. The play continues to set up a shared body whose brutalism 'measures' the quality of self. That Cloten wishes he was one of the 'Iacke-slave[s]' getting a 'belly full' of satisfaction (II. i. 22–3) confirms that he too shares in the desire which takes Iachimo, the play's tangible 'Iacke', into Imogen's 'trunk'. Once there (II. iii), playing at one moment the 'jack-in-the-box' and, as he leaves telling the chime—'One, two, three: time, time'—the 'Jack of the clock', Iachimo suggests how Shakespeare sets up a pattern of repetitive naming wherein desire and agency continually double up, producing and reproducing the shared figure, at once single and multiple, of the competitive body politic.[11]

The courtly world is a duelling one, where mercenary preoccupations shade into lewd puns. There is little difference between Cloten's gaming and Iachimo's gamble; the language is identical: 'Your Ring may be stolne too . . . I should get ground of your fair Mistris; make her go backe, euen to the yeilding' (I. v. 92–110), boasts Iachimo, his figures those of duelling and land, the poaching and engrossing which is courtly sexual conquest. Imogen's 'ring' is her wealth, her husband's

---

[11] *OED*, 'Jack', respectively nos. 18 and 5, 1 and 2, 6. 'Jack-in-the-box' is a gambling game, a thief or cheat, the springy toy or, interestingly, a contemptuous appellation for the consecrated host (*OED* 2), suggestive for Cloten—one of the Jacks—as a gross parody of the sacrament. Further, a 'jack' can connote a machine for turning the spit in roasting meat (*OED* 7), cf. Cloten-Posthumus' carcasses, eventually 'ouer-roasted' in sacrifice (V. iv. 153).

love-troth, and her pudendum, just as the 'Backe-side' where
Cloten ventures his 'Steele' (his sword, larceny, and penis)
evokes the blind stab of the coward, the secret haunt of the
debtor, and the rectum of the rival (I. iii. 11–12). Sexual rivalry,
then, metaphorizes commercial ambition: to be 'in debt',
Cloten's sorry fate, is to fail in both fornication and credit-
worthiness.[12] The city-cum-court environment is miasmic, obsessive, paranoid with the imperatives of self-constructing
masculinity. So, to be stolen is also to be violated sexually,
which then puns on the 'stale' as prostitute. Imogen later applies
the pun to herself ('Poore I am stale, a Garment out of fashion',
III. iv. 51), while early on she enjoys the thought of 'prick[ing]
The goer backe' during her suitors' desert duel, her 'Needle'
made a familiar 'Steele' of compensatory desire (I. ii. 99–100). A
degraded courtly discourse is somehow irresistible. She too prepares for sacrifice upon the phallic altar: 'Had I bin Theefe-
stolne, As my two Brothers, happy' (I. vii. 5–6).

It is such over-concentration, such neurotic fascination with
the body's capacity for disobedience and embarrassment, which
facilitates Shakespeare's reworking of the romance 'body politic'. The puns, oddly abstracted from any morality, speak a kind
of nervousness, as if the rules of etiquette are in abeyance. One
can discern a lack of polite comfort, a communal body breaking
into uncertain forms, and a background of swirling civic mobility. Cloten's bellicosity, for instance, keeps colliding into homo-
or auto-eroticism. The hopes to kiss 'the Iacke', to have his belly
stuffed full of 'satisfaction'. It is said of Posthumus in the duel
that 'he fled forward still, toward your face': the agnominatio
suggests 'forward steel' or erect penis, charging in the 'face', or
the buttocks, of Cloten (I. iii. 14–15). When Posthumus' body is
called a 'passable Carkasse', this quibbles on its penetrability, as
well as its desirability, while a 'through-fare for Steele' still more
luridly evokes the anal passage (I. iii. 8–9). At times his companion lords pun quite compulsively: 'nor crop the eares of them'
puns on 'arse' and 'ass', as folly and sodomy are again Cloten's
beastly burden (II. i. 13); Cloten's 'Oathes' are 'curtall[ed]', or
castrated into the impotence of a 'Capon' (II. i. 11–25). Cloten's
own protest is the most telling: 'every Iacke-Slave hath his belly

---

[12] Cf. Dante's infernal triune of buggery, usury, and blasphemy: *Inferno*, XI.

full of Fighting, and I must go vp and downe like a Cock, that no body can match' (II. i. 20–2). Absurd, pitiful, obscene, and rather menacing, Cloten's sense of self-lack is both personally characteristic and metonymically appropriate: he envies his fellow gallants their duelling plenty, but more pointedly compares their replete bellies, stuffed full with each other's masculinity, with his own frustrated maleness. His very body becomes a lonely angst-struck penis, waggling brave but sterile in a 'self-figur'd knot' of absent satisfaction. At such moments Cloten's body seems to replace, or to analogize, his lumpen intelligence: the sum effect of his manners suggests not only verbal clumsiness, but the knockabout potency of embodied malapropism. That such a physical-linguistic figure can 'be' the body politic suggests how distant the present state is from secure analogies or elegant orders. For the point is that the 'whole', the organic body politic, must be conceived historically in terms of its disseverance. This history soon finds its most plangent symbol: Cloten-Posthumus' decapitation, in which Cloten's clotpole is left 'empty' of all sense, money, and seed. Early moments like this, where Cloten is shrunk into his own little trunk, anticipate and generalize the movement toward brutalized impotence.

Cloten wants to be the ascendant self-creator, enjoying the profane luxuries of his position. Instead he is ridiculed as a fiscal debtor, a sexual impotent ('oathes' equals testicles), and a discursive borrower. In such a context any 'satisfaction' is likely to be second-hand, given value by vicarious or voyeuristic nourishment. Accordingly, Cloten's fantastical will imagines a veritable apotheosis of the plagiarist's imagination, involving a kidnap, a plunder, and a cuckolding piece of ventriloquism:

With that Suite vpon my backe wil I rauish her: first kill him, and in her eyes; there shall she see my valour, which wil then be a torment to hir contempt. He on the ground, my speech of insulment ended on his dead bodie, and when my Lust hath dined ... to the Court Ile knock her backe, foot her home againe. (III. v. 138–46)

Cloten's 'speech of insul[t]ment' recalls, and in his eyes revenges, his humiliated 'oathes': the 'speech of insultment' is nothing less than Cloten's onanistically wound-up penis. That his fantasy is at this moment shared by Posthumus reinforces its epitomic stature; in the courtly milieu at least, it is of such stuff that dreams are made on, even when transported, as here, to the unbuttoned liberties of the wild.

Throughout the play Cloten treasures anticipations of another duel with Posthumus, a duel perfect in its 'single oppositions'. His recurring dream is of solipsistic possession, a metamorphic doubling of Cloten's 'Glasse' into body and property:

How fit his Garments serue me? Why should his Mistris who was made by him that made the Taylor, not be fit too? . . . I dare speake it to my selfe, for it is not Vainglorie for a man, and his Glasse, to confer in his owne Chamber; I meane, the Lines of my body are as well drawne as his; no lesse young, more strong, not beneath him in Fortunes, beyond him in the aduantage of the time, aboue him in Birth, alike conuersant in generall seruices, and more remarkeable in single oppositions. (IV. i. 2–15)

Cloten's own body, then, is the temple of the 'oppositions' he desires; his mirror, likewise, sends back an image of his rival. Similarly, the woman he would possess is incorporated into his self-conception. He imagines wearing the princess as he does her husband's clothes; pre-emptively, their flesh is his own. Cloten always duels with himself, this self in turn is always whatever he opposes: at such moments he is the body politic. When he seems narcissistic, then, drooling or drowning in his own reflection, Cloten is staging the violent contradictions of the British nation itself.

Shakespeare here creates bodies that get their identity less from some ennobling presence of mind or soul than from the metaphors and metonyms that their 'parent' language invokes. The characters don't adjudicate upon metaphorical decorum, like for instance a Hamlet might; they are used by it, made by it. In *Cymbeline*, none of the characters are within sight of any sovereign self-consciousness. Hamlet rebukes his 'friends' for trying to play him like a 'Pipe' (III. ii. 361): in *Cymbeline*, by contrast, Shakespeare's metaphors do just this. His characters are played, instruments of surrounding designs and impulses. *Cymbeline* here practises an almost pornographic aesthetic principle, quite separating gratification from affect and the physical from the emotional. A self-regarding language fills in for any 'natural' performance. The play's crucial set pieces—Iachimo's stealthily semiotic rape of Imogen (II. iii. 11–51), Posthumus' rage against her 'pudency so rosy' and his own 'woman's part' (II. iv. 153–86), Imogen's gradual deification, limb by limb, of her 'husband's' corpse (IV. ii. 308–33)—each evoke erotic possession through the concentrated savouring of a single bodily part. Imogen's cinque-spotted mole, her blushing face, her 'ring', are soft-porn pictures, barely sublimated, of a barterable pudendum. The 'woman's part' is here manipulated into pure symbol and possession of male desire. But as the persistent puns around Cloten show, the male body is similarly implicated, similarly a 'passable Carkasse' liable to be chopped up and chewed over as the subject of competitive ambition. The conceptual habit depends upon metonymy, where the part stands for the whole: this in turn is indicative of the dialogue's rootedness in the microcosmic body. But the concentration upon discrete or severed features is such that these members take on a life, a magnetism, of their own. Rather than simply signifying the cohering mass to which they belong, they announce their own separation. Crucially, though, it is a separation into fetishism, into an eroticism of dismemberment.

In *Cymbeline* Shakespeare is developing that radical conception of theatrical metaphor—language given a metamorphic, almost coagulative potency to become as much 'mass' as that which empirically is physical—which finds consummate expression in Caliban. The images, anally retentive as they are, disengage from the necessary reality of the action. They construct a vast field of supra-characterological discourse, dancing over the exchanges like an antic, profane chorus, rattling, skeletal, almost posthumous in the way it is collected out of the old bones and redundant obscenities of masculine banter. Partly, the superfluity of such punning—all that perfervid concentration upon the sexual trumping of one's neighbour—simply represents the excreta of a decadent environment. But Shakespeare does not allow the words to die. The 'phallocentric' puns in fact collect together and pre-empt the future. The effect of this is to reify, to fetishize, and to valorize such language as an abiding principle and energy of historical reality: a kind of central,

controlling imagination—Shakespeare's and/or the audience's
—fixes upon apparently wayward discourse a price, a value
correspondent to the rampant commodification of desire, of
body, and of language. Metaphor becomes a kind of new god,
endowed with powers of creation and judgement. Indeed distinctions between 'metaphor', 'metonym', and the 'literal' become difficult to make sense of; there is no sanctioning reality
from which the trope gains its strength or its reference. Shakespeare's method provokes a near-Nietzschean perception
that there is, finally, nothing but metaphor, here of lost wholeness and compensatory desire. At the very least, his figurative economy is a metaphor of a world in which the great
analogical chain of being lies in pieces, separated links lying
mocked and messy, offering novel freedoms, awaiting renewed
incarcerations.

To say that Shakespeare's language and characters are, in
the world of the play, microcosmic, is to say that they accommodate and harness an environment which the 'larger' story
will magnify or amplify; hence metaphor's energy here of impulsion, or predictive capability. Consider the ostensible political
'heart' of the play, the battle between Romans and Britains.
The rival nations' stand-off is chronicled in the same language
as is used to describe the duel of Cloten and Posthumus. A
'passable Carkasse', a 'throughfare for Steele', 'Stand me',
'Stand you'—the sense of a body brutalized but somehow civic,
or of a 'Sacrifice' oscillating between profanity and purification—all are reprised in the battle's 'strait Lane . . . ditch'd, and
wall'd with turph' (V. iii. 7–14), in its cries to the Britains
of 'Stand, stand', we 'will give you that Like beasts, which
you shun beastly' (V. iii. 25–8). At the fight's end the Romans
are slaughtered with the 'backe doore open' (V. iii. 45), just
as earlier the 'strait passe was damm'd' with dead Britains,
'hurt behinde' (V. iii. 11–12). As in the duel between Posthumus
and Cloten, the insults and the bravery are interchangeable,
subject and object collapsing and indistinct; one thinks of
Troilus' erotic fear that he should 'loose distinction' in his
joys, 'As doth a battaile, when they charge on heapes The
enemy flying'.[13] The repeated references to being hurt 'from

---

[13] *Troilus and Cressida*, III. ii. 24–7.

behind', 'with length'ned shame', like 'beasts', suggest how chivalry is ruined by a prevailing cowardice, or by intimations of buggery which linger to stain even the ragged threesome's heroics. The point to note is how the text gives forewarning of these larger degradations in the entangled bodies of Cloten and Posthumus. One is a reeking 'Sacrifice', the other a 'passable Carkasse'. The twinned armies become one monster, eating its own, consuming itself. The antagonists' entwined bodies are civically anthropomorphized into gargantuan correlative animation. The first, comically inept duel, then, marinates the bodies for the battlefield.

Just as it prepares for a debunking version of martial valour, the punning which surrounds Cloten's body, preparing for the symbolic portent of his death, also parodies the desire for some kind of saviour. Here again one sees, within the putatively irenic discourse of romance, the subversive intimacy of Shakespeare's 'body language'. 'I gaue him satisfaction', Cloten protests after a second duel. Alongside the now-familiar profane referents, the text suggests Cloten as a sacrifice, an atonement for the world's sins. The lord says 'you reek as a Sacrifice', suggesting an unpleasant mixture of steaming breath, moist clothes, burning flesh, and bloodily pungent perfume. When the sardonic lord ridicules Cloten as the crowing cock ('you crow, Cock, with your combe on' II. i. 26) it might be another profane reference to some antitypical 'saviour'. Much of Cloten's role enacts a kind of severing and sharing around of his 'passable Carkasse'— the epithet passes effortlessly from Posthumus to Cloten—for the benefit of others, and perhaps for a more bracing propitiatory ambition. Or again, the over-determined 'ayre' of the first duel seems to hover and return, in the form of Imogen, when the soothsayer interprets the 'Mollis Aer' of Jupiter's tablet (V. v. 447–53). The echo may suggest Imogen as a kind of fumigator, cleansing the dolt's rank airs; equally, however, there is a suggestion of identity between Cloten and Imogen, each able to distil and evaporate into all, sharing the play's symbolizing links between micro and macro. Cloten's insinuative significance is not ultimately tied to a living body: as if resisting decent cremation, his humours are imperfectly buried. It is, then, archly appropriate that his *doppelgänger* should be called 'Posthumus'.

THE WINTER'S TALE

The idea of a saving majesty is often intrinsic to conventional romance. The redemption might be mainly chivalrous, a noble paragon to praise and emulate, but equally it might invoke the term's full weight of judgement and grace. In *Cymbeline*, the role of Cloten suggests an ironical debunking of any such claim that revelation might begin at court. Shakespeare's scepticism here has a political cachet. For King James sanctioned the apocalyptic mantle of the true prince. Wrapping himself in the garments of Apocalypse, James confirmed and exploited the unique role of kings in God's plan.[14] Apocalyptic readings of contemporary history, then, might confirm the Establishment as the legitimate arbiter of chaos or crisis. James's commitment, however, was less robust than some of his publications implied; he withdrew from the violent fervours inevitable to last age purgations, seeking to ward off those militants still eager to discover in Revelation stirringly radical instructions. Fancying himself as the mediator between apocalyptic enemies, and in the case of militancy aware of the constraints imposed by a light royal purse and a country resentful of taxation, James preferred peacemaking. His son Henry, by contrast, seemed to embody a hopeful romantic mythology.[15] Enthralled by the plumed valour of France's Henri IV, dressed as it was with an authoritarian panache and machismo, the young Prince Henry gloried in tilts and jousts, hoped to establish a new order of chivalry, and was from deep within his Protestant being fired by crusading, reformatory ambitions. Even his renowned chasteness might suggest the pattern for a new male Britomart. Those aspects

[14] James made two separate commentaries on Revelation. Upon his succession in 1603 he reissued the Calvinist *A Fruitefull Meditation*, first published in 1588, and in later years offered another *Paraphrase on Revelation*. In 1609 he published *A Premonition*, elaborately 'proving' that the Pope was Antichrist. James wrote a sermon on Rev. 20: 15, 16, published in his *Works* in 1616. He took the view, fostered by John Knox, that prophecies dealt almost exclusively with affairs of state, and were therefore of especial relevance to princes. See Katharine R. Firth, *The Apocalyptic Tradition in Reformation Britain 1530–1645* (Oxford, 1979), 131–2; David Norbrook, *Poetry and Politics in the English Renaissance* (London, 1984), chs. 7 and 8.

[15] See Roy Strong, *Henry, Prince of Wales and England's Lost Renaissance* (London, 1986); R. Malcolm Smuts, *Court Culture and the Origins of a Royalist Tradition in Early Stuart England* (Philadelphia, 1987).

of his father's court which had served the gall and ink of the satirists—the Scottish invasion and undeserving minions, the profligacy and luxury, drunkenness and swearing, the daily counsels neglected for the joys of the chase—were to be expelled in the zeal for temperance and holiness. The cult of Henry accelerated once he began establishing his own household toward the end of 1609. His investiture as Prince of Wales in June of 1610 canonized a genuine popular hero, the cynosure of impatient eyes. The political programme emanating from St James's Palace thus links putative arms with epic romance, the loyal genre of British history.

But whereas writers as diverse as Dekker and Browne found inspiration in the young prince, such urgent calls for piety and violence receive an almost ironic echo in Shakespeare's late plays. The implosive, hysterical, often hilarious violence of *Cymbeline*'s anxious upstarts offers one measurement of such loathness; the fate of Mamillius in *The Winter's Tale* offers another:

Arch. You have an vnspeakable comfort of your young Prince Mamillius; it is a Gentleman of the greatest Promise that euer came into my Note.

Cam. I very well agree with you, in the hopes of him: it is a gallant Child; one, that (indeed) Physicks the Subiect, makes old hearts fresh; they that went on Crutches ere he was borne, desire yet their life, to see him a Man. (I. i. 35–43)

Succinctly, and as if pre-emptively to disappoint them, Shakespeare evokes apocalyptic Christian anticipations. The 'greatest Promise' can invoke the specific 'promise' made by God to Abraham of Christ, panning out to welcome the blessed nationhood of a 'promised land'. Similarly, the 'Crutches' all would live on while waiting for the king to have another son (I. i. 45–6), may pun upon the cross or 'crutch' of crucifixion and hence, again, the 'promise' of a new kingdom. Characteristically, however, the language confuses any halo of optimism. Camillo's words can be taken as simple praise, hinting at magic, as people extend their normal lifespan for the joy of seeing the boy a man; equally, they suggest a prevailing climate of illness. His earlier apprehension that the kings' friendship 'cannot choose but braunch' is similarly poised between optimism and decline (I. i.

24): it might mean grow and prosper, as if a grandly spreading tree; or it can connote a tearing and splitting, all union splayed by a cuckold-horn, or by the forked tongue of falsehood. The context is one of hope made hesitant by unpronounced trepidation, and by a furtive desire for alternatives.

This nervousness is the overture to Sicilia's crashing catastrophes: Leontes' paranoid tyranny and, its immediate consequence, the impugning of the queen and death of the prince. But even though Shakespeare so squarely undermines simple royal or revelatory triumphalisms, the question of the prince's great 'Promise' remains alive, left begging in his precipitous disappearance. Why does he go? Where does he go? If he in his own person remains securely dead, is anything reborn or redeemed from his sacrifice? What exactly is the role of the boy who gives the play its name? It has been shown how multiple, specular, ventriloquial, and trope-twisted Shakespeare's characterization can be, and how it is through these methods of characterization that Shakespeare orientates his genre's sense of occasion and opportunity. So, in the absence of a salvational royalty, how does Mamillius, and his 'sad' tale of 'winter', harness romance's engagement with authority, violence, and transformation?

Leontes turns to his son the moment it becomes apparent, to him if to no one else, that his wife and 'brother' are lovers. For the next few minutes the king smothers Mamillius with narcissistic attentions, abruptly fondling and questioning his child as if to a daily glass. The boy is harangued by his father into knowledge: a brisk martialism, the curious study of faithless faces. But the relationship is more symbiotic than that of teacher and pupil. For the father relies upon the boy's veracity, upon the mirror of his face and answers. Cause and effect between the two works like twinned reflexive pedagogy. The boy says 'I am like you say' (I. ii. 208), suggesting a correspondent obedience, perhaps terrified like Ariel's: the father's words 'make the man'. 'Why, that's some comfort', replies the king, rejoining with stark irony Archidamus' optimistic invocation of the prince as romance's apocalyptic 'comfort'.

At the same time as the scene toys with such nascent messianism, it recalls a mythical source of deliverance in a pure Edenic pastoral. So, Mamillius is the frisky lamb or 'wanton Calfe', the pure fresh animal who knows 'not The Doctrine of

ill-doing' (I. ii. 67–70; 126). Taken thus, he becomes a resurrected figure of the un-'tript' guiltless spirit. However, he is also
his epithets' puns. Mamillius' staging of pastoral hope is, like
the 'red blood raigns' of Bohemia, as nubile as comedy. Time
and again Leontes' soubriquets for his child invoke salacious or
roguish implications: 'Bawcock', 'neat . . . Captaine', 'wanton
Calfe', 'Sir Page', 'sweet Villaine', 'Most dear'st, my Collop',
'my young Rouer' (I. ii. 121, 126, 135–7, 176). Leontes' avidity
is always close to dissevering or dehumanizing Mamillius' body,
much as *Cymbeline* effects upon Cloten's. He will isolate particular parts in an urge to discover or retrieve his own power.
His metaphors give a tantalizing literalism, magnetic and kinetic, to the physical contiguity of father and son. They are 'like
as Egges', as if encased in shared embryo, a state of whole
potential to which Leontes would return. Or his son is his
'Collop', the father's flesh grafted in the son to grow and replicate (I. ii. 130; 137): Mamillius is here distilled into a slice of
meat as if cut from the master's joints, a re-embodied phallus
joining the 'Dagger' as a 'dangerous' instrument, liable to 'bite
it's Master' and disrupt that Eden which a child's innocence
might otherwise befit (I. ii. 156–60). The son is made a kind of
metonym of the father, or a synecdoche shared mutually, each
able to act out whole the other's part. One consequence of this
is that the 'boy eternal', Mamillius, is already scioned to a
rougher stock: that of his father. Innocence is precipitously
sophisticated; it is a necessary casualty of the play's proxying
architecture.

Leontes brings out with fuller menace the consequences of
this narcissistic transference of desire from father to son:

> Looking on the Lynes
> Of my Boyes face, me thoughts I did requoyle
> Twentie three yeeres, and saw my self vn-breeched,
> In my greene Veluet Coat; my Dagger muzzel'd,
> Least it should bite it's Master, and so prove
> (As Ornaments oft do's) too dangerous.
>
> (I. ii. 153–8)

Polixenes' 'lamb' is here threatened by the biting snake of
knowledge, at once phallic and satanic. Leontes sees the same
incipience in his son. The crucial word is 'requoyle': there is

aversion as well as helplessness in his need. It is a violence which
will destroy its object. And this is where the particular occasion
of the speech is telling. Leontes is trying to explain the 'distraction' he has shown when seized by thoughts of his wife's
unfaithfulness and his son's illegitimacy. He moves from
Hermione's 'practis'd Smiles As in a Looking-Glasse', to the
mirror of his son's motions, to a vision of himself, grotesquely
reflected, as the monstrous embodiment of the world's 'infection' (I. ii. 116–17; 145–6). In describing himself in his son
Leontes identifies the juvenile root of his 'hardning' brows;
coterminously, he identifies in the ornament which would prove
'dangerous' a metaphor for his wife, she whom Bohemia wears
'like her Medull, hanging About his neck' (I. ii. 307–8).
Mamillius' 'promise' is made to absorb the 'Imposition' of tax-
ing experience (I. ii. 74).

Leontes' last words to Mamillius are 'Goe play (Mamillius)
thou'rt an honest man'. But the command is sheer menace,
made so by the word's earlier repetition as suicidal rhetorical
mockery:

> Goe play (Boy) play: thy Mother playes, and I
> Play too; but so disgrac'd a part, whose issue
> Will hisse me to my Graue. Contempt and Clamor
> Will be my Knell. Goe play (Boy) play.

> (I. ii. 187–91)

The 'play' he would have his boy enjoy is hopeful and ingenuous, like the goblins' 'tale' he shall soon seek to tell; the 'play' he
imputes to his wife is adulterous; while the 'Play' he sees himself
in is at a theatre, representing the abrogation of royal control
over narrative. All three merge together in the contempt of his
'issue', hissing him into ignominious disappearance: this 'issue'
represents his audience and, of course, his children. Without
knowing it Leontes acknowledges that critical identity—of children and community—which the rest of this 'play' must pin its
hopes upon. The problem for Mamillius is that, although implicitly part of the contemptuous audience, he is equally implicated in the king's 'play' they so excoriate. He is, then, for an
audience as much as for Leontes, a figure both of hope and
disappointment, of 'Promise' and a kind of treachery. Mamillius
is no more free or self-constructing than is Cloten; his childish

imitations might be seen as a variation upon Cloten's dim vacancy or even Pericles' generic senility: striking metaphors for
figures who are written, spoken, bespoken, by the discourses
that surround them. So, like a child shooting marbles before
war's cannon, Mamillius being sent thus to 'play' sets off rather
than relieves the court's violence. Like the eponymous 'sad tale'
which the boy would tell, his 'play' too is a meta-dramatic
crystal:

> *First Lady.* Shall I be your play-fellow?
> *Mam.* No, Ile none of you.
> *First Lady.* Why (my sweet lord?)
> *Mam.* You'le kisse me hard, and speak to me, as if I were a Baby
>   still. I loue you better.
> *2 Lady.* And why so (my Lord)
> *Mam.* Not for because
>   Your Browes are blacker (yet black-browes they say
>   Become some Women best, so that there be not
>   Too much haire there, but in a Cemicircle,
>   Or a halfe-Moone made with a Pen)
> *2 Lady.* Who taught 'this?
> *Mam.* I learn'd it out of Womens faces.
>
> (II. i. 4–11)

Mamillius proves that he is not a 'Baby still' by adopting the role
of apprentice court jester, a place hitherto unfilled. Correspondingly, his words, like Feste's or Lear's Fool's, are as prescient of
his master's follies as of things to come. Having told the lady he
loves her 'better', she expects a little precocious flattery. Instead
Mamillius offers an awkwardly bookish lecture, rehearsed as if
by rote, on the art of face-painting. He refers his wisdom to
authority ('they say'), a tutoring influence picked upon by the
lady. 'Who taught 'this?', she asks, and Mamillius' vaguely
cynical answer ('I learn'd it out of Womens faces') persuades
one to take the question seriously: Hermione 'did not nurse him'
(II. i. 56), whilst Leontes coddles and cajoles the child into
becoming his precocious double. The lady seems amused, sur-
prised, worried at the child's rapid escalation from 'baby' to
post-adolescent, ripe with the wisdom of a beauty's connoisseur
and unillusioned about the sources of wonder. The boy's advice
seems tempered by a censoriousness which might quickly warp

desire into disgust. Mamillius' pedantry thus imitates his father's erratic rhetoric earlier which, asserting the fact of his
paternity, depended upon two typically oxymoronic proofs: the
face tells true, even when this truth encodes a lie, and women are
comprehensively false (I. ii. 128–35). Mamillius too, in the very
detachment of his appraisal, seems prepared to discover in one
day's 'loue' tomorrow's arch-betrayer.

This is reinforced by his odd insistence that the black brows
should be in a 'Cemicircle, Or a halfe-Moone'. Certainly this
gives a shape to the brows, but beyond that it seems obscurely
to picture a state of divided government. At two other points
Leontes' tyranny is associated with a governing moon more
capricious than constant ('you may as well Forbid the Sea for to
obey the Moone, As (or by Oath) remoue, or (Counsaile) shake
The Fabrick of his Folly', I. ii. 426–9; 'these dangerous unsafe
Lunes i' th' King, beshrew them', II. ii. 29–30). The full 'circle'
is a symbol of completion and harmony, or of the spheres
of universal correspondence. Likewise, the full moon evokes
beauty, fertility, chastity, and control. The half-moon, by contrast, is an uncertain guide for the ship of state, too akin to the
destructive sea, and like it a topos of fickleness. Again, the micro
and the macro converge in the turbid metaphors at court. Bartered by the whims of vanity, decoration, and sex, the moon is
as prone to profane and violent falls as are the thoughts and
words of the king. Thus, a 'halfe-Moone' is a colloquialism
for cuckold, its crescent decline shaping the horned 'pash' of
Leontes' bestial mirror. A waning moon becomes the duped
or duping parent of illegitimacy: 'Score a Pint of Bastard in the
Halfe-Moon', cries Hal, aping the 'tinkers' in advertising impure
wine.[16] As with Leontes, Mamillius' enigmatic words—indeed,
they are stiltingly spoken as if ventriloquized through some elder
spirit—are made to luxuriate in, or obtusely to desire, what is
adulterated.

His further insistence that 'there be not Too much haire
there' seems to barber the woman's brow into elegant horns. In
A Mad World, My Masters Middleton lists characteristics of
women acting 'against kind', including in the litany 'To wear
half-moons made of another's hair', suggesting the 'periwigs' of

[16] *1 Henry IV*, II. iv. 27.

sexual craft and duplicity, perhaps rendered necessary by the scabs and baldness—one of the work's particular obsessions—resulting from the pox.[17] Likewise learning 'out of Womens faces', Mamillius uses the same map of the nation as his father, who moments earlier was spying treason in 'the Neb' and 'Byll' and the 'practis'd Smiles' of his wife (I. ii. 183). The adulterers' 'padling Palmes and, pinching Fingers' are, like Mamillius' lady's 'Pen', the 'Virginalling' instruments of duplicitous art (I. ii. 115–16, 125). Just as Leontes understands in Hermione's body a symbol of his authority's vast and accelerating dissolution, Mamillius' advice to the lady would seem to memorialize a giant bite from erstwhile lunar authority.[18]

Mamillius' strange reading of women's faces looks forward and back to crucial moments in the story's narrative of a court destroying itself: to Leontes' vision of adultery, treason, and illegitimacy, and then, a consequence of this, to the wild storm which attends the simultaneous deaths of Antigonus and his crew:

> What colour are your eye-browes?
> *Lad.* Blew (my Lord).
> *Mam.* Nay, that's a mock: I haue seene a Ladies Nose
> That ha's been blew, but not her eye-browes.
>
> (II. i. 13–15)

In a different court, where the 'centre' had not been stabbed, one might expect the question to be about the lady's eyes. But Mamillius, like Leontes, cannot put his 'brows' away. The moment echoes Leontes' command seconds before his collapse: 'Looke on me with your Welkin eye', he says to his son (I. ii. 136), as if in desperate bid to retain faith in a collapsing epistemological 'centre'. From this moment, however, the 'Browes' suffer a 'hardning' as 'a Cuckolds Horne' 'stabs the Center' like a main-mast 'boaring the Moone' (I. ii. 138–46; 268–9; III. iii. 91–2). The 'blew' with which the lady claims her brows to be

---

[17] *Works of Thomas Middleton*, ed. Bullen, vol. iii, III. iii. 101–2; *A Mad World, My Masters*, ed. Standish Henning (London, 1965), III. iii. 92–3. 'Periwigs' replaces 'half-moons' in the 1640 edition.

[18] Compare Hotspur's protest: 'See how this river comes me cranking in, And cuts me from the best of all my land A huge half-moon, a monstrous cantle out' (*1 Henry IV*, III. i. 94–6).

coloured cannot escape the context of a kind of blindness, authority's light shut out, which attends the previous appeal to the 'Welkin eye'. Furthermore, just as the 'Welkin' doubles to mean both the colour 'blue' and the vast sky and heavens which in an organicist vision represent order, so does the 'blew' as teased out by Mamillius evoke both the colour and the wind, whether it be the wind of destructive weather as in the central storm scene or, as in the young prince's joke, the sneeze 'blown' from a lady's indecorous body. Still more, Mamillius' 'blew' takes on the violence of Leontes' decentring 'stab'. Like the 'sneaping Winds' (at I. ii. 13, Polixenes' fearful phrase for what Leontes similarly senses, the assault from below upon monarchical absolutism) of the simultaneous storm and bear, the boy's 'blew' might be a bruising fist. So, Mamillius's 'mock'—again the same verb which animates both sea and bear as they swallow crew and nobleman (III. iii. 99–100)—endangers the blue brow of clarity with an almost insurrectionary collision of energies. The analogies which Mamillius is made to orchestrate, quite beyond his will, are hardly auspicious. As with the incestuous censorships at Antioch, Leontes' narcissistic possession of his son suggests the dangers attending inherited monarchy. Eschewing counsel and disdaining the common voice, such courts are prey to caprice, irrationality, and self-destruction.

Father and son, therefore, are concordant and symbiotic. However, Shakespeare's method here of homologous or synecdochal characterization does not depend upon royal or even familial contiguities. In *The Winter's Tale*, narrative and political responsibility operates as if through Chinese dolls, one figure both hidden and discovered in another. Just as the significance of Cloten is discovered in surrogacy, prophetic metaphor, and what one might call posthumous capability, so too is Mamillius' role as the latent 'Promise' of repair or redemption constructed through allusion to and conflation with many figures and moments throughout the play. Shakespeare's development here of shared voices—harmonic, contrapuntal, internally dissonant— suggests a narrative technique common to both medieval and renaissance romance. Eugene Vinaver has written of the way analogy can work as a substitute for psychological cause, and of how the techniques of 'entrelacement' and 'amplificatio' dilate and interrupt a set of stories or tropes over vast narrative distances.[19] An event or figure will appear, vanish, reappear, never completed but forever supplemented by its accumulating precedents. Subtle resemblance, analogous juxtaposition, casual allusion, horizontal reference: through such means the story garners movement, veracity, even profundity. While in the Arthurian schemes individual desire may be dwarfed by the epic scale, and some supernatural or other supra-rational power might enter the psychological absence to claim government, in Shakespeare's work, as in Spenser's, the technique serves as another means of opening out the tales to multiple, often competing, agents. And it is through just such means that Mamillius possesses posthumous magnetism, the power to influence and inform quite beyond the presence of his voice or body.

With what seems perfunctory abandon Mamillius is whisked off to his death. But the play is, as it were, constantly aware that Mamillius will not live to fulfil 'the hopes of him' (I. i. 37). As Archidamus says, closing the scene's coy prognostications, 'If the King had no Sonne, they would desire to live on Crutches till he had one' (I. i. 44-5). The proleptic irony is clear enough, predicting a displacement of the 'promise' from one son, Mamillius, to the other, Florizel, an effective synonymity which the respective fathers quickly confirm ('My Brother Are you so fond of your young Prince as we ...? ... So stands this Squire Offic'd with me', I. ii. 162-72). But the manners of the opening scenes hardly encourage one to trust monarchical interpretations: that they seem to prepare us for the facile and unfussy replacing of one son for the other might warn us that more complex consequences are brewing. For Mamillius' demise is a kind of inaugurative ending, a denial of a certain type of exclusive courtly romance. This is emphasized by the eponymous frame of the boy's fable: 'tell's a Tale ... As merry as you will', asks Hermione; 'A sad Tale's best for Winter: I have one of Sprights, and Goblins', replies Mamillius. As with his earlier tutorial, the boy's tone is oddly portentous, neurotic, even possessed; a meta-dramatic spirit takes the boy's 'play' hostage. Resisting gaiety himself, Mamillius reminds those who watch of the supposed comedy they've all paid to enjoy (II. i. 23-6).

---

[19] Eugene Vinaver, *The Rise of Romance* (Oxford, 1971; repr. Cambridge, 1984).

Pre-emptively doomed as Mamillius is, his words have the alienating, lingering cachet of a prophetic ghost: to appropriate the play's title is to say, 'adue, adue, Remember me' (*Hamlet*, I. v. 91). It is as if at the same time as he is preparing to vanish he is also being prepared for a role as the audience's narrative medium. Like the storm's conjunction of 'things dying' and 'things new borne', the extinction of one type of 'promise' here implants the need for others. And, therefore and therein, a new type of romance.

The 'merry' old tales of valour, innocence, and virtue are, as if poisoned by Leontes' 'knowledge', no longer sustainable. Mamillius' mime—he acts out the telling of his tale whilst Leontes thunders away on another part of the stage—suggests the last faint strands of a song out of time. A dwarfish non-narrator, Mamillius' preference for sadness and his compulsion into silence evoke a waning epilogue to a mode no longer tolerable. Simultaneously, however, he appears like an Induction, introducing the 'Sprights, and Goblins' which the rest of *The Winter's Tale*, in various guises, will represent. This future beyond his death is then prepared for with supernatural trappings, tragi-comic like the bear: 'doe your best, To fright me with your Sprights: you're powrefull at it' (II. i. 27–8). Again like the bear, Hermione's adjective for her son ('powrefull') surprises by its portentousness. It seems to connote his status as a narrative medium, the ubiquitous verbal telepathy of the story now being orchestrated as if by ghosts, as the rest of the play reaches back to make his tale unfold itself. Romance becomes a communal seance. We don't hear Mamillius tell his tale: *The Winter's Tale* goes on to do it for him.

The most obvious 'character' in Mamillius' tale is Leontes himself, the man who, his crime revealed, 'Dwelt by a Churchyard'. Repeatedly his role is meta-theatricalized, most pertinently when he portrays himself as the contemptible player. His physical descriptions, all 'rough pash' and infected brows, sculpt the king as a kind of devil-cum-goblin; he calls himself a 'pinch'd Thing; yea, a very Trick For them to play at will', as if one of Autolicus' puppets in the rogue's irreverent 'motion' (II. i. 51). But the tale must travel out to the country which his father so denies and derides: to the world of Sir Smile and his neighbour, among that audience, taunted by the king, yet still

expecting less masochistic satisfactions (I. ii. 190–204). Consequently, it is the storm scene which is pivotal in continuing
Sicilia's censored tale: here the court explodes into the country,
into novelty and wilderness, the necessary clearing-house of old
corruptions. Antigonus' prayer for the baby Perdita's safety had
called upon 'Some powerfull Spirit' to instruct the kites, wolves
and bears to put aside savagery and nurse the feral exile (II. ii.
184–8): Antigonus adds to Mamillius' cast-list, confirming how
the tale is amplified throughout time and place, mutating from
prophetic voice to the manifestation, in this case, of Bohemia's
sheep-stealing wolves, its mocking bear, and the 'kite' Autolicus.
Upon reaching these 'Desarts', Antigonus recounts his vision of
Hermione, supposed by him and us dead: 'I haue heard (but not
beleeu'd) the Spirits o' th' dead May walke againe' (III. iii. 16–
17): gasping, spouting, and shrieking, Hermione's ghost gives a
terrifying posthumous voice, not only to the queen, but to her
son's promise of spirits. Moments later, the daemonic bear and
the fairy-child, the 'Changeling' Perdita, add to the sense that
the stopped tale is afoot (III. iii. 116–17).

Such momentum accelerates with the singing entrance of the
'coll pixci' Autolicus, who with his 'she-angel' smocks, his false
benedictions, his magical transformations as if a troupe of
'sprites' in one, seems the very fit of a maleficently entertaining
goblin (IV. iii–IV. iv). The dancing saltiers (IV. iv. 325–45) and
the miraculously metamorphosing 'statue' (V. iii. 120–55), returning to the queen's ear wherein the tale was first whispered,
complete its circle through court and country. And, immanent in
all of this are recollections of the opening scene and its predictions of princely 'comfort': Mamillius' disappearance recalls
myths of 'sleeping heroes', like Edward VI, myths that would
find invocation at moments of crisis, promising the restoration
of lost peace and plenty. Here is where the more predictable
analogies of one young prince with another play their part;
Mamillius is indeed recapitulated in Florizel and Perdita. But the
point is that they alone do not carry such responsibility; it is a
dialogical burden which all of Bohemia struggles with, competes
for, juggles, and finally shares.

Earlier, Hermione seems to anticipate the implications of her
son's silenced story: 'One good deed, dying tonguelesse, Slaugh-
ters a thousand, wayting vpon that' (I. ii. 92–3). Hermione's

intended meaning is simple enough: she seeks praise, asserting
the need to publish virtue so as to encourage its emulation. As
usual, however, the speaker cannot legislate the discourse's dilating meanings: her striking language poses a meta-dramatic
challenge regarding interpretation of her son's death. For the
'thousand, wayting vpon' the tale are the play's audience, anticipating their comic romance, and, by analogy, the commonwealth of people seeking a model in their prince. To silence
Mamillius is to kill not only the exclusive, aristocratic romance
which the play from its inception appears to both invoke and
undermine, but also any hope that the transformatory optimism
of the genre might be brushed up into something new, something less beholden to courtly violence. As Hermione implies,
the courtly epitome must discover meaning and quality in its
wider, 'multitudinous' consequences. As has been seen in
Leontes' court, the boy is a type of screen, not only of encroach-
ing violence and hilarity, but of more furtive hope and discreetly
nurtured honour. His 'Promise' is the burden of romance hope,
in all its ambivalent engagement with fractious place, fractured
time, uncertain belief. As Archidamus avers, Mamillius offers an
'vnspeakable comfort': this is true, with stern irony, in the sense
that initial hopes of the boy are driven into dust. So, any
'comfort' is literally 'unspeakable', because the prince is dead
and disappointment everyone's duty. However, at the same time
the hope stays afloat through the inaugurating pregnancy of its
utterance. It won't be spoken directly, but the quality of any
'comfort'—ineffable, supernal, disgusting, drunken, beyond civility: each a version of 'unspeakable'—is what the play sets out
to discover.

4

Country Matters

PASTORAL romance's conventional recoil from court venality always makes it to a limited degree 'anti-courtly'. However, the usual assumption is that Shakespeare dramatizes a truth gone missing, an assured ideal whose blessed vessels are exiled amid forest or cave, awaiting discovery and return. In the opening chapter I argued that it is misguided to base one's understanding of Shakespeare's romances upon the supposedly inviolable distinctions and hierarchies which underlie a traditional courtly pastoral. Consequently, having examined the self-destructive courtliness which leads to this diaspora, it comes now to question the rural situation's possession of a spa-like capacity to refurbish an ideal made shabby or precarious by central corruption. The countryside here has a double capacity: it both recapitulates the problems of the centre, and evokes a place over which a traditional courtliness has little control. Shakespeare's wildernesses, his deserts, fields, and caves, thereby remain historically accountable: they show a world both beyond and in competition with the court.

Shakespeare's romances here contribute to a re-emergence of the pastoral-cum-georgic milieu as a locus for political criticism.[1] The so-called 'Spenserian poets', for instance, used Virgilian tropes to channel their nationalistic diagnoses.[2] Invariably such work was critical of perceived malaise at the centre, and nostalgic for the vigour of an already-romanticized Elizabethanism, whether focused in the queen herself, in her naval glories, or in dissident aristocrats such as Essex and Sidney. Drayton's *Pastorals* were revised in 1606 so as to mix conventional evocations of virgin spirits and sheep-shearings

---

[1] Anthony Low, *The Georgic Revolution* (Princeton, 1985); cf. Annabel Patterson, *Pastoral and Ideology: from Virgil to Valéry* (Oxford, 1988).

[2] They included Michael Drayton, George Wither, Phineas and Giles Fletcher, William Browne, perhaps Samuel Daniel. See Norbrook, *Poetry and Politics*, ch. 8; Joan Grundy, *The Spenserian Poets: A Study in Elizabethan and Jacobean Poetry* (London, 1969).

with the standard bucolic liberty to shadow shepherds with dark
and often bitter political allegorism. Pastoral here enjoys coun-
terpointing simplicity with iniquity; apparently ingenuous idylls
may carry an ironical, indeed parodic, edge. Even Drayton's
monumental act of topographical love, *Poly-Olbion*, mixes its
celebrations of provincial fertility with satire; it should not then
be surprising that the passion, the professional pride, and something of the inclusive populism of Drayton's georgic pastorals
are thematically similar to the anatomizing invectives of his
Owle and *Moone-Calfe*. Similarly, William Browne's *Britan-
nia's Pastorals* includes stringent criticisms of oppressive and
expropriative rural practices, as of the inglorious idleness of
Jacobean foreign policy. The Spenserian influence is doubly
present: both in Browne's leisurely dilations of threatened virtue, and in his impatiently Protestant politics.[3] The important
point is how each feeds the other; Browne's investment in the
cult of Prince Henry, for instance, evokes pastoral's fascination
with exiled or marginalized 'truth'. Shakespeare's sometime collaborator, John Fletcher, was similarly sensitive to the need to
historicize his country's mythographies.

There is much in this creative environment to suggest the
orientation of Shakespearian romance. However, there are certain ways in which Shakespeare's use of pastoral is distinctive. A
consistently 'Protestant' line is difficult to maintain: Guiderius
and Cloten, for instance, are equally militant, while prophecies
of the redemptive prince Mamillius are answered directly with
his death. And Shakespeare's idylls are not structured around a
separation of eulogy from satire, or of 'happy' from 'melan-
cholic' allegory. Shakespeare allows such basic and elegant contrasts, but always complicates simple generic inheritances. Take,
for instance, the famous sheep-shearing scene in *The Winter's
Tale*. It alludes constantly to familiar models; but equally it
eludes them. It is exactly similar neither to Drayton's 'Ninth
Eclogue' which, despite its 'Clownish King', is basically a precious celebration of flowering virtue, nor to the bitterly allegorical moments of Drayton's 'Sixth Eclogue', in which James is
ruefully characterized as the 'cold Northern breath' that now

---

[3] *The Poems of William Browne of Tavistock*, ed. Gordon Goodwin, 2 vols.
(London, 1893); Helen Cooper, *Pastoral: Mediaeval into Renaissance* (Ipswich,
1977), 168–86.

blasts the once 'pleasant Heath'.[4] Bohemia is a place slightly apart, not beholden to meta-generic expectations. The articulating responsibility Shakespeare gives to his own networks of metaphor means that the plays don't finally depend upon Virgilian amplification or allusion, or upon the kind of fragmentary 'quotation' which Annabel Patterson has suggested was an eloquent and readily available political shorthand.[5] Certainly the plays have characters who speak dutifully 'Virgilian' sentiments—Belarius, Florizel, Gonzalo—but their obedience to topographical expectation is rarely able to explain or possess a scene's energies. The place and its myths may be familiar, but each are played upon with Shakespeare's characteristic polytropical density. Generic 'place', then, is less a settled bucolic patch than an edgy terrain, under threat of conquest, and sown, plotted, and disrupted by metaphorical energies anything but slavish to custom and convention.

The release in *The Winter's Tale* from brumal Sicilia to sunny Bohemia is conventionally seen as an escape into hope and innocence. Similarly, *Cymbeline*'s hidden princes, despite being surrounded by the confused contentions of war, exile, and vengeance, are usually understood to frame an artless, ingenuous correction to the corruptions of the centre. Pastoral is fresh, therapeutic, and somewhat fantastical. However, in stressing the various ways in which courtly turbidity and conflict expects and requires the country for its further expression, I have been anticipating a more hybrid and materialistic, more accountable version of the romantic idyll. In both plays, preparatory metaphor comes relentlessly true. Whether through the clamorous amplification of Mamillius' 'sad tale', or the magnetic surrogacies effected by Cloten's duelling body, romance here questions the linguistic and political unanswerability of the ruling élite. The insouciance of authority cannot survive Shakespeare's densely woven analogies.

A crucial figure here is Autolicus, both in his parodying of hegemony and in the way he is given the power to embody and ventriloquize a wider community. Autolicus' strangely verisimilitudinous deceptions fulfil Leontes' conviction that

---

[4] *The Works of Michael Drayton*, ed. W. J. Heber, 5 vols. (1956; repr. Oxford, 1961), ii. 564–70.
[5] Patterson, *Pastoral and Ideology*, 140–1.

'All's true that is mistrusted' (II. i. 48): such narrative hypallage, or interchange, where the lying rogue gives ironic vindication to the mad tyrant, suggests how unsettled is Shakespeare's land-locked sea-shore of a romance world. Perhaps rather paradoxically, Cymbeline's rumbustious heir apparent, Guiderius, works similarly. Just as Autolicus might appear quite detached from the ministrations of authority, so too might Guiderius seem sublimely untarnished by its violence: Autolicus floats in and out at an entertaining tangent from the main issues, Guiderius descends as a lusty saviour able, through his similar indifference to policy, to cut through the dross into things pure. Each case would thus be amnesiacally complicit in the genre's fabled, sanguine conservatism. But to understand Autolicus as transcendently apolitical might be implicitly to forgive Leontes his tyrannies; to embrace in Guiderius a magically noble warrior may be to endorse a politics of helpless primogenitive reverence. Such detachment is untenable within Shakespeare's romance architecture: Guiderius is as implicated in the play's mutating 'public' body as Cloten or Posthumus. For these plays are anything but forgetful. The forward and backward text confers a complexly interrogative mode of pastoral, of idyll, and of wilderness.

BOHEMIA

Leontes' madness is characterized by increasingly hysterical predictions of aberrance. Certain that his wife's adultery has mocked all propriety into a dizzying spin, Leontes then dares order into chaotic inversion, conjuring calamity and destruction should his conviction be mistaken. In other words, wrong or right, Leontes heralds a sharded world, unutterably split, await-ing some new birth through the breach. In many ways it is Leontes who is responsible for all that 'is' Bohemia: his treatment of Perdita, Camillo, and Polixenes dictates that country's basic direction, which can in turn be understood as a broad-based, long-cogitated response—not, it might be said, always a renunciatory one—to absolutism. But more than this, Leontes gives textual seed to Bohemia through his own mistake-riddled metaphors. Repeatedly and unconsciously, the false fool tells true. Asserting the truth of his fatherhood in the face of woman's mendacity, Leontes lists, as indubitable epitomes of falsehood, the very agencies which go on to impel the play (I. ii. 130–5): 'o're-dy'd Blacks', suggesting the bleaching sheet of king and rogue; 'Wind' and 'Waters', evoking the storm and bear; and 'Dice', wished 'false' by 'one that fixes No borne 'twixt his and mine', representing not only those who seem, at different times, to steal what is Leontes' (first Polixenes, then Apollo), but also the transgressive gamesmanship of Autolicus. Or again, he harangues Camillo with the justice of his 'vexation', mocking the notion that he would, 'Without ripe mouing to't', thus 'Sully' his sheets into 'Goades, Thornes, Nettles, Tayles of Waspes' (I. ii. 325–33). His marital bed becomes a flax-wench's hedge. 'Could man so blench?', he then asks, and by 'blench' he denotes 'deceive oneself'. But the punning association is with 'blanch', or bleach, which may mean equally to whiten or to blacken. Black can be white, order inverts: nothing is sacred. His vision of sheets, bleach, and hedge is a nightmare of relativism, as mocked impossibility wobbles into present fact: he does indeed 'so blench'. Of course such a self-fulfilling process is Leontes' curse from the first; he makes 'true' that which he fears:

> . . . Barbarisme (making me the precedent)
> Should a like Language vse to all degrees,
> And mannerly distinguishment leaue out,
> Betwixt the Prince and Begger.
>
> (II. i. 84–7)

For the play mimics, or 'mocks', the king's world of haunted *non sequitur*: what cannot follow does, as the story builds out of collapsing antinomies. In due course, then, Autolicus enters singing of his vocation: 'The white sheete bleaching on the hedge . . . Doth set my pugging tooth an edge, For a quart of Ale is a dish for a King' (IV. iii. 5–8). Leontes' vision of horror returns, but now transformed into an impudently familiar present. The befouled 'sheete' of power becomes a barterable black-market commodity, a topsy-turvy imminence foreshadowed in Autolicus' larcenies: not simply stolen linen, but licentious beds, aggressive trade, subversive scripts. Like the fishable 'Pond' and opened 'Gate', the promiscuously exchangeable

sheet heralds the levelling chaos and competitive free-for-all
which Leontes both fears and ensures.

Simon Forman recalls, with memorable precision, the Globe's
own initiation into the pedlar's mysteries: 'Remember also the
Rog that cam in all tottered like coll pixci'.[6] A 'coll pixci' is a
mischievous sprite or hobgoblin, a perfect fit for Mamillius'
silenced tale. As a 'colt', the pixie was proverbially lascivious,
and a cunning kind of cheat. The basic reference, though, is to
the rank of 'coles', or synonymically, a 'cole-prophet', one prac-
tising dissimulation, a sharp card or dice, or, most pregnant
of all, mysterious, perhaps bogus, prognostications. As John
Heywood has it, 'ye plaie cole prophet who taketh in hand, To
knowe his answere before he do his errande'.[7] The adjective
Forman uses to describe Autolicus' entrance is difficult to decipher from the script of his diary: it is probably 'tottered' but
may be 'tattered'. 'Tottered' might suggest a reeling drunk, a
storm-tossed ship or, as in *The Tempest*, a 'brained' state;
'tattered' suggests an idly chattering ragamuffin. It is in the gap
between the former's intimations of symbolical plenitude, and
the latter's disdainable triviality, that Autolicus moves, repeatedly upsetting assumptions as to exactly where significance and
agency might lie: 'You haue of these Pedlers, that haue more in
them, than youl'd thinke (Sister.)' (IV. iv. 217–18).

Pastoral often relies upon Arcadian disguise; the thing about
Autolicus, however, is that the security of an underlying truth,
linked as it were genetically to a home and rank and name,
simply recedes into absence. As Forman's intimations of a
haunting gypsy suggest, Autolicus is a strangely disconnected
figure, operating without relation of dependence to any other
character. He claims many pasts, none definitive, all fleeting yet
somehow returnable; he has served the prince, and indeed
claims a father: 'My Father nam'd me Autolicus, who being (as
I am) lytter'd vnder Mercurie, was likewise a snapper-vp of
vnconsidered trifles' (IV. iii. 24–5). What is striking here is how
inadequate is any claim of origin: by invoking such a feckless
patriarchal model, Autolicus strangely annihilates the parent,
who becomes at best a solipsistic abstraction, an idea of tena-
cious transgressiveness. As if inverting Leontes' tyrannical

---

[6] See *Winter's Tale*, p. xxii.
[7] *OED*, 'Cole-prophet'.

narcissisms, Autolicus folds father into son with knowing irony: 'My Father . . . being (as I am)', he says, as if to imply that he is his own progenitor's existential predecessor. This power of self-creation, self-naming, is in a sense the basic affect of Autolicus' act; he repeats the trick time and again, even naming himself, 'Autolicus', as the perpetrator of his own mugging (IV. iii. 98–103). In thus eluding conventional hierarchies of origin, Autolicus can be as innovative, reactionary, or recapitulatory as his moment demands: decorum becomes as capricious as wind or waters. He consummates the collapse into unstable oneness of the precedent father and son, Leontes and Mamillius, whose identity both expressed and prepared for violence, wilderness, and novelty. Autolicus now embodies, or energizes, all such competitive pressures. And in not being linked to a defined home, Autolicus in a sense lives out the romance trope of the abandoned foundling. In this he 'is' the world after the diaspora, before fanciful return and closure. And to the extent that Autolicus—like Caliban—remains outside of centripetal returns, his role continues to defy conventional 'romance', thereby suggesting a new definition of both genre and future.

That such a figure is Bohemia's chief soliloquizer suggests the decentring directions in which Shakespearian characterization is here travelling. Autolicus is uncanny at turning things inside-out, dissolving oppositions in likeness, disengaging from 'subjective' autonomy: 'If I make not this Cheat bring out another, and the sheerers proue sheepe, let me be vnrold, and my name put in the booke of Vertue' (IV. iii. 116–18). His words suggest both a simple pun—he'll make the farmers as silly as their flock—and a reflexive crib—his particular 'motion' re-enacts masters in servants, the great in the low, rich in poor and, time and again, the product in the producer. Hence his own sardonic, utterly atheistic, imitations of the powerful, whether the precise punishments of a king (IV. iv. 785–95, cf. IV. iv. 426–42) or the spellbinding surprises of an oracle (IV. iv. 609–15, cf. III. i. 8–11)). He pretends to dare the narrative to undo 'him'. But what he 'is' forms and unforms, a vaporous solid like Mark Anthony's clouds, folding from one thing to another, ripe with arresting reference but finally captured by none (*Anthony and Cleopatra*, IV. xiv. 3–13). He is a semiotic tease, invoking and subverting the realist-nominalist distinction, seeming to endorse and mock both at once. Thus, he is his name, and nothing more, an empty sign; or his name is he and all he does, impishly faithful to the real; or he is a page of a book, created a canting prig by genre, belonging and beholden only to fiction; or he is pure materialism, written upon or rolled like the 'sheets' he traffics in, barterable, stealable, readable, beddable, but without soul or substance beyond such utility. But Autolicus speaks entirely knowingly, and as such retains a power to possess 'himself': he hints that it is he, should he fail in his mission to gull, who will write the book, cross out his name, tear out the leaf. Autolicus' role, then, mimics an entire social exchange: as he says of himself to the clown, 'Very true sir: he sir hee: that's the Rogue that put me into this apparrell' (IV. iii. 100–1). He creates, becomes, and consumes his goods: which, of course, include all subsisting notions of 'Play'.

Autolicus is a figure augmented and mythologized by report.[8] He watches himself perform, annotates his own intentions and victories, gives a life and a past to himself solely by telling 'himself'—his audience—what he shall do or has done. Autolicus' role is littered with his wayward, unverifiable curriculum vitae. At his own word he has been or is minstrel, beggar, prodigal son and pimp, pardoner, balladeer, merchant and courtier, gambler, pick-pocket, thief and whorer, festive king, satyr, puppet-master and bailiff, ape-bearer, estate-owner, bigamist, and bagatelle-man, haunter of wakes, fairs, hangings, and bear-baits. What is often thought to be missing in this play—the veracious world of markets and men, village and strife—is thus found in Autolicus, the cipher of a nation's fears and dreams: 'Euery Lanes end, euery Shop, Church, Session, Hanging, yeelds a carefull man worke' (IV. iv. 685–6). With great economy he embodies historical turbulence: Autolicus is made to act out various prevalent varieties of social hunger and mobility. He encapsulates his surrounding environment, as Caliban does, but from an almost opposite direction: he has been freed from service; he preys upon others; he has moved from physical constriction into the liberties of an open-skied

---

[8] Compare *Henry VIII*'s 'historicism', in which so much is reported rather than 'dramatized'; a critic's task becomes largely to decipher the conflicting versions of events as variously reported. See Peter Rudnytsky, '*Henry VIII* and the Deconstruction of History', *Sh. S* 43 (1992), 47.

libertarian world; the energies he ventriloquizes or dresses in or those of his will, often stolen from the insufficient agency of others.

Correspondingly, Autolicus' first song, tumbling in as the serenading 'coll pixci', does more than celebrate an insouciant carnality. It is a meridian overture, a harbinger of blossom and leaf, and a geographical efficacio of both its singer's and Bohemia's politics. One is tempted to call it an *aubade* as well as meridian, of spring as well as summer: he invokes growth yet subverts linearity, is both nascent and complete. As with Caliban, semiotic compression invokes experiential capaciousness. This is Shakespeare's new decorum: character works as if through amplified puns, dilated metaphors inscribing an appropriately agitated sense of historical occasion:

> *When Daffadils begin to peere,*
> *With heigh the Doxy ouer the dale,*
> *Why then comes in the sweet o' the yeere,*
> *For the red blood raigns in y winters pale.*
>
> *The white sheete bleaching on the hedge,*
> *With hey the sweet birds, O how they sing:*
> *Doth set my pugging tooth an edge,*
> *For a quart of Ale is a dish for a King.*
>
> *The Larke, that tirra-Lyra chaunts,*
> *With heigh, the Thrush and the Iay:*
> *Are Summer songs for me and my Aunts,*
> *While we lye tumbling in the hay.*

(IV. iii. 1–12)

Autolicus here is at his most galvanizing, an ebullient messenger of 'High-day, freedome'. His invitation to an unfenced saturnalia is stirring, even tactile, to the senses, but the actual lyrics confuse the apparent clarity of his recklessness. Initially the minstrel's place of delight seems clear: it is the 'dale', the common bursting with the colour and sensuality of open liberty. Immediately this evokes thoughts, if not of cockaigne, then of the kind of communal harmony at the heart of the fishermen's wistful 'jangling' in *Pericles* (II. i. 41). It is the triumph, again, of what Leontes so fears: the opened 'Gates', the absent 'Barricado', of sexual and economic promiscuity. Autolicus appears to confirm this: 'For the red blood raigns in y winters pale'. The 'red blood' repairs the brumal claustrophobia of Sicilia: lust, exertion, laughter, and beer connote energies which then seem to flow into a Shrove or May Day kind of rollicking. Gates are spread wide, fences razed, hedges overleaped, as the incarcerating 'pale' is redeemed into the 'sweet' ancient garden, everbody's playground.

But the minstrel's place is more ambiguous than this. His logic is both contiguous and contradictory. Autolicus' 'red blood' reigns 'in' the pale: this might mean 'in place of', but it also allows for the fences still to be standing. Autolicus becomes less a new-world wonder than a dilation of the old world: an animator, duly translated from court to country, of the consequences of the court's fears and desires. One need only consider plausible referents of 'pale' to see how Autolicus' song here mediates a host of significances set up in the putatively more 'serious' era years past: the territory of a specific dominion; the definer of civility, exiling to 'beyond the pale' the wild and woolly 'hedge-pugges'; a vertical stripe or band on a heraldic shield; or the fence of the engrossing farmer. Autolicus' song establishes his situation as somehow 'on the fence', a manipulative, detached relationship to both dale and pale that is flaunted similarly when, at the end of the bucolics, he departs pissing upon another hedge (IV. iv. 827). His urine expresses a cavalier indifference both to those who define their sovereignty through the 'pale',[9] and those who might live amid the thorns. Autolicus won't rest in the social role he appears to adopt.

Thus, he brings the festival to life by foretelling, coterminously, the imminence of its demise and its transformation: 'if you did but heare the Pedler at the doore, you would neuer dance againe after a Tabor and Pipe' (IV. iv. 183–5). As with Mamillius' 'tale' earlier, old-fashioned entertainments are at once appealed to and left behind. Things more audacious, and perhaps disorientating, grow from within the framework of the familiar. Such moments beckon new rhythms, novel discourses, for which Shakespearian romance is here a macrocosm. Autolicus' merchandise therefore both parallels and strangely threatens the stuff of the play. His ballads, for instance, are meta-vignettes, telling tales of mythic, moral, and mercenary

---

[9] Compare Claudius' 'there's such divinity doth hedge a king', *Hamlet*, IV. v. 123.

inversion. The first records a usurer's wife, pregnant to the tune of twenty money bags and possessed as a consequence by appetites—for adders heads and toads carbonadoed—as lascivious and grotesque as anything conceived in Leontes' dystopia (IV. iv. 263–73). Again, then, untrammelled sexuality feeds into and upon the chaos of rampant 'capitalism'. The 'Faiery Gold' of Perdita is usurped by a naked materialism, multiplying out of nothing into a usurer's infernal paradise. Autolicus' microcosmic art here hurries the world of the play into its consequences. The ballad taunts the audience with a surreal vision of emerging socio-economic 'truth': Autolicus exploits while satirizing those energies which threaten old romance. His second ballad (IV. iv. 276–82) seems similarly committed to abolishing the priorities of fairy-tale: it too reprises Bohemia's violent moment of destruction and 'rebirth', the devastations of storm and bear. A 'Fish' appears upon the coast, singing against the cruelty of chastity: it recalls Hermione's appearance in Antigonus' dream, recounted, like the ballad, at the 'coast'; it similarly recalls Perdita, who also 'appeared vpon the coast', an undeciphered 'character' speaking to the shepherd not of chastity but of 'behind-doore worke' (III. iii. 47; 70–6). Autolicus' ballad, then, reverses the moral order of the play's pivotal scene: now it is chastity which should be punished. But this in turn can suggest Leontes' catastrophic inversions of propriety: 'all's true that is mistrusted', 'your actions are my dreames', says the king, wreaking the same kind of retributively somersaulting justice as the ballad's fish, who petrifies a chaste woman into 'cold' form just as Leontes apparently does his 'too hot' wife into the cold stone of a tomb or statue.

Popular ballads would often enjoy extravagant reversals, as if mockingly to suggest a riotous or apocalyptic 'world turned upside-down': mice eat the cat, distaff beats a sword, an ass rides on its master's back. The impulse behind them is carnivalesque, the brief fantasies of misrule. But Autolicus' ballads go further, seizing upon the play's catalytic instabilities, and offering themselves as the new 'promise', the 'witnessed' authority, of the world that swirls around the sheep-shearing. For Mopsa's hermeneutic faith is both absurd and prescient: 'I loue a ballet in print, a life, for then we are sure they are true' (IV. iv. 261–2). This is not a play, after all, to enshrine dogmatic epistemologies; the minstrel's media are no more nor less 'lies' than the disputed oracle, the 'nothing' seduction, the 'changeling', the non-statue, and so on. We are left not so much with a world of vertiginous relativism as one in which all evidence requires a double-take, and in which status, devotion, and the decorum of the moment are palpably up for grabs.

Autolicus is sublimely unsentimental, and contemptuous of nostalgic mollifications. He is a galvanizer, but one who understands rather than empathizes with his subjects: hence the sense that he acts upon and alters them with something of the invincible energy of embodied economics, an impersonal 'mode of production'. Autolicus' meta-commentary upon both the play he is in and the authorities it inscribes is perhaps most starkly apparent in describing his coup in singing his songs and selling his trumpery:

My Clowne (who wants but something to be a reasonable man) grew so in loue with the Wenches Song, that hee would not stirre his Petty-toes, till he had both Tune and Words, which so drew the rest of the Heard to me, that all their other Sences stucke in Eares: you might haue pinch'd a Placket, it was sencelesse; 'twas nothing to gueld a Cod-peece of a Purse: I would haue fill'd Keyes of that hung in Chaynes: no hearing, no feeling, but my Sirs Song, and admiring the Nothing of it. (IV. iv. 607–15)

The moment's triumph alludes to the classical tale in which Autolicus' spiritual parent, the precocious Mercury-Hermes, comes into his own by doubly duping the great Apollo: first he steals his flock, and then the magnetism of his lyre seduces Phoebus not only into letting him retain his gains, but into giving him a power of divination. The allusion perfectly encapsulates the audacious, iconoclastic larceny of Autolicus' role, and more particularly his splendid acceleration of a world in which young, shape-shifting, unpredictable agencies ('I was only born yesterday', is Hermes' wide-eyed evasion) enter the gaps in power created by the negligence or folly of monolithic authority.[10] But the pedlar's magic is also less benign, less novel. His thraldom thieves on three fronts: mind,

[10] See 'Homeric Hymn to Hermes', in Hesiod, *The Homeric Hymns and Homerica*, ed. and trans. Hugh G. Evelyn-White (1936; 2nd edn. London, 1948); Ovid, *Metamorphoses*, II. 674–706.

money, and genitals. He pretends to please the dreams of his audience; but they sink instead into the sleep of Caliban, waking to find the impotence of castration, the choicelessness of poverty, and something like the triumph of state violence. For Autolicus takes up here an accumulating dialectic of homologies. Describing how he amasses his revenue out of his 'Bowget' (IV. iii. 20), he invokes the power of taxation or 'imposition'. Speaking of 'Honestie', 'Trust', and 'benediction', he returns squarely to the hopes, already strained, of the opening scene, and thence to the 'comfort' retrievable from a resurrected romance tale. This 'time of Lethargie' (IV. iv. 615) recalls Archidamus' resolve to entertain with 'sleepie Drinks', a resolution already translated into the destruction of folk fairy-tale by Leontes' poisonous 'cordial' (I. ii. 316–18). Autolicus' speech might furthermore be understood as a parody of a church-going congregation, himself the charlatan priest ('tromperie') or Chaucerian Pardoner. He invokes redemptive desires surely enough, but his figures of pastoral are mere 'Chowghes', rustic boors, nosing into dead flesh and worthless chaff: that is, into the communal husk of traffic, the bargain and banter of merchandise. This is the new god of the age, turning full circle into a tyranny as emasculating, and perhaps as silencing, as Leontes'.

Autolicus' increasingly pitiless dystopia, given liberty to goose-step its own merry dance of death, would have 'not left a Purse aliue in the whole Army'. His comedy becomes what it should mock and relieve (IV. iv. 619–20). A strange image of a somnolent, lobotomized country, it seems a long distance from the 'Ha, ha'-trumpet with which the speech begins. Autolicus doesn't create the barrenness he exploits, but rather strips it to a skeletal absoluteness. The dissipation, even destruction, of carnival 'oneness' is a symptom of a failure of popular political agency. The cupidity with which Autolicus unloads his pack represents a type of community brainwashing which, while holding out the illusion of participatory enfranchisement, in fact dupes into defeatist obediences. At such moments, then, Autolicus' floating power of surrogacy mediates between recent and imminent versions of tyranny, one totalitarian, the other chaotic; the latter has a certain cachet of liberty, but is in practice hardly less destructive than is despotism. Traditional festivity, like its pastoral cousin, cannot be fenced off from surrounding climes. In Shakespearian romance, the 'posterns' have been opened, and a tempestuous new world comes rushing in.

WALES

Shakespeare envisages various kinds of 'countryside' in his late plays. They vary in wildness, as they do in the debts owed to poetic or mythic precedent. But whether a magic island, a ship-wrecked shore, a fenced pastoral, or an impossible inland beach, all in some sense offer an alternative to established order and, consequently, an environment capable of inaugurations, of beginnings. Such places evoke not only a kind of parallel world to a disappointing present, but a community's past or future, a world before present forms have been built, or after they have disintegrated. The desert, forest, cave, or rock permits the contingent suspension of court or city's law, of its harshness or even necessity. Order becomes less immutable, and so more open to challenge and revision. But the putative novelty of wilderness is in practice an intimate engagement with competing pasts. Political discourse in the renaissance held that there was an intimate connection between the conditions of origin and the quality of any ensuing form; they held little faith in innovations or improvement that were not somehow patterned by the original 'genetic' environment. So, in returning to 'scratch', the country scenes represent the soil in which any 'romance hope' must take root and thence prosper. At its most penetrating, Shakespeare's evocation of wilderness suggests both a people's contested past and, through a literalization of foetal, savage, pre-civil metaphors, a howling absence out of which language and cities may be built: this is the *The Tempest*'s originality. In *Cymbeline*'s Welsh scenes, Shakespeare contents himself with an exploration of distinctively British origins: the audience look at the mountaineers as if at their own evolving selves, growing from pagan primitivism to an imminence just ahead of the Jacobean moment.

The talismanic 'Milford-Hauen' directly evokes legitimating Stuart rhetoric: James located his inheritance, originally from

Brute and later from Henry of Monmouth, at this famous port.[11]
But to invoke is not necessarily to agree: Shakespeare is never
Whitehall's bard, praising some insular courtly line. The geography of Wales, for instance, evokes an inclusive, independent,
local sufficiency. The tributary stream which flows between
haven and court, as between provincial country and imperial
seas (IV. ii. 35–6, 151–3), suggests the myriad rivers and brooks
which, in Drayton's *Polyolbion*, are the distinctly uncourtly
source of national virtue and fecundity. Furthermore, the 'rock'
of nationhood, evoked by the cave in which live the king's 'lost'
sons and their guardian-abductor Belarius, was not beholden
to courtly aesthetics. It was rather like the raw material for
sculpture, to be chiselled and cut as interpretation dictated.
Thus, Drayton describes the series of tableaux in his massive
map of British history and topography as 'artificiall caves, cut
out of the most naturall Rock' which will show the 'ancient
people of this Ile in their 'lively images'.[12] The 'caves' here are
partly the classical sources which Drayton uses as a model, and
partly a kind of amorphous, primal, unbuilt Britain which his
mythopoeia can then populate. The cave, then, is both literary,
a promise of plastic poetic form, and a type of womb, expecting
birth.

It is true that bucolic rocks were a familiar setting for Jacobean masques.[13] Belarius would have his boys imaginatively
transform their rock, as if by ineffable 'Nature', into the 'Roofes
of Palaces' (III. iii. 84), just as the prince Oberon does in
Jonson's masque in honour of Prince Henry. But whereas Cloten
may represent a type of antimasque—though emanating from
within the court, like the false alchemists in *Mercury Vindicated*—Cymbeline's sons are far more wild and antic than
would normally be countenanced by the majestic closures of

[11] This 'Happy port of Union' was invoked in Samuel Daniel's masque, *Tethys
Festival: The Complete Works in Verse and Prose of Samuel Daniel*, ed. Alexander
B. Grosart, 4 vols. (London, 1885), iii. 301–24. Nevertheless, Daniel's work, like
Drayton's, was often implicitly critical of James.

[12] *The Works of Michael Drayton*, ed. Heber, vol. iv, pp. iii*–iv*, Preface to
Polyolbion.

[13] 'Rockes? Nothing but Rockes in these masking devices! Is Invention so poore
that shee must needes ever dwelle amongst Rockes?', George Chapman's 'Masque of
the Middle Temple and Lincoln's Inn' (1613), *A Book of Masques in Honour of
Allardyce Nicoll* (London, 1967), 67.

Jacobean masque. Whereas the 'Cave' evokes pastoral's liberty to counterpoint and arraign central corruption, it is also resonant here of mystery and savagery, of rebellious cabals, gnomic old seers, wild-men, bears. Consequently, their savage den suggests a potential simply to get the diaspora wrong and, like the forest's flailing creatures in *Mucedorus*, or the hapless cave sage in *The Rare Triumphs of Love and Fortune*, to render the promise of hidden, heroic redeemer a gauche, brutal, or anachronistic joke.

The boys' presence at the obscure birthplace of dynasty frames a strange, time-travelling promise. Like Romulus and Remus, together they promise a great city, as yet unbuilt. Of course this city is 'Lud's Town' which, named after Cymbeline's grandfather, already awaits them, its walls securely founded. But the point of such anachronisms is to assert the simultaneity, ideologically and in a sense sensuously, of past and present and, more than this, the imperative to assess one's own achievements against the models to which one appeals for legitimation. Thus, for most of the play Cymbeline's court is simply a Renaissance one; but when the Romans enter demanding tribute, it reverts back to the first century AD and to the confused batch of semi-legendary assumptions that surround the reigns of the Celtic leader Cunobelinus, or Kymbeline, and his sons Guiderius and Arviragus. A series of beginnings are foisted together, with a casual nod to historical accuracy, so as to suggest a basic climate of judgement and inauguration: the hunting austerities and tribal rites of aboriginal man; the Roman state under Augustus Caesar; the life of Jesus Christ and the inception of his Church; the incipience of the British island's independence from the Roman Empire. Cymbeline's mythical descent from Brut, the legendary founder of Britain, and Brut's own emulation of his great-grandfather Aeneas, the father of Rome, add to the sense that the power to originate, and the terms that such novelty establishes, are here being tested. As they were continually, of course, in the Jacobean context which seems to hedge and interpenetrate such prehistory. The notorious anachronisms, therefore, are neither careless, inelegant, nor flippant: the juxtapositions of one age with its distant cousin are *Cymbeline*'s alternative to the palinodal accountabilities of *The Tempest*.

Shakespeare's anachronisms do, however, contribute to a framing irony regarding the Welsh scenes' prophetic veracity. Rather than serendipitous fortune or destiny, the boys' residence at the birthplace of dynasty is the consequence of treason and larceny: a den of the thieved. Such incongruity is crucial to the Welsh scenes' historical engagements. Indeed they might have formed a model for Brecht's 'epic' theatre of alienation: nothing in these hills is quite at home, no affect quite innocent or response secure. As it stands, the whole scene near Milford is hedged by a stagey, almost camp, kind of comedy. The boys' nobility lurches into earnestly cogitated atavism: 'What thing is't, that I neuer Did see man dye, scarce euer look'd on blood, But that of Coward Hares, hot Goats, and Venison?' (IV. iv. 35–7). Wavering between childlike stolidities, knock-about rumbustiousness, and a finger-wagging instinct for aphorism, the princes invite sophisticated scepticism; one thinks of Philaster's gauchely exuberant role-playing. The irony extends to Belarius who, though he fills in certain essential information, seems quite inadequate as an 'authorial' figure. Rehearsing pastoral criticism of the court as if by some compulsive motor reflex, he appears caught in a generic time-warp, blissfully unaware of the past twenty years' stage-history, and of a medium that has grown briskly sceptical of old-fashioned pieties. So too his relentless sententiae upon the boys' princely blood, and upon the difference this forges between themselves and all baser creatures. Belarius' status as the play's catalytic traitor works less to judge his 'treason' sharply than to ironize his subsequent self-framing as a repository of ancient virtue and obedience. *Cymbeline*'s pastoral has trickier aspirations than effortless aristocratic restitution; this is evident from the briefest recollection of Imogen's extravagant paean to the bucolic patch ('this same blessed Milford. And by'th'way Tell me how Wales was made so happy, as T'inherite such a Hauen' III. ii. 60–2), when her passage is preparing a brutal satisfaction, quite beyond irony's etiquette, of her wish for a 'smothering of the Sense' (III. ii. 59). The play's previous upholders of degree, one may recall, are the twin dupes of the evil queen, Cymbeline and Cloten; it is appropriate that the fledglings should meet their 'destiny' only through the flat refutation of their parent's will.

One should not expect, then, a simple contrast between ancient virtue and modern degeneracy when, stuttering and foam-
ing and ready for excision, misrule's satyr-prince, Cloten,
arrives and so marks the hidden princes' reunion with imperial
destiny. For one thing, Cloten too comes from Holinshed, as a
king of Cornwall, chronologically subsequent to Cymbeline,
Guiderius, and Arviragus, but also the father of that Mulmutius
whom Cymbeline celebrates as that ancestor who 'Ordain'd our
Lawes' (III. i. 56–7). Once more Shakespeare chooses from
history in such a way as simultaneously to invoke and confuse
the question of precedence: Cloten can be a distant great-grandfather of the lost princes, just as he can be the *nouveau riche*
interloper who, through his mother's marriage, presumes sovereignty. To Belarius, meanwhile, Cloten evokes the previous
generation at court, and so evinces the presence in Wales of that
privileged venality which pastoral likes to criticize. Guiderius'
role, too, is only partially one 'of' the past. More pertinently, he
is a figure of incipience. So, when Cloten meets the mountain
men there is a strange sense that each represents to the other
both a past and a present. For the meeting between Cloten and
Guiderius stages something like the ultimate duel for which
Cloten has prepared.

Consequently, the collision sparks off a symbiotic trade of
insults, as the appellations of transgression become comically
interchangeable. Thus, Cloten enters complaining, 'I cannot
finde those Runnagates, that Villaine hath mock'd me' (IV. ii.
62–3), meaning respectively Imogen, Posthumus, and Pisanio.
Belarius, his own crime tipping at his tongue, hears himself
hunted: 'Those Runnagates? Meanes he not vs? . . . We are held
as Out-Lawes' (IV. ii. 63–7). Seeing them flee, Cloten rejoins
Belarius's self-accusation: 'Some villaine-Mountainers? I haue
heard of such. What Slaue art thou?' (IV. ii. 70–2). Guiderius
stays to confront the queen's son, and does so by returning the
insult and democratizing the tags of infamy: 'A thing More
slauish did I ne're, then answering A Slaue without a knocke'
(IV. ii. 73–4). Cloten replies in kind—'Robber . . . Law-
breaker . . . Theefe'—and so shares out further the illegality he
himself had boasted of when seeking to charm the ears of his
mistress (II. iii. 70–4).

The point is partly one of synonymity; equally, it is one of

anonymity. Everyone awaits a proper name: it is another register of a nominal return to beginnings, a fluidity which nourishes
anxieties about unstable rank and unlegislatable transgression.
Belarius recognizes that the court will identify them as outlaws
who 'May make some stronger head': the growing head is an
image of sedition from the provinces (IV. ii. 139), echoing the
identical metonym, used by Cloten, to describe the 'growing'
head of the 'dangerous' Posthumus (IV. i. 16–17). The play is
premissed upon instability at the geographical and ideological
centres, and Wales represents such instability's dilation and
consequence. To thus 'return to scratch' is to scrutinize those
namings which, when buttressed by custom, assume ineffable
authority:

> *Clo*. Thou iniurious Theefe,
>   Heare but my name, and tremble.
> *Gui*. What's thy name?
> *Clo*. Cloten, thou Villaine.
> *Gui*. Cloten, thou double Villaine be thy name,
>   I cannot tremble at it, were it Toad, or Adder, Spider,
> 'Twould moue me sooner.
>
> (IV. ii. 86–90)

Like the 'burst[s]' and 'snatches' of his voice, Cloten's shaky
hold upon the dignity of a name epitomizes the play's spreading
indecorum. The Welsh subversion of proper names corresponds
to Bohemia's howling bear and *The Tempest*'s primal roaring: it
suggests a community in hiatus, cultural discourse unbeholden
to conventional dictation. Guiderius here flattens out the grand
presumption of Cloten's name by according superior awe to the
amphibia of a lapsarian, diluvial wilderness. These pre-bour-
geois intimations are brief, used mainly to continue the comic
derogation of Cloten. Still, they express a pervasive nominalism
wherein authority survives, not through 'natural' eminence, but
through possession of varieties of violence.

Cloten, it will be recalled, is out hunting for Posthumus,
determined to destroy his 'mean'st' rival while himself dressed
up in Posthumus' clothes. A combination of low birth, restlessness, envy, and emulation find a symbol in that 'mean'st garment' which, earlier (III. iii. 86–158), the jeering Imogen had
claimed warranted more respect than Cloten's 'noble and

natural person'. Cloten wants to kill Posthumus and rape Imogen while wearing this 'mean'st garment'; to do so is to both mock and usurp Posthumus' potency. Pisanio gets for him the suit with which Posthumus took leave of his wife (III. v. 155); the garment Cloten duly wears, then, is an amalgam of both moments. In a characteristic and oft-repeated exchange, one moment, one figure, takes on another's power: so, Cloten rolls into Posthumus, the meanest garment into the lover's farewell suit. This helps explain Imogen's mistake over the dead body, while symbolically contextualizing Cloten's appearance: he evokes Posthumus both as Imogen's erotic memory and as the beggar or 'Squire's Cloth' of Cloten's opprobrium (that Cloten's insult rhymes with his own name further suggests the play's doubling self-figurations). Dressed thus, in a kind of magnetic, chameleon cloth, Cloten animates the same kind of socially epitomic pun as did his earlier games and duels. He is both pauper and prince, potential and achievement. Again, the 'shift' of Cloten's 'shirt' figures the humour of the body politic: like a child's game, whoever wears the shirt is somehow 'on'.[14]

Confronting the mountaineer, therefore, Cloten fancies himself the exemplar of achieved dignity. Instead his appearance suggests a factitious materialism which it is up to his opposer, if any, to gainsay. However, rather than offering a pure image of inheriting noble virtue, a clear-eyed heroism which the present should revere and recover, Guiderius in turn presents to the indecorous Cloten as much a specular as a corrective relation. Neither admits the reflection, but the comic portent of the combat rests in doubled-up desires of emulation and escape. Thus, if Cloten's garment partially makes of him a base wretch, he is in turn greeted by a correspondingly unenfranchised interloper. At the same time, both men represent the desire for extravagant social mobility: the cavemen's relentless theme is the prison of their home, the barrenness of custom, while

---

[14] In John Speed, *The History of Great Britaine* (London, 1611), 180, the historical period of 'Cunobeline' (Kimbeline) is illustrated with drawings of two 'ancient Britaines', one civilized and one wild. The rougher one's body is painted and damasked all over with the figures of lion's heads; he holds a severed head in his hands, identical to his own, with another clot-poll, again identical, on the floor by his side. This coalition of effects unerringly evokes the triumvirate of Guiderius, Posthumus, Cloten.

Cloten's inscrutable past makes his achievement of greatness itself a kind of satisfaction of the princely boys' glorious ambitions. Furthermore, of course, the mountaineers unknowingly possess what Cloten wants to achieve: royalty blessed by legitimacy. The moment is almost Oedipal, as Guiderius at once emulates, internalizes, and kills his precursor. Opposition is swallowed into likeness.

Of course, an audience will be far from impartial; Guiderius' scorn for authority is thrillingly libertarian:

> *Gui.* . . . Thou art some Foole,
>   I am loath to beate thee. . . .
> *Clo.* Nay, to thy meere Confusion, thou shalt know
>   I am Sonne to th'Queene.
> *Gui.* I am sorry for't: not seeming
>   So worthy as thy Birth.
> *Clo.* Art not afeard?
> *Gui.* Those that I reuerence, those I feare: the Wise:
>   At Fooles I laugh: not feare them.
>
> (IV. ii. 85–96)

The moment has something in common with mischievous exchanges such as *Measure for Measure*'s Lucio with the 'Duke of darke corners' (IV. iii. 156), or Strumbo's mockery of Albanact in *Locrine* (II. iv. 82–8), where festive iconoclasm shades into home-spun independence. But Guiderius isn't simply 'comic', and he doesn't stop with the winking joke. And although the preceding action assures us that Guiderius is justly scornful, it remains a big leap, and one perhaps outside the customary permissions of comedy, to meet disdain with homicide.[15] The assassination of Cloten may evoke a persuasively homely justice, as if law before King Lud. But, as I have been arguing, such tribalism is not the scene's only historical frame. The pastoral characters are nominally 'outlaws', but this needn't translate into a preference for anarchism, however righteously vigilante. For Guiderius takes the very foundation of legitimate government—the rule of law—and baldly mocks its irrelevance:

[15] Although compare Clyomon's killing of King Thrasellus: 'My Lord and King, I thee defie, and in despite I dare Thee for to say thou art no Prince, for thou a Traytour art': *Clyomon and Clamydes: A Critical Edition*, ed. Betty T. Littleton (The Hague, 1968), 1363–9.

> [T]he Law
> Protects not vs, then why should we be tender,
> To let an arrogant peece of flesh threat vs?
> Play Iudge, and Executioner, all himselfe?
> For we do feare the Law.
>
> (IV. ii. 125–9)

A necessary question, consequently, is whether his violence enjoys a protective halo of romance. Can genre pre-emptively
neuter political accountability? The fledgling princes emerge
from familiar fairy-tales, surging with preordained courage, and
this protects them against a punctilious legalism. Nevertheless,
their immunity from political seriousness is by no means absolute. For Guiderius particularly shares in the play's architecture
of moral and physical transference. Thus, granted his desire to
confront Cloten alone, he peruses him as if in his own glass,
repeating the same self-appraising ritual as Cloten moments
earlier performed upon Posthumus:

> ... What are thou? Haue not I
> An arme as bigge as thine? A heart, as bigge:
> ... Say what thou art:
> Why I should yield to thee?
>
> (IV. ii. 76–9)

Shakespeare here has Guiderius size up his opposite with a
telling echo of Shylock's 'hath not a Iew hands, organs,
dementions, senses, affections, passions ... if you pricke vs do
we not bleede? ... and if you wrong vs shall we not reuenge'.
The prince is threatened, perhaps tempted, by the Shylockian
crime of aping the violence of his customary oppressor: 'The
villainy you teach me I will execute, and it shall go hard but I
will better the instruction' (III. i. 52–66). Interpretation will
partially depend upon how much one endorses the wistful
antinomianism which is so often romance's latent architectonic:
a preordained definition of grace frees a chosen few for the
violence, and then from the accountability, of historicity. The
moment also recalls Cloten's own defiant belief that the British
'straight Armes' are fully able to counter the Roman: Guiderius
joins Cloten, Posthumus and the rest on the side of an impatient
patriotism (III. i. 38–9). But more than this, Guiderius endorses
a competitive self-assertion, dangerously familiar, based in the

separation and valuation of discretely potent limbs. A body politic enthralled by dismemberment is, if not the Welsh norm, still a temptation. Does Guiderius, then, either emulate or take on the 'humour' of Cloten?

Asserting the assassination's rough justice, Guiderius seems to claim a cerebral difference between himself and the vacuous Cloten:

> This Cloten was a Foole, an empty purse,
> There was no money in't: not Hercules
> Could haue knock'd out his Braines, for he had none:
> Yet I not doing this, the Foole had borne
> My head, as I do his.

> (IV. ii. 113–17)

However, Shakespeare's language is at once literally descriptive and figuratively prescient. The 'head' that the victorious prince bears is both held decapitated in his hand, and, metaphorically, 'borne' on his shoulders: Guiderius becomes a kind of hydra, giving renewed birth to what was Cloten. Other heads will grow out of Cloten's severed one: like many a fairy-tale monster, it generates with fearsome spontaneousness. Guiderius carries in his own being the weight of the mutating corporate body, the action's magnetic 'passable Carkasse'. Just as, earlier, Cloten had anticipated incorporating into his body those of his specular enemies, the text here passes into the victor's own person whatever energies animated the 'arrogant peece of flesh' that was Cloten (IV. ii. 127).

However, it is not simply that Cloten's desires, the pressures of his carcass and its sacrifice, are transferred into the savage young prince. For a start, neither Cloten's clot-pole nor his trunk quite die. With the former sent down the stream in mocking embassy to his mother, and the latter soon the subject of Imogen's mistaken, microcosmic blazon, they retain their capacity to emblematize, both as separate members and as a severed whole, the current state of the British body politic. This very posthumousness of Cloten renders the tenor of Guiderius' behaviour significant. For Guiderius' dubious privilege of bearing the 'empty purse' is also the power to readdress its priorities for purchase, sense, or potency. Granville-Barker has remarked of Guiderius' nonchalant confession of murder that it shows 'young prince and young savage in a sentence'.[16] Civility is not effortlessly achieved. Violence remains the community's unwanted origin, a stubborn precedent and persistent temptation. Guiderius in his triumph is not yet free from the illegality and corruption represented by his enemy.

And indeed, in another of the play's starkly arresting transformations, Guiderius' bellicose relish is suddenly counterpointed by 'Solemn Musick':

> The matter?
> Triumphes for nothing, and lamenting Toyes,
> Is jollity for Apes, and greefe for Boyes.
> Is Cadwall mad?
>
> (IV. ii. 190–5)

Mistakenly, the scornful Guiderius thinks the music is for Cloten. For the 'ingenious Instrument' sounds for Fidele-Imogen, and so represents exactly the 'greefe for Boyes', felt by boys, which the happy murderer condemns as nursery-school silliness. His tale of the tossed clot-pole jars like a rude libretto against a floating requiem, and the clashing arts serve to isolate or freeze the moments in stark mutual judgement. Cloten's body, even in death, is 'remarkeable in single oppositions': the music is also for him, as his body makes a 'shift' into Imogen's. Cloten has reached his long anticipated moment of 'Sacrifice'. But the propitiation, rather than cleansing all anxiety, augurs in other symbolical beasts, equally addled, atavistic, mistaken. As Belarius says of Cloten, summing up his strangely posthumous physique: 'his Honor Was nothing but mutation, I, and that From one bad thing to worse' (IV. ii. 132–4). This scene, then, shows Cloten's 'Honor', like his 'humour', passing respectively into Guiderius and Imogen.[17] The question here asked of the British polity, in *Cymbeline* as in the other romances, is this: must such mutation, as Belarius has it, be from bad to worse?

[16] *Prefaces to Shakespeare, Second Series* (London, 1930), 284. Brian Gibbons, *Shakespeare and Multiplicity* (Cambridge, 1993), 39, sees in Guiderius the 'cheerful callousness of Jack the Giantkiller'.

[17] The Folio has here 'Honor' for 'humour', which is Theobald's emendation. Both fit Cloten's mutating being: 'humour' suggests the mix of temperamental and physical; 'honor' destabilizes aristocratic achievement.

The Welsh scenes, then, 'hunt' for a place, a moment, an act or ritual or instinct, which might canonize some legitimating inaugural presence. But there is no such clarity. Antiquity, wherever it is located, offers no transcendent source, no originary surcease. Unlike, say, Drayton's 'Ballad of the Battle of Agincourt', Shakespeare's recourse to regions far and battles distant does not locate stirring heroic models, whether to swell present hopes or make stark the present's lack. Empire's beginnings, too, are tetchy and ambiguous; to blandly usher mythic precedents into political service is to sustain the kind of rhetorical euphemism and obfuscation which these plays invoke but rarely if ever endorse. Nothing, neither character nor artform nor topos nor myth, can escape the tangled complicities of analogy.

5

Magnetic Island and Islander in
The Tempest

As its historical reception has time and again attested, *The Tempest* is a work of anticipation, forever poised, like Ariel in the bough, upon the aching pulse of modernity. And in its magnetic island, Shakespeare offers the consummate incarnation of his 'ur'- or anti-worlds, those wild places which magically precede, escape, judge, and sublimate the 'split' communities of convention. Wilderness can suggest beginnings, and, in *The Tempest*, Shakespeare goes back further even than the cave primitivism of *Cymbeline*. He transports scene and motive to a kind of primordial formlessness, in which he replays and reassesses the movement from absence to order, desert to city, and, crucially, from silence, aural chaos, and pre-articulate sonorousness into the voices that organize political community. Simultaneously, the island is a place where memory—private and communal, mythical and imaginary, traumatic and tender—can be replayed, repaired, or revenged. In some ways the wilderness will be like a dream, the cathartic expression of repression. Habitual fears and desires, shaped by oppression of state or suppression of self, can find surprising enactment. One may call it a political unconscious, a play-field in which desire and censorship, assuming disguise, bring their struggle to the light. In one sense, the wilderness may be no more than what was or is, an illusion of escape which is in essence pure recapitulation, the always and already defeated. From an alternative perspective, the fields of licence can seem inherently radical, expressing longings or anxieties which, achievable or not, stand as a defiance of current order. It might be at once dystopian and utopian, a revolving kaleidoscope in which beauty and beast appear and fade and interchange, perception contingent upon perspective.

In epitomizing the romance wilderness, *The Tempest*'s magic island also epitomizes Shakespeare's radical refurbishment of the romance genre. Constructions of the island will therefore double as reflexive commentaries upon the play itself, upon its appropriate franchise and ambition. In turn, the adequacy or otherwise of a character's sense of the island—its sounds, shapes, memories—will be one register of their intimacy to historical process, and of their ability to comprehend or apprehend the pressures out of which novel forms may swell. For Shakespeare's romance wilderness remains the most modern of generic places.

The attitudes here of the two 'bad brothers', Anthonio and Sebastian, can serve as introduction to the island's peculiar provocations. Dumped against their will amid this palingenetic, cosmopolitan genre, they take on the part of critical sophisticates, in both aesthetic taste and political faith anti-romantic and atheistic. What is most remarkable is that these two, alone among the shipwrecked, accept their strange environment with a quite unperturbable phlegmatism: magic is as banal as evil. Romance often seeks a Sidneian poetics, transmuting banality's dross into golden hope; Anne Barton's word for the rogues' wit, 'prosaic', encapsulates their disdain for all such pretty alchemy.[1] They affect disbelief in the island's magic, as in its delicacy or beauty (II. i. 56–65). A Jonsonian cynicism spices their adjectives: to be 'subtle', for instance, is resonant less of learning beyond the rational and familiar than of the wiles of materialistic desire (II. i. 41–4). One is reminded here of Jonson's rogue alchemist, Subtle, whose wonder is the spurious electricity of simple craven appetite: Anthonio and Sebastian would be pleased with such a 'play', one whose positivist logic could only renew their cynicism in its mastery. Faced with the courtiers' awe at the island's suspension of normal cause, they haul perception back into what it needn't fear or envy, the dappled mundanity of custom. They require pedestrianism, clipping the heels of those they pass. Above all they are nominalist in political philosophy. They do not accept neoplatonic homologies of place and word, or beauty and worth, or if they do only to the extent of exploiting the susceptibility of others to this charade, and recognizing the manipulability of signs and badges: 'looke how well my Garments sit vpon me', says Anthonio to justify

---

[1] *The Tempest* (London, 1968), 153.

usurpation (II. i. 267), certain that fate is as casual and possessable as a ducal name. They would mock the pure past worlds which Prospero wants, and for which Caliban and Ariel rebel; so too transformations without error or fall, back into a crystal halcyon.

This implies a relationship to the legitimization of authority almost unique in these plays. To the cynics, both desire and law rest in possession, in the possession of one's desire. Not even upon his *coup d'état* does Anthonio, in line with usurpation's customary practice, seek out precedents or lineage to justify his arrogation. Prospero had earlier told Miranda of his brother's monstrous faculty of self-birth, of extempory innovation: 'one Who hauing into truth, by telling of it, Made such a synner of his memorie To credite his own lie' (I. ii. 99–102). Where the moment's lying 'credite' thus foments its own magical surplus, there can be no debts left owed to the past. Anthonio scorns and ignores the politics of origins, and would have Sebastian, more fearful of ghostly imperatives, follow his own opportunistic example.

Anthonio's persuasions to fratricide and assassination repeatedly enforce his difference from the prevailing Janus-minded perceptions of history. He disdains Sebastian's excuse of 'Hereditary Sloth' (II. i. 218), identifying such inertness with a fearfulness of will. He would bury Gonzalo with the dismissive epitaph of 'Lord of weake remembrance' (II. i. 227), as if to align the counsellor's irritating senility with his future absence from all relevant chronicles of their time. The 'little memory' which will be accorded Gonzalo chimes with the present insignificance of their being 'cast againe' from the swallowing sea (II. i. 228, 246). What matters, Anthonio avers, is now: it avails them nothing to worry upon any other agents of 'destiny'. Therefore, 'what's past is Prologue; what to come In yours, and my discharge' (II. i. 248–9). It is a beautifully unfussy philosophy, wherein past events share their teleology with a prologue to a play: friendly and inviting to those who await the real thing, but fundamentally negligible. The real action, for Anthonio, will be performed by them, extempore. And this play, too, will construct as its abiding principle one of existential unaccountability, of a history without echo: Alonso is as 'dead' as the 'earth he lies vpon', Gonzalo an 'ancient morsell' of fusty meat, the rest of their little band as available as themselves to read time according to Anthonio's radically innovative watch: 'They'l tell the clocke, to any businesse that We say befits the houre' (II. i. 284–5). The past, then, is as distant and irrelevant a country as Tunis, the dark hole 'beyond mans life' (II. i. 242) to where the stupid Alonso has cast his daughter and, now, his surviving hope of umbilical authority. Anthonio's icy politics prefer a wasteland of diminishing impedimenta. But whereas other 'romance deserts' are hollow with longing and shimmer with mirage, Anthonio's particular wasteland is purposefully atrophied, emptied of nostalgic affect, uninterested in community, and free from dreams of retrieval. Anthonio thereby articulates a corrosive assault upon the foundations of both old and new romance.

The twin cynics appear to recognize how the island plays upon people's hankering for as-if magical transformation; also its homesick, childlike, even foetal, seductions, so intimate to secret longings for instauration. What they deride, then, is something akin to art itself, and certainly the kind of art which, as here, appears to 'run away from nature'. So, when Gonzalo's relentless flattery turns into a licentious mythography (Dido, recast as Claribel, returns to bless our alliance), it is met with characteristic scorn. Gonzalo and Adrian have engaged in a mild enough debate about 'Widdow Dido', warding off depression, finding assurance of self-power in their access to supposed historical fact: '*Adr.* . . . . You make me study of that: She was of Carthage, not of Tunis. *Gon.* This Tunis, sir, was Carthage. *Adr.* Carthage? *Gon.* I assure you Carthage' (II. i. 78–82). So far so pedantic: but now Anthonio and Sebastian transform Gonzalo's fastidious mistake into a kind of charter of concupiscent romance. Their language goes marvellously beyond their moment, hurdling the cynics' habitually cramped and pithy decorums; in deriding the play and its island, the recalcitrant Jonsonians offer unwilled celebration of both:

> *Ant.* His word is more then the miraculous Harpe.
> *Seb.* He hath rais'd the wall, and houses too.
> *Ant.* What impossible matter wil he make easy next?
> *Seb.* I thinke hee will carry this Island home in his pocket,
>   and giue it his sonne for an Apple.

Ant. And sowing the kernels of it in the Sea, bring forth
more Islands.

(II. I. 83–9)

In effect they leave Gonzalo behind; the old counsellor's wishful
fidgeting with the past is never this sensitive to the island's
potential. Their choice of ludicrous metaphor is doubly ironical:
first because in due course they are indeed upbraided by circumstances, by a world which, renouncing Neapolitan garments, is
coloured by childhood's fabulous spectres, by harpies, goblins,
and vanishing feasts. And second because both 'Apple' and
'Harpe' evoke the island's magic with perfect acumen. Their
dismissiveness, then, is an unerring, paradoxical entrée to the
play's politics.

As if alive to the geography's effortless microcosms, they
imagine the apple as an incredibly shrinking island. Such sweetly
fecund fruit can, with gratifying facility, be popped into one's
pocket, evoking the dream of possession shared by Prospero,
Gonzalo, Sycorax, Caliban, Stephano, and Trinculo. It suggests
the 'lunatic' dislocation of the rogues' vow to lift the 'Moone
out of her spheare' and 'go a Bat-fowling' (II. i. 177–80), as it
does Stephano's identification as the 'Man ith' Moone', descended now to effect his antic government (II. ii. 138–9). The
apple thus prepares for the way the play challenges Prospero's
presumption of being the island's sole author and authority. A
boy's bite into the apple would scatter the meticulous prepara-
tions of the mage, trumping his project's ethical hubris with a
jolly jape from the fair. A massive dispersal of authority is
predicted when, to spout new islands, the pips are tossed carelessly to sea. Similarly, the archipelagian geneses of the child are
a geographic analogue of Caliban's desire to people the isle with
his likeness; kernels equals testicles (I. ii. 351–3). Sovereignty on
the island is juggled, threatened, or barterable, its glories both a
mundane and a presumptuous ambition; Sancho Panza, too,
would be governor of an isle. Quite beyond their will, the
aristocratic materialists here prepare for Prospero's overthrown
charms at the play's end, and for the way the temptations,
privileges, and responsibilities of power are handed over to an
audience set free with Ariel.

Anthonio and Sebastian invoke so as to mock *The Tempest*'s
miscellaneous Virgilian heritage: Aeneas, bucolics, and eclogues

meet in the apple-isle, a magical distillation of literature's quest for new worlds and boisterous growth, for a magnetic fecundity or imperializing blossom. But what they would deride into a fairground folly the rest of the play is asserting as history's poignant, if elusive, necessity. So, the apple anticipates Ariel's secret abode beneath the 'blossom', a spirit of freedom awaiting, perhaps inciting, fructification: it may be the fruit promised by the spirit's libertarian incipience, a consummation of nostalgic dreams of release (V. i. 94). The magic apple here metamorphoses out of a Bartholomew Fair cravenness into the island's most wistful dreams of replenishment. The 'new-dy'de' visions that the island inspires (II. i. 61), of renewed health, recovered lives, salved sin, and restored power, are linked, through Gonzalo's 'sonne', with the childhood which seems to correspond to and then emanate from the magic desert's inverting treats. The cynics' joke distils the radical 'kernel' which is the island: scepticism, like so much else, must endure transformation. 'What impossible matter wil he make easy next?' (II. i. 85): Anthonio echoes the exasperated Ben Jonson, as the old pedant ('he') turns archly into Shakespeare, mocking the political and artistic authoritarianism of his flat-footed rival.[2]

So, there are profound aspects of the play's struggle with memory and history which the bad brothers' philosophy is ill-equipped to reach. The island's deepest resources of hope, although often ironized or brutalizing, survive their piggy-to-market materialism. The cynics seem far distant from the shrill erroneousness of Leontes; but not unlike the erring King of Sicilia, Anthonio and Sebastian express their would-be mastery in ways that rebound upon them, 'coming true' in ways they cannot foresee, and so suggesting how the island's historical impulsions do not keep time to their own cold hearts. For instance, they are about to kill Alonso and Gonzalo when Ariel wakes Gonzalo; Sebastian and Anthonio explain their sword-drawn postures as defence against the bellowing of beasts:

> *Seb.* (Euen now) we heard a hollow burst of bellowing
> Like Buls, or rather Lyons, did't not wake you?
> It strooke mine eare most terribly. . . .
> *Ant.* O, 'twas a din to fright a Monsters eare;

[2] Harry Berger Jr., 'Miraculous Harp: A Reading of Shakespeare's *Tempest*', *Second World and Green World: Studies in Renaissance Fiction-Making* (Berkeley, 1988), 147–85, sees the harp as a metaphor for Prospero's art and power.

To make an earthquake: sure it was the roare
Of a whole heard of Lyons.

(II. i. 306–11)

They lie; they've heard no such noise. Caught *in flagrante delicto*, they draw knowingly on myths of desert islands, hoping to exploit their audience's gullibility. Yet their descriptions exactly echo the howling of Ariel in Sycorax's pine, a song of both freedom and tyranny, and chime with the cacophony which is the island's symphonic historicism. A strange ventriloquism inhabits their joke, denying the power of disdain or condescension, and insisting that other voices, silenced at court, will here be heard. Once again, their decorums are too positivistic; like the citizen-critics in *The Knight of the Burning Pestle*, they inhabit the wrong play, resisting its charms at the same time as perfectly apostrophizing its radicalism. It is then their worldview that appears redundant. As it is, this scene is littered with verbal and situational anticipations of the imminent drunken rebellion (for example, II. i. 198–204; 216–18; 221–5; 244–7); they at once deny and predict the island's intoxications. In inventing the terrible 'bellowing', Anthonio and Sebastian mockingly conjure a style of kitsch, a past found in popular fable which, all around, is coming back to life as the island's reality. For there's a whole expectant community, a universe of hunger, in the howling of an Ariel or Caliban. The two slaves, swelling with longing, encapsulate Shakespeare's futuristic romance wilderness: that sophisticated derision keeps on leaking hints of this future suggests the imminent inadequacy of an Italianate courtly discourse.

The Tempest never denudes Anthonio and Sebastian's astringent machiavellianism of all coherence. The rogues alert one to the need—from a divergent place but with similar effect to Caliban—to scrutinize that which seems conventional, dazzling, or inevitable. On various levels the play exposes the euphemizing of bare power through romance tropes. Certainly, their mockery of Gonzalo's 'Golden Age' reflects a pathological resistance to idealism, untimely amid the ebb and flow of the island's wistful 'yellow sands'. But still their scorn is necessary and corrective. As Anthonio dismissively notes, 'The latter end of his Common-wealth forgets the beginning' (II. i. 153–4): he remarks specifically upon Gonzalo's shifty rhetoric, rendering him 'King' upon an isle without 'Soueraignty'. Gonzalo's rhetoric would occlude his ideology, and the cynics will have nothing of it; they know how fictions serve annexational desire, and how such desire requires the very letters, guns, and engines which Gonzalo would eschew. As always in these plays, Shakespeare doesn't romanticize indigenous place or person. The cynics are thus given partial authority: Caliban's designs upon Miranda clearly conform more to Anthonio's scorn ('all idle; Whores and knaues', II. i. 162) than to Gonzalo's prelapsarian fantasy; so too the monster's embrace of weapon, wine, and contract law. Romantic dreams don't thereby sink dead in the sludge—indeed Gonzalo's has a carelessly resistant quality partly ensured by the punctilious sarcasm of his audience—but they must battle for currency in a dialogue with scepticism.

The rogues' multiple refusals thus point to the possibility of dissent. More importantly, however, the fact that it is they, vain and craven as they are, who capture the claims of prosaic empiricism, frees up the play to be impossible, radical, wistful; epistemological margins stay malleable. To not take issue with the rogues' scepticism is to undress the emperor before he begins, like seeing *The Wizard of Oz* backwards. One needn't glorify Prospero's wizardry to resent such deconstruction, not least because it denies purpose to the play's equally magical paraphernalia of analogous desires, the barks, bottles, and bombards of others' roaring fantasies. Sarcasm and denial are always easy, but rarely in the vanguard of dreams or justice. Caliban is, 'no doubt, marketable' (V. i. 266), but much else as well: both island and islander refract beyond the cynics, beggaring their materialist political vision.

ROAR, CURSE, VOICE: THE ORIGINS OF LANGUAGE AND COMMUNITY

The island is fashioned aurally. Its dramatization of historical origins is figured in sound, or in sound's absence. In one version of genesis, perhaps, there was the word; before such beginning, though, one might infer silence. Silence is a type of scratch, a beginning from which things might build. But the silence itself may prescript that which will fill the absence: for silence is not only an opportunity, but a kind of perfection. It can be the habitat of a prelapsarian truth, pristine and hallowed, to which a return must be the dutiful teleological trope. Consequently, it will particularly symbolize spellbound obediences, hushed and reverent as a church. At times the wonder of the place—the metaphysical stillness, for instance, implied in the 'odde Angle of the Isle' where Ferdinand sits sighing, 'cooling of the Ayre' with his arms in a 'sad knot' (I. ii. 222–4)—seems to construct a kind of motionless silence as both the necessary environment and ultimate moral of Prospero's lesson. On other occasions it seems that the island's geography is itself released into anthropomorphic animation as, suitably amazing and disorientating, it forces apprehension of things unspeakable:

> Such shapes, such gesture, and such sound expressing,
> (Although they want the vse of tongue) a kinde
> Of excellent dumbe discourse.
>
> (III. iii. 37–9)

The evident silence of that which is new and unknown prepares the old world, through a form of instantaneous undressing and judgement, for both renunciation and, if they apply themselves to the available possibilities, refurbishment. Alonso and friends are, as Prospero would repeatedly have Caliban, bitten by the 'spirits' of their sin and stunned into preparation for grace. The sense of silence plays upon their temperaments in such a way as to pre-empt their apparent choice: if not necessarily Christian, the pregnant, alienating internalizations effected by such stillness seek for renewed piety and order. But as Prospero says, relishing his 'meaner ministers': 'a grace it had deuouring', as if the silence of wonder must share its spoils with his waiting pack of watch-dogs (III. iii. 83–7). For Prospero's work, like his world, is imperfect, and silence too straitened a habit for his impatient interventionism.

Accordingly, the play's music is not that of a swain's lyre. The patient yearnings of Arcadia, its gentle admonitions of sophistication, are surrounded and altered by an atmosphere of dissonance. It resembles nothing so much as its apparent agent, the sea: Shakespeare's ambition seems at times to chime with Joyce's in *Finnegans Wake*, as sleep, dream, language, and desire find source and model in the cerebral currents of swirling water. More broadly, the island's sounds match its capricious, strangely 'individuating' weather: they boom, crash, and retreat, dilate to a murmur and hum before rising to a roaring crescendo which, in its fall, prepares once more to thunder. Lyrical delicacy exists, but only in the context of bombarding percussion, of snapping strings as if torn from the guts of living calves. For the noise of the island is as plangent and squealing as it is mesmerizing.[3] Take Ariel's hypnotic song over Ferdinand:

> *Come unto these yellow sands,*
> *and then take hands:*
> *Curtsied when you haue, and kist*
> *the wild waues whist:*
> *Foote it featly heere, and there, and sweete Sprights beare the*
> * burthen*
> *Harke, harke, bowgh wawgh: the watch-Dogges barke,*
> * bowgh-wawgh.*
> *Hark, hark, I heare, the straine of strutting Chanticlere*
> * cry cockadidle-dowe*

(I. ii. 377–89)

It describes something exquisite, ethereal, as if the dance of printless foot, as the perfection of mime possesses each sense, its beauty simultaneously quelling the elements. Aesthetically, its closest partner might be the masque, or the particular moment in the masque where collective courtly dance passes into the tranquil, perhaps paralysing, apotheosis of revealed perfection. But, on this island, such soundless harmony can intimate only the briefest escape: unlike the witches in Jonson's *The Masque of Queens*, swept suddenly away in a wash of music, 'scarce suffring the memory of any such thing', the bark and bite of the island's antimasque is never quelled.[4] Instead, the ocean's magical 'whist' is as precarious as the decorous curtsying, its

---

[3] The play's music expresses the emerging 'musical humanism', which stressed the rhetorical, ethical, affective quality of music, giving priority to its textuality; it could declare, persuade, deceive, inflame, seduce, or punish, like any language. See D. P. Walker, 'Musical Humanism in the 16th and Early 17th Centuries', in *Music, Spirit and Language in the Renaissance*, ed. Penelope Gouk (London, 1985), 1–71; John Hollander, *The Untuning of the Sky: Ideas of Music in English Poetry 1500–1700* (Princeton, 1961), 147–61; 195–206; David Lindley, 'Music, Masque and Meaning in *The Tempest*', in Lindley, ed., *The Court Masque* (Manchester, 1984), 57 ff.

[4] ll. 345–59, Herford and Simpson edn, vii. 301.

existence both contingent upon and shattered by the omnipres-
ence of the watch-dogs, as by the ominous crow of the proudly
'strutting' cock. Aristocratic comforts, then, like the delicacy of
courtly music, require an atmosphere of unceasing surveillance.[5]

The immanence implied in Ferdinand's question, 'Where
shold this Musick be? I'th aire, or th' earth?' (I. ii. 390), cap-
tures sound's polyvalent creativity. If the 'sweet ayre' here
seems courtly in its Orphic seductions, Ariel's later intervention
among the drunkards, banging and whistling with tabor and
pipe, evokes through appropriative manipulation—much like
Autolicus—the militant festivity it intends to subvert. The pied-
piper Ariel charms high and low from earth and air equally: the
two moments find a common accompaniment in Ariel's watch-
dogs, whose dutiful choric bark is later unleashed into the
hunting vengeance of 'Fury' and 'Tyrant'. The watch-dogs take
up a music whose instruments are revealed, from this perspective, as the sleepless vigilance of martial law.

It would be misleading to identify the island's music solely
with Prospero's authority: Ariel's serviceable tabor emulates the
thumping rhythms of Caliban's marching catch, anticipating
insurrection, while the tricksy spirit later enjoys his own song of
blossom and freedom. But each is defined, indeed only given
purpose, by opposition to the omniscient orchestrations of
Prospero. Music in this play expresses the motives of power:

> Me thought the billowes spoke and told me of it,
> The windes did sing it to me: and the Thunder,
> (That deepe and dreadfull Organ-Pipe) pronounc'd
> The name of Prosper: it did base my Trespasse.

> (III. iii. 96–9)

The bass instrument which here terrifies Alonso into guilt likewise frightens Trinculo into muddy bed with Caliban. The
clown names the cloud a 'foule bumbard' for various reasons (II.
ii. 21), one of them being the booming thunder which gives to
the foulness a voice. The bombard is a bassoon, interpreted by
Alonso as his old adversary's accusatory 'organ-pipe', and by
Caliban as his master's 'spirits' (II. ii. 3–4), doing the mage's

---

[5] Tom Paulin, *Minotaur: Poetry and the Nation State* (London, 1992), 162, notes
how Ariel's song is a variation upon a children's play-song about the beggars coming
to town, suggesting the kick and contempt in the island's apparent blandishments.

bidding despite their rooted hatred. Trinculo, meanwhile, prefers to see in the weather a kind of spherical ale-house, washing the world in liquor. This of course introduces Stephano's 'bottle', a further challenge to, and interpretation of, the 'book' of Prospero to which the 'brewing' atmosphere is correspondent. Roaring, then, expresses government, emulation, and dissension. But it also, as the condition and genesis of such contention, projects back to origins.

Accordingly, one might think of the alternative inference about the world before its inaugurative word: that is, not silence and emptiness, but the vibrating disturbance of disordered sound, of a clamour unmediated by meaning. In this case, origins do not begin with a peace that passes all understanding, but with a chaos awaiting annexation. Antediluvian or post-revelatory, the bare sound of the magic island evokes a plasticity out of which civilization may mutate. The island's sounds are a strangely fecund mixture of howls, breaking waves, and mesmeric harmonies. If one withdrew the human agency much would still remain: the snarling dogs, thunderous skies, screaming trees, perhaps a reminder, sardonic or not, of the cosmos's harmonious spheres. If roaring can suggest society marooned in a baby's babble, its violence might also connote the same state's ending, cursing in the mouth of revelation, a refusal of grace abominable to any Omega silence.[6] Such onomatopoeic discourse can evoke a time before etymological trace; the plays can then seem to rebuild a language, and a state, if not from scratch then with a memory duly informed by the calamities which inform huge violence. The free-form fluidity of sound is both an aspect and analogy of an environment where human institutions are optional, contingent, or simply absent. A noisome prehistory, therefore, evokes the constructed, arbitrary evolution of civilization: *The Tempest*'s repeated return to just such noise suggests how it retrieves history's rootedness in conflict and the consequent tendentiousness of attempts to monopolize amorphous or original permissions. The play will then trace, elliptically and impressionistically, the steps of linguistic evolution, and so the processes through which structures of dominance and subservience become canonized and naturalized in language.

[6] Rev. 22: 3, 4. 'And there shall be no more curse.'

The movement from amorphousness to form, then, appre-
hends more than physical birth: it is a microcosm of the struggle
for language. Thus, both a part and a tentative civilizing of
roaring is the curse, throughout the island more ubiquitous than
poetry. The instinctive resort of court, clown, and monster,
cursing can imply the tenuousness of speech or the precariousness of possessions: its peremptoriness is a sign not only of
violence but of a pressure of transition. Much of the political
restlessness, for instance, of a Hotspur from one angle, a Iago
from another, might be epitomized in their quickness to curse.
In early Shakespeare cursing is linked to an overleaping politi-
cian—curser and cursed—whose atmosphere of colloquial
vitriol establishes both nominal illegitimacy and a thrilling complicity with the audience; one thinks of Jack Cade, or the hunch-
backed Gloucester. Of course, a curse can become merely
rhetorical, a repetitive habit: but such cursing is not the register
of the magnetic island, where the pain attending each curse of
Caliban's replays the original violence done his gullibility. The
elliptical pith of imprecations is apt in a place where, at each
turn, the body is unfree and the mind jealous for liberty. In this
context the curse can be as elemental as a scream strained
through a lexicon.

Equally characteristically, insults will be roared in mutual
political disdain. Such is the play's discursive overture as, on the
unstaunched ship, each voice is 'mocked' by the roaring elements, they in turn roused by the curse of Prospero: 'A plague
——vpon this howling: they are lowder then the weather, or
our office: yet againe?' (I. i. 35–8). Here the boatswain com-
plains of the aristocrats and their 'cry within'; Sebastian requites
the insult: 'A poxe o' your throat, you bawling, blasphemous
incharitable Dog', reduced by Anthonio to a concise accusation:
'you whoreson insolent Noysemaker' (I. i. 40–4). The vessel
suffers rival authorities—king of Naples and master of the
ship—and each side's 'noisemaking' is an attack upon the
other's conception of applied power. Importantly, the two
nominal leaders are not only ineffectual but somehow absent:
the master disappears into his 'whistle', Alonso below to his
prayers, while the thunderous envelope of noise drowns the
ensigns of either. Ship-master and prince, locked unseen within
their 'Bark', add their curse, prayers, and whistles to the

howling fugue. Authority's articulacy is flattened into a music barely distinguishable from calamity. Intimations of baptism, as the ship sinks, conflate with an awareness of awful, comic, contingent judgement, Prospero's 'mock' a little like Bohemia's bear's. In this way the terrible noise, the master's shrill whistle drowned by a phalanx of emulative jeers, evokes the bickering ignominy of a civilization lost. They return to an Eden already sophisticated, already Babelic, denying clear origin and naming. In other words, a rebirth into earth, or into the imperfections of memory and loss.

The overt vocabulary of the howling is a slanging match between 'noble' and 'citizen'; but its further annotations are held in Gonzalo's choric cry: 'we split, we split, we split' (I. i. 61). Conceived of as a secure, organic vessel, the unsplit ship can be a symbol of order, the cabin a kind of home correspondent in its safety to a nurturing maternity. The 'split' figures the breaking apart of the ship of state and all that travels in her: master and crew, king and attendants, father and son, husband and wife. As such, the 'split' is a return to the confusions of the individual confronted with independence, with an existential and experiential loneliness. Hence Gonzalo, his losses having already flashed through his mind ('Farewell my wife, and children, Farewell brother' I. i. 59–60), offers a comically desperate contract with fate: 'Now would I giue a thousand furlongs of Sea, for an Acre of barren ground: Long heath, Browne firrs, any thing' (I. i. 64–7). He pleads, that is, for a kind of wilderness, a desert which pre-dates that empire-building which has wrought the Neapolitans such destruction. He will spill out from the 'split' ship, then, into a kind of beginning.

And, in due course, Gonzalo's prayer becomes a prophecy of those who do indeed seek to construct brave new worlds on the island: the aridity of his transformed dystopia accords with both the environment in which Caliban and his confederates pursue their plot ('Here's neither bush, nor shrub to beare off any weather at all: and another Storme brewing' II. ii. 18–19; 'Tooth'd briars, sharpe firzes, pricking gosse, & thorns' IV. i. 180), and the waste land which facilitates and accords with Anthonio's amorality ('as' twere perfum'd by a Fen ... The ground indeed is tawny' II. i. 46–52). Each of these rebellions, in different ways, expresses the consequences of a 'split' world. But the implications of such a split go beyond the basic motive-forces of the play: familial jealousies, internecine ambition, under-class aspiration, or the violence inherent between master and slave. The trade proposed in Gonzalo's last-ditch prayer is of 'a thousand furlongs of Sea' for a plot of 'barren ground'. The sea here represents, partly, the vast hubris of imperial ambition, the apparent folly of believing man capable of sovereignty over tempestuous nature: Gonzalo invokes, then, the heights of humanity's presumption, whether Prospero's art or Alonso's continent-spanning conjugal diplomacy. At the same time the sea represents the terrible carelessness of mothering: the amneotic fluids break, flushing the child from the womb's warm safety to the barren acres of daylight.

The storm, then, invokes ends and beginnings, the violence of secular judgement and the pain of birth. The consciousness of a 'split' thus connotes on the one hand the political subject's divorce from authority, and on the other the emerging subject's need to construct a language capable of dealing with a frightening and unaccommodating environment. This is where human imperfection begins its battles. For the imputed perfection of the imagined origin will loom as a kind of ur- or master-text awaiting imitation. Hence the 'split' between desire and instrument. For Lacan, the individual yearns constantly to return to the wholeness, the self-possession, of a pre-linguisticism figured by identification with the mother; but the subject can only be defined in terms of that law and language, identified with patriarchy, whose irresistible hegemony pre-empts the split from the imaginary origin. Language, therefore, must always express an absence, a desire rooted in division and bifurcation. Notions of origin, therefore, recede coterminously with those of a centre. The necessity and magnetism of such teleologies is, like rainbow's gold, matched only by its elusiveness.

The romances take on board such a recessive source and dilating centre, not as a charter for nihilism or, indeed, a reactive totalitarianism, but as the reflective application of an uncertainly humanist historiography. The repeated separation from a soothing organicist source, whether godlike regent or uterus, confirms the imperative that manageable structures of belonging be constructed; this is the dilemma of any society as of any individual. Such society will seek to construct institutions which best correspond to the perfect government inscribed, as it were, in the cultural memory, and blessed with the attributes—loving, forgiving, attending justly and equally to all—of a kind god or parent. But all the time such inscriptions must negotiate that 'split' which, in the relationships of words as much as subjects, renders breaches hard to heal. The world splits into wilderness and asks a fundamental question: what can grow from the breach?

As the fissured ship presages, nothing on the island can long escape the alpha and omega of a roar: in its storms and imprisonments, rebellions and punishments, it is the play's plangent register of historical change. A formative trope is repeated throughout the play: roaring attends incarceration within a bark, cell, or shroud, before splintering open into a form created out of the mutual violence of the containment and its resistance. A rumbustious onomatopoeia, consequently, remains a kind of impermeable register of political desire, which to staunch is as effectless as a cork in a hogshead or a lid on the wind. These births out of the dark supply a kind of rhyming exergasia throughout Prospero's lengthy account of his and others' histories. They all link together to 'conceive' the world of the island, strangely concatenating as it is of both shape and word.

For example, Prospero metaphorizes the loss of his dukedom in terms of a 'princely Trunck' suffocated by the ivy of his brother's parasitism (I. ii. 86–7). Anticipating the 'clouen Pyne' within which Ariel was imprisoned, and forced like Ariel to suffer the 'tune' of his oppressor (I. ii. 85), there emerges from Prospero's incarceration a birth as diabolical as the beastly progeny of the spirit's howl. So, Prospero conceives of his sibling trust as 'a good parent' (I. ii. 94); he duly begets his opposite, Anthonio's mendacious regime. Anthonio then becomes the figurative parent, as once again the future's midwife works from within howling, incoherent entrapment: 'ith' dead of darkenesse' the 'gates of Millaine' vent the ex-duke and his 'crying' child (I. ii.130–2). Two further pregnancies, consecutive and competitive, complete Prospero's narrative: having groaned beneath his 'burthen' of grief, supplementing the water's sharp fury 'with drops full salt', his daughter's smile raises in him an 'undergoing stomach' of 'fortitude' (I. ii. 152–8). Imagining himself as a kind of *post facto* mother, Prospero's tumescent metaphors adopt responsibility, respectively, for Caliban and Miranda. The community's future will be bartered through the birth and life of each.

The ostensible cause of Prospero's grief is his usurpation and exile: it is this which is his original 'burthen'. But now, as has been seen, this 'burthen' mutates into an anticipation of Prospero's 'bad' child, Caliban. Furthermore, Prospero pictures his very boat of exile through the familiar prison-and-roar tableau; only now the metaphor begins to mould a body:

> In few, they hurried vs a-boord a Barke,
> Bore vs some Leagues to Sea, where they prepared
> A rotten carkasse of a Butt, not rigg'd,
> Nor tackle, sayle, nor mast, the very rats
> Instinctiuely haue quit it: There they hoyst vs
> To cry to th' Sea, that roard to vs; to sigh
> To th' windes, whose pitty sighing backe againe
> Did vs but louing wrong.
>
> (I. i. 144–51)

The cantankerous misshapenness of the 'rotten carkasse' seems prescient of the ugly thing their 'sea-sorrow' weepingly comes upon: Caliban. The 'Barke' is another in the play's symbolical death-traps, suggesting that the physicality of Caliban is both an image of the oppressive politics which cause the repeated incarcerations, and such a black hole himself, screaming with the potential to confer 'new worlds'. More specifically, Prospero speaks of the bark as he does later of his ward ('as with age, his body ouglier growes, So his minde cankers' IV. i. 191–2), marrying as ideological cousins his brother's treason to Caliban's recalcitrance. Prospero's 'Thing of darkenesse', Caliban, rhymes with and recapitulates Anthonio's deed in the 'dead of darkenesse' (V. i. 275). In meeting Caliban, the rueful Prospero both retrieves his past, and finds the dark 'plot' of his future.

Prospero's metaphors, then, betray his complicity in both his own usurpation and, by extension, the creation or discovery of Caliban. And furthermore, he prepares for the amoebic screen that is Caliban. For the island's monster here embodies not only the brutal motives of secular dukedom but the cursing burdens of such politics' victims. At the same time, he is part of the new life born from apparent death. Like an embodied roar, Caliban is always in a process, simultaneously, of becoming, ending, suffering, and punishing, agent and object symbiotically, with all the violence such collapsing binaries can muster. Caliban has a metamorphosing capacity to be history, to embody in process political ideology. One function of this narrative of roars and barks, then, is figuratively to prophesy, in a sense to create through telepathic language, Caliban. He may not resolve anything, but he will offer something, apparently tangible, in and upon which to test the motive and justice clamouring in the noise.

As so often in these plays, then, places apparently distinct in space and time at certain points conflate and share their histories. Prospero will replay Milan on the island, and in turn the inhabitants of the island before Prospero's arrival will, in the accounts we get of their prehistory, supply the pasts to which the two exiling shipwrecks—first Prospero's, and then Alonso's—return their members. The roars of wind and mouth spawn a communal rebirth; as with Milford-Haven's quarrellers, society is envisaged at its belligerent and pugnacious source. Language, like the flailing ship and its members, echoes its meta-cry: 'we split, we split, we split'. What should one expect out of all such rebirths into linguistic and political materialism, into the fissiparousness of earth?—What, indeed, but Caliban?

CALIBAN: NATURE AND NURTURE

In the creation of Caliban Shakespeare refines the analogical processes which, in all the romances, allow single moments or characters to stand for a complex community or cultural transformation. Caliban embodies the processes, not only that surround him, but that are narrated as having preceded him: he makes tangible the engagement of political discourse with origins. Accordingly, the 'real' Caliban remains as elusive as one's own moment of birth, accessible, and then imperfectly, only through report.[7] The island surrenders a sequence of interpretations which serve both for our knowledge of Caliban and

[7] Peter Hulme, *Colonialist Encounters: Europe and the Native Caribbean 1492–1797* (New York, 1986), 108, writes: 'Caliban as a compromise formation, can exist

as a sounding-board for the interpreter's own fears and desires, their own paradigms of moral and political order. He becomes each of the things he is called, discretely and in aggregate, always both less and more than any possessive definition.[8] His is a figure preternaturally intimate to metaphor, to connotation rather than denotation: figurative language, by turns limping, licentious, contagious, finds in him strange form. And yet language is and is not 'Caliban'; like the porter's drink, it makes and it mars him: the equivocating descriptions render his body fluid, at ebb and flow like the travelling oceans. Hence his name, the badge by which one might find him a home, is an endlessly circulating, always imperfect anagram, evoking places, persons, and beasts that span the globe, invariably returning to some hybrid notion of an exoticism that, nearly, consumes its own kind.[9] 'Caliban' is, like the play, *sui generis*, a work finally owning neither genetic nor generic paternity. For instance, the disgusted rhetoric of disease propagated by Thersites, Pandarus, and later Timon—Greece and Troy are a scab, a botchy sore, a boil or bone-ache—may suggest something of Shakespeare's conception, building Caliban's role as an opprobrious cipher of others' malice, or confusion, or self-hate, a festering 'body politic'. But still, 'he', or 'it', is something more, an anti-neoplatonic essence, awaiting capture, inviting empathy, eluding both.

Trinculo, for instance, perambulates around the prostrate Caliban, niggling at the thing's species:

What haue we here, a man, or a fish? dead or aliue? a fish, hee smels like a fish: a very ancient and fish-like smell: a kinde of, not of the newest poore-Iohn: a strange fish: were I in England now . . . there, would this Monster, make a man: any strange beast there, makes a man . . . Leg'd like a man; and his Finnes like Armes: warme o'my troth: I doe now let loose my opinion; hold it no longer; this is no fish,

only within discourse: he is fundamentally and essentially beyond the bounds of representation.'

[8] Anthony Pagden, *The Fall of Natural Man: The American Indian and the Origins of Comparative Ethnology* (Cambridge, 1982), 10–11, notes the inadequate descriptive vocabulary of Europeans in America.

[9] 'Caliban' itself has often seemed an anagrammatic corruption, whether of 'Cannibal', 'caribbean', 'Cauliban' (the gypsy word for 'blackness') or sundry others of increasing exoticism; for survey of speculations see Alden T. Vaughan and Virginia Mason Vaughan, *Shakespeare's Caliban: A Cultural History* (Cambridge, 1991), chs. 1 & 2.

but an Islander, that hath lately suffered by a Thunderbolt. (II. ii.
24–37)

In the end, Caliban has to be the thing that Trinculo has not yet
actually met: an 'Islander'. A little like the word 'romance',
Trinculo's choice registers taxonomic inadequacy; it means
a question mark. On the one hand Caliban is 'before' humanism, both reversing and reliving Ajax's regression from
blockish thug to prehistoric cretin: 'Hee's growne a very land-
fish, languagelesse, a monster' (*Troilus*, III. ii. 263). And yet, like
the child Perdita, he is a figure of futurity: but a future laden
with ancient burdens. His fish-flesh, like his 'rore', is preternatu-
ral, before words yet chronicling of history. As a fish Caliban
may invoke the Christian allegory, numerous puns upon genita-
lia, and, through the 'poore-Iohn' of Trinculo's recoil, any old
fool at a fair.[10] But then, being but 'halfe a Fish, and halfe a
Monster' (III. ii. 28) Caliban reprises the fishermens' scene in
Pericles, where the bouncing and tumbling 'porpas', 'half fish,
half flesh', was not only the harbinger of a storm but, by the
fisherman's contiguous allegory of wrongs righted and lands
returned, of a new and 'washed' world (II. i. 23–43). For the
Greeks the dolphin, similarly fish-and-flesh, was the 'uterine
beast', revered by Apollo and the ocean's equivalent to Delphos,
each symbolic of non-being and beginnings.[11] At the less mercurial end of creation Caliban is 'thou Tortoys' (I. ii. 318), equally
antediluvian, but slow, slothful, antique. Caliban's scaly body
will link to the sea, and so to the play's originating tempest; it is
as though he renders fluidly manifest the roaring wind and
chiding storm. Similarly, the elusive mix of fish and fluid will
suggest the primal waters of creation, whether of the womb, or
sperm, or the deep oceanic sludge. This makes Caliban both
unspeakably aged and, as though still floating in the protective
uterus, as young as the moment, awaiting shape and mind.[12]

[10] Compare the pig-woman Ursula in Jonson's *Bartholomew Fayre*, who, with her
servant 'Mooncalf', seems to draw upon aspects of Caliban.
[11] C. Kerenyi, 'The Primordial Child In Primordial Times', in C. G. Jung and C.
Kerenyi, *Science of Mythology: Essays on the Myth of the Divine Child and the
Mysteries of Eleusis* (1949; repr. London, 1985), 49–51.
[12] G. Wilson Knight sees Caliban being 'dragged painfully up creation's stair' (p.
237). His analysis is firmly imperialist, but all the same full of an acute sense of
Caliban's intimacy to historical energies: 'Caliban is ... process incarnate ... He is

Some of his insulting or derisive appellations indeed evoke Caliban as a kind of foetus brought to air, unfinished, molested, aborted, yet magically posthumous (II. ii. 25–6; I. ii. 367; II. ii. 107, 135–6). To Prospero, Caliban is the 'Hag-seed' (I. ii. 367): he can grow up and back into the 'blew ey'd hag' he came from (I. ii. 269). The drunkards call him 'Moone-calfe', defined by Pliny as a 'lumpe of flesh without shape, without life', but nonetheless 'a kind of moving it hath'.[13] This evokes with alluring piquancy Caliban's netherland status, in so far as others sense and manipulate him: a status subhuman, almost inanimate, like wet clay. The name itself evokes the governing hemispheres awry, the moon erratic and the tides confused. Linguistically, 'Moone-Calfe' invokes bifurcation, things 'double-tongued . . . unstable, or double-minded'. The phrase was often used with a political edge, to slander impudent schemes or idiotic labours: the sort that 'Democracy' or a 'Parliament', other many-headed monsters, might seek to foist on a suffering state.[14] Predictably, Drayton's lengthy poem, 'The Moone-Calfe', provides Caliban's prodigious gloss.[15] Conceived by the Devil or by violent rape, Drayton's elephantine sea-monster (50–6), a babe of 'unnaturall pollution' (124), is meticulous punishment for a world gone to seed:

> The World's in labour, her throwes come so thick,
> That with the Pangues she's waxt starke lunatick . . .
> Dropsied with Ryots, and her big-swolne bulke
> Stuff'd with infection, rottennesse, and stench
> But when as man once casts off vertue quite,
> And doth in sinne and beastlinesse delight,
> We see how soone God turns him to a Sot.

> (5–17; 695–7)

Drayton parabolizes the sot in a series of old wives' tales, narratives detailing various of the avarices, fornications, and

---

heavily weighted down on rails of time, and cannot move from them . . . Caliban is a *sub specie aeternitatis* study of creation's very inertia and retrogression in laborious advance, growing from slime and slush, slug and furry beast, to man in his misery and slavery, though shot through with glory; and learning, in his own despite, the meaning of lordship and grace.' *The Crown of Life: Essays in Interpretation of Shakespeare's Final Plays* (London, 1947), 240.

[13] *Pliny's Natural History*, Holland's translation (1601).
[14] *OED.* 2b.　　[15] *Works*, ed. Hebel, iv. 166–202.

treacheries which so diabolically impregnated the globe (1373–83). The grotesque moon-calf, conceived as the world's come-uppance, embodies the 'Ile of Ideots'. Drayton himself, whether through stubbornness or *faux pas*, was ostracized from worth-while patronage. In satires like 'The Owle' and 'The Moone-Calfe' he vents his spleen, excoriating the injustice and de-cadence at the Jacobean court. Drayton and Shakespeare had acquaintances such as Southampton in common, who shared the colonial interest.[16] Drayton may have written 'The Moone-Calfe' as early as 1607: if Shakespeare transposes anything of its furious import into his characterization of Caliban, then it is in the direction of microcosm, of the monster taking on the sins of promiscuous, mutating, plaguish corruption. The allusion might register a wry topicality in *The Tempest*'s ambivalent apprehen-sion of disorder and its responsibilities.[17]

Caliban's sensitivity to language feeds into the nuanced poli-tics of his role. He recalls the arrival of Prospero, for instance, with a palpitating quickening of spirit, a warmth and flutter which makes more arresting his bitter self-castigation:

> [W]hen thou cam'st first
> Thou stroakst me, & made much of me: woudst giue me
> Water with berries in't: and teach me how
> To name the bigger Light, and how the lesse
> That burne by day, and night: and then I lou'd thee
> And shew'd thee all the qualities o' th' Isle,
> The fresh Springs, Brine-pits; barren place and fertill,
> Curs'd be I that did so.
>
> (I. ii. 334–41)

---

[16] Drayton celebrates Hakluyt in 'To the Virginian Voyage' (1606), ibid. ii. 363.

[17] Shakespeare probably saw 'The Moone-calfe' in manuscript. One of Drayton's old wive's tales, that of Mother Bumby, corresponds in enough details to *The Tempest* to suggest a sustained analogue or influence. The resident witch can float her island, sell the winds, stay the moon, and eclipse the light (ll. 861–5); she controls various 'Bastard creature[s]', 'Halfe men, halfe Goate . . . A Beare in body, and in face an Ape: Other like Beasts yet had the feete of Fowles, That Demy-Urchins weare and Demy-Owles' (ll. 877–840). Her closest disciple is one 'ill-favoured *Babian*', a master of counterfeit, a 'Jipsy', 'juggler', 'mountebank' (ll. 888–901), her 'very Hermes' (l. 986). They are eventually vanquished by a Wizard, skilled in 'black and gloomy arts' but seeking to banish evil, who adopts the guise of the witch and Babian respectively, causing her to despair and drown herself. S. Naqi Husain Jafri, *Aspects of Drayton's Poetry* (Delhi, 1988), 146–51, links the Wizard with Prospero.

As part of Caliban's encapsulatory power of 'being' history, he is gifted here with a double-time apprehension, ensuring that the wounds reopen, as he is shafted, new and tender, all over again. He feels the moment as if new, casting back as though uncovering some unwounded heart, white as veal; he is in the past, living it with the ingenuousness of revelation, resentment cast off like a hairshirt. So Caliban relives the wonder of a child, liberated into naming's powers and permissions. The exile's words are received as the harmonious extension of physical coddling, swallowed as if musical accoutrement to the berry-soup. Caliban thought a 'name' as guileless and inevitable a property as a fresh spring, believing, with the instinctive gullibility of wonder, that Prospero's introductions were to a world of boundless communal myth. The moment's poetry, then and now, belies its economics, as fruit's ripeness does its fall. For simultaneously he suffers hindsight, with all of its unblinking irony and reproach. And so back it comes, the stark and sudden cast to the now, and its loss, bereavement, and slavery. His final expostulation ('Curs'd be I . . .') replays the parched rasp of anguish as, played for a fool, 'love' is withdrawn and mastery and malediction begin. Of course Prospero sees in his slave's autobiography the most craven revisionism; but this judgement, fair or not, is itself ironical testimony to Caliban's rhetorical gifts. And yet, as his reminiscence itself attests, Caliban retains a sense that language can serve love, that it can be faithful. Hence the ambivalence of his nostalgias, galvanized so familiarly by Stephano's wine, with their all-too-human shifts through idealism and delusion, ignominy and service, violence and retreat.

A prolonged debate among Augustan editors about the uniqueness or otherwise of Caliban's language was provoked by Nicholas Rowe's report of a conversation among some of London's most eminent public figures, including Viscount Falkland, Chief Justice Henry Vaughan, and the jurist John Selden, which concluded that 'Shakespeare had not only found out a new Character in his Caliban, but had also devis'd and adapted a new manner of Language for that Character'.[18] The particular

---

[18] Nicholas Rowe, *Some Accounts of the Life of Mr. William Shakespeare* (Michigan, 1948), p. xiv. See Brian Vickers, ed., *Shakespeare: The Critical Heritage*, ii: *1693–1753* (London 1974), 197.

'antique' or 'grotesque' air of Caliban's speech is recognized because it eludes convention: it differs from both the controlled and muscular rhetoric of Shakespeare's noble figures and the profane and witty prose of his commoners. Dryden said of Caliban's language that it is as 'hobgoblin as his person'.[19] However, the contending editors, such as Warburton, Heath, Holt, and Johnson, fail to establish what it is about Caliban's speech which makes it resonant of 'brutality', or the 'grotesque', or in what way 'his 'Stile is peculiarly adapted to his Origin'.[20] It is not quite, as Johnson avers, satisfied by Caliban's 'brutality of sentiment'. It seems more helpful to think in terms of barbarism; this will link to and extrapolate the sense, suggested by Holt and Heath, that Caliban's language evokes his origins. His 'gabble' is barbarous in the sense of being before recognizably civilized—Greek, Italian, English—language. So, his speech evokes both a state of howling unerudition and his subsequent passage into 'humanism'. He enumerates sun and moon half like a child, puffed with his new words. Caliban recounts how Prospero taught him 'how To name the bigger Light, and how the lesse That burne by day, and night' (I. ii. 337–8): both torches are alive with inspiring, awesome, dangerous energy ('burne'), making as if inevitable the proverbial association of each with power beyond the mortal. Caliban takes metaphors back to a manner of inaugurative or formative principle. They become inherently reflexive, reliving the processes or relationships which make language, and the social priorities they frame and then control, simultaneously so unstable and, once learned, so easily assumed. Caliban's language is indeed so tactile, a simulation of things autochthonous, as itself to suggest flesh; metaphor and mass are here tantalizingly inseparable.

The play takes Caliban, through recollection or recapitulative representation, along a path from barbarism to a sophisticated verbal mimeticism. Early on, Shakespeare gives to Caliban's language a supple kind of naïf-literalism. Sophisticated speech abstracts and ellipticizes, or yokes, in the service of economy or

---

[19] *Essays of John Dryden*, ed. W. P. Kerr. 2 vols. (London, 1900), i. 219.
[20] See *The Works of Shakespeare in Eight Volumes*, ed. Alexander Pope and William Warburton (London, 1747), i. 19; John Holt, *Some Remarks on The Tempest* (London, 1750), 28; Benjamin Heath, *A Revisal of Shakespeare's Text* (London, 1765), 9–10; *Johnson on Shakespeare*, ed. Walter Ralegh, (Oxford, 1908: repr. 1959), 66; Parker, *Johnson's Shakespeare*, 112–26.

speech-reflexive satisfaction, disparate concepts and words into union. By contrast, Caliban's early speech is noun and task based, returning to a more juvenile register of 'this equals that'. It expresses a genesis of habits, of controls and customs normally taken for granted ('Water with berries in't'). He might, of course, now employ the knowledge acquired, but much of the point of this moment is to return us to the ingenuous wonder before disillusionment, and thereby to mimic an awakening veracity. Throughout the play his cadences are lilting and pellucid, his rhythms quick, curious, gliding; Caliban's intent is always as clear as the 'fresh Springs' with which he requites his education (I. ii. 340). There is an eagerness of description, particularly in his namings of flora and fauna, or the geography of land and sky, freshening his words as if still crisp with dew. Unlike the static relationships of sign to signified of habitual language, or the thoughtless rehearsal of stock-phrases, Caliban's language is still permeated by the kineticism of matter itself: like his body, it tells a tale of process and surprise, a fluidity that is not a detached backdrop but an affective, effecting contiguousness to the individual experience. It is childlike, pastoral, in a way that, for instance, the sophistication of Polixenes' 'twyn'd Lambs' (I. ii. 70–5) memory quite precludes. Much of the empathy Caliban evokes comes from the way his language, when enthusiastic, taps into communal desire for golden days, unspoiled beauty, halcyon leisure. He enjoys a sparrow's mind, quick and delighted to garnish desire with linguistic novelty: thus, for instance, his wary but proud quotations, 'utensils' and 'non-pareill' (III. ii. 94, 98), and his hobgoblin invocation, a little like Othello, of stiffly surprising names, made exotic and threatening by their formality or specificity: 'paunch him', 'cut his wezand', or 'I am full of pleasure, Let vs be iocond' (III. ii. 88–9, 115). Caliban's choice of words overlays his violent intent with comedy; he wears them like bright new clothes, all self-aware and conspicuous, and one effect is momentarily to detach his language from its message, concentrating attention upon the vocabulary itself. Accordingly the clothes are those of his master, with Caliban absurd, charming, accident prone—yet resolutely proleptic—in his father's suit. The 'monster' oddly appropriates the 'promise' of Prince Mamillius.

His grammar is in part an emulation of Prospero and Miranda, and the monster's graceful iambic pentameters might be considered a small triumph of civility. At times he betrays the rhythms of court, speaking with an antithetical, almost euphuistic symmetry.[21] But he uses such rhetoric knowingly, even parodically; decorum is shaken, and the unctuous violence of ruling discourses made palpable ('Do that good mischeefe, which may make this Island Thine owne for euer, and I, thy Caliban, For aye thy foot-licker', IV. i. 217–19). For Caliban is hardly transcendent: his irony and nominalism when egging Stephano on toward the murder, so distinct from his word-pleased wonder in less contemptuous moments, draw him close to the sheer efficiency of Anthonio. Caliban remains the perfect hybrid, a hobbling goblin belonging here, there, and nowhere. He cannot forswear his education; there's no undressing back to aboriginal simplicities. Caliban, then, doesn't simply achieve language as he might long trousers: rather, he continues to figure and suffer the 'roar', the violence which lies latent in linguistic history. This roar is pre-linguistic; it is inherent in slicing the howl into syllables; and it is the measure of the resistance and desire which humanizing and humanism can provoke but never satisfy. This is Caliban's curse.

The roar, then, is the soundtrack to Caliban's growth. From the moment he was littered, the island has been terrorized by its own pregnant ululation: that of Ariel, imprisoned in a pine by the mother Sycorax. As narrated by Prospero, the spirit's tomb-cum-womb frames a primal archetype, not only of numerous other arrested histories, but of the passage, epitomized by Caliban, from anarchic babble into articulate service:

> Into a clouen Pyne, within which rift
> Imprison'd, thou didst painefully remaine
> A dozen yeeres: within which space she di'd,
> And left thee there: where thou didst vent thy groanes
> As fast as Mill-wheeles strike: Then was this Island
> (Saue for the Son, that he did littour heere,

---

[21] Anthony Pagden, 'Identity Formation in Spanish America', in Pagden & Nicholas Canny, eds., *Colonial Identity in the Atlantic World 1500–1800* (Princeton, 1987), 88–9, records a 1591 judgement that the Spaniard born in the Indies 'speaks in a manner so polite, courtly, and elaborate . . . with such a rhetorical style, neither forced nor artificial but natural'.

> A frekelld whelpe, hag-borne) not honour'd with
> A humane shape.
> *Ar.* Yes: *Caliban* her sonne.
> *Pro.* Dull thing, I say so : he, that *Caliban*
> Whom now I keepe in seruice, thou best know'st
> What torment I did finde thee in; thy grones
> Did make wolues howle, and penetrate the breasts
> Of euer-angry Beares; it was a torment
> To lay vpon the damn'd, which Sycorax
> Could not againe vndoe: it was mine Art
> When I arriu'd, and heard thee, that made gape
> The Pyne, and let thee out.

(I. ii. 277–93)

Most particularly, Ariel's experience seems to replay an 'ascent' from barbarousness into language. Stuck in a dungeon prehistoric to names and syllables, he surrenders all but pure voice or potentiality. This voice, though, is stripped of all semantics: besotted by pain and denial, it groans rather than speaks. Ariel's condition is akin only to the negative states, before birth or in death, awaiting or forgetting words. A kind of 'foetalism' is then implicit in the womb-like pine, although one whose birth is deferred until, and conditional upon, the necessary doctoring of a powerful 'Art'.[22] This art—civil or daemonic—can deliver the voice from its inarticulate burden. Prospero releases Ariel from his howling prison, and in doing so bestows articulacy. Language, then, is a Faustian pact. It confers the gift of bourgeois self-knowledge, but only within an immanent frame of service: subjectivity equals subjection. Gratefulness ushers in obligation, as Ariel's beginnings describe Caliban's.

But Ariel's experience in Sycorax's death-womb seems not only to mimic, but in a way to cause, Caliban's maleficent origin: Prospero claims that Caliban was vented from an alliance between witch and devil, the perfect 'littour' from such a 'clouen Pyne' ('Clouen' evokes the gaping womb, splitting of identity and the foot of the devil; 'Pine' evokes the tree or voice of torture, denial, and longing). Tortured for stubbornness, Ariel is twisted into a daemonic kind of evangelist. The spirit's

---

[22] Jacques Lacan, 'The mirror stage', *Écrits: A Selection*, trans. Alan Sheridan (1977; repr. London, 1989), 4, says 'foetalization' is used by embryologists to connote what he sees as the 'real *specific prematurity of birth* in man'.

howls have an insidious, counter-reformatory effect on those who hear: 'it was a torment To lay vpon the damn'd' (I. ii. 289–90), reminds the menacing magician, conflating the claustrophobic blackness suffered by Ariel with the 'torment' of hearing the mill-wheel clack and roar. This is where Caliban tumbles into and out of 'Ariel's' story, a listening presence both then and now (I. ii. 282–3). For he is here recounted as an orphaned, feral creature, both 'humane' and not, but as yet without words, a mere gob on the landscape. The infernal racket seems to 'penetrate' Caliban's breast, become a voice identical with and descriptive of himself. He joins with the howling 'wolues' and 'euer-angry Beares'—the ranks of 'the damn'd'—reinvented, as if by a mirror of sound, in their savage opprobrium. The hellish scream makes beasts over again into beasts, re-engendering the diabolical and recondemning 'the damn'd'. Throughout the play, 'syllables' are rendered physical by Ariel. The 'frekelld whelpe, hag-borne', seems the inevitable product, even prototype, of Ariel's howl. The history of language, then, reflects, records, and reinforces the history of power relations. Caliban's relation to both language and desire is contained in his relation to the island's music, its language of murmur and roar. For instance, he is lulled to sleep by 'noises' that lead him to dream upon the 'clouds' which, when he wakes, are the 'bombards' of thundering denial (III. ii. 137–41); harangued into service, his life is a cacophony of cries and moans ('Ile racke thee with old Crampes, Fill all thy bones with Aches, make thee rore, That beasts shall tremble at thy dyn', I. ii. 370–3). Caliban's very being—in his mind, his language, his 'rock', his labour—repeats Ariel's traumatic burial and coming-to-be in the pine. The spirit's imprisonment is a kind of parenting process, spawning and then socializing Sycorax's child.[23]

The point is that the play shows the process, as constant as its music, of Caliban's parentage. And he knows the score himself: amid the hushed pragmatism of his assassination tread, Caliban ruefully acknowledges how his shape, and the contempt it attracts, are the construction of a peremptory spoken command: 'if he awake, from toe to crown hee'l fill our skins with pinches, Make vs strange stuffe . . . we shall loose our time, And all be

[23] Kerenyi, 'The Primordial Child', 28, notes the currency of myths in which the mother '*is* and *is not* at the same time'.

turn'd to Barnacles, or to Apes with foreheads villainous low'
(IV. i. 232–4, 247–9). Indeed, the slave not only chronicles, but
augments his own painful evolution:

> All the infections that the Sunne suckes vp
> From Bogs, Fens, Flats, on *Prosper* fall, and make him
> By ynch-meale a disease: his Spirits heare me,
> And yet I needs must curse.
>
> (II. ii. 1–4)

The slave wants to do what the master has done to him: turn
torturous intent into hideous form, self-serving metaphor into
mass. He wants the island's foul vapours to precipitate and
coagulate into a suffering subject called 'Prosper'. But the 'Bogs,
Fens, Flats', the home of infection, evoke nothing so consummately as they do Caliban.[24] It suggests the pivotal symbiosis, or
rather parasitism, of Caliban and Prospero: inch-meal, they feed
off each other. As Ferdinand says of Prospero, and as we might,
ironically, of Caliban: 'he's composed of harshnesse' (III. i. 9).
So, 'make him By ynch-meale a disease', says the slave, 'his
Spirits heare', and descend to perform just that:

> . . . But they'll nor pinch,
> Fright me with Vrchyn-shewes, pitch me i'th' mire,
> Nor lead me like a fire-brand, in the darke
> Out of my way, vnlesse he bid 'em; but
> For euery trifle, are they set vpon me,
> Sometime like Apes, that moe and chatter at me,
> And after bite me: then like Hedg-hogs, which
> Lye tumbling in my bare-foote way, and mount
> Their pricks at my foot-fall: sometime am I
> All wound with Adders, who with clouen tongues
> Doe hisse me into madnesse.
>
> (II. ii. 4–14)

Caliban is 'made' by the simple physics of the operation:
pinched, he becomes blotchy; frightened, he is made timorous
and drawn; pitched in the mire, he's rendered smelling and
filthy; sent lost through the dark, he becomes confused, aimless,
his intimacy to the land mocked along with all dominium;
bitten, he is scarred and lumpy, bleeding and diminishing; his

[24] Wilson Knight, *The Crown of Life*, 235: Caliban 'is Shakespeare's imagery of
stagnant pools personified'.

feet stuck full with hedgehog-pricks, he must limp, become more afraid to move, further erupting in scars, bruises, swells, and pain, as fear of the ground reinforces his alienation from the land, his sense that all that was known and loved is now lost; woven by adders, he is made short of breath, reptilian, perhaps bone-broken; hissed into sin and 'madness', he discovers the justifying answer to the state's cruelty.

The point about Caliban's tortures is that they are not an isolated sentence. There is no healing back to an indigenous comfort. Even as he speaks he sees another spirit coming, so dives flat to fulfil the promise of 'earth' and its stupidity. Furthermore, Caliban is forever incorporating into his restless cellular structure the bodies of the things that torment him, devils all. Urchins, Apes, hedgehogs, adders: they embody the 'born deuil', here narrating the incessant, never-complete process of this birth into suffering and need. Caliban evades generic taxonomies as much as, at the play's end, he eludes romantic closures; he remains as definitively unfinished and cumulative as history and its verdicts. Caliban, then, is not simply a born beast, ugly because unregenerate; Prospero's allegations of devilish parentage are famously unverifiable, perhaps merely more grist for the cursing mill (I. ii. 321–2; V. i. 272–6). The violence Caliban suffers, and the language he learns, together refute the claims of Miranda and Prospero that he is somehow a neoplatonic invert, 'a borne-Deuill, on whose nature Nurture can never sticke' (IV. i. 188–9). Indeed Prospero at one point apostrophizes both this intimate geneticism between body and mind, and the way the action replays Caliban's development (if that is the right word), his accelerating command of and captivity to the language and logistics of civilization: 'as with age his body ouglier grows, So his minde cankers' (IV. i. 191–2). Prospero's bitterness here proposes his ward as a kind of anthropological mutant, his mind the very image of a slowly ulcerating sore, a creeping, malignant, crab-like cancer which turns the healthy cells of learning and civility into abnormality, division, and decay. In this way Caliban not only subverts, but reverses, the ethical teleology of Prospero's 'project'. But whereas Prospero is mourning the pointlessness of his educative 'pains', one might instead interpret his words as reinforcement of Caliban's own judgement, that the master's education was all too successful. For, just as

Caliban harks back to a lonely halcyon, so does Prospero imply that each step of his slave's maturation—physical and mental—has been one step further away from (a perhaps never-achieved) perfection. This needn't imply any Rousseauesque primitivism—a purity of origin which the play resolutely occludes—but does suggest that Caliban's 'Western' education prepares him, more and more, for emulation, ill-temper, and depravity ('canker'). Caliban may be a referent-leaping 'other' to Eurocentric man, but never exclusively; more presciently, he is the mirror of governing rhetoric and ideology, its image and accuser, likeness and inversion. Caliban can punish this learning, this receptivity, but only through a linguistic violence whose inevitable victim must be himself. Caliban's parent is just such processes of violence; symbiotically, his resistance, his desire to remake himself, can only feed upon and reiterate such a diasporic origin. To make is to return and to fragment: like the cloven tongue, the language of creation is split.

6

Violence and Freedom

'So foule a skie, cleeres not without a storme':[1] an issue ringing in the wind in each of the romances is the place of violence, not only in government, but in dissent, idealism, transformation. Each play enjoys magnetic scenes of great primitive violence, tempting or tempted by a raucous, clamorous, ambiguous comedy. One might think of Imogen's hysterical blazon over Cloten's headless corpse; the Bohemian shepherd's report of a murderous bear and flapdragoning storm; Trinculo's bibulous arithmetic, half-toast, half-prophecy, assessing whether his party's crapulence might cause the state's coterminous totter; and, to a lesser degree, the sudden abduction of Marina by pirates. The significance of these moments is rarely simple. Their political cause or motive is often sublimated into things grotesque, extreme, fantastical, a kind of inversion of the way, in the traditional romance surcease, conflict is sublimated within generic resolution. They both fear and celebrate imminent catastrophe. The frequent resort to noise and chaos at such moments may itself suggest the unspeakableness of the seduction, or the indefinability of the desire. The destruction effected by storm, beast, drink, or sword appears to foretell, rehearse, or even desire the passing of an epoch. Some kind of unknown future beckons; various kinds of ending or displacement have begun. But if romance is a genre of imminence, even of anxious innovation, it is equally, in Shakespeare's hands, the genre of repetition, where genesis is rebirth and where revelation, whether spiritual or rebellious, is most often recapitulation. A vaguely chiliastic sense then mutates into, or contextualizes, the resonance of nostalgia. The challenge for criticism is to acknowledge how such moments—their awfulness, their paranoid comedy, their histrionic sense of beginnings and ends, the wistfulness which hedges their extravagance—are as definitive of Shakespeare's romance as the beautiful abused heroine.

[1] Shakespeare, *King John*, IV. ii. 108.

The pivotal desert scene in *The Winter's Tale* anticipates in miniature what *The Tempest*'s magic island amplifies: 'how the poor soules roared, and the sea mock'd them: and how the poore Gentleman roared, and the Beare mock'd him, both roaring lowder then the sea, or weather' (III. iii. 98–101). The multiple roaring can evoke punishment and reprieve, destruction or opportunity. A certain decadent miasma can be swept away; the awfulness may consume itself; the tumult might simply disappear, like the bear does, an anonymous force of motiveless annihilation, briefly replete. The very casualness and inarticulacy of the violence can lend it the neutral quality of fate, of insentient opportunity. Hence, occasionally, the comically blithe brutality with which the 'sauage clamour' is witnessed: Leonine displays an almost sublime indifference ('let her go') when the pirates swoop down to relieve him of the task of murdering Marina, and is then phlegmatic, indeed expectant, as he prepares to watch them 'please themselves' on the maiden (IV. i. 97–102); having mourned the loss of sheep, ship, and nobleman, the shepherd and his son display a perfect moral opportunism when the storm's gift to them is 'Faiery Gold' ('We are luckie (boy) . . . Let my sheepe go', III. iii. 123–4). As much as anything, terror here is the framework, the permission, for mundane ambition. At the same time, Shakespeare's recourse to wordless, atavistic onomatopoeia evokes violence as both necessity and redemption: destruction permits transformation.

Shakespeare's late romances always retain a sniff of the wilderness; this is so even at their most courtly or mercantile, as Leontes' 'bawdy planet' or Mytilene's piratical brothel might suggest. It is in such a scent, given flesh by the bear, or by the strange island, or by the princess Imogen's dream and then destiny of being thief-stolen, that the romances ensure the constant influence of indecorous desire. Such desire needn't be sphere shattering. Resistance might take the form of criticism, or of a wish that the monarchical prerogative not intrude upon certain important liberties; often the plays seek space for a less fettered agency, and expect government to be neither cloistered nor unaccountable. There are various registers of such an implicit civic contract: *Pericles* appears to advocate, like a nagging but prudent diplomat, the necessity of consultation; Paulina remains within the court but insists upon her caustic counsel.

But what about the case where opposition ceases to be decorous, when it is rude and vulgar either of person or manners? For the claim to possess a legitimating salvational violence may not be the sole province of nature-shaking tyrants such as Prospero and Jupiter.

Perhaps the discourse most casually available for the dramatization—and oftentimes the implicit ridiculing—of rebellious violence was the carnivalesque.[2] As readily identifiable in Coriolanus' rhetoric of disgust as in the euphoric, inverting bacchanalia envisaged by Cade, the vulgar festive body was the indecorous vessel of popular desire. But, equally and paradoxically, festivity has often been understood as the mollifying or manipulative agent of the state. Seasonal feasts always combined solemn worship with grotesque iconoclasm, thanks for labour with extravagant idleness. The engines of obedience purr on throughout their putative derailing: 'high-day' celebration in turn requires normative productivity. James, indeed, encouraged popular customs as a sign of submission to his prerogative and the legitimacy of his proclamatory power.[3] Festivity becomes cathartic, violence expelled for the peace of the machine.[4]

The argument that festivity is basically a 'permissible rupture of hegemony' has been argued particularly as a counter to the somewhat ahistorical utopianism of Bakhtin, which identifies in carnival both a 'site' and a discourse of potentially genuine radicalism.[5] Here one needs to distinguish the symbolics from the achievement of desire. For the popular liberties celebrated by

[2] For detailed historical appraisals of festive rituals see: François Laroque, *Shakespeare's Festive World: Elizabethan Seasonal Entertainment and the Professional Stage*, trans. Janet Lloyd (Cambridge, 1991); Leah S. Marcus, *The Politics of Mirth: Jonson, Herrick, Milton, Marvell and the Defense of Old Holiday Pastimes* (Chicago, 1986); Peter Burke, *Popular Culture in Early Modern Europe* (London, 1978); Michael Bristol, *Carnival and Theater: Plebeian Culture and the Structure of Authority in Renaissance England* (London, 1985).

[3] James's *Basilikon Doron* noted the utility of traditional customs in governing the lower orders: *The Basilicon Doron of King James VI*, vol. i, ed. James Craigie (Edinburgh, 1944). Stuart encouragement of old popular festivities met with opposition from Puritan landowners in parliament. They would associate luxury at court with a model and licence for the intemperate games of the countryside. Marcus, *The Politics of Mirth*, 3–9 ff.

[4] Particularly influential here has been C. L. Barber, *Shakespeare's Festive Comedy* (Princeton, 1959).

[5] M. M. Bakhtin, *Rabelais and His World*, and *The Dialogic Imagination: Four Essays*, ed. Michael Holquist, trans. Caryl Emerson and Michael Holquist (1981; repr. Austin, Tex., 1986).

Bakhtin are not to be measured in suffrage and charters. The bursting of homebound constraints, for instance, is exemplified less in a Dick Whittington pilgrimage to the city than in the defecation and copulation which houses one's true freedom, one's links to the living-and-dying communal body. Bakhtin therefore proposes a populace whose 'utopia'—typified by the liberties and impudence of laughter—is quite ineffective and fantastical if considered in linear or nominal terms.[6] Bakhtin's analysis might be historically imprecise, but it is emotively accurate. The politics of carnival are often intrinsically romantic, the essence of the feast found in nostalgia and fantasy.

But the circumstances of carnival tend to defy facile dichotomies, such as between razing wildness and herd-like submission. The Shrove Tuesday apprentices, with their ritualized attacks upon brothels and at times playhouses, might suggest a suitably cathartic edge to carnival; and indeed, throughout Shakespeare's period popular protest would always find impetus or occasion in festivity, often organized by the apprentices' 'Abbeys of Misrule'. The festive can be a catalyst of struggle, or a source for radicalism's emblems when inversion rituals take on 'reality'. However, other regular London festivals defy assumptions either of subversion or obedience. The Ascension Day feast, with its nosegays, beer, and bread, like the milkmaids and dancing of May Day, suggests rural ties and perhaps recent immigration, whereas Midsummer affirms civic pride, St Bartholomew's a hybridized commercialization.[7] This contextual variousness suggests the need to develop sinuous models of subjectivity and its available language of resistance. Festivity wasn't ineffably scripted by 'the state', though it may often have served the desires of more localized authority, like a particular trade or mayor. Holiday modes might therefore channel the rights of some emerging agency or interest, neither identifiable with, nor really against, a centralized authority. 'Creative disrespect', 'demystification', a force against the 'monological', here come to evoke less a subversive and unanimous crowd

---

[6] *Rabelais and His World*, 123; cf. Keith Thomas, 'The Place of Laughter in Tudor and Stuart England', *TLS* (1977), 77–80, which argues that laughter often served intolerance, conformity, malice.

[7] Peter Burke, 'Popular Culture in Seventeenth-Century London', in Reay, *Popular Culture*, 36–8.

than corporate or subcultural aspirations within a modern polity.[8]

The popular insurgency desired by *Pericles'* fishermen evokes a traditionally 'conservative' grotesque inversion ritual. Using the metaphor of the voracious whale consuming the small fry, they attack the 'rich Misers' who engross and expropriate the common parish. The piscatorial protest invokes a commonplace rhetoric shared with their georgic partners on the land: 'We would purge the land of these Drones That rob the Bee of her Hony' (II. i. 46–7). They take pride in their labour—accounting equally as enemies the enclosing lords and the similarly otiose beggar class—but their fantasy of inverting resistance takes its tropes, predictably, from festivity: 'when I had been in his belly, I would haue kept such a iangling of the Belles, That he should neuer have left, Till he cast Belles, Steeple, Church and Parish vp againe' (II. i. 40–3). They countenance a reparatory vomit, a regurgitation of the parish to its true owners and origin. However, their challenge to hegemony is hardly subversive; Pericles' instinct is cheerfully to patronize their 'prettie morall[s]', so familiar and decorous is their carnivalesque fable (II. i. 35). For they have no intention of forcing the issue: 'if the good King *Simonides* were of my minde', is the fisherman's necessary caveat, and their rebellious nostalgia will wait either upon just such change or upon some other aristocratic chevalier to relate their grievance at court (II. i. 43–4). The scene does not dramatize a dormant or doltish working rank, but the carnivalesque here serves brisk good nature, hierarchical order, and due process. They take pleasure in sharing the 'Flesh for all day [holiday?]' with the refugee (II. i. 81), and call the sea a 'drunken Knaue' when, in answer to their fable, it 'cast[s]' up the dishevelled stranger (II. i. 57–8): the fisherman's metaphor might suggest a casual, tolerant familiarity with just such drunken knavery, but at the same time it connotes things inept and wasteful. There is little sense here that the tropes of carnival will be the ferment of insurrection; instead, they convey restlessness, robust criticism, and an unsleeping popular mind.

The romances' most obvious example of rebellion—the crapulous plot against Prospero—similarly exploits the

---

[8] See Peter Stallybrass and Allon White, *The Politics and Poetics of Transgression* (London, 1986), esp. introd. and ch. 1.

discourse and opportunity of carnival. The music and geography of the scene are familiar, as motives and manners from elsewhere—the plottings of Anthonio and Sebastian, Gonzalo's utopia, Prospero's storm—discover the dramatization which the play elsewhere denies. Furthermore, Stephano's sea-shanty overture directly transplants the ship's crew onto the island ('*The Master, the Swabber, the Boate-swaine & I*', II. ii. 47): the drunks can develop the opening scene's intimations of roaring disrespect, and act out the consequences of the vessel's 'split'. The text therefore implants the drunks' slapstick bravado as magnet and analogy. Importantly, carnivalesque rebellion is given a context which insists that its temptations and lessons are at the very heart of civic endeavour.

Appropriately, therefore, throughout the subsequent licentiousness, a subversive exhilaration is permitted its brief exultation, but repeatedly denied the liberty of unaccountability. Accordingly, Caliban's transferral of service from Prospero to Stephano has invariably been understood as a dishonourable 'horse-pisse' masquerading, briefly and delusively, as cockaigne (IV. i. 199). As so often, the putative repair proceeds upon recapitulation, upon a movement backward in time: Stephano repeats Caliban's indoctrination into language and slavery. Recapitulation, then, confers renewed and still more ignominious capitulation. This appears to confirm Caliban's entrapment within an expropriative ideological process wherein he has no choice but to take on the shape demanded by his possessors. And such bondage is nowhere more insidiously pervasive than in the high jinx of carnival. Hitching up with Caliban, a 'holiday-foole' incarnate (II. ii. 29), the court servants are ushered out of their entrepreneurial guises into an archetypal festive fantasy. The drunks will become lords of an island, where water is wine and the book of law a bottle. Subsequently the play briefly makes carnival, like so much else, pay its promises. So, there is brief euphoria ('high-day, freedome', II. ii. 186–7), a cavalier indifference to propriety ('drinke to me', III. ii. 3), the frisson of collective calamity ('the State totters', III. ii. 6), bad-temper ('A pox o'your bottle, this can Sacke and drinking doo', III. ii. 77–8), recriminations ('Beate him enough', III. ii. 83), until, finally and thankfully, the objective correlative of the stinking-pond, manifesting the wise hindsight of the hangover, festivity's crapulent, mind-sogging deterrent (IV. i. 171–84; 196–211). So, approximately, goes the conventional ticking-off, reading the drunks as a derisive diversion.

However, it might be argued that such determinism is insensitive to the empathies and desires here engaged. For the drunkards express a *joie de vivre* which should neither be ignored nor, once noticed, patronized into oblivion. The mutable quality of audience reception here suggests the politics of these scenes. One digests a play as it proceeds—engaged, bored, reflective—in ways that defy prediction and unanimity. Moments will exist for themselves, have memory beyond the temporal moment. The communication will not find all purpose in an epilogue, or in some surceasing teleological elegance. One's leisured enjoyment and vicarious desire can, coterminously, be fugitive, secretive, mischievous, or brutal.

The simple tale of irrationality foiled, of indecorum rendered serviceable, thus tells only a small part of the drunks' significance. Trinculo's prophecy, for instance, is both a distillation of drunken abdications and a casually wrought magnet of the oddly angled isle: 'Seruant Monster? the folly of this Iland, they say there's but fiue vpon this Isle; we are three of them, if th'other two be brain'd like vs, the State totters' (III. ii. 4–6). Instead of regeneration, festivity invites self-destruction: the booze brains them as they would the 'Sorcerer', shafting their minds like a 'logge' through the skull (III. ii. 86–9). Any solidarity is paradoxical—divided we stand, together we fall. But Trinculo choruses more than carnival's millennial disintegration. His predicate is 'brain'd like vs', invoking any intelligence that correlates to the drunkards', or partakes of the same heady 'Bumbard'. The clown's folly finds analogues in the neighbouring brains on the island: not only the log-bearing bondage of the lovers, or the treasonous nihilism of the criminal aristocrats, but, as the drunkards' orchestration through the bombard (cloud-bottle-book-gun-music) implies, Prospero's own capricious omniscience. Indeed one might go further: the dangerous imminence in Trinculo's tope is aroused by the sense that the homologies orchestrated throughout the play's tottering 'State'—between past and present, Europe and the island, high and low, civilized and savage, master and servants, mage and witch, slave and slave—might all momently be hustled together, stripped into indistinction, only to blow up in hilarious explosion like some apocalyptic head-butt.[9]

But the peculiar intimacy of Trinculo's hypothesis suggests, still further, that the irresponsibility of festivity carries its own political franchise, not dependent only upon parodic analogy. '[T]he state totters', cries Trinculo, his euphoria as careless and anarchic as Guiderius' when, king of the wilderness, he sends Cloten's head flying like a football. In neither case is empathy safe or sensible, but each moment pulsates with the reckless liberties of romance. Shakespeare's use of the genre continually undresses convention, sends it naked or disguised into nativities which, as here, might be at once promising, treacherous, and precarious. Trinculo's prophecy depends upon such exile into beginnings; it is a jester's version of a habitual romance trope, discovering hilarity in the imminence of loss, in historical helplessness. Similarly, the laughter parodies renunciation, Prospero's solemn, diligently organized mission.

The point is partly about the attractiveness of violence, its seductiveness, the frisson of mocking the sturdy balance-sheet of justice: Bohemia's bear effects a similar callous comedy. Such impulses are the tempter's lair of romance, one of the seductions putting such pressure upon temperance and decorum. As Yeats interprets Shakespeare's tragic victims, awesome epitomes of 'civilisations put to the sword': 'Gaiety transfiguring all that dread'.[10] One must, I think, countenance the potency of just such gaiety, apocalypse a joke, failure a kind of satisfaction, in the political sense of these plays; one sees it in Autolicus' casual embrace of accident, and here again in Trinculo's toast. Such fecklessness resists measurement; it is a process, like getting drunk is, which exists for itself, its own wastefulness. But it can be as prophetic, as politically serious, as any succession to nominal government: the politics of carnival, then, subsist less in achievement than in its denial, in the way the process requires effluence and fluidity. Paradoxical as this may seem, it says much about popular participation in politics, and about the elusive empathies which the plays supply. The politics are metadramatic: theatre itself (or indeed the process of reading) is an

---

[9] Compare Drayton, 'Moone-Calfe', 39–46.
[10] 'Lapis Lazuli', *The Collected Poems of W. B. Yeats* (1933; repr., London, 1981), 338.

example of politicized festivity, a site encompassing, in mutual, unappeasable tension, both desire and disappointment. Fictions needn't 'come true', on or off stage, to express meaningful interventions in matters of both state and the soul.

One must give a nuanced reading, then, to the fact that Caliban seems perfectly happy to trade renewed bondage for a razing of recent history's mistakes. There is far more here than a born slave's lolling subservience. For among the sublimest desires which the age could countenance is an appropriation of hindsight, the arrogation of the past and, so it follows, of legitimate heritage. And here one must realize Caliban's craft, his linguistic and logistic subtlety. For Caliban offers Stephano a contract: knowing Prospero's race to love titles and hierarchy, Caliban dangles to the butler the carrot of 'King'; in return, he gets his own past repaired (and recall that it is now Caliban who possesses knowledge, of island and language; who will choose carefully his revelations; and who thereby retains a reservoir of power and resilience, e.g. III. ii. 64–6). So, Caliban's rebellion, his historical revisionism, offers a moment where the place of language, not only as the imperative and seal of authority, but as an instrument of resistance and subjectivity, discovers a symbolic epiphany:

> No *more dams I'le make for fish,*
> Nor *fetch in firing, at requiring,*
> Nor *scrape trenchering, nor wash dish,*
> Ban' ban' Cacalyban
> Has a new Master, get a new Man.
> Freedome, high-day, high-day freedome, freedome
>   high-day, freedome.
>
> (II. i. 180–7)

The duties in Caliban's refrain record his role as symbol of a vast serviceable community, at best georgic, at worst slavish. One might compare a different vision of peace and plenty: Cranmer's prophecy of Elizabeth at the close of *Henry VIII*, evoking a golden age when 'Euery Man shall eate in safety, Vnder his owne Vine what he plants; and sing The merry Songs of Peace to all his Neighbours' (V. iv. 33–5). The praise is for labour without whipstock or alienation. In its familiar evocation of a happy state both past and deferred, *Henry VIII* transforms its reflexive, forward-and-backward prophecy from the speculative into the specular: the Jacobean public are forced to look at themselves, to judge the appropriateness of Cranmer's 'Oracle of comfort'. A similar invitation gives the tension to Caliban's more boisterous 'comfort'. It is a renunciation, from commodity into cockaigne, which could hardly but strike chords with a significant section of a commercial theatre's franchise.

One might compare the tough and tender priorities of *Locrine*'s Strumbo and his cobbling mates:

> We Coblers lead a merie life (Dan, dan, dan, dan)
> Void of all enuie and of strife (Dan diddle dan)
> Our ease is great, our labour small (Dan, dan, dan, dan)
> And yet our gaines be much withall (Dan diddle dan).[11]

This simple air, combining the festive, the pastoral, and the georgic, is violently adumbrated by a captain pressing Strumbo into military service: 'King Nactabell, I crie God Mercy, what haue we to doo with him, or he with us?' (II. ii. 60–2). The call to arms violates an industrious peace which the play, comically but meaningfully, invests with an almost anticipatory nostalgia. That is, the fact of war circles around the cobblers' blithe insulated domesticity. The context already demands a shattering of the moment's sweet self-sufficiencies, so that in the act of witnessing it, as it were, one wishes for its return from the dead. Apart from this the play recounts distant dynastic quarrels and, somewhat more animatedly, the ambivalence of adulterous love. So in some sense it is in this moment, or moments like it, that the play locates its 'romance' heart. The cobblers' ballad gets this romance energy partly from its suggestions of contemporaneity. Thus, while most of the play fights battles of the first millennium, Strumbo and friends could inhabit any Elizabethan village. Their peace and productivity are the popular audiences', given a tinge of romance by the threats which make them wistful and familiar; intimations of England and nationalism will further secure this. But within such associations, and probably unacknowledged, is the relationship of these home-grown moments to generic types or precedents which help make romance the medium of shared dreams: their song is pastoral, because it

[11] *Locrine*, II. ii. 1–8.

sings of the simple man in a peaceful enclave far from the strife and corruption of court; it is georgic, because it measures the hard-working, productive Happy Man, parochial and isolated, unlearned but idyllic; and it is festive, because it is communal, bacchanalian, and inherently dismissive of authority. The cobblers' harmonic refrain—'Dan, dan, dan dan, Dan diddle dan'—is the heartbeat of this merry unanimity. Its very meaninglessness celebrates an independence from obedient utility, its juvenile rhythms being as close as language gets to the simple iteration of the free body's nonchalant sensuousness. It may be no coincidence, then, that it is just such a guildhall chant to which Caliban turns to assert his own rhyming liberty: 'Ban' ban' Cacalyban . . .'. Whether understood as innate and pursuant to the body unrolled into voice, or as the splintered memory of a folk-song which, along with fables of the moon-man and his dog, Miranda had rehearsed in happier times (II. ii. 141–2), Caliban's autistic rhythms might evoke a specific sub-genre of self-mythologizing popular romance.

It is important here to recall the exact moment of the play. Whatever the justice of Caliban's claim to sovereignty, and whatever the emotive pull of his rebarbative wassail, high spirits soon mutate into obsequious, recriminative brutality. Significantly, however, this does not happen yet; it does not happen until Shakespeare has allowed Caliban his moment of basically untarnished celebration. He says nothing more vicious than a curse upon the 'Tyrant' that he serves (II. ii. 162), violent enough but hardly more guilty than an echo. Ariel has not yet entered to shadow optimism with surveillance. There were no set half-time 'intervals' in Shakespeare's time, but it is this moment, more than any, which appeals to modern directors. The reason is simple: the first half ends with a bang and a laugh, with hope and high spirits and a certain complicitous expectation. So, to some extent the scene permits the thrill of sudden release, the intoxication of emancipation before logistics set in.

Furthermore, Caliban's song is one link in an amplified harmonic chain. Resigning thus from service, Caliban offers antic anticipation of Prospero's resolve to 'abiure' his art and set free his myriad 'demy-Puppets' (V. i. 33–57). There may be a grand kind of sadness in Prospero's renunciation, but this hardly quashes the dignity of the freedom thereby given his servants, or its facilitation of that for which Caliban's song clamours. Caliban twice claims a frustrated political alliance with Prospero's 'rabble': 'they all do hate him As rootedly as I', he claims, while earlier asserting that they would never torture him if the mage did not 'bid' them to do so (II. ii. 4–7; III. ii. 91–3); and indeed, Ariel's example may suggest a mutinousness tamed only by Prospero's books. Caliban's claims of solidarity, unrefuted as they are, reinforce the experiential centrality of his slavery. His song of freedom may garner a further communal blessing through identity with the more decorous, if no less utopian, aestheticism of Ariel's song ('Merrily, merrily, shall I liue now, Vnder the blossom that hangs on the Bow', V. i. 88–94). And again, Caliban's anthemic celebration evokes Miranda's own self-castigation, likewise reversed into admiration by an audience: 'but I prattle Something too wildely, and my Fathers precepts I therein do forget' (III. i. 57–9). The recurrent appeal of such vitalizing, even bacchanalian defiance challenges any latent generic authoritarianism.

Furthermore, Caliban is not alone in his slavery: others might empathize with his mutinous brooding. Ferdinand, too, is forced by Prospero to lug logs around, humiliated into performing a dirty and arduous task in which there is no 'profit' or justifying cause but the ownership and power of another. As with Caliban, it is desire for Miranda which causes the punishment; of course here it is prelude rather than postscript, but still there seems an obscure link to Caliban in terms of Prospero's wish to enforce a penitence—here anticipatory—which might cleanse the longing of all salaciousness. Ferdinand, like Caliban, rejects any such ascetic morality: the two lustful males remain joined in faithfulness to a belief in free agency, and to a desire equally political as sexual. Ferdinand sees his 'wodden slauerie' as akin to having the 'flesh-flie blow my mouth' (III. i. 63), meaning to have an insect deposit its eggs in his dead flesh, or more particularly his dead 'mouth'. In his simile he rather becomes Caliban, a lump of flesh reproducing bacterial mutations out of itself; that the 'flesh flie' is also a pun on the penis reinforces how the prince is forced to accommodate Caliban's opprobrious symbolics, muddying neoplatonic distillations at the same time as, ostensibly, the scene shows beautiful prince and princess assert their ineffable connectedness. Ferdinand's loathsome trope posits his body and voice being taken over by some foreign power, which then arrogates to itself the privilege of self-reproduction out of the flesh of the subjected: like Caliban's life, it encapsulates both ideology in process and the endemic, silenced, state of the masses. That which the victimized 'subject' understands to be discrete and individual is taken hostage by a multitude—here of flesh-flies—who constitute a kind of physical correlative to his moral, political, vocational servitude. The prince's physical unease makes him dream, amid disgust, of escape back into beauty: again, just like Caliban. Ferdinand's flesh-flown mouth invertingly rationalizes, or at least understands, the rebellious violence of the oppressed.

Up to this point, Caliban's kinetics have been those of forced labour, slothful and grudging. His new language, by contrast, is the intoxicant of choice. He longs to share the land once more, as he did before, but he wants neither to be tricked into revelation nor bullied into discoveries. He vows to 'show thee a Iayes nest, and instruct thee how to snare the nimble Marmazet: I'le bring thee to clustring Philbirts, and sometimes I'le get thee young Scamels from the Rocke: Wilt thou goe with me?' (II. ii. 169–72). His movements would be as light and fleet as Ariel's, a darting facility which, momentarily, evokes a magical conflation of the servants. Fletcher's *The Faithfull Shepheardesse* has a similar moment when the Satyr longs to serve Corin, the virtuous maiden. Fletcher's eager servant seems to poise the topoi of Ariel and Caliban: 'Shall I stray, In the middle Ayre and staye, The sayling Racke or nimbly take Hold by the Moone, and gently make Suite to the pale Queene of the night, For a Beame to give thee light? Shall I diue into the Sea, And bring the corall, making way, Through the rising waves that fall In Snowy fleece?'[12] This forms part of Fletcher's epilogue: the satyr epitomizes a kind of consummating, reverential service. Shakespeare's similar moment, by contrast, is a persuasion to insurrection. The contrast is a telling indication of the way *The Tempest* lends to Caliban's rebellion so many of the tropes and gestures of humanity and legitimacy. A buoyant linguistic tactility, then, helps explain the moment's complicitous magnetism, as we half share, half amusingly patronize, his enthusiasms. For

---

[12] John Fletcher, *The Faithfull Shepheardesse: A Critical Edition*, ed. Florence Ada Kirk (New York, 1980), Epilogue, 242–51.

above all he is like a child, but one with his own domain. Caliban wants to invite an 'adult' to share in his joy: but the sense is that he is off, regardless, to play. The closing question ('Wilt thou goe with me?') might even suggest Caliban as the master; he is initiating things, choosing his moments of exertion and their particular object ('sometimes I'le . . .'). He glories in a new master, but his servitude, however disgusting or congenital it might seem, would, if it could, exist alongside a noble and generous consensual humanity. Indeed there is now in his voice an arresting sense of novelty, as if, having absorbed Prospero's philological education, Caliban now begins his own project of reappropriative naming. The notorious power of Caliban's secret 'Scamels' to elude European or American referent has been used by Stephen Greenblatt to affirm the independence and integrity, the 'opacity', of Caliban's construction of reality.[13] These strange things, clustering on Caliban's own private 'rock', out of mind's eye and beyond proof, are a chimerical partner to the 'one thing [Sycorax] did' which stands in the place of Caliban's full parentage. Together they suggest the defining desire for personal 'origin' and 'end', each symbiotically 'under erasure', each powerfully necessary in the search for dignity and identity.

It is therefore important to take care in assessing the particular service into which Caliban leaps. 'These be fine things, and if they be not sprights: that's a braue God, and beares Celestiall liquor: I will kneele to him' (II. ii. 117–19). It is not so much Stephano as his liquor which, with the force of revelation, arrests Caliban. The butler is either a priest administering the blasphemous sacrament or, as Caliban's grandiloquent naming permits, a millenarian wonder, floating on his butt in a burlesque second coming: 'Ha'st thou not dropt from heauen?': 'Out o'th Moone I doe assure thee. I was the Man ith' Moone, when time was' (II. ii. 137–9). Stephano's characterization as the man in the moon both reinforces the moment's festive roots and insinuates how such popular dreams, the froth and bubble of marginalized fantasy, can possess a persuasive and even affecting potency. The Man in the Moon was (then as now) the name of at least three alehouses in

---

[13] *Learning to Curse: Essays in Early Modern Culture* (New York, 1990), 31.

London, one of which was notorious as the home of the city's most devoted drinkers. Stephano becomes the grand burlesque initiator, as if to a fraternity, a low-life alternative to the exclusive halls of power.[14] But, for Caliban, the moon's evocation recalls his education by Miranda and, therefore, confirms his sense that some kind of original, originating power has descended to lend him aid: 'My Mistris shew'd me thee, and thy Dog, and thy Bush' (II. ii. 134–5). Stephano's fairy-tale phrase, 'when time was', thus signals Caliban's return to his childhood, to the namings of Prospero and Miranda when once they 'made much' of the moon-calf. In turn, the butler both adds to and reprises Caliban's engenderment. The quality of this particular 'Man ith' Moone', therefore, not only recalls but can reappraise the formative principles behind both authority and subjectivity; throughout the play the moon is a figure, possessed by Anthonio, Sycorax, Prospero, of political power. And, just as in his first scene, Caliban's memory of happier times veers between tenderness and vengeance. He longs to both reclaim what was lost and punish those who—at once heroes and villains of his nostalgia—robbed him. Again, then, nostalgia flows into rebellion.

The connection between Caliban's nostalgia and his rebelliousness is epitomized, and in a sense founded, in the way his insurrection picks up the promise of his mesmeric dreams. For dream too can be a kind of uprising, time-travelling and transformatory. Caliban's famous account of his 'long sleepe' travels through tenses in a fashion intimately suggestive of his dream-scape's wistful itinerance, a vertiginous movement through forgetfulness, futurism, and then a violent lurching for what is lost. As sensuous as it is cerebral—like his freedom

---

[14] In *The Man in the Moon, Discovering a World of Knavery under the Sun* (1663; repr. Guernsey, 1977), a series of fantastical tales from the Antipodes, Greenland, Faryland, etc., including a sequence involving a diplomatic war fought out through an invented language, the man in the moon is both the all-seeing storyteller—'who hath been so long Absent, that you may well think him lost in some inchanted Island'—and, it seems, a pimp-pandar at the 'Moon' pub-cum-brothel. The man in the moon also suggested an overseeing prognosticative faculty, bringing outlandish news or predicting fates with a sage relish. In *The Man in the Moone, or, The English Fortune Teller* (London, 1609), the man, called 'Fido', offers a series of moralistic, gruesomely unforgiving pictures of various sinners' fates. See J. O. Halliwell, ed. *Early English Poetry, Ballads and Popular Literature of the Middle Ages* (London, 1851), vol. xxix.

song—Caliban's unquiet sleep offers vaporous rehearsal for his rebellion:

> Sometimes a thousand twangling Instruments
> Will hum about mine eares; and sometime voices,
> That if I then had wak'd after long sleepe,
> Will make me sleepe againe, and then in dreaming,
> The clouds methought would open, and shew riches
> Ready to drop vpon me; that when I wak'd
> I cri'de to dreame againe.
>
> (III. ii. 135–41)

Stephano picks up the dreams' political intimations, identifying thoughts of a 'braue kingdome' in the moon-calf's phantoms (III. ii. 142–3); and, as the monster notes with an Oedipal relish, it is the tyrant's custom, too, in the afternoon to sleep (III. ii. 85–6). The enthralment of dream-clouds, then, typifies the island's permissions regarding subjectivity and power. The 'subiect' is seduced by a beauty which seems to be his alone, a form of flattering solicitude or homage to imminent and deserved self-metamorphosis. But seen from the perspective of social engineering, the dream-text is hypnosis, the script the master's. The music is the enslaving means of production, a mollifying opiate, an interpellation into obedience dressed up as choice. And yet, the waker's cry is not merely for slothful consolation, or forgetful abandon; subversion is contained, certainly, but not its attractiveness. Prospero's 'subiect' stays coiled in his private world, forswearing allegiance to anything but tardy and chimerical opportunity. And, as the humming and bombards suggest, the central storm scene shows the agency of such catalytic clouds passing beyond Prospero's customary sanctions. Suddenly the cloud—the bombard transmogrified into a bottle—does indeed seem to 'drop' riches upon Caliban. He need no longer 'cry' to dream again, but can instead 'howl' his song of satisfaction. The same verb, 'drop', makes Stephano the agent of Caliban's seditious fantasy. In other words, his service isn't as contemptible—indeed isn't as serviceable—as may first appear. Stephano appears to Caliban as if his own creation, his own rival to Prospero's ability to conjure spirits up out of fantastical will: Caliban has rubbed his lamp and at last a genie has appeared. 'O braue Monster; lead the way', say the scenes' parting words (II. ii. 188). The tone is amused, but still it can imply that Caliban has grabbed for himself the 'braue' laurel of his, like Miranda's, 'new world' (V. i. 183). His 'God', then, is the 'riches' of escape, of freedom. Its status as festive licence is reinforced by this source in dream; but by the same token the crabby, fleeting, artificial fabrications of alcohol are thereby given their own dignifying contextualization.

Caliban worships a desire which, in its defiance of 'bestial' determinism, can define what it is to be a subjective individual agent. *'Has a new Master, get a new Man'*: he resolves to 'make' himself anew, become a 'Man' and not a monster, defying rather than succumbing to the various exploitative 'makings' of Prospero, Trinculo, and Stephano. He will resign into a different service, his head held high. 'Get a new man', turn a new leaf: Caliban's transformation can suggest a communal, utopian evangelism. One might consider the play's previous song, that of Stephano as he entered:

> *The Master, the Swabber, the Boate-swaine & I;*
> *The Gunner, and his Mate*
> *Lou'd Mall, Meg, and Marrian, and Margerie,*
> *But none of us car'd for Kate*
> *For she had a tongue with a tang,*
> *Would cry to a sailor goe hang.*

(II. ii. 47–52)

The 'Master' and his men are here virtually indistinguishable, co-operative members on ship or land, collected within the category of 'sailor'. Similarly, the ship which suffers the opening tempest is controlled nominally by the 'Master' but in fact by the 'labour' of his 'men', with effective verbal authority conferred upon the boatswain in cantankerous opposition to the nobles. The master's invisible whistle, in turn, competes against Prospero's invisible roar. Authority is competitive rather than singular. Like Caliban's gods, to serve one might be in the hope of trumping another, or at least of performing one's own purpose—taking in the top-sail, digging for pignuts—with coherence and exuberance. Caliban's embrace of the new 'Master', then, might be yet another way in which his rebellion reprises the inclusive vigours and devotions of elsewhere in the play. He wants to get on the ship, find joy and worth despite or in confutation of the tyrant's splitting roar. If this sounds vaguely Whitmanesque, then that might be a measure of the scene's strangely refractive foretelling of the Americas; a measure of this is the way certain Caribbean poets and dance-masters have recognized and adopted Caliban's fracturing rhythms as tribal and independent, the throb and gyre of an indigenous song more in tune with the island body, with its sense of place and duty, than colonial cadences ever could be.

Caliban's 'high-day' breaks down the usurper's pioneering, emasculating language, cracking its oppressive unity and inscrutability: 'Ban' ban' Cacalyban Has a new Master, get a new Man'. His own name, bestowed by his master, is turned into a dissevering rhyme, like a thumping drum of insurrection: 'Ban' ban'', he bangs, reiterating a new kind of fundamentalist resistance. Like the 'rore' which it echoes and splits, he harnesses violence to an onomatopoeia whose faithfulness to the urgings of the body momentarily fractures conventional semantics. Furthermore, Caliban's implicit return to an anal and genital register ('caca') suggests how he is dredging up an imagined preternaturalism, concomitant with a refusal of the master's voice. His language would cherish a purer and more perfect subjectivity, recalled from deep within his being or his memory. One might recall here Kristeva's 'semiotic' language, a constant kinetic impulsion of linguistic heterogeneity, resistant to the organizing hegemony of what she calls the 'symbolic' master language. Her 'semiotic' is a realm of 'contradictions, meaninglessness, disruption, silences and absences', a kind of pressured, combustible communication which is the individual's most intimate channel to that which is felt to be indigenous or original.[15] Its putative source is what Kristeva calls, after Plato, the chora or enclosed space or womb, that fiction of the pre-symbolic child. Endless 'pulsions', anal and oral, constitute this chora, perceivable only as disruptive pressure upon or within the parent's language. Kristeva leaves open this space as one for the individual subject-in-process to attempt to express or effect their world.[16] One can recall here how Ariel's tree, littering Caliban in

---

[15] Toril Moi, ed., *The Kristeva Reader* (Oxford, 1986), 13.

[16] Julia Kristeva, *Revolution and Poetic Language*, trans. Margaret Waller (New York, 1984), 142–50 et al. Kristeva's work here proffers a less deterministic view of the subject than Lacan's.

its wake, works as a prison-cum-womb (I. ii. 274–93): the spirit emerges from his captivity, first into new syllables of service and eventually into a 'high-day, freedome' no less exuberant than Cacalyban's. Caliban's howl, too, finds source in 'the barke of a Tree' (II. ii. 123–4). As has been seen, Caliban's nostalgias are never simply for some pacific maternity, his rebellions never simply against paternal authority. But his cackle of freedom does indeed split the father's speech as if in exultant return to an originality before nominality.

Caliban is experimenting with the sudden breezy liberty to play with what he has been taught. Instead of the every-hour tutorials, curiosity oppressed by pedagogic imperatives, he can now twist and turn his name inside and out, dilate, abbreviate, and deride, both accepting and then reorientating the heritage of language. For rather than a wholesale destruction of the conquering language, Caliban's lexicon-splitting syllables propose a chopping and chiselling, an accenting and bias, which might adapt the conqueror's speech more felicitously to a retrieved and revamped dominium. For a joyful moment he is detached enough from his body, and from the name that is controlled along with it, to play with this name as if with building-blocks or a bauble. Partly this indicates the familiar dislocation of drunkenness; more importantly, it intimates a realm of utopian capture which, a happy dagger, the alcohol leaves hovering before his eyes. He attains a benign possession of that wizardry which customarily, and much more violently, arrests and compresses, fractures and mocks, his flesh and its enigmatically generic title.

However, nowhere on the island can language escape doubleness, and Caliban's corroboree remains ambivalent: at once a chant of birth, freedom, war, and death; as much a paean to his own lucky escape as a trumpet call to any fellow oppressed. The final line's caesura poises something of this see-sawing historicity: '*Has a new Master, get a new Man*'. Half prepared grandly to enter the future, half drawn back into a recriminative derision of his past, Caliban dares the old 'tyrant' to find new dupes of his humanizing blandishments. His farewell to Prospero is scornful but oddly knowing: high art will demand other slaves ('*get a new Man*'). Caliban's grim, wry, bitter conviction of civility's missionary remorselessness suggests a deep pessimism about how securely the 'high-day' might ever be shared. And furthermore, Caliban's body, even in celebration, remains racked by the antinomies of his curse. His song twice 'ban[s]' himself, his own name: but the verb is ambiguous. The first 'ban' can be a proclamation of Caliban's power, a summons to arms against his master; the second can be its own mutiny, like his 'ynch-meale' fantasy turning into an imprecation against himself, as if accusing his own, rather than Prospero's, outlawry. Similarly, in prefixing his name with the extra 'Ca', Caliban 'compounds' his own entwinement and representation in that which he curses, his manipulation by a master-text. For his innovation evokes the vast range of bad or evil compounds associable with the Greek 'Caco'.[17] Most obviously, he is made a curse of excrement: 'Caca' equals faeces and 'ban' is a public announcement, often a malediction. A whole baggage of ill-humours, diseases, and foul sounds are marshalled to the banner of his howling rebellion. The implicit opprobrium seems based in Caliban's twin indecorousness: physically putrid and linguistically vituperous, he remains the mutating disease in body, while his voice speaks 'cacology', or evil report.[18] History remains as palinodal and antinomic as the language, cacology or eulogy, that figures it.

Caliban cannot channel his subjectivity into freedoms independent of the structures which enslave him. His imperfect resistance therefore suggests a manner of 'ideology' in process. Nevertheless, one must adopt a more supple and diachronic understanding of ideology than for instance Althusser's, wherein ideology reproduces and serves the relations of production, 'interpellating' subjects, with a minimum of coercion, into

---

[17] John Florio, *Queen Anna's New World of Words* (1611; repr. Menston, 1968), 72–3, lists many Italian words, invariably rude or violent, with the 'caca' or 'cacc' prefix. For example: 'caccima' = bitch with whelps; 'cacchinare' = to laugh unmeasurably loud; 'cacchera' = a hen cackle; 'cacciuolare' = to thump or bang; 'cacalegge' = scorner of the law; 'cacafuetta' = a shitten-hasty fellow; 'cacaria' = shitten tricks, trifles, toies; 'cacciafrusto' = sting; 'cacafuoco' = hot violent fellow; 'cacafotto' = a pisse-kitching, a drisled-asle, a durty flurt, a shitten slut. Often the 'caca' seems to work like pouring hot faeces over whatever concept is at issue: in this sense it works as an adjective of wasteful carnival, quite without Rabelaisian optimism.

[18] George Puttenham, *The Arte of English Poesie*, ed. G. D. Willcock and A. Walker (Cambridge, 1936), 260, notes the Greek 'cacemphaton, we call it the vnshamefast or figure of foule speech'.

positions as worker, owner, and so on, rendering them the grateful vessels of hegemony.[19] When Caliban recounts the effect of the humming music, and the listless dreams of sovereignty with which they enthral him, he recounts with a perfect, poignant unconsciousness the mix of charm and awe which achieves obedience. Nevertheless, he is never a piece of unreflective social machinery. While the play acknowledges the psychology of obedience, it doesn't rest with it. Caliban as subject is a rebel, his condition one of 'moodie' rebuff.[20] His dreams seem less to seduce him into acceptance and gratitude than to render the gap between desire and achievement more vexing. Consequently, his example suggests how one should modify deterministic views of ideology, or of power as some immanent Foucauldian network of subjection and paralysis. The desire for change and apprehension of difference work within cultural reproduction, making its physics more unstable, fissiparous, and hopeful than a mass brand from above might countenance. Caliban can't escape ideology, indeed in a sense does only reproduce it; but still he does not do so in ways that the 'state apparatus' would wish to implant.

In many ways, then, Caliban is Shakespeare's ultimate mutating metaphor, a cerebral, instinctual, emotional, and visceral symbol for both his old-and-new genre and for man-in-history. The strange islander is, simply enough, the west writ strange, his struggles those which have been and shall be. And nowhere is this archetypal historicity more arresting than in his scrap (ennobling quest? humiliating lurch?) for freedom:

> Flout 'em, and cout 'em: and skowt 'em, and flout 'em,
> Thought is free.

(III. ii. 119–21)

These are the words of the song which Stephano has taught to Caliban, and which Caliban, at that moment of intense 'pleasure' when he believes his *coup d'état* imminent, asks his

[19] 'Ideology and Ideological State Apparatuses (Notes toward an Investigation)', *Lenin and Philosophy and Other Essays* (New York, 1971), 127–86.

[20] Compare Greenblatt, 'Martial Law in the Land of Cockaigne', in *Shakespearean Negotiations*, 137–8 ff., who argues that Prospero epitomizes a government policy of arousing 'salutary anxiety . . . [which] blocks *secret* wrath and inward grudging . . . potential anger gives way to obedience, loyalty, and admiration'.

confederates to sing. The song works, then, not merely as con-
tinuation of Caliban's mutinous soundtrack. It is the constitu-
tive, indeed the constitutional, language of Caliban's brave new
world, as novel and as revelatory as the 'quicke Freshes' of his
geographic repossession (III. ii. 66). For Stephano's 'catch' of
freedom partly reprises, partly replaces, and partly supplements
the language which Caliban first learnt from Prospero.
Prospero's language, with its introductions to authority, hierarchy, and service ('how to name the bigger Light, and how the
lesse'), is the language through which Caliban pursues his plot.
What is most remarkable about his persuasions to assassination
is the sheer knowingness of his rhetoric: he moves from the
quick mastery of political taxonomy ('I am subiect to a Tirant',
III. ii. 40), to arguments of dominium versus illegitimacy ('by
Sorcery he got this Isle', III. ii. 51), to an unctuous imitative
courtliness, an expedient parody of the primrose path to violence and thence obedience ('I do beseech thy Greatnesse giue
him blowes', III. ii. 63). At the same time, Caliban retains access
to his sense of the new, his ingenuous delight in innovation and
discovery; with marvellous economy, Shakespeare both recapitulates and continues the 'natural's' precocious learning curve.
As always, Caliban is much in one, and his 'hobgoblin' language
aptly conveys a whole sequence of waiting, competing futures.
In the midst of his plot, then, Caliban is a kind of child, a
practised malcontent, a court-schemer to rival a Cecil and,
almost, a tyrant in wait. At times his rhetoric almost flies off the
handle, his eagerness bloating into atavism. His impatience with
his confrères, too, suggests a type of contempt, a barely suppressed indignation at their fecklessness; consider the remarkable balancing act, impudence, impatience, and mastery barely
reined in by efficacious decorums, of Caliban's 'Pre-thee (my
King) be quiet' (IV. i. 215). Somehow, Caliban's greater pride
and dignity is concomitant not only to his intelligence and his
relative linguistic control, but to an almost antinomian indul-
gence toward the violence necessary for his ends. In all of this,
the Oedipal student suggests his master, the torturing moralist,
Prospero.

    In this way, Shakespeare's representation of rebellion could
not be more unillusioned, anticipating the terror and banality of
any 'new' regime, while at the same time evoking the genuine

thrill and idealism of a glimpsed revolution into justice. This ambivalence is perfectly captured in Caliban's newly learned song. It appears to be a simple proverbial catch, appropriate to their brief high-day beyond authority's surveillance. Annabel Patterson has noted how the proverb took its place in a tradition of popular resistance: there are parts of the mind free from coercion or censorship, from the conformities and obedience which, as Stephano as much as Caliban is aware, necessity provokes.[21] At the same time, the proverb was often used to indicate the harmless, impotent, almost solipsistic quality of thought: think what you like, as wild or woolly as you like, but still it will not change a thing. 'Thought is free' only in so far as it is translatable into neither words nor action. However, it is unclear whether the lyrics to the song defy or endorse any such pessimism. To flout, cout, and scout basically means to deride, mock, or insult, a jeering disdain ('flout') which might find effect in a spying contempt for liberty or opposition ('scout'). So, these somewhat self-proud verbs—like Caliban's earlier 'ban, ban' at once exhilarating and vituperative, libertarian and intolerant— are as appropriate for a mischievous subject as a vindictive monarch. The phrase, 'Thought is free', therefore, is poised tantalizingly between garrulous provocation and its silent defiance; the flouting and scouting might equally be an expression of 'free thought' as the oppressive tactics which cause the harassed subject to take refuge in such 'free thought'. The confederates, then, inhabit both sides of an equation which posits both their present and, should the plot succeed, their destiny: they sing of the sweet surreptitious compensations of an unenfranchised but still hopeful and critical subject; they fight for freedom against a mocking panoptical violence which, given the chance, they in turn will replicate.

This brief catch thereby encapsulates much of romance's paradoxical politics. In a sense the song, like theatre, is self-sufficient, its impulses satisfied in the shared act of its singing. Such compensatory art suggests a utopian form of escapism, a no-place of perfect, or perfected, desire. And yet the song's projections are equally dystopian, a charter of failure or despotism, and its rhythms those of replicatory violence. And

---

[21] *Shakespeare and the Popular Voice*, ch. 7.

furthermore, like so much of the play's 'wild whist', the song's putative escapism rehearses both imminent praxis and, foreseeably, in the world predicted by the play, all kinds of rebellious intoxications. This song, then, takes its place amid the rest of the island's dissonant, argumentative, historically over-determined music. And, again, the uncertainty regarding politi-cal agency, the sense that a maelstrom of longing and frustration is at work in the anti-melodic noise, is focused in an ambiguity about source. Stephano has taught Caliban the song, but it is the monster's 'pleasure', his particular 'desert island disc'. However, perhaps under the influence of drink, perhaps as a sign of inescapable dissonance, the drunks get the tune wrong. As if on cue, the invisible Ariel supplies the missing tune with tabor and pipe. The most obvious interpretation is that the spirit, an agent of his master, flouts and scouts the would-be scouters and flouters. That is, Ariel proves that, at the very most, the rebels have their 'thought' while all else belongs to the powerful: the moment represents a perfect 'recuperation' of subversion. Dis-ruptive agency belongs, truly, to 'the picture of No-body' (III. ii. 124–5). However, whilst Ariel's music leads them to the foul-stinking pond and to the 'infinite loss' of their bottle, it does not lead them, and least of all Caliban, to a renunciation of their plans. Indeed, one might understand Ariel the tabourer as the rebels' martial drummer, playing the 'ban, ban' of their freedom march as they 'advanc'd' toward the sleeping tyrant. In other words the song retains its sensory rebelliousness: Ariel plays on a 'pipe' which might be the flute of the rebels' 'flout'; like 'vnback't colts' they act out their 'cout' (IV. i. 176). Together, however vainly, they fulfil the song's invigorating verbs.

And what of Ariel's role? The spirit, aching for freedom, serves the master. Yet, one might ask, how does Ariel know the tune of the freedom song? The spirit is in a way as coiled as Caliban, a spring waiting for release. Ariel knows the easiest way to the self-concordant 'air' is through a few hours more of service. But whereas the play mainly shows the spirit as 'corre-spondent' to Prospero's syllables, their very first scene shows just how much desire simmers in Ariel beyond the 'liberator's' possession. 'Thought is free' is Ariel's song, too, and in a sense the very slogan of the spirit's being, so abstract, so out of the moment, so imminent in deferred promise. The thought that 'thought is free' must energize Ariel's slavery: as the hope to which to clutch, payment for pains, compensation, perhaps, for semi-fraternal treacheries.[22] For in the spirit, too, Shakespeare's politics are epitomically romantic: fired by dreams, unillusioned about methods, wary, critical, wise-eyed about absolutist whimsy; but hopeful that, somehow in some rainbow-scarfed end, freedom might be more than a furtively cherished 'thought'.

---

[22] That a strained brotherhood between Caliban and Ariel is at the very source of Shakespeare's conception might be suggested by his namings: Caliban and Ariel rhyme with, contain, and amplify Cain and Abel.

7
Women and Romance

WHAT is the place of women in Shakespeare's revamping of romance? The political dialogues that this book has been identifying may suggest qualities that some feminist thinking has identified as prototypically 'feminine'. The dilated centre, the fluid body, varieties of 'other'; diffuse and multi-centred desire;[1] the sea as a mothering source; narratives of gap and absence; a body politic not determined solely by the phallic head; a dialogical structure whose puns and connections stress varieties of both sexual and political unconscious; and a teleology which complicates the simple supremacy of lawful violence:[2] all such things might connote a feminized textuality and politics.[3] However, one need not identify 'female' qualities only in essentializing, universal metaphors.[4] Many of the battles

[1] Rejecting phallocentrism, Luce Irigaray writes: 'But *woman has sex organs more or less everywhere.*', *This Sex Which Is Not One*, trans. Catherine Porter, with Carolyn Burke (Ithaca, NY, 1985), 28. See Gayle Greene and Coppélia Kahn, eds., *Making a Difference: Feminist Literary Criticism* (1985; repr. London, 1988), 84.

[2] Alice Jardine, *Gynesis: Configurations of Woman and Modernity* (Ithaca, NY, 1985), 25–7, 34, analyses how male theorists, like Derrida and Lyotard, have displaced gender onto a textual figure of femininity, a space coded as feminine or maternal which can figure and confront the breakdown of 'phallogocentric' master discourses of various kinds. This metaphorization of woman is partly, then, a male appropriation of feminine voice.

[3] Helene Cixous and Catherine Clément, *The Newly Born Woman*, trans. Betsy Wing (Manchester, 1986) depicts woman in terms of elastic ability to accommodate otherness of various sorts. The liminal woman—sorceress or witch—is the site of what is repressed in culture, while the hysteric is archetypally double-tongued, a quintessential female duplicity. See Elizabeth D. Harvey, *Ventriloquized Voices: Feminist Theory and English Renaissance Texts* (London, 1992), 54 ff. In *The Weyward Sisters: Shakespeare and Feminist Politics* (Oxford, 1994), Dympna C. Callaghan, Lorraine Helms, and Jyotsna Singh collaboratively explore the possibilities for feminist criticism of a kind of discursive 'bricolage', incorporating Marxist dialectical materialism, humanist historicism, and psychoanalysis.

[4] For criticism of essentializing notions of woman's voice and character, as well as of ahistorical conflations of misogyny with established 'patriarchy', see Diane Purkiss, 'Material Girls: The Seventeenth-Century Woman Debate', in Clare Brant and Diane Purkiss, eds., *Women, Texts and Histories 1575–1760* (London, 1992), 69–101; cf. the Jungian-style feminine archetypes in Linda Bamber's *Comic Women, Tragic Men: A Study of Gender and Genre in Shakespeare* (Stanford, Calif., 1982).

identified as at the hub of feminist aspiration are played out, for example, through the biographies of Prospero's two slaves. Caliban's ambivalent entrance into the namings of his master might suggest the dilemma of female subjectivity, whose only medium for justice, dignity or, indeed, malice, is the language of pre-emptive 'patriarchy'. The political marginalization even of noble women will at times make them as-if 'natural' symbols of the struggling subject.[5]

Furthermore, gender in these plays is always prone to be manipulated by symbolism and analogy beyond biological determinants: one might consider certain of *The Tempest*'s pregnant vessels—Gonzalo's 'unstanched wench' (I. i. 47–8), Ariel's cloven pine (I. ii. 277)—so as to see how multiple figurations of the state and the subject proceed from and return to a kind of battered but resourceful femininity. Or again, the creative asexuality of Ariel: s/he is Prospero's slave, a role customarily associated with the masculine. But Ariel's is a kind of linguistic slavery, a correspondence which not only withholds consent but generates meaning beyond the patriarchal command: Patricia Parker has noted how the Renaissance adage that 'women are words, men deeds' stands behind the 'male anxiety about the feminisation of the verbal body'.[6] As Prospero's 'language', then, Ariel's slavery has a feminine labileness. Playing sea nymphs, harpies, and Ceres as much as tabor and pipe, Ariel's elusive, libertarian servitude straddles the sexes, eluding definitive gender. Similarly Caliban, who from one perspective is a kind of phallic insult, seems profoundly inhabited and impelled by feminine energies: his nostalgia for the maternal; his identity with the lunar; his fluidity; a 'fish'-like primordialism which evokes the womb or pudendum as much as it might the phallus; and, adapting Kristeva's terms, his anti-'symbolic' embrace of the disruptive 'semiotics' of a feminized 'chora'. Gender is metaphoric as much as 'real', the genre itself potentially hermaphroditic.

---

[5] Burke, *Popular Culture in Early Modern Europe*, 28, argues that one might see 'noblewomen as mediators between the group to which they belonged socially, the elite, and the group to which they belonged culturally, the non-elite'. Fictional heroines usually choose their partners, a rare privilege within social elites but normal lower down the scale. See Barbara B. Diefendorf, 'Family Culture, Renaissance Culture', *RQ* (1987), 661–81.

[6] *Literary Fat Ladies: Rhetoric, Gender, Property* (New York, 1987), esp. ch. 5.

If gender in these plays is thus split—atomized, mutable, diffused—then it suggests that the 'traditional' male-gendered understanding of pastoral romance requires qualification. For whereas each story's nominal teleology is patriarchal, emotional investment and often narrative organization are, almost as unremittingly, feminized. A foolish or venal male hegemony is altered and humanized by the incorporation, as a persuasive instrument of power and decision-making, of a 'feminine principle' based not only in the faithfulness of chastity but the eloquence of the female tongue. For instance, Paulina in *The Winter's Tale* is mocked early on as a scold, but the cheap laughs are turned quickly upon their purveyors as the matriarch's verbal defiance is harnessed into thrilling protest against Leontes' tyranny. Paulina has no particular title, no nominal sovereignty. But when the scene shifts back to Sicilia she is shown contesting with various male counsellors for the determining power behind Leontes' throne. She appears to have manœuvred herself into a position where half the court, Leontes included, is petrified of stepping on her toes. It is to her 'councell'—the word carries a specifically political connotation—that Leontes has been taught to accede: 'Good *Paulina*, Who hast the memorie of *Hermione* I know in honor: O, that euer I Had squar'd me to thy councell' (V. i. 49–52). The king is responding here to Paulina's characteristically fierce rebuttal of 'those Would have him wed againe' (V. i. 23–4). Remarkably, in pursuing this line Paulina outlines a strident advocacy of a nominated rather than inherited monarchy: 'Care not for Issue, The Crowne will find an Heire' (V. i. 46–8). She dismisses as trivial Leontes' earlier obsession with the honesty of his 'issue': to be thus slaves to 'blood' is less likely to arrive at sound government than if one judges and appoints upon merit. Whereas Dion argues for the king's remarriage on the grounds of 'What Dangers, by his Highnesse faile of Issue, May drop vpon his Kingdome, and deuoure Incertaine lookers on' (V. i. 27–9), Paulina sees more perfidious danger in forgetting and ameliorating the king's past tyranny. Her indifference to 'Issue' might be interpreted as a rebuke to the agnatic mania of Leontes earlier in the play. Paulina's role—as her faithfulness to both the oracle and Father Time suggest—is one which facilitates inauguration, whilst taking the past with her: as a narrative 'dominatrix' she protects comic lore, at the same time as insisting that feminine agency and completeness are intrinsic to the genre's, and the state's, happy organization.

Discovered variously in mother, wife, lover, worker, friend, and child, free and virtuous womanhood is a crucial focus of romance's search for sanctifying origin. If patriarchal 'legitimacy' is to survive, the polity must assimilate the political symbolics of such womanhood, and most particularly of the royal daughter. Nevertheless, because the patriarchal order is never finally dislodged, it is often argued that the woman's apparent autonomy is illusory.[7] The power structures of Shakespeare's period always remain in place at the play's end, and men continue to command the positions of authority. But to erase the marks of feminine agency because the framing plot is irredeemably patriarchal seems curiously unkind to an audience who, as the play proceeds, will have spent anxiety or approval upon just such defiance or self-definition. The presence of many women in Shakespeare's audience may have demanded some kind of echoic satisfaction, an at least partially feminized theatre;[8] one might identify an analogy with the popularity of romance tales among female readers.[9] Such popularity might further suggest how putatively obedient closures need not disempower the female. Marriage might be the ultimate patriarchal institution, but it could also permit women access to means and place, albeit often only through the *de jure* permission of the husband.[10] The channelling of feminine desire into marriage may suggest the need for a more supple notion of gender politics

[7] e.g. Marilyn L. Williamson, *The Patriarchy of Shakespeare's Comedies* (Detroit, 1986), 112, 150; cf. Stevie Davies, *the Idea of Woman in Renaissance Literature: The Feminine Reclaimed* (Brighton, 1986), 129–42, who sees power being restructured around the nurturing female.

[8] Linda Woodbridge, *Women and the English Renaissance: Literature and the Nature of Womanhood 1540–1620* (Urbana, Ill., 1984), 266, argues that the presence of women at the theatres directly influenced drama's representation of women; cf. Kathleen McLuskie, *Renaissance Dramatists* (Hemel Hempstead, 1989), 95–6.

[9] Helen Hackett, ' "Yet Tell Me Some Such Fiction": Lady Mary Wroth's *Urania* and the Femininity of Romance', in Brant and Purkiss, *Women, Texts and Histories*, 39–68.

[10] Kate Lilley, 'Blazing Worlds: Seventeenth-Century Women's Utopian Writing', in Brant and Purkiss, *Women, Texts and Histories*, 102–33, notes (p. 128) that women utopists in the second half of the seventeenth century wrote of marriage in both positive and negative terms.

than an ugly sense that the wife becomes a serviceable and silenced chattel.[11] Furthermore, the 'feminine' should not, even when embodied regally, be understood entirely homogeneously. For instance, there are symbolic differences according to the heroines' marital status: whereas the bride symbolizes promise, a map of the state's integrity, the wife or mistress will invariably emblematize the possession, inherently jealous and nervous, of private or public property. Both *The Winter's Tale* and *Cymbeline* play upon the wife's instability as an emblem of social order.

So, if Shakespeare understood politicized femininity in mainly metaphorical terms, it must still be recognized how various are the ways in which metaphor can relate to achieved reality: it can compensate for denials, reflect proprietary violence, fill in for the tardiness of achievement, describe the engines within social machines, or deconstruct the arrogance of authority. The heroines partly work, then, as just such amplified metaphor, ripe with alternative promises for an unstable society. For the romances are rooted as much in promise as achievement; at times they are almost a kind of 'science fiction', tempted by whimsical schemes and unlikely experimentations. The heroines' independence and itinerance is a version of the plays' embrace of the liberty of wilderness. It should be taken seriously as an expression of political desire.

The role of the 'heroine', then, is encapsulated in neither her 'character' nor her ultimate social 'fate'. These two things themselves may work in contrapuntal tension: a sceptical or ironically minded heroine may be politically 'ahead' of the putative denouement; she articulates a challenge which the patriarchal generic teleology can neither accommodate nor quell. Alternatively, the heroines can work as meta-theatrical scapegoats: undeservedly battered and bruised by the casual tyrannies of the genre, by cruelties of metaphor or situation, they alert one to generic and socio-political inequity; their treatment within the play is challenged, counterpointed, by an audience's sense of

---

[11] Often the question depends upon how much faith one stores in agency or expression which ultimately remains bounded within 'patriarchal' forms: see Coppélia Kahn, *Man's Estate: Masculine Identity in Shakespeare* (Berkeley, 1981); Carol Thomas Neely, *Broken Nuptials in Shakespeare's Plays* (New Haven, 1985); McLuskie, *Renaissance Dramatists*.

what is 'fair'. The heroines thereby provoke an alternative version of both genre and society, within the cage, as it were, of the reigning hegemony. However, the heroines are not reflexive exemplars: they are never given the privilege of perfect choric consonance. They can at times be stiff, unbending, lacking the mischief and audacity of Shakespeare's medium; the surrounding text, restless with echo and shadow, can equally embarrass or undermine the heroines. If they carry something of romance's projective facility, they do so in dialogue with the more antic, equally inclusive, figures such as Autolicus, Cloten, and Caliban.

Furthermore, the romance heroines evoke a tradition (typified in Dekker's work) in which the princess is symbolical vessel of the ideal nation or true church. Such symbolics tap into a proto-'Elizabethan' discourse, emerging in response, first, to a growing disillusion with the new king, and second, to the blossoming at court of a new Prince Henry and Princess Elizabeth, who it was thought might harness a radicalized nostalgia for the old queen's golden age.[12] When Shakespeare's heroines are exiled into cave or forest, for instance, they evoke Elizabethan figurations of the chaste princess, their very powerlessness symbolizing the country's resourceful, imperturbable self-sovereignty; as Elizabeth said to her 1576 parliament, 'If I were a milkmaid with a pail on my arm, whereby my private person might be little set by, I would not forsake that poor state to match with the greatest monarch.'[13] A beleaguered but proud Virgilian bucolic serves a monarchical populism wherein princess and her public can protect and analogize one another. And indeed, in *The Winter's Tale* and *Cymbeline* Shakespeare appears to be reworking *The Thracian Wonder*, an Elizabethan romance which celebrates in particularly effusive fashion the tradition that the commonweal finds creative womb and nourishing breast in the figure of the old queen. Here the shepherd princess, Ariadne, is the object of the comically harmless but still competitive desire of every man in the play, her stepfather and son included; the climax involves

[12] Queen Elizabeth was decisive in developing literary symbols of the nationally embodying princess. She was Defender of the Faith, Bride of Christ, 'renovator temporis', as well as Diana, Ceres, Cynthia, Phoenix, the Vestal Virgin, Astraea, and so on. See Frances Yates, *Astraea: The Imperial Theme in the Sixteenth Century* (London, 1975).

[13] Quoted in Louis Montrose, ' "Eliza, Queene of shepheardes" and the Pastoral of Power', *ELR* 10 (1980), 113–82 (p. 156).

a rebellion of nobles and commons against the court where she is held prisoner: 'Let us see our Queen, And if she have received the smallest wrong, A general ruine shall o're-spread the Land' (G2ʳ). As far as her massed rebels know Ariadne is not actually any kind of queen; it is purely a pastoral appellation. But the absoluteness with which the identification is insisted upon suggests not only how effortless is the link between pastoral grace and majestic microcosm, but the way in which the fictional heroine is rendered the apogee of popular desire. To reclaim their 'fair Ewe', accordingly, is to justify a brand new 'Holiday' (G1ʳ⁻ᵛ). The climax of the denouement's multiple revelations is the king's declaration of a 'Holiday in the remembrance of the Shepherds Queene' (H4ʳ): she becomes a kind of mascot of happy self-sufficiency. And the play's final words confirm the flattering correlation of the gazed-upon shepherdess and a majesty identifiable specifically as Queen Elizabeth: 'When was there such a Wonder ever seen? Forty years banisht, and live still a QUEEN!', wherein the fourteen years which the plot actually spans are conflated with the forty years of the old queen's glorious reign (H4ᵛ). Shakespeare's heroines, too, must encounter their own 'causes'—in the sense of where they come from and what they symbolize—as Elizabeth so cannily did in her rhetoric, in the 'country'.

That Shakespeare dramatizes the birth of the virgin princess in *Henry VIII* might suggest that a latent or nascent Elizabethanism is common to all of his late romances. However, the 'heroine' of *Henry VIII*, the young princess who attracts the praise most familiar from *Pericles*, *Cymbeline*, *The Winter's Tale*, and *The Tempest*, is the rather ambiguous figure of Anne Bullen. The very brittleness of Anne's precedent—the historical awareness that rhetorical idealism and popular applause could not in her case withstand the claims of flesh and realm—helps one give a political perspective to the tropes of celebratory, even redemptive, royal femininity. Thus, part of the significance of Anne is in the way she animates or even mirrors the common will:

> [W]hile her Grace sate downe
> To rest a while, some halfe an houre, or so,
> In a rich Chaire of State, opposing freely
> The Beauty of her Person to the People.

Beleeue me Sir, she is the goodliest Woman
That euer lay by man: which when the people
Had the full view of, such a noyse arose,
As the shrowdes make at Sea, in a stiffe Tempest,
As lowd, and to as many Tunes. Hats, Cloakes,
(Doublets, I thinke) flew vp, and had their Faces
Bin loose, this day they had beene lost.

(IV. i. 65–75)

Just as the Field of the Cloth of Gold was eulogized in terms so
extravagant as to suggest self-destruction (I. i. 1–45), so too here
the exaltation teeters upon anarchy or delirium. The image of
heads being tossed about like hats recalls Trinculo's prophecy of
a state tottering, as indeed the comparison of the popular acclaim to the 'many Tunes' of a 'Tempest' at 'Sea' might suggest
Shakespeare's frequent resort to just such weather to evoke the
clamorous demotic voice. Shakespeare hands the powers both of
observation and description to the people; they, not she, possess
the power of portraiture. He lays double entendres like land-
mines, making of the coronated queen a kind of Doll Common.
Her chair of state evokes a bed; her beauty 'freely' opposes the
people, like a general hymen; the people have a 'full view' of her
self-display, and return the compliment with flying doublets.
The text enjoys rupturing decorum: idealizing gestures, practica-
ble politics, and the aggressiveness of desire cannot discover
endlessly harmonious surcease. Anne's status as a highly contentious figure of recent history brings to the surface the kinds
of tension which underpin each of Shakespeare's romance
heroines.

Henry VIII thus offers various perspectives upon the homology of princess and people, a homology which the play seems to
understand as both volatile and necessary. Thus the Porter at the
door of the palace as, within, Elizabeth is named: 'Blesse me,
what a fry of Fornication is at dore? On my Christian Conscience this one Christening will beget a thousand' (V. iii. 34–6).
It is unlikely that these lines are Shakespeare's, but Fletcher
seems here to be working to a plan which emphasizes how
prosperity depends upon popular energies that, although exuberant and indecorous, can be kept roughly harmonious while
united in praise of a promising royalty. The Lord Chamberlain
comments further: 'Mercy o'me: what a Multitude are heere?

They grow still too; from all Parts they are comming, As if we kept a Faire here?' (V. iii. 66–8). This is one of various occasions when the crowd around the palace can be accommodated descriptively only in analogies with carnival. The descriptions of railing wits and flying meteors, of clubs, pebbles and bitten apples, suggest rapid ochlocratic movement and a whirling, merry kind of violence. In so far as the excitement is in praise and expectancy of the princess it unites the mob; but the evocation hardly seeks to play down the fractural, fissiparous allegiances which otherwise take over. Hence, for instance, the 'Habberdashers Wife' who, as if a citizen rival of Elizabeth, draws 'forty Truncheoners' to her succour before herself getting 'quartered', these youths in turn being unendurable to all but a rowdy rump of fellow thunderers (V. iii. 38–65).

The important point is how Shakespeare informs his female characters with popular energies and responsibilities. Paulina bestrides *The Winter's Tale* as a straight talking comic figure; Leontes' identification of her as a city shrew, a Dame Partlet, is inadequate but not irrelevant. Her direct manners combine with her hostility to despotism to make of Paulina a partial populist. One can see, then, how her dialogical responsibilities flow outwards, become maternally capacious. There are moments in *Henry VIII*, which is similarly based around the transference of hope and responsibility from women to child, that serve to animate the franchise implied in Paulina:

> Great belly'd women,
> That had not halfe a weeke to go, like Rammes
> In the old time of Warre, would shake the prease
> And make 'em reele before 'em. No man liuing
> Could say this is my wife there, all were wouen
> So strangely in one peece.
>
> (IV. i. 76–81)

The one-in-all and all-in-one so characteristic of a romance surcease is here epitomized by the shared imminence of birth. The crowd becomes a wife and mother, the coronation a midwife. The movement expects, then, that moment of origin which is the constant dream of the historical and romantic imaginations, and which finds a prototype in the closing blessing and baptism of Elizabeth. But this multiple proxying both accompanies and complicates the royal birth. The pregnant women seem careless not only of their burdens but of their familial identity. They seem to be grabbing for themselves a phallic violence ('Rammes'), so that the sense of seamless coherence is troubled by the evaporation of patriarchal property; such movement might strangely amplify the independence of the lone 'turtle' Paulina. At the same time, looking forward as it does to the births that will proceed, it seems to prepare for a revamped hegemony in which women—and one woman in particular— will arrogate a new power to energize the desires of the masses.

Popular participation is rarely dramatized unproblematically by Shakespeare, and in asking his heroines to escape the ivory tower, to 'open' their mouths and bodies to sometimes indecorous environments, the plays invest in and expect from their young princesses something of the difficulty and caprice of serious political agency. They are never merely bland vessels of blessing and reconciliation. Unlike allegorical polemics such as Dekker's *Whore of Babylon*, the romances don't 'apply' any militaristic or crusading line; a fuzzy halo of renovation may surround the heroines, but they are not to be strait-jacketed by patriotic symbol. The princesses themselves may treat the responsibility sarcastically. Hermione certainly does before her fall, and Imogen likewise at times exploits or ironizes the rhetoric of reverence which hovers around a princess. Such a gestural, almost impressionistic political role is almost inherently neutering; it can veer toward hagiography, toward the silence and silencings of a petrified icon, a statue of liberty, justice, truth, or patience. Shakespeare's heroines are too alive for monumentalized silence, their avidities and passions at times quarrelling with whatever more euphonious symbolics are at play. This, like their scrupulous linguistic integrities, allows their roles to both harness and complicate populist responsibilities. They can indeed 'be' the people, but they are also intelligent subjects struggling, in what has become a bourgeois commonplace, for an unpre-empted identity, less beholden to male desire and its consequent myths and categories. Their discursive function, then, goes well beyond the representation of womanhood, or of particular women in specific circumstances; they become archetypes both of the emerging individual subject and of the emerging political masses. Clearly, these various responsibilities

cannot always be complementary, and often one finds the heroines' roles devolving into difficuties, caught within ideological
antinomies, or uncomfortably straddling contradictions of manner, motive, or metaphor. But it is this very unrecuperated,
unfinished quality that is the measure of their integrity within
Shakespeare's exploratory, transformatory mode of romance.

MARINA

Marina holds in poise *Pericles'* basic sources of optimism: on the
one hand courtly grace, on the other communal equity. She does
not work merely as an aristocratic paragon; somewhat like
Pericles earlier, when he rose from the sea as if answering the
fisher's prayers, Marina is textually prophesied, and works to
negotiate the aspirations of the commonalty that precedes and,
in a sense, permits her. For if Pericles and Thaisa are her parents,
they are so only through the good grace and 'armour' of the
fishermen: if one is to understand Marina's responsibilities, one
must come to terms with the shared agency of her genesis. The
fishermen hope for a restorative belch from their great mother
the sea. The story responds with a sequence of watery births:
first Pericles and his armour (and his 'amour' with Thaisa); next
their child; and then mother and daughter each reborn a second
time from the sea which appears to have ended them. Communal optimism, therefore, will seek for consummation in
the one who bears the sea's name: Marina. Her resistance and
repair find a precedent, a kind of script, in the fishermen's
restitutive fantasy.

Marina's responsibilities, then, are established through those
forces which 'make' her. In the later plays, it is the moment
of escape to the wilderness which establishes both the destructiveness of courtly turbidity, and the need for more inclusive,
if conflictory, political dialogues. In *Pericles*, such roaring
delivery, or deliverance, is given principally in two scenes:
first, Marina's birth at sea, and second, her abduction and
enslavement. As with so many of the births and rebirths in
The Tempest, as with Perdita's roaring delivery, it is the environment of genesis that must establish the terms of any irenic
closure. Marina's knows such environment only from report.

Significantly, the tale Marina knows by heart is that of her nurse, Lychorida:

When I was borne the wind was North . . . My father, as nurse ses, did neuer feare, but cryed good seamen to the Saylers, galling his kingly hands haling ropes, and clasping to the Mast, endured a sea that almost burst the decke . . . When I was borne, neuer was waues nor winde more violent, and from the ladder tackle, washes off a canuas clymer, ha ses one, wolt out? and with a dropping industrie they skip from sterne to sterne, the Boatswaine whistles, and the Maister calles and trebles their confusion. (IV. i. 55–67)

Marina's nativity recalls exactly the kinds of co-operative endeavour which the romances appear to endorse. She gives voice not only to her father, but to an unnamed sailor's fatalism, the boatswain's labour, and the master's urgent authority. This 'dropping industrie' ensures not only the boat's safe passage but, delivered in the same rush of water, the child's tenuous life. The chronicle's heroes double as collective midwife, in turn folding into the nurse's warm and animated memories. There is a manner of transference, then, between 'Lucina', goddess of childbirth, and Lychorida, she who actually oversees the birth of the 'Poor inch of nature'. Pericles himself effects the conflation: '*Lychorida—Lucina*, oh! Diuinest patrionesse and my wife gentle To those that cry by-night' (III. i. 10–11). If one completes the trinity by including the labour, both embryonic and chiliastic, of the seamen ('Blow, and split thyself', III. i. 44), one will begin to see the type of new world discourses promised by Marina's inception: that is, multiple not only of agent but occasion. One might compare here the multiple tale-tellers in *The Winter's Tale*: Marina's nativity tale is the gift of her nurse. The little we see of Lychorida, candid, stern, respectful toward yet unafraid of chiding the great, suggests that she conforms to Shakespeare's customary court servant (III. i. 15–27). Marina is similarly robust and practical when faced with her own unforgiving necessities. The voices which inform her are not solely those of her blue blood and royal guardians.

However, Marina's subsequent history is often one of savage oppression, effecting her repeated separation from both courtly grace and communal equity. Both at Tharsus and Mytilene she is abstracted as an iconic sign, separate from intelligence, desire, and virtue, a fate brutally parodied in Dionyza's 'posthumous' construction of a 'monument' in 'glittring goldé characters' of praise (IV. iii. 42–5). Simultaneously marmorealizing and destroying Marina's wonder, her manipulative epitaph is a courtly version of the brothel's death-trap. There too she is a 'piece', a 'sign', a 'parragon', as nameless as the pooped 'stuff' of the pander (IV. ii. 17–143). She lives in 'report', in 'proclamation', in verbal 'picture', a text to be written upon, morsel to be chewed, or soup lewdly to be stirred. The body is a conglomeration of disseverable and possessable members ('I haue cryde her almost to the number of her haires', IV. ii. 91–2). Unlike any Bakhtinian regeneration, when food and flesh are endlessly reconstituted, even from manure, into new life, both whore and whoremonger are soaked or masticated into extinction: 'the poore Transiluanian is dead that laye with the little baggadge' (IV. ii. 20–1). The brothel allows no space for the body beyond its commodification. There is neither private subjectivity nor public homogeneity, but only members for the machine.

In this way, the exchange of the brothel might be seen as a vicious extrapolation of romance characterization itself. That the brothel was linked culturally and geographically to the theatre may reinforce a sense that both institutions are the fantastical playgrounds of male desire. However, whilst the brothel scenes show Marina being, almost literally, 'put together' out of available mythic or generic remnants, our sympathies are at odds with such expropriations. To the extent that the brothel scenes are meta-theatrical, they point to a generic discourse far from sanguine about masculine violence, and one which, as a crucial part of its purpose, seeks to deconstruct and then transform imprisoning conceptions of the female. Partly this imperative reflects Marina's own stubborn will; she retains possession of a language uncolonized by her oppressors. Equally, however, the resistance is the genre's own, a power rooted not so much in the heroine's transcendent independence as in the play's own faithfulness to its revivifying discursive sources.

For Marina's slavery in Mytilene reprises the tempest of her birth ('the stuffe we haue, a strong winde will blowe it to peeces, they are so pittifully sodden', IV. ii. 18–20). Contributing to the clashing discourses in the brothel, then, is the memory within Marina's lexicon of Lychorida's exciting nativity tale; whether

speaking warm affection or bitter disdain, there is a consistent
demotic presence in the young girl's voices. The text therefore
both proffers and mitigates bifurcatory 'class' clichés. It is fundamental to recognize how Shakespeare doesn't allow either the
audience, or Marina herself, to rest with saving mythic dichotomies. Her chastity is of course fiercely royal: if violated, her
precedent would be Lucrece rather than Mary Magdalene. But
just like the other romance heroines, Marina is as much a
talisman of the subject as of regal virtue. She shares things with
those who, both 'Lord *and* Lowne' (IV. vi. 17, my italics),
employ her: and this means equally the audience, and the popu-
lation of the brothel.

Like those of Pericles earlier, Marina's responsibilities are
finely poised between those of leader and subject. With the
governor being the stew's champion stallion, a measure of resistance becomes essential to the very survival of romance. Marina,
sold into a slavery as ideologically deterministic as Caliban's,
must provide it: 'If you were borne to honour, shew it now, if
put vpon you, make the iudgement good, that thought you
worthie of it' (IV. vi. 91–3). Marina defends her chastity
through recourse to a fundamentally political argument: in trying to rape her, the governor dishonours equally his class and
those who sanction his rule. She identifies two possible sources
of his authority—birth or election—which find partners in Marina's own franchise. Wherever located, power should respond
to high and low alike. Marina becomes an exemplar of justice,
fulfilling the responsibilities of her mixed origin: in rebuking,
and thence repairing, the governor's permissive iniquities, she
redeems the fishermen's similar indignation at mercenary
cannibalisms winked at by authority.

However: that Marina is unaware of any such role is part of
the point. There is a kind of reigning consciousness throughout
the play that is never captured by a single choric figure. This
consciousness derives from the risky hybridity of the genre, and
from the way the text invokes old modes in ways that straddle
respect and irony, neither endorsing nor annihilating traditional
valencies: the effect is to transform the tropes of hope, give time-
grafted, custom-honed images a flinty kind of modernity. Marina is crucial here. She embodies a perfect virginal royalty,
fulfils consummately the archetypal brief, and yet is forced into

accommodations which the symbolism would conventionally
preclude. It is not that it was unusual for the princess to 'represent' the nation; what is striking about Marina's role is that her
discourse is not granted its own generically hedged ontology. In
a sense Shakespeare gives to the situation the unsettling charge
of a pun amid reverence. Marina is both 'gazed on like a Comet'
(V. i. 86) and sized up as meat on a rotisserie (IV. ii. 128–30).
And the maiden's own words, too, leak into and out of this
world that would rape as much as praise her. Hence the disquiet
of critics facing the brothel scenes: the text brings to the air
those silences and assumptions which buttress aristocratic
proprieties; hierarchy gives way to debate. Here she abuses the
servant Boult:

To the cholerike fisting of euery rogue, thy ear is lyable, thy foode is
such as hath beene belch't on by infected lungs. (IV. vi. 166–8)

It is Coriolanus who cries, 'You common cry of Curs, whose
breath I hate As reeke a'th rotten Fennes', but the scalding
tongue of the young princess adopts a similar register. However,
what she sees as simply contemptible—a belch from infection—
is elsewhere in the play the agent of regeneration; both the
fishermen and Cerimon recognize how unruly vomit might
faciliate repair. Further, Marina speaks viciously not only of the
brothel's patrons and its hosts but, it would seem, also of those
other 'poore', 'rotten', 'Creatures' forced into 'continual action'
(IV. ii. 6–9): they are included in the reference to 'foode', a
heavily ironical appellation which at once mocks and reinforces
the resident discourse of contempt and consumerism. But before
Marina herself arrives in the brothel, it is the horror of her
fellow captives' careers which establishes the place's iniquity; in
turn, it is the knowledge of these other girls' death-sentence
which gives the framework for the heroine's own resistance.
Shakespeare lends the 'poore three' surviving whores a kind of
indirect voice. Marina's fury is thus less equivocal than the
moment's 'conscience'. Those whom she disdains as dishonest
'Tib[s]' the previous scene has already given a bleakly predetermined biography: the bawd has brought eleven bastards up to
puberty, thence into service and an early grave (IV. ii. 13–15).
The poor whores remind one of nothing so much as the 'little
ones' eaten up by the rapacious rich of Pentapolis. Or again, her

claim that the bawd and pandar are not as 'bad' as Boult, 'Since they do better [Boult] in their command', seems a perverse application of 'degree', mocked by the surrounding evidence.

As so often in *Pericles*, bibliographical confusion both causes and mirrors wider uncertainties. It may well be that Shakespeare 'came upon' a Marina in the original play who was a more simple example of conventional pastoral princess; he complicates her figure in line with his renovation of the old genre, but for whatever reason—a corrupt text, a half-baked job—traces of something gauche and simplistic remain. When she pleads with Leonine for her life, Marina seems almost to parody the idea of living innocence: 'I neuer killed a mouse, nor hurt a fly, I trod upon a worm against my will, But I wept for't' (IV. i. 77–9). It is often specious to explain egregious writing as the work of irony; but if one compares Marina's naïvety here to, say, Perdita's scrupulous integrity, it is difficult to draw any conclusion (textual corruption apart) than an ironizing invocation of an impossible, almost solipsistic archetype which, to regain any currency, must haggle with possibility, community, and the quickening tensions of genuine political discourse.

Empson writes of the 'electric nausea' aroused here by Marina's 'tear-jerks', and identifies a similar 'bad taste' in the gallants leaving the brothel to 'hear the vestals sing'.[14] But if there is 'false sentiment' and 'telling lies' in these and like moments, it might best be understood as a product of Shakespeare's generic translations: one's scorn or disbelief comes because the context does not allow self-forgetting idolatries; nor does it place redemptive trust in supernal star-gazing, or indeed in any bad art. It is working instead toward a re-placing of romance idealism, not only within the contemporary moment, but in the theatrical wake of works like *Lear*; after the awe and horror of Cordelia's corpse, it is difficult to believe that Marina's lachrymose pacifism is a true register of the necessary heroine. Her performance once in the brothel is of course more vital and compelling, but still, I would suggest, in a fundamentally *rhetorical* sense. That is, her speech encodes not so much ineffable truths as political persuasion, her tropes to be weighed and judged for contextual decorum. This, like the scene's intermittent

[14] Empson, *Essays on Shakespeare* (1986; repr. Cambridge, 1988), 236–7.

tonal ambiguities, points to the need for a nuanced awareness of how her role works in creative asymmetry to cliched romance exemplars.

Such presentments of ideological strain are typified by the sudden plaintive relativization of Boult's tawdriness:

What wold you haue me do? go to the wars, wold you? wher a man may serue 7 yeers for the losse of a leg, & haue not money enough in the end to buy him a woodden one? (IV. vi. 169–72)

In a sense the awkwardness of this exchange, the mutually felt embarrassment, comes from a collision of genres. The brothel scenes are, like the brothel patrons, a sore and bald presence. Here the assumptions behind the characters' respective discourses, usually tacit and latent, are brought unsettlingly to account: Marina makes Boult face his degradation, while his response makes her words echo, if not with ignorance, then with harshness. Shakespeare gives to the man who would rape her a socio-political context which immediately explains, if it doesn't justify, his calling; similarly, he gives to innocence the voice of experience. In other words, Marina's situation struggles free of myth, of hagiography, to become materially possible. She is thereby asked to accommodate what her experience leads her to hate: the open spawning body.

The effect is to dislocate decorum out of certainty. Furthermore, Marina's preaching, far from the 'diuinitie' of which the rutters, bewildered into repentance, speak (IV. v. 4), rather apes the visceral metaphors of her imprisoners. Marina's speech dissuading Lysimachus from rape—notoriously abbreviated in the quarto—is, as Wilkins reports it, a balanced and eloquent piece of oratory. But again an arresting mix of discourses is apparent: 'Is there a necessitie (my yet good Lord) if there be fire before me, that I must strait then thither flie and burne my selfe?'.[15] She conflates evangelical metaphors of impending hell-fire with metonyms of the pox. Typically, the indecorousness has been used in itself to argue for textual corruption.[16] As is the case with Caliban, language is Marina's main weapon, and it may be that the clashing genres, working like a particularly inhospitable

---

[15] Wilkins, 'Painfull Adventures', 535–6.
[16] S. Musgrove, 'The First Quarto of *Pericles* Reconsidered', *SQ* 29 (1978), 390–1.

pun, force her words into unattractiveness. When she too slips into the tropes of the 'common shores of filth' (IV. vi. 173–6), one recognizes the moral of Tharsus, the ease with which rectitude is bent and guttered, the physical contingency of decorum. The exchange thus epitomizes the romances' intermittent indifference to feminine desire, as it were sacrificed to a linguistically 'forward and backward', supra-characterological, prophetic memory.

Marina's escape into the 'Honest-house' might in many ways seem to prefigure an exclusive, aristocratic denouement. The arts she practises are courtly and decorous: she sews, sings and dances 'like one immortall' (V. Chorus, 3–8). Arriving on the barge so as to minister to the surly Pericles, she takes upon her being the responsibilities, perfected earlier by the charitable Cerimon, of magical healer (V. i. 70–8). Coaxed into revealing her true identity, Marina rejoins her royal stock. And it is above all Marina's persuasive language, a direct contrast and repair to Pericles' silence, which allows this return to nourishing origin; her narrative prowess is itself a kind of midwife. But here one needs to recall the implications of public speech. Denied by Antiochus, travestied by Cleon and Dionyza, leased out to a bawd by Lysimachus, honest consultation and informative communication is the oft-betrayed register of good government. Pericles' silence, and the hirsute inhospitability of his appearance, are foes equally to decorum as to the populace. But the populist element to the question is further entrenched by the link throughout the play of educational speech to nourishing food: each is a type of sustenance. Just as in *Coriolanus*, where to possess public rhetoric is to control the bread, the circulation of speech and food offers a graph of power.

Pericles' silence has a deleterious effect upon his people's produce: while the king lies entombed in his ship Hellicanus asks for fresh 'prouision', 'wherein we are not destitute for want, but wearie for the stalenesse' (V. i. 56–7). Marina, by contrast, 'starues the eares she feedes, and makes them hungrie, the more she giues them speech' (V. i. 112–13). She endows, that is, something like the gratifying frustrations of suffrage: the sense is of long-endured denials, an anxiousness to make up for lost liberties, and the difficulty of discovering some shared and replete surcease. In other words, a return not to dearth or forgetfulness, but to the clamour and conflict of a healthily expressed franchise.

It is Marina, then, who supplies the fresh provision for which the ailing ship of state yearns. Pericles' impulse is to interpret Marina's revelatory beneficence in ethereal terms: she is a 'Fairie', a second 'Iuno', the archetype of 'patience' (V. i. 111, 138, 153). But the text grounds her continuing presence in Mytilene with a quite unillusioned commercial imperative: 'her gaine She giues the cursed Bawd' (5 Chorus 10–11). A dialectic is established between this corrupt expropriation and her more idealizing association with a plentifully husbanded land. Her voice, that is, does not descend like Diana's from the stars, but carries now the burdens of a rather brutally material education.

Of course, Marina's principal focus at the end is upon her parents. She belongs, she has a home, and these things have a simple and exquisite emotional pregnancy. But this return to source similarly represents a return to the sources of community: the wandering royal child is also the lost nation. Thus, the only words which Marina does say after being renamed and re-blessed as Pericles' 'child' (V. i. 212) confirm a theme which unites the foetal, familial, and political: 'My heart leaps to be gone into my mothers bosome' (V. iii. 44–5). Marina rehearses romance's favourite trope, the umbilical return which can banish all corruption and ensure all safety. Marina's desire exactly duplicates and corrects the 'original' cannibalistic, matricidal transgression of the Antiochan princess: both daughters in a sense 'feed' on the mother's flesh, but whereas one eats it away, the other gives and draws nourishment. The consequent sustenance is not only to the princess, but to the people whose desires she can animate or deny. The Antiochan crimes, one will recall, included massive denials of liberty, voice, and consultation. Marina's leap into her mother affirmatively denies such denials, whilst reinforcing how nascent and uncertain, how hedged by primal violence, must any new world be. Pericles' own longing for a cathartic-cum-vaginal 'gash' also recalls the tale's insistent pulse of self-destructiveness, and suggests an abiding impulse to leap beyond civic accountability into silent or violent immolations. The old goat Lysimachus becomes a Fortinbras figure, insisting that events answer to his 'iust beliefe': it is to his secular scepticism, oblivious to supernal music, that Marina is joined

(V. i. 236, 261). Her betrothal to the revisionist lecher follows the tale's source, but in so far as it means anything must tend, once more, to make one question the verity of generic habit. Marina's homecoming thus recalls, as it questions, the conditions of her 'making': the future returns into the care of a 'midwife' which, like a ship on the sea, is at one level ordered and hierarchical but, beneath that, many-headed, garrulous, and potentially tempestuous.

IMOGEN

Cymbeline is premissed upon the disobedience of its heroine, not only to her father, but oddly to the romantic genre: Imogen is the perfect princess who, at the play's start, is already a wife, and so already—perhaps—beyond the tradition's preference for the blushing unpaid promise. Another context's hopeful closure—the happy ever after betrothal—here curdles, like spilt milk, into disappointing commission. The situation is characteristic of this play: desire is somehow out of kilter, its satisfactions precipitous, belated, or anachronistic; dichotomies collapse into muddle and indistinction; fairy-tale clarities are invoked to be doubted. And the woman's part, too, is one of ideological disjunction.

Imogen is often far removed from the Swinburnian paragon of grace under pressure, displaying instead an array of violent or defiant motives. Indeed it is striking how closely her first scene anticipates our introduction to Caliban: her father calls her a 'disloyall thing', 'vilde one!', 'Past Grace? Obedience?', tells his wife to 'pen her vp' and ends with a splenetic, visceral curse further reminiscent of Prospero's furious tortures: 'let her languish A drop of blood a day, and being aged Dye of this Folly (I. ii. 62–89). As a woman she shares a certain inherent powerlessness with the slave; coterminously, she shares the slave's rage, and, in Shakespeare's day if not our own, no doubt exceeds the slave in eliciting the support of an audience projectively indignant at her imprisonments. Imogen, then, is both identifiably gendered, a female exemplar, and a more generally unsettling political presence. Her first words declare a libertarian verve and irony, 'O dissembling Curtesie! How fine this Tyrant Can tickle where she wounds' (I. ii. 14–16). A hankering after novel adventures forestalls conventional placidities. Sidney's *Arcadia*, for instance, most suggests the early Imogen when Philoclea, aware of the horror of lesbian love, yet stays resolute to whatever infamy or humiliation her passion must deal.[17] Imogen's temper is sauced by an adversarial self-regard, a vanity that enjoys a certain vituperative pride ('The Shees of Italy should not betray Mine Interest, and his Honour: or haue charg'd him... T'encounter me with Orisons, for then I am in Heauen for him', I. iv. 29–33). 'Oh for a Horse with wings' (III. ii. 49) expresses much of this leaping ambition; she would be Bellerephon, slaying the chimera that oppose. Imogen wishes first to elope with a commoner, then to be rushed off-centre by daring strangers ('Had I bin Theefe-stolne, As my two Brothers, happy', I. vii. 5–6). Elizabeth had made bucolic self-dramatizations conventional. But she did so from the epicentre, from a position of possession: Imogen uses her wilful marginality as a prototype for a femininity which depends less upon defiant chastity than defying the monarch. She yokes as partners the illegal and the ideal, dreaming upon, and indeed anticipating, a subversive pastoral ('Blessed be those How meane so ere, that haue their honest wills', I. vii. 7–8). Imaginatively Imogen joins her brothers, flings hierarchy and succession to the wind, and allies her hopes with the only naked treason in the play.

Imogen's ambition is restless, marooned in a domesticity too quiescent and unquestioning: 'I would they were in Affricke both together, My selfe by with a Needle, that I might prick The goer backe' (I. ii. 96–100). At times punctiliousness narrows into conceits of comprehensive destruction: 'I would haue broke mine eye-strings; Crack'd them, but to looke vpon him, till the diminution Of space, had pointed him sharpe as my Needle: Nay, followed him, till he had melted from The smalnesse of a Gnat, to ayre' (I. iv. 14–22). Her emotions are at once lovelorn and damagingly potent; the instinct is one of violent immolation, of herself, her lover, her world. Imogen appears to cherish her abandon and violence; hence her conceits' escalating hysteria, the sense that she must sustain its fire until her very being burns itself to vacancy. At the same time a self-glorifying

---

[17] Sidney, *The Countesse of Pembrokes Arcadia*, 1590 version, ed. Albert Feuillerat (1912; repr. Cambridge, 1939), Bk. 2, ch. 4, pp. 173–5.

quality, centred in Imogen's fast grip upon her weapon, reflects a longing for a punishment which she herself must deliver. Her rhetoric's grandstanding quality suggests one eye on her 'parents', as though she is the grown child still cocking a snook; at the same time, she will survive her lover too, another sacrifice to her desire, to its absolutism and righteousness. It is almost as though Imogen has to reach a state of waste, a razed field, as the only place worthy of and correspondent to her self-defining virtue. She is more Antigone than Juliet. It is then not so much her husband *per se*, but rather her own unappeasable hungers, the nourished sense of lack of a self-furious subject—unrecuperated energy and angst, rebellion, a need to dare and to lose—that itself seems to give her passion its pulse. In all of this archetypal, insurrectionary helplessness, Imogen suggests no one, perhaps, as much as she does Caliban: in his heroines, too, Shakespeare offers epitomes of romantic subjectivity, under strain, pushing at the edges, crucially unfinished.

However, the text itself seems to nobble Imogen's 'horse with wings', and to frustrate the aspirations of both woman and subject. She races out to the wilderness of her dreams only to find that it is, in fact, a killing field; the irony is brutal and, from certain perspectives, as misogynistic as her husband. Even though Imogen survives the proposed assassination plot, she must realize that none of the men who love her can, at heart, abide her reckless self-will. So, as though to drum the message of deference home, Imogen agrees to 'play the man', and perforce begins to weaken. Her brisk capitulation into lassitude the moment she dresses in doublet and hose is as far removed from the 'quicke-answer'd' and 'quarrellous' wag Pisanio prepares one to expect as it is from her character hitherto, which has indeed approximated to such 'sawcie' appropriation of the masculine (III. iv. 155–66). It may be another of the play's jokes that Imogen weakens into faintness and embarrassment only after she takes on the tedium of a man's life. Pisanio indeed seems to joke upon just such popular inversion of 'official' gender stereotypes: 'You must forget to be a Woman: change Command, into obedience' (III. iv. 155–6). But explanations for her change have invariably been in terms of patriarchy's resurgent hegemony: Imogen is trimmed and tamed, her impudence and independence suffering a tacit but forceful rebuke.[18]

However, there are less sociologically absolute explanations for Imogen's increasing placidity: her husband is faithless and wants her killed, sufficient cause one might think for depression; she walks a long way in the wilds, gets tired, sick, and is then drugged into sleep and confusion. Meanwhile, she never loses an independence of mind, moralizing in overtly political terms as she encounters novel freedoms and fears (III. vi. 6–15; III. vii. 54–9; IV. ii. 32–6). She doesn't cower, and avoids any stereotypical dependence upon men's greater strength; indeed, as she sickens, her wish is rather to be left alone, a form of pride as much as modesty or thoughtfulness. The increasingly 'feminine' airs that surround Imogen in Wales are more to do with the mountaineers' lyrical encomiums of her—rhapsody (IV. ii. 48–56) and then monody (IV. ii. 218–29, 258–82)—than her own softening. Furthermore, while these commentaries upon her nature suit Imogen's new status—no longer the rebellious recalcitrant of court, she is now a humble supplicant, physically unprotected, but shining in her beauty and gentleness and hence worthy of the boy's wonder—they do not capture her being or her function. The text's sense of Imogen remains balanced between the myth-hewn figurations of others and her own self-definitions: like Caliban, she is informed by, yet beyond, any discrete appellation, whether insult or praise. Hence the violence of her 'coming to life' after drugged sleep: the scene has been floating in mellifluous eulogy for the 'sweetest, fairest lily' (IV. ii. 201), before suddenly it explodes with the lily's profane metamorphosis ('Ods pittikins: can it be sixe mile yet?', IV. ii. 293). Imogen's waking idiom is confused but familiar, evoking the itinerant, rumbustious iconoclast so disruptive to the court's due order: 'Oh! Giue colour to my pale cheeke with thy blood, That we the horrider may seeme to those Which chance to finde vs' (IV. ii. 329–32). Clearly, an audience is not meant to settle upon some new washed version of the princess, prim and decorous.

---

[18] e.g. Ann Thompson, 'Person and Office: The Case of Imogen, Princess of Britain', in Vincent Newey and Ann Thompson, eds., *Literature and Nationalism* (Liverpool, 1990), 79–86. Alan Sinfield, *Faultlines: Cultural Materialism and the Politics of Dissident Reading* (Oxford, 1992), ch. 3, considers examples of feminine discontinuity, when 'continuous interiority' collapses under the strain of 'perfunctory closure' and patriarchal ideology.

However, as with Caliban, Imogen must be approached as a textual and cultural 'screen'. She is both thinker and thought, actor and acted upon. In other words, she does not quite control her own representation. For not only the male characters, but the text itself, construct Imogen as might a voyeur, cruel, objectifying, at times pornographic. She is made the victim not only of others' words and wishes, but of her own. Her language repeatedly rebounds upon her. Always these pay lip service to conventional proleptic irony. However, instead of resting with a wry kind of situational rhyme, they retrospectively undermine the original statement by implying a kind of desire or responsibility for the humiliation. There seems a willingness to allow the play to hurt women, callously, just as its characters would. Occasions of Imogen's textual exploitation are numerous. To mention only some obvious examples: her invitation to Iachimo to keep his jewels in her bedchamber, where she shall 'pawne' her 'Honor' for their safety and truly yield his 'Trunke' (I. vi. 193–210); her jibes to Cloten about Posthumus' 'meanst Garment'; her riposte that 'He neuer can meete more mischance, then come To be but nam'd of thee' (II. iii. 133–4); her euphoric anticipations over Milford, comparing her own haste to 'one that rode to's Execution' (III. ii. 71). At other times Imogen's irony consciously offers herself as victim. 'Obedient as the Scabbard' (III. iv. 80), is Imogen's vicious pun upon her presumed status as a 'Strumpet'—scabbard is a translation of vagina—and so on her supposed relish in 'striking with the scabbard', or in rendering her husband a cuckold. 'The Lambe entreats the Butcher', she cries (III. iv. 97), mockingly endorsing the way her clear script is twisted, through others' pathologies, into something masochistic.

The moment which most infamously embarrasses Imogen is her mistaken blazon over her enemy's dead trunk (IV. ii. 296–332).[19] Falling upon Cloten's body, she is made temporarily complicit in the regime that, from various directions, would have her raped, killed, or stopped. The necrophilic union

---

[19] In *Clyomon and Clamydes*, ed. Littleton, ll. 1532–73, Clyomon's golden shield, laid over the vanquished king of Norway, makes the princess Neronis think that her lover is dead. Providence's quick descent to forestall Neronis' despair emphasizes just how unrelenting and unformulaic is Shakespeare's treatment of Imogen.

appears to fulfil such rapacious desires: wiping her face in the remnants of that of her 'husband', Imogen paints with antic grimness a post-coital tableau of bloody dehymenization; once more the play shames her 'pudencie so Rosie' (II. iv. 163). As Belarius fears, then, Cloten's body indeed does have 'a taile More perillous then the head' (IV. ii. 143–4). Imogen's imperilled propriety, her disembodied 'taile' or pudendum, becomes a metaphor of centrifugal corruption and civil commotion. At the same moment as sister and brother share this 'bloody Pillow' (IV. ii. 363), tempting chaos ('For Nature doth abhorre to make his bed With the defunct, or sleepe vpon the dead', IV. ii. 357–8), the queen mother suffers 'A Feauor with the absence of her Sonne', and lies terribly 'Vpon a desperate bed' (IV. iii. 2–6). Lucius records the droll curiosity of necrophilia; back at court, the queen writhes as if incestuously jealous, her son's returning 'clot-pole' suggesting a kind of executing incubus upon the devilish mother. With Imogen already the creeping succuba, the two women's fates momentarily conflate: it is difficult to measure the purpose or extent of Shakespeare's homologous ironies here, but at the very least Imogen's travails suggest how difficult it is to battle out of oppression or complicity into the kinds of transformation and clarity which, back at court, Imogen's pastoral appropriations might have imagined. Like the 'single opposition' of Cloten and Guiderius and the battle between Britain and Rome, Imogen's grief for her lover-cum-enemy serves primarily to replicate the conditions of the opening duel between Cloten and Posthumus. Desire both proceeds from and devolves upon a sacrifical 'Carkasse'. But Imogen here doesn't only embrace such dead matter in Cloten. The moment's hybridity suggests that she too becomes part of the thing sacrificed; it is a piquant symbol of her textual exploitation.[20]

But if Imogen is mocked or humiliated by the text's apparent infelicities, she is hardly alone. Almost definitively, the play's esoteric analogical structure, with its frequent recklessness as to affect, frustrates 'bourgeois' hankerings for empathy. The

---

[20] Cf. Philip Brockbank, 'History and Histrionics in *Cymbeline*', *On Shakespeare: Jesus, Karl Marx, and Other Essays* (Oxford, 1989), 281, who, like many critics, sees 'a triple sacrifice' of 'an innocence that will revive, an animal barbarity which is properly exterminated and a duplicity (involving Posthumus) which has still to be purged'.

pervasive irony is further grounded in the way the text subverts
the very generic stereotypes it depends upon. Consider some of
the other supposedly virtuous figures: rarely can a stage king,
short of slapstick mockery, be so embarrassed by his play as is
the eponymous 'hero' here. Cymbeline's subtly wrought senility
evokes, in a sense, the superannuation of any 'straight' genre,
whether historical, pastoral, or romantic; his sharded mind, an
egregious mix of Shallow, Prospero, and Claudius, is both an
indictment of inherited authority and an ironical counterpoint
to the play's audacious eclecticism. Irony is also the measure of
Cymbeline's lost sons. Bursting with courage and 'nobility', they
are given a gauche kind of forthrightness which makes them as
ridiculous as refreshing. As the ignorant *idiots savants*, they do
what, in a sense, nobody expects or wants: they pay pastoral's
promises, embodying the mode's incessant purity of motive, its
distrust of the court, its sanctimonious certitudes and robustly
unaccountable violence, and bring the lot to a courtly centre
where none of these things can pass off without censure, compromise, or ridicule. That is, they are rendered dramatically
unreflexive in a piece of work almost neurotically aware of its
own generic sources, of the parent(s) it must emulate and, in a
sense, kill. The noble Roman, Lucius, suffers still worse treatment: he walks on to the stage as if from one of Shakespeare's
'real' Roman plays, puffed with an honour and stoicism quite
unsustainable amid the play's abiding irreverence. Imogen's
blithe neglect of Lucius' expectation of deliverance from execution is indicative of *Cymbeline*'s generic recklessness, its refusals
of piety and expectation.

Consequently, there is nobody but the heroine to take up
audience desire. It is only Imogen, with her maverick mix of
facileness, obduracy, exhibitionism, self-subversion, and true
love, who comes close to the play's erratic sense of unresolved
possibilites, latent conflicts, and uneasy rapprochements. And
here is the hint as to the direction of Shakespeare's next two
romances: the play needs figures of the 'wilderness' able
to embody and accelerate popular desire, but to do so with
theatrical economy. A new decorum is necessary: one which
magnifies, which allows for many in one, for magical metamorphoses, for projections which are both in and beyond the
moment, impossible, desirable, potentially equally destructive as

transformative. Hence, therefore, the storms, the bear, Autolicus, Ariel, and Caliban. *Cymbeline*, like *Pericles*, although eccentric, itinerant, hugely experimental, remains tied to history and precedent in ways that frustrate the audacity of Shakespeare's romantic political imagination. Imogen, having set up a turbulent threat and promise, needs to be able to pass the responsibility onto others; she could 'return' to her role as princess, secure the framework of generic and political order, yet without abdicating the more dissonant energies which her initial rebellion sets in motion. But there is no such figure. The language of the play is bursting with restlessness and challenge, but it is an energy which none of the characters is capable of harnessing; it is supra-characterological. This does not make *Cymbeline* any less tremulous or nascent in its politics than the other romances; all of them are 'unfinished', rife with unrecuperated desires, in ways that are scrupulously faithful to Shakespeare's (as our own) anxious historical moment. But in the other plays, Shakespeare more securely separates the princess, as a symbol of unity and security as well as the populace, from the anxious and perhaps destructive desires which surge in subject and country. Autolicus and Caliban, for example, work in creative, unsettling counterpoint to Perdita and Miranda. In *Cymbeline*, by way of contrast, the turbulence remains bound up in the nation's princess. Consequently, Shakespeare makes the basic archetype informing Imogen—that of embodied virtue, remaining the 'right way up' howsoever assaulted—take up a fearful strain. Imogen's humiliations epitomize the play's intermittent indifference to 'natural justice', a cavalier, almost obtuse, mischief which, like so many of the romances' implosions into wilderness—mental or geographic—suggests both the discords within decorum and the unreal or tenuous quality of putative resolutions. She is battered by error and absurdity, but can do nothing but dust herself off and carry on because the play doesn't separate the symbolics from the physicality of the princess. She suffers the tensions and aspirations for which she might, in a more decorous world, be mainly the talisman. This is why she cannot in the end be folded away into some preordained niche. Hers is a role of inclusive promise, awaiting and embodying liberties as yet denied. One can talk of 'ragged prophets', such as in a way Autolicus and Caliban are, proleptic in their very resistance to hegemony; and Imogen too, whether penned up, smeared with blood, bashed to the ground by her husband, is similarly both prescient and frustrated, punished ragged in her devotion to novelty and will. Hence, I think, the bruised but almost jack-in-the-box violence of Imogen's famous words to Posthumus:

> Why did you throw your wedded lady from you?
> Think that you are upon a rock, and now
> Throw me again.
>
> (V. v. 261–3)

In a way the words, at once earthy and fantastical, reflect a return to 'herself', and to her inchoate, surging, chiliastic sense of lack and need; in another way they are a perfect expression of her ambivalent capture, hostage to a genre whose constraints she seeks to burst, and to a masculinity whose violence she both rebukes and invites; or again, her words reprise the uproar of the Welsh scenes, and most particularly the moment when Cloten's head is hurled from rock to creek with anarchic ebullience. Once more, it is difficult to disentangle the turbid textual connectedness. But one thing is clear from the heroine's final expression of her passion: whatever one's expectations of this framing union between princess and 'pauper', one cannot dismiss those energies, often illicit, which have hitherto given Imogen the power to stretch, to soil, and at times to tear, the garments of decorum and possibility.

PERDITA

Much that is incipient or highly contested in Marina and Imogen finds lucid and confident expression in Perdita. With his grown-up 'changeling', Shakespeare goes far beyond the simple pastoral pun of a queen dressed as a shepherdess. Perdita speaks a maturely turned 'common-sensical' philosophy, attentive with a kind of saint-like inclusiveness and humility to the desires of her ignorant peers. She respects that which is provincial, homely, and modest, mistrusts frills and painted faces (IV. iv. 10, 22), and nurtures a quietly stern conviction of the injustice if inevitability of state suppression (IV. iv. 17, 39–40). She is hostile to fictive fooling because it detracts from a power and security drawn from place, custom, and a sense of rooted legitimacy. Only if without this anchor of humbleness might the king's terror frighten her: 'or how Should I (in these my borrowed Flaunts) behold The sternnesse of his presence?' (IV. iv. 23–4). Aware of material compulsions ('Out alas; You'ld be so leane . . .' IV. iv. 110–11), she is yet unprepared to accept with Camillo that a lack of 'Prosperitie' will pall the mind as well as the cheek (IV. iv. 574–8). This implies what her 'father's' riches may belie but her stormy history ensures: that she has indeed suffered the 'Affliction' of an outcast, toughening rather than diminishing her resolve. As she earlier reminds Florizel, 'your Greatnesse Hath not beene vs'd to feare' (IV. iv. 17–18). All the time Perdita is both of and outside the court, her wisdom as appropriate to green velvet as to the 'greene-sord' (IV. iv. 157). Her ignorance of the fardel's surprises must confirm rather than withdraw her provincial bona fides. So, while Perdita's 'innate' gentleness is an ideological bedrock of the play, it is partly this regal grace which asserts her 'pastoral-cum-georgic' ethics as worth respecting. There is no irony in her loyalty, nor any sense that its farming and customs are beneath her notice. The disparate origins here succour one another.

Perdita seems consciously to resist the types of patriarchal manipulation which subsist even within the encomiums that celebrate her. Hitherto in the play male discourse—Leontes', Polixenes', Antigonus'—has stressed woman's violent instability: her open body, wagging tongue, painted face. Perdita, by contrast, and like her mother, is unafraid of sensual fulsomeness, her body alive with nascent sexuality. She seeks a *via media*, the gentle but elusive ambition of unmorbid desire ('What? like a Coarse?' 'No, like a banke, for Loue to lye, and play on: Not like a Coarse: or if: not to be buried, But quicke, and in mine armes', IV. iv. 129–32). Her wishes suggest a subtle defiance of the masculine need to possess and somehow paralyse the female. Perdita's suspicion of masculine violence or scurrility links to her distrust of the arts of disguise, flattery, and seduction: she recognizes the affinity of such aggressions to loss and enslavement. Aware that her discourse is being taken hostage by festivity's pre-emptive rituals ('Sure this robe of mine Do's change my disposition'), she is an avid censor of pretension, but also of enthralment and dictatorship. Hence the little morals in her flower-giving: they are not prescriptively hostile to sex, but to the precipitous abdication of that which the man will not and cannot return.

Consequently, her enthusiasm to make love to Florizel remains hedged by fears not only of physical pain but of abandonment: 'The Mary-gold, that goes to bed with' Sun, And with him rises, weeping' (IV. iv. 105–6). Perdita's sexuality implies a social liberty and perhaps mobility which she would not have trampled upon. Thus, while one may allegorize such a 'Sun' with a bedding monarch, it is not a simple equation of awe. Here Phoebus might be a licentious ruiner of girls, or in his power a kind of rapist. Equally, Perdita does not restrict her sun to kings, or even to prince's mistresses: Dorcas and Mopsa should receive its radiance, while the 'weeping' flower may simply bear dew, a sign of crisp, fresh health, much like Perdita herself. Consequently there appears to be an incipient democratizing of the sun: rather than the person or property of the monarch, the sun is an immanent motion and energy, received by all, enfranchising of all, including the king:

> I was not much a-fear'd: for once, or twice
> I was about to speake, and tell him plainely,
> The selfe-same Sun, that shines vpon his Court,
> Hides not his visage from our Cottage, but
> Lookes on alike.
>
> (IV. iv. 443–7)

Perdita's 'selfe-same Sun' sets out a position thoroughly rejecting of absolutism's possessive assumptions. 'Cottage' and 'Court' shall unite in her spring.

For Perdita's example does not stand alone. It contributes to the play's general interest in the decorum of aspiration and enfranchisement. Advocating a watering of the blue blood and a widening of franchise, Polixenes' horticultural eugenics annotate Perdita's behaviour, both its pride and presumption:

> [You] see (sweet Maid) we marry
> A gentler Sien, to the wildest Stocke,
> And make conceyue a barke of baser kinde
> By bud of Nobler race. This is an Art

> Which do's mend Nature: change it rather, but
> The Art it selfe, is Nature.
> . . . Then make you Garden rich in Gilly'vors
> And do not call them bastards.

(IV. iv. 92–9)

His tutorial would grant the power for such manipulations to the aristocrats ('gentler Sien'), but this again serves unknowingly to endorse the example of his son. Perdita's immediate response is one of brusque dismissal:

> Ile not put
> The Dible in earth, to set one slip of them:
> No more then were I painted, I would wish
> This youth should say 'twer well: and onely therefore
> Desire to breed by me.

(IV. iv. 99–103)

Her response garners narrative moment from its backward allusiveness. Characteristically the text is playing with dark memories, sowing new meanings as the old ones die. For Perdita's proscribing of the 'bastards' evokes her particular amplification of Mamillius' sad tale. This tale was cried down amid calumny of the new-born 'bastard', and Mamillius declines, according to the false father, 'Conceyuing the dishonour of his Mother' (II. iii. 13). At the most basic ledger of justice, Perdita's disapproval of bastards would correct Leontes' lunatic parenting. Her resistance evokes Hamlet's attacks on face-painting (III. i. 144), public dishonesty finding its symbol in a harlot's mask. Thus Perdita echoes, but rebukes, Mamillius' justification for loving one of his ladies 'better' because of her particular way with beauty's artificial 'Pen' (II. i. 7–11); as I have argued, this moment certifies Mamillius' embroilment in the bawdy malaise, as the coloured brows picture the state's fractured globe of rule. The daughter will oppose not only the terms of artifice within which his tale is constructed, but the political mess which hastened both its conception and its silencing: aristocratic exclusiveness and fear of the people ranking stark and foolish among Leontes' mistakes. However, Polixenes' tolerance toward the bastards is as necessary as Perdita's distrust of falsely configuring art. The king recognizes how things wild and unhoused—like Perdita— can be nurtured into improvement. Quite beyond the intention of either, Perdita is framed as the potential embodiment of both responses.

If one is searching for simple verisimilitudes, such doubleness may seem absurd; but in the dialogical context it is rigorously appropriate. For there is a fullness, with nothing brittle or factitious, about the way Perdita can enact both 'Shepherdesse' and 'Queene' whilst, paradoxically, being identical to neither. She gives honour to both in a way that no one else in the plays quite achieves. If there is some force which unites her two identities, then it is a vaguely Platonic one, founded in a kind of meeting between her own cherished but half-hushed 'sincerity', and an audiences' similarly private, perhaps in Shakespeare's time incipient, sense of inner dignity. Whilst she is repeatedly invoked in terms of mythical types—pastoral praise apart from Polixenes 'excellent Witchcraft' and 'Enchantment'—she makes it a point never to be captured by any. Indeed, there is a strange sense that even the role she is given in the play itself is one of the 'borrowed Flaunts' which, to please her 'guests', she must endure against her more grounded will: 'I see the Play so lyes, That I must beare a part', she says (IV. iv. 655–6), stepping out of the action, much like Autolicus, to both decry and surmount its magnetic mendacity. This is to suggest a high degree of meta-theatricality: Perdita evokes a kind of centred integrity which the genre barely allows. She is never quite 'in' the moment, invoking instead a true 'her' which must be inferred from her denials of self-presence: 'me (poore lowly Maide) Most Goddesse-like prank'd vp . . . I should blush To see you so attyr'd: sworne [swoon?] I thinke, To shew my selfe a glasse' (IV. iv. 9–14). Unlike, say, Cloten, there is no adequate 'glasse' for her in the play's world; she is drawn into Shakespeare's characteristically specular drama ('beare a part'), but demurs from giving the image legitimacy.

The sheep-shearing is in a basic way a reflexive representation of pastoral drama. Consequently, the heroine's detachment from her function, the way her mind is constantly elsewhere—her flower-giving, for example, satisfies the day's game whilst more privately and pertinently reiterating her fears—suggests how her own self-definition is peculiarly anticipatory. Yet such definition is not really bound up in becoming a princess, although of course it is bound up in her love for Florizel: the point is one of desire that exceeds while not despising custom. This can be generalized in political terms as something like liberated agency, and in generic terms as a thorough transmutation beyond those old, static, imprisoning modes in which the men of the play still like to figure her. So, Florizel's courtly-pastoral decorum is to frame his appetites in 'metaphysical' conceits; he thinks that to praise his love in terms of myth is to ennoble her: 'These your vnvsuall weeds, to each part of you Do's giue a life: no Shepherdesse, but *Flora*' (IV. iv. 1–2). But it is just such reversion to textually constructed beauty that Perdita abjures. In herself, her own subjectivity—and such vaguely 'essentializing' notions of character seem to make a curious return in Perdita's fierce and unillusioned self-possession—she seems both to apprehend and get beyond the archetypes which half-subvert both Marina and Imogen. She is a powerful presence, looking ahead both to nineteenth-century heroines, like the Brontes', and to the gradual suffragist reforms which would follow upon a burgeoning consciousness of the dignity in honest desire.

But if Perdita's virtues suggest a pattern for the future, they must find particular influence upon her lover, Florizel. And indeed, the terms used often evoke a kind of sensuous pedagogy. As the shepherd says of her suitor: 'he says he loves my daughter, I think so too; for neuer gaz'd the Moone Vpon the water, as hee'l stand and reade As 'twere my daughters eyes' (IV. iv. 173–6). The gaze is upon the water rather than the moon: waves and tides are 'reade', as if the book of rule, the moon gleaning its script from its customary servant. These waters, as so often, will analogize a political estate, only here without caprice or violence; the gaze precludes such petulance, conferring instead an awe almost immobilizing. Florizel's love thus arrests time: 'I wish you A waue o'th Sea, that you might euer do Nothing but that: moue still, still so: And owne no other Function' (IV. iv. 140–3). The lyricism is exact, savouring the feeling of joy as it is felt, and in a sense it is carping to complain that Florizel's wish to freeze history ('still, still so') is irresponsible and forgetful: such negligences are at the core of their love. However, thus mesmerized, Florizel repeats the drugged idolatry of Autolicus' choughs. Leontes has displayed the tyranny of fallen 'Affection', and Florizel serves the same concupiscent master ('I Am heyre to my affection', IV. iv. 482). Furthermore, he displaces his own affect onto its cause, suggesting, as did his embrace of the masque-like qualities of the feast, a narcissism not entirely unlike that which Leontes sees mirrored in Mamillius. Thus, Florizel's delight seeks to celebrate by paralysis, his lover fossilized in endlessly recurring perfection. As with Leontes' figurative transformation of his wife into cold stone, Florizel's 'affection' is one of various anticipations of Julio Romano's consummating sculpture: repeatedly, such 'art' vacillates, much like Perdita in Florizel's vision, between wonder and collapse. It thus links with earlier petitions, to be 'red with mirth', to 'strangle such thoughts' (IV. iv. 47, 54), where violence chases exuberance, an impatiently leering reaper. 'Carpe diem' always contains such implications, but the difference with Florizel is that he possesses the means to compel the obedience he seeks.

Perdita's flower-giving shows her aware of her situation's sexual ambiguity: Florizel aestheticizes, without quite banishing, the will to rape. Perdita perhaps takes note of the ambiguous morality of Florizel's anthropomorphism, adopting as it does models in Jupiter's descent as a bull to rape Europa, Neptune's as a ram to deceive Bisaltis (IV. iv. 26–31). These gods, in Florizel's somewhat gauche translation, 'bellowed' and 'bleated' their unilateral success; Florizel's own luxurious metaphors are a similar male mating cry, which Perdita firmly recognizes and rebukes. Florizel's strangles and arrests, his 'owne no other Function', can take on rather menacing contours. As if part of her role as proleptic repairer, then, Perdita quells her beau's hyperbolic poetasting just as she resists his anaesthetizing, and aestheticizing, of political function: 'I cannot speak So well, (nothing so well) no, nor meane better By th'patterne of mine owne thoughts, I cut out The puritie of his' (IV. iv. 381–4). Her words appear to defer to Florizel's sophistication, but in fact reverse the modest expectation, interpreting his words in terms of her own thoughts. Semiotic and political 'mend[ing]'— anticipatory, shadowed by threats, sustained by the romantic idealism which the genre's utopianism permits if only contingently endorses—is at least potentially in her hands.

Thus Perdita's cheeks, like those of the shepherd's wife, are warmed with 'blushes': once more, the red blood reigns in place

of wan and pale winter. Here, however, it is the hue either
of embarrassment or some kind of guilty thrill: 'He tels her
something That makes her blood looke on't', observes Camillo,
offering a familiar pun about Perdita's noble birth (IV. iv.
159–60). But the moment also evokes Florizel's command
to Perdita to 'Be merry', to 'Strangle' her fearful thoughts of
transgression, discovery, and arrest, and to 'be red with mirth'
(IV. iv. 40–54). Uneasy with his embrace of disguise and his
extravagant praise, Perdita soon rebukes Ferdinand for false-
ness: she seems to understand the royalist quality of his praise
(IV. iv. 145–6), as she does the 'painted' face, as a register of
artifice. And as she does so she further complicates the scene's
sense of 'blood': 'but that your youth And the true blood which
peepes fairely through't Do plainely giue you out an vnstain'd
Shepherd With wisedome, I might feare (my Doricles) You
woo'd me the false way' (IV. iv. 147–51). The quality of 'blood'
here has become infinitely elusive: she says his 'blood' tells
true, when she knows she tells an untruth; if he does have
'true blood', then it is that of a prince and not a shepherd;
consequently, she chastises him for using his 'blood'—his breed-
ing, his lust, and the way the two combine to construct his
fantasy of paralysing courtly flattery—to seduce her 'falsely'.
The 'blood' then returns to one of the denotations in Autolicus'
song: the red-stained sheets of defloration (compare IV. iv. 105–
6; 122–4). She still speaks partly for and from her country
station; unlike Marina, Perdita doesn't have to struggle for
sexual, and implicitly political, empathies.

Shakespeare's romance heroines, then, are not simply vehicles
of wistful or nostalgic utopianism. In a sense the plays here
permit a doubling-up of prophetic import: the socio-economic
compulsions embodied in an Autolicus are in dialogue with
the aristocratic, populist optimism of the heroines. But such
optimism is hard fought and, in the case of the overburdened
Imogen, as tenuous as her own hold upon decorum. And in
none of the plays is it a question simply of angel and beast.
The princesses are forced to get amongst it in ways that might
remind one of Elizabeth's precarious years under lock and
key. A similarly inclusive suffrage animates the heroines as
much as it does the rogues. Together, as two sides of a coin,
or criss-crossing visions of historical desire, the twin groups

construct interpenetrating prolepses. These works are not satisfied by the cursory patriarchalism of the generic skeleton, any more than their heroines are the inert vessels of a wistful pastoral tradition.

8

Endings

THE chapters so far have argued that Shakespeare's febrile use of metaphor, and the diffusion of narrative authority and responsibility among competing voices or agencies, creates a politically restless genre which offers a robust and often irreverent challenge to providentialist or conservative teleologies. And yet, it may be argued, one cannot wish away each play's harmonious surcease: however ragged the ride, the plays end in a courtly and royalist haven. Mistakes are resolved, families reconcile, disruption ebbs to silence. And, like the tragic hero's death, such placation accords entirely with audience expectation.

But what exactly does this mean? A play has to end, but it doesn't follow that an ending equals closure, like some mathematical equation where the preceding figures combine inexorably to form the final sum. There are large elements of convention in generic expectation, and, in the theatre, a sense that a contract has been fulfilled. But commercial obligations neither end nor define the matter; conversations, phrases, arresting sights, play in the mind's eye both before and after the play's putative denouement. The act of reading merely emphasizes such hermeneutic freedom, and the medium's resistance to any remorseless narrative 'bottom line'. One doesn't forget empathies or abjure affiliations: an ending will rarely provoke retrospective revision of emotional or intellectual investments. And in works ripe with invention and novelty it is by no means certain that convention must carry the day. The dramatist might follow the form, bow to the strictures of source or plot, whilst informing the ending with equivocations and imperatives perhaps unusual in terms of generic history but dialectically faithful to the work at hand. One important question, then, is whether the forces and conflicts that have driven the action are in fact resolved, or whether they in some sense subsist within the ending's putative transformations. The political status of Shakespeare's romantic 'teleology' (if indeed there is one), will therefore partly depend upon the continuing currency of any forward and backward dialogues.

The late plays are sometimes thought to share discursive priorities with the Jacobean court masque, particularly as it matured in Jonson's careful hands, where misrule, in the form of an antimasque, is quite swept away by the serendipitous appearance of some principle of grace or personage of majesty. To be sister to the masque, then, is to be courtly, idealistic, and hierophantic. But the currency of any such relation requires careful scrutiny. Does some epiphanous divinity descend as ultimate authority, free from Shakespeare's networks of allusion and recapitulation, and so from the complicities and complications they inscribe? Is any single figure given a meta-dramatic completeness, able perfectly to embody the functions of either playwright or play, and so to speak for the text's sense of proleptic decorum? Or do Shakespeare's borrowings from this courtly form, like his appropriations of things classical, work mainly to serve his work's abiding principles of multiplicity, heteroglossia, and unassuaged desire?

Criticism's quests for a meta-dramatic exemplar have usually rested upon Prospero, the magician bullying his puppets into grace. And certainly Prospero's nature, like his project, typifies the ambivalence of the genre's bridling of desire. At once titanic and elegiac, wistful and vicious, the mage embodies romance's sibling temptations toward both chaos and order. Indeed, it is the very sense that Prospero's appetites at times threaten his mission that suggests how Shakespeare's wizard, even as he epitomizes the romance world's ambitious turbulence, cannot quite encapsulate Shakespeare's art: the play itself, so contrapuntally terse, has a self-possession denied each of its characters. Prospero lacks an ultimate power to define the play's 'generic brain'; its temper is often more mischievous than moralizing; and as in all the plays, there are demotic energies, both brutal and thrilling, which challenge any strict taskmaster. Might the pulse of these plays—their proleptic orientations, the manners of their players, their appeal to an audience—find comparable measurement in an Autolicus, or even a Caliban?

Autolicus' pack, or what he at another point calls his 'bowget', evokes the bustle and litter of a public theatre's tiring-house: songs, tunes, ribbons and gods, ballads, benedictions, table-books and points, a vast array of clothes and accoutrements fit for any disguise. Part of this pack is his songs. As if the theatre's own resplendent book-keeper, Autolicus sings to the click of counted cash: 'he singes seuerall Tunes, faster then you'l tell money; he vtters them as he had eaten ballads, and all mens eares grew to his Tunes' (IV. iv. 185–8). But his meta-dramatic potency extends beyond being some mascot of consumerism. His very being is an effect of his art. Autolicus appears to be created out of the tunes he sings; they sustain him as food and money, in turn bestowing the power to recreate others in the image of his ditties. He eats, they grow, as if sharing the sensory experience: the receptive organs of each become mutual, as the body of Autolicus engrosses and becomes, tautologically, the communal mind which he figures and shapes. Autolicus is here given a potency familiar from Pygmalion, that of making alive, manifest, and danger-ously seductive the inanimate fancies of art. Coterminously, his hurly-burly dazzle of songs distils the play's echo-ripe harmo-nies, at once competitive and complementary, successive and simultaneous.

Indeed, Autolicus' mimetic reflexiveness seems to have been plotted from the very choice Shakespeare made of his name, probably derived from Ovid. In *Metamorphoses*, the infamous thief is the first of twins, one born of Mercury, the other Apollo. Shakespeare, however, appears to conflate in his rogue the qualities of Ovid's twins, making him the son of both gods:

> Now when shee full her tyme had gon, shee bare by *Mercurye*
> A sonne that hyght *Awtolychus*, who provde a wyly pye,
> And such a fellow as in theft and fliching had no peere.
> He was his fathers own sonne right: he could mens eyes
>   so bleere,
> As for too make y black things whyght, and whyght things
>   black appeere.
> And by *Apollo* (for shee bare a payre) was borne his brother

Philammon, who in musick arte excelled all farre all other,
As well in singing as in play.[1]

An intermediary between heaven and earth, Mercury is the
perfect dramaturge: he can be playwright or director, summon-
ing actors, dancers, and precedents, the ringmaster of a supernatural circus.[2] But, as Jonson's *Mercury Vindicated* suggests,
the reputation of Mercury was dubious; impudence and
unpredictability often upstaged the obedient supernatural messenger. Golding's preface to Ovid glosses him thus: 'the suttle
sort that use too filch and lye, With theeves, and Merchants
whoo to gayne theyr travell doo applye'.[3] He adapts precedents
from scurrility or divinity as the moment's exchange demands.
In 'hermetic' alchemy, similarly, wisdom and folly coincide in
popular exchange: the wing-foot god conflates with the mystical
sage, Hermes Trismegistus, in turn either teacher or pupil of
Moses, and so custodian of the mysterious wisdom that priest,
magician, and king must seek to discover.[4] A further analogue
might be mercury's quicksilver capacity to absorb other metals:
magically, and as it were romantically, it can accumulate,
transform, and yet retain its identities. As an emblem and
example of the medium's processes, then, the mercurial
Autolicus challenges the play's nominally supreme justice
and narrator, Apollo. However, Autolicus is also Apollo's
son: might he be the 'heir' for whom the community on
'crutches' awaits, and in whom they are mocked? This inheriting
capability adds a further political cachet to the mercurial
presence in the pedlar's pack, as, emulating Hermes' duping of
Apollo, Autolicus not only enthralls and steals the 'army' of
his nominal host but turns his gullible audience to 'stone'
and acquires the power of prophecy (IV. iv. 596–620).
The play's arts are thus plotted in its rogue's etymology.
As Hermes, he is god of hermeneutics, the archetypal interpreter, wherein to 'interpret' means both to narrate and to

---

[1] *Shakespeare's Ovid Being Arthur Golding's Translation of the Metamorphoses*,
ed. W. H. D. Rouse (London, 1961), XI. 359–66. (Hereafter *Golding's
Metamorphoses*.)
[2] e.g. in *The Rare Triumphs of Love and Fortune* (ll. 204–56).
[3] 'The Preface too the Reader', 65–6.
[4] See e.g. Douglas Brooks-Davies, *The Mercurian Monarch: Magical Politics from
Spenser to Pope* (Manchester, 1983), 1–13 et al.

decipher; as the stealer of Apollo's flock, this Mercury is a threat to the Delphic law; and, as a son to the same Apollo, this minstrel is a challenge to our very definition of the Apollonian—or as so often in critical history, the Shakespearian—voice and progeny.[5]

Autolicus' magic is naturalistically bogus, but dialectically real enough. Accordingly it again takes up an eponymous mantle, his multiplying arts invoking the romance mode's investment in dreams of blessing and perfection. His smocks are advertised as if 'she-Angell[s]' (IV. iv. 211), while his 'Tromperie' seems so 'hallowed' as to bestow a 'benediction' (IV. iv. 598–603). Autolicus boasts of his mesmeric prowess at the fair in terms which directly echo Cleomenes and Dion's description of the voice and thunder at Delphos: the sound of the oracle so surprises Cleomenes' 'Sence' that he is 'nothing' (III. i. 10–11), while Autolicus' 'Nothing' leaves 'no hearing, no feeling, but my Sirs Song', 'all their other Sences stucke in Eares' (IV. iv. 615). His arts shadow Florizel's amatory idolatry: 'When you sing, I'ld haue you buy, and sell so', says the prince, exactly anticipating the 'Pedler at the doore' who 'singes seuerall Tunes, faster then you'l tell money' (IV. iv. 137–8; 183–6). In such moments Autolicus' role ridicules the sheer promiscuity of reverence. Shakespeare is presenting a succession of ironical epiphanies, putatively revelatory moments in which wonder tussles with disbelief: the surprises of the fardel and statue offer further instances of an art, both spellbinding and stealthy, whose patron 'saint' appears to be the pedlar.

At times Autolicus' entertainment seems intimately to chime with romance's projective optimism, mediating between past and future with alluring, mysterious propheticism. For instance, his 'occupation' is to bear his part in song (IV. iv. 296–7); he sings with the two peasant girls:

[5] See 'Homeric Hymn to Hermes', a tale which with great economy suggests Autolicus' meta-dramatic capability; *Golding's Metamorphoses*, II. 846–79; Joan Hartwig calls him 'a kind of 'fallen' Apollo'. *Shakespeare's Tragicomic Vision* (Baton Rouge, La., 1972), 117–20. The mythical Autolycus was himself famous for stealing people's cattle. Interestingly, his daughter married one Laertes, who was widely suspected to have been cuckolded in the birth of their son Odysseus by Autolycus' foe, Sisyphus. Edward Tripp, *Dictionary of Classical Mythology* (London, 1988), 128.

> *Aut. Get you hence, for I must goe*
> *Where it fits not you to know.*
> *Dor. Whether?*
> *Mop. O whether?*
> *Dor. Whether?*
> *Mop. It becomes thy oath full well,*
> *Thou to me thy secrets tell.*
> *Dor. Me too: Let me go thether:*
> *Mop. Or thou goest to th' Grange, or Mill.*
> *Dor. If to either thou dost ill.*
> *Aut. Neither.*
> *Dor. What neither?*
> *Aut. Neither.*
>
> (IV. iv. 298–306)

The love-triangle theme is familiar from Sicilia and Bohemia alike, reprising the terms of Hermione's trial and disappearance, and the clown's courting of both Mopsa and Dorcas. Autolicus' song dramatizes himself in the roles, equally, of the shepherd-clown and of Hermione. His wordless and inexplicable exit prepares for a more mysterious reappearance: '*Then whether goest? Say whether?*' (IV. iv. 309), he leaves the girls imploring. Partly we know the answer: he's off to sell more stuff, in broader terms he's 'sworne' to facilitate the 'Money's a medler' market (IV. iv. 323), oral communications and bartered goods making way for the world of printed texts, cash and contract, the individualism of copyright. Beyond that, however, Autolicus' pack is preparing for Hermione's return: hence the enigma of the song's protagonist's departure, an enigma unsatisfied by mercantile explanations. It is rather about longing, love, and romance, and so about the desire for a consummating clari-fication of mystery, the dream of fictive return and closure. Autolicus at such moments prepares for the kind of encircl-ing satisfaction which his own role, through its manifold recapitulations and parasitic interventions, impishly teases and defers. Of course he again defers such satisfaction, puncturing the girls' naïve longing, akin to that of an unsceptical audience ('I loue a ballet in print, a life, for then we are sure they are true', IV. iv. 261–2), with a sharp commodifying shaft: 'And you shall pay well for 'em' (IV. iv. 315). But such commercial imperatives are part of his roles' capaciousness. So, the song prepares for the

return of the unreconciled, disappearing loved one, whilst
maintaining Bohemia's edgy obsession with bartered virginities:
'fits', 'oath', 'Grange' and 'Mill' are all ripe with the surreptitious pressures of harvest-time. As when Leontes' starved
eyes prey salaciously upon his unknown daughter, Autolicus'
arts teeter between wonder and depravity. His role 'as' theatrical mimesis therefore takes on the play's desire, alongside
its mischief and its profanity, for some kind of centripetal
return. Through Autolicus, then, the play works out alternative
distributions for romance's traditional investment in the
supernatural.

Autolicus eventually loses his reflexive capacity to propel the
arts of the play: the microcosmic 'Farthell',[6] which had been
represented by the sheets, budget, and pack of the pedlar, is
transmuted into the package attesting that the shepherdess is in
fact Leontes' abandoned child. However, the ensuing revelations continue to suggest his hand: 'such a deale of wonder is
broken out within this houre, that Ballad-makers cannot be able
to expresse it . . . This Newes (which is call'd true) is so like an
old Tale, that the veritie of it is in strong suspistion' (V. ii. 24–6).
The wider play, the silenced 'tale' of Mamillius, and the tall
ballads of Autolicus are here yoked together with the fulfilled
oracle as mutually supplementing fantasies. As the play's multiple narratives have suggested all along, popular ballads and
courtly tales together contribute to the hybrid that is romance.
But the identity of each analogous form to the full revealed
'wonder' is definitively imperfect: 'I neuer heard of such another
Encounter, which lames Report to follow it, and vndo's description to doe it' (V. ii. 58–9). Shakespeare uses the gentlemen
here to offer ironical commentary, both vindication and apology, upon his 'Tale's' risky generic appropriations. Their
circumlocutions and *non sequiturs* reflect the inadequacy of
courtly discourses, a redundancy confirmed by their appeal to
baggy popular traditions. Ridiculing the action as the most
hoary old cliché, they yet celebrate its audacity as an entirely
new genre, magically self-created. Yet, counter to any such

---

[6] A fardel could denote a box or package; a burden of sin and sorrow; the
advantage of profit; a book of collected sheets, like Autolicus' ballads; or a mask or
disguise as in French 'farder': like Autolicus' 'bowget' or packe', therefore, it can be
a metaphor of both the play and theatre.

ingenuous boast, they identify in this odd new-old mode a curious meta-destructiveness. Discursive origin is abandoned, and language's truth-telling power is undone, lamed into limping metaphor. So, typically paradoxically, the gentlemen appeal to empirical proof by asserting a prevailing power of sensuous delusion: 'Most true, if euer Truth were pregnant by Circumstance: That which you heare, you'le sweare you see, there is such vnitie in the proofes' (V. ii. 33). Hearing 'becomes' sight, the mind's eye fills the place of the absent body. It is a charter for poetic imagination, but also one in which 'blind' faith is the only recourse in the face of disappearing proofs: the events 'cannot bee spoken of', the encounter 'vndo's description to doe it', but it is exactly such description upon which we are asked to rely (V. ii. 44, 59). In literal terms, the scene unravels to a familiar 'nothing'; emotively, the very same rarity evokes presentments of genuine wonder. Shakespeare is relishing the denouement's crucial paradox, that of the long-delayed 'unspeakable comfort'. Whatever is in the air, it cannot be 'truly' spoken of: the art folds and turns between miracle, chimera, and joke.

The sense, then, is that one cannot *know* truth, but that whatever it might be, it rests in the possible coherence of opposite extremities: 'There was speech in their dumbnesse, Language in their very gesture: they look'd as they had heard of a World ransom'd, or one destroyed' (V. ii. 13–15). As Traversi notes, a 'grave' and pious Christian vision is 'half-revealed'. However, the point of these nebulous, teasing, apocalyptic invocations is that the other 'half', that which mocks or doubts or leaves half-baked, confounds the certainty of any epiphany.[7] Instead, the moment is characteristically unfinished, a teleological diffidence rooted in multiple recapitulations and therefore an unresolved, perhaps conflicting sense of what is imminent. For example, the gentleman's hesitancies recall the pleonasms and occupatio which, in the play's first scene, half-undermine similar assertions of princely conciliation; 'Nothing but Bon-fires' is an ambiguous call of celebration, suggesting the violent doubleness of the earlier storm, and an abiding sense that novelty, generic or political, stands on a cliff-edge of sheerness and destruction;

---

[7] Derek Traversi, 'The Final Scenes', in Kenneth Muir, ed., *The Winter's Tale: Casebook* (Glasgow, 1968), 174.

at the same time, the moment confirms the play's stubborn disappointing of chiliastic violence, a kind of agnosticism sketched in the scene's insistent comparison of oracular wonder to a dubious 'old tale'. Furthermore, the whole scene is partially ironized by the fact that the gentleman seeks words to describe and verify that which is already known by the audience to be true. 'Yond Crickets shall not heare it', said Mamillius (II. i. 31), but we already have: there is no unwonted return to teleological master-narratives, nor to the privileged possession of secrets withheld from the commonalty.

A kind of tolerant mischief, then, characterizes the extravagant circles of utopian romance. The tone of the gentlemen's reports is at once wide-eyed and winking: 'The Dignitie of this Act was worth the audience of Kings and Princes, for by such was it acted. . . . that which angl'd for mine Eyes (caught the Water, though not the Fish) was . . . his Daughter . . . Who was most Marble, there changed colour: some swownded, all sorrowed' (V. ii. 80–92). Discreet jokes—about the impudent role-playing of the King's Men, the sexiness of the shepherdess, the audacious trick about to be played upon the audience—threaten the moment's solemnity with more iconoclastic imperatives, textually both ahead and behind. So, despite our partial foreknowledge, the audience is hardly omniscient: we know nothing, yet, of Hermione's survival, and the scene lays wry jokes preparing for the moment when we too, like the witnesses of Delphic or fairground magic, will be dumbstruck in credulous admiration. If anything is sovereign, it is, tautologically enough, the text itself. Or, more particularly, metaphor: no single authority or denotation carries the day; interpretation and prediction rest in the stealth and surprises, the unrecuperated promises, of Shakespeare's analogical architecture.

It has seemed to many that at the play's end Autolicus is a neutered figure, bereft of both vitality and influence. However, there are ways in which his role continues to operate reflexively. For instance, his promise to the clowns to 'amend' his life is clearly to be taken with a pinch of salt; like Merrythought in *Pestle*, he parodies the genre's redemptive pretensions. And if he is folded into uneasy accommodation with the newly inclusive state, then this serves, I think, to confirm rather than deny the prophetic responsibility with which Shakespeare invests him.

For Autolicus has from his first entrance been characterized by an ability to embody both past and future, centre and margin. Thus, it should not be thought that his disappearance into normality is some kind of betrayal, or even disappointment, of his customary purposes. For Autolicus has not hitherto been separate from the power structures of the play's environment. Not only does he anticipate the play's main action in being 'whipped' from court to country, but his role once in the country is often one of recapitulation: the 'centre' cannot be forgotten when his circus occupies the 'margin'. Equally, his role is one of incipience: he animates, and prepares for the triumph of, nascent social and economic relations. One of the by-products of Autolicus' initial 'otherness', his exuberant nonconformity, is that it allows the activities in which he indulges to seem abnormal, liminal, or novel. For he is obviously much more than a 'sturdy' vagabond, one of the banes of Jacobean England. He is in fact the future as well as the past incarnate. He supplies what the festive crowd want, as if the metamorphosis of their desires: so it is as their future, their ambivalent consequence, that Autolicus achieves first his expropriative triumphs and then his integration and anonymity.

Consequently, his initial strangeness, the widely felt wonder that such gifts should descend, also works as a kind of confirmation that the action of the play spans a long period of time, a generation or more within which his dazzling mobility and splendidly useless goods can seem less exotic, and more an invitation to share in the future markets of plenty. Again, then, his role depends upon labile time-frames: speaking literally, he doesn't enter until sixteen years have already past; in terms of the dialogical effect, however, Autolicus' role, like that of the shepherds, replays the play's move toward a less stratified and exclusive—if hardly less foolish—polity. Similarly, the folding-in of Autolicus at the end—both figuratively in that he partakes somewhere in the statue, and in real terms in that he loses his mercurially reflexive manners and becomes mainly another player for preferment—reinforces how, throughout the romances, metaphor works as a prognosticative force. That is, the energies, vicious or virtuous, which he had figuratively predicted are now barely distinguishable from the broadened patriarchy now at court. Much of this still awaits fruition, its promissory quality shared, and set to wrangle, with the more idealistic princesses. Yet it is perhaps this maturing of metaphor into action which, ironically, proves the continuing authoritative potency of Autolicus even as he seems, rather lamely, to disappear. The arts and desires he animates can no longer be kept on the margins, exploited by a knowing few: Autolicus achieves his art's destiny which, in a way oddly like Prospero's, demands that he shrink into banality. For his triumph is the purchase of his goods, the acceptance that he does indeed tell true; with pack and book both empty, with nothing left to teach, both Autolicus and Prospero pass into that audience, on and off stage, whom they once so astounded.

And, still more precisely, Autolicus prepares for the equally mercurial Julio Romano, reputed to have created the statue of Hermione. This of course is one of the denouement's many opaque jokes: there is neither statue nor sculptor. Furthermore, Shakespeare's choice of Romano reinforces his discourse's rootedness in iconoclasm and mischief: the Italian was famous as a pornographer, suggesting more than anything the 'Dildo's' and 'fowle gap[s]' of Autolicus' pretty love songs (IV. iv. 196–9).[8] The textual manner, while not perhaps sarcastic, is irreverent, alive to broad-jawed 'sea-side' humour: 'Euery winke of an Eye, some new Grace will be borne' (V. ii. 110–11). And yet, however arch Shakespeare's jesting, the descriptions of Romano's work stand as an epitaph of idealizing art and, consequently, of the romance genre's more breathtakingly transcendent pretensions: '(had he himselfe Eternitie, and could put Breath into his Worke) would beguile Nature of her Custome, so perfectly he is her Ape' (V. ii. 96–9). The main outlet for Shakespeare's mischief here is the casually echoing, overdetermined quality of his verbs: 'beguile' suggests trickery, while to 'Ape' draws in not only the mockery of previous imposters but the shaggy intercessions of bear and satyrs. Autolicus calls himself the 'Ape-bearer', the haunter of 'Beare-baitings', able to 'beare his part' (IV. iii. 92–9). He too has the power, mostly but not entirely figuratively, to bereave people of their 'purses', of their minds and power and money (IV. iv. 616). Furthermore,

---

[8] In Jonson's *Alchemist*, II. ii. 44, the libidinous Epicure Mammon refers to 'dull Aretine', the satirist who wrote pornographic verses to accompany Romano's pictures.

the ravenous bear too is a further version of Apollo, god of all plastic energies: suspended between 'art' and 'nature', it lickingly sculpts its children into shape.[9] 'Iulio Romano', it would seem, has been seen on stage after all: 'Thither (with all greedinesse of affection) are they gone, and there they intend to Sup' (V. ii. 101–3). The text here is busy ensuring that familiar tropes—eating, mockery, affection—remain in play. Beast, minstrel, and sculptor, like Chinese dolls, are discovered one inside another.

And these recapitulations do not vanish with Romano; they rather find further manifestation in the statue's apparent depetrification. Hermione's reappearance already enjoys a metadramatic prestige as the ostensible satisfaction and completion of Mamillius' tale of 'Sprights, and Goblins': the climax's faithfulness to this tale's multiple narrators suggests the play's continuing disappointment of linear or univocal teleologies. For an ambiguous indecorousness endangers the straight face of reverence. Robbing the senses of its beholders, the apparition recalls, as much as it repairs, the earlier destructive, 'mock'-ing', creativities of sea, bear and thief. Furthermore, Shakespeare's false deaths and fake art, disarming simple empathies, appear partly to be transforming clichéd stage tricks. In Marston's *The Dutch Courtesan*, for instance, Beatrice wakes from her swoon and sees the lover whom she had believed dead. Immediately she assumes she is in heaven (V. ii. 36–81): fatal charades and rebirths into grace had become eminently mockable. Shakespeare's Ovidian memory further reinforces the ending's subtly poised politics. Two statues here contribute: not only Orpheus's famous tale of Pygmalion's Galatea, but the 'filthy *Propets*', turned initially into the first prostitutes, then into stone, by a Venus enraged by the denial of her divinity. It is in response to this double horror that Pygmalion builds his sensual altar.[10] The twin Ovidian precedents suggest the same mix of flouted divinity, petulant authoritarianism, and over-heated puritanism that so splits Sicilia. What is important here is the ambivalence of Pygmalion's example, as the strength of his desire transforms

---

[9] Compare Jonson: 'It is said of the incomparable *Virgil*, that he brought forth his verses like a Beare, and after form'd them with licking.' *Discoveries*, ll. 2449–50, in *Ben Jonson*, ed. Herford and Simpson, viii. 638.

[10] *Golding's Metamorphoses*, X. 255–67.

cold stone into warm flesh. The renaissance juggled alternative interpretations: Pygmalion's triumph might affirm the glorious transcendence of love, imagination, faith, art; alternatively, it might seem a fugitive, illicit, onanistic refuge, an act of narcissism, misogyny, and intemperance.[11] Accordingly—and as with Paulina's wondrous marble—fears of black magic haunt the dream come true. The forebodings are justified by the fate of Pygmalion's grandson. The child of flesh and ivory has a son, Cinyras, whose 'cursed seede' discovers the 'wicked womb' of his willing daughter, Myrrha, as pathologically obsessed with her creator as was Pygmalion with his creation.[12] Incestuous solipsism, as much as the civilizing arts of temperate government, compete as Pygmalion's heritage.[13] The resurrective principle hovers between redemptive wonder and dangerous transgression.

The Winter's Tale may well have influenced the court masque's similarly ambiguous use of the trope. In Thomas Campion's *The Lords' Masque* the contest over illegal and sanctioned enfranchisement is symbolized in the power to give life to statues.[14] By contrast, in Jonson's *Mercury Vindicated* Mercury, speaking for James and Nature, seems to mock the dissimulation of the 'statues dance', as if parodying the claims of Campion's masque.[15] The effect of Hermione's statue upon the audience is thereby suspended between the spellbinding and the larcenous. If the depetrified stone does indeed seek to canonize the play's own methods, then it is an epiphany summed up in the phrase, hovering like a reflexive crib over the revelations,

[11] Charles and Michelle Martindale, *Shakespeare and the Uses of Antiquity: An Introductory Essay* (London, 1990), 77, notes how Marston's *The Metamorphosis of Pygmalion's Image* (1598) is 'a poem by turns satiric, voyeuristic and lubricious'. Compare Jonathan Bate, *Shakespeare and Ovid* (Oxford, 1993), 234: 'All these dark contours are removed.'

[12] *Golding's Metamorphoses*, X. 312–13, 350–590 (538).

[13] George Sandys published a commentary and translation of *Metamorphoses* (Oxford, 1632), in which he seems ill at ease with Pygmalion: the statue 'may be some virgin in whom Pygmalion was enamoured, who, long as obdurate as the matter whereof she was made, was mollified at length by his obsequiousness'. See Martindale and Martindale, *Shakespeare and the Uses of Antiquity*, 78. One might compare Autolicus' ballad of the cold fish who wouldn't exchange flesh.

[14] *The Lords' Masque*, ed. I. A. Shapio, in *A Book of Masques*, 97–123.

[15] Jonson, *Mercury Vindicated*, ll. 126–34. Jonson's dialect grotesquerie, *The Irish Masque*, parodies Campion's *Somerset Masque*.

'mock'd with Art' (V. iii. 68). The revelation scene is startling and audacious, but in the same way as any magnificent live performance can be. It confers no higher truths but the yearning for such, a privilege it both grants and, albeit gently, ridicules. Hermione is wrinkled after all, the creases on her face figuring the corresponding lesions upon a smoothly marmoreal aesthetics. Transcendence is compromised by identity, linguistic and situational, with more temporal media. Resolutely 'forward and backward' in its organization, the play's time-frame remains resistant to simple linearity. Consequently, a metaphor for Shakespeare's punning architectonic might simply be Autolicus, the winking ringmaster behind the curtain. The surviving media are not all ambivalent: the personality and beauty of Perdita draw forth a consensually magnetic gaze, an awe and reverence similarly stealing the senses of her 'proselytes' (V. i. 104–9). But Shakespeare's willingness to locate numerous proxies for his own inventiveness, his own dubiously wrought omniscience— and the playful, tolerant trust this implies in the facility of metaphor—itself metaphorizes a political stance unafraid either of popular acclaim or of a certain experiential raggedness not to be tidied by authoritarianism either of state or script.

CYMBELINE AND JUPITER

The descent of Jupiter in *Cymbeline* is engineered in knowing fashion, as if to draw attention to something nominal and dispensable in those authorities that are conventionally, and as if naturally, accorded the privilege of reverence. Thus, the belatedness of Jupiter's appearance is itself a cause for scepticism, and together with his hop-scotch verse a signature to many critics of the belated interpolation of the whole scene into an already complete work.[16] For the play's action is basically

---

[16] See, for example, the 'Prefatory Note' to J. C. Maxwell's Cambridge edition of the play by John Dover Wilson, pp. vii-x, concurring with Granville-Barker's judgement that Shakespeare could not possibly have written 'the jingling twaddle of the apparitions'. E. K. Chambers, *William Shakespeare: A study of facts and Problems*, 2 vols. (Oxford, 1930), i. 486, believes it a 'spectacular theatrical interpolation'. Maxwell, however (pp. xi–xv), prefers the modern consensus which follows G. Wilson Knight in *The Crown of Life* and accepts it as 'Shakespearean'.

finished, its circles effectively straightened, when the thundering god pronounces his 'prophecy'. Jupiter himself suggests that to be 'delayed' is to be delightful, as if he had intended only at the end to emerge from behind the screen, the great director, to gain the palm.[17] But in the light of Antioch's riddle and Apollo's oracle, each of which at least frame basic patterns for the plot, Jupiter's teleological asymmetry would appear to emphasize that the stakes and government of the future rest in mortal hands.

Jupiter's glittering, meretricious appearance is prone to accident or absurdity. A great deal here depends upon the staging, and if the revelation is to come off with any solemnity then the dangers of tinniness, of creaking or cumbersome or trivializing machinery, must be overcome. Of course it is quite possible, given the requisite money and technology, to evoke power through spectacle. Leah Marcus has identified familiar Jacobean applications in Jupiter's descent, as he quashes the threats of the Leonati to an appeal beyond his justice, asserts a guiding paternity, and voids an enigmatic tablet. So, Jove, riding on an eagle, delivering sulphurous but ultimately benevolent thunderbolts, evokes the iconography of James; so too does the god's pedantic self-advertising, and his compulsion to declare his prerogative in print.[18] But even if one grants that Jupiter's descent is supposed seriously to symbolize the intervention of authority, then Shakespeare's text can still seem designed more to undercut than praise the god's percipience. And indeed, for the Jacobean stage to represent Jupiter in less than reverential terms would hardly translate as gross sacrilege. In Posthumus' dream his father upbraids Jupiter's 'Adulteries' (V. iv. 33). In *The Winter's Tale* Florizel alludes to Jupiter's wooing of Europa in the form of a bellowing bull; Golding reminds his readers that Jupiter's deception was employed to 'winne his foule desyre'.[19] Thomas Heywood's *The Golden Age*, performed around 1611, puts

---

[17] Northrop Frye associates Jupiter with Shakespeare's machinery of plot, a 'projection of the author's craftsmanship': *A Natural Perspective: The Development of Shakespearean Comedy and Romance* (New York, 1965), 69–70; 125.

[18] Marcus, *Puzzling Shakespeare*, 140 ff.

[19] *Golding's Metamorphoses*, 'Preface', l. 36. 'That all theyr Goddes with whoordome, theft, or murder blotted be, Which argues them too bee no Goddes, but worser in effect Than they whoose open poonishment theyr dooings doth detect.' (ll. 30–2)

another tale of mendacious divinity onto the stage in the form of Jupiter's rape of Callisto ('nay let your skirt be raised . . . You are too wanton, and your hand too free . . . Oh God you tickle me').[20] As Florizel suggests, the pagan gods enjoy 'Humbling their deities to loue', taking the 'shapes of beasts'. In the great classical tradition, gods can be as nubile and capricious as their 'subjects'.

In *Cymbeline*, Jupiter's absent authority is the context, and perhaps the cause, of the various young men's petulant self-fashionings. As we learn from the egregiously supernal scene, Posthumus had two brothers, killed in battle, whose ghosts admonish Jupiter and threaten to fly his justice (V. iv. 91–2). In doing so they exactly evoke the tone of impatient, independent martialism struck by Cymbeline's two sons. Further, both Posthumus' parents die before he was 'ript' from his mother's womb: this makes him the child of reigning power, in a way as plastic and permeable as Caliban. Sicilius Leonatus upbraids Jupiter for parental absence or negligence: 'Whose Father then . . . Thou should'st haue bin' (V. iv. 39–41). The parental absence translates as the crisis of viable authority. *Cymbeline* searches vainly for a 'son of Jupiter', as if a pure inheritor from the king of gods. Instead it shares out success and ignominy, the sniff of sovereignty, among all its young warriors: 'Wert thou the Sonne of *Jupiter*', says Imogen to Cloten, 'and no more, But what thou art besides: thou wer't too Base, To be his Groome' (II. iii. 125–8). Her main point here is that no dignifying title can raise Cloten from the pit of his nature, but she expresses it in such a way as firstly to invoke and immediately to deny the redemptive majesty of Jupiter: the god could have coined Cloten and still he would be counterfeit.

The point is not only the conflation of the play's young men as Jupiter's nearly-sons, but, as if a consequence or correlative of this unconsummated parentage, the sense that 'Jupiter' cannot, here in Britain, represent or control what it is that defines 'virtues'. Erica Sheen has noted how Jupiter's descent from the

---

[20] See Heywood, *The Golden and Silver Ages*, ed. J. Payne Collier (London, 1851), II. i, pp. 33–5 (D2); Heywood also left foul papers of an unfinished play, intended for performance, which was picking presumably popular excerpts from the *Ages* to create a 'new' compilation, entitled *The Escapes of Jupiter*, ed. G. R. Proudfoot, The Malone Society (Oxford, 1978).

heavens contrasts unfavourably to the 'rock', or the rear-stage trap, from which the Leonati emerge and which throughout the play is the stolid proof of British self-subsistence. Jupiter's airy sky, appealed to vaguely and to little effect by Belarius, recalls a transcendent authority which the youthful characters repeatedly ignore in search of more grounded ambitions and secular models.[21] The movement is away from the sanguine endorsement of transcendence. Whereas the closing 'bloody' peace sees Cymbeline head for the temple to thank the gods with sacrifices, the surrounding agencies suggest a much more tangled momentum which finds its model less in any authoritatively surceasing interpretation than in the theatrical auditorium itself. Thus, even at the moment of serendipitous unmasking, purpose and focus are crossed and interpolatory:

> See
> *Posthumus* Anchors vpon *Imogen*;
> And she (like harmlesse Lightning) throwes her eye
> On him: her Brothers, Me: her Master hitting
> Each obiect with a Ioy: the Counter-change
> Is seuerally in all.

(V. v. 393–8)

The description here evokes not only the hushed, expectant quality of an audience, but the particular type of vision required at this moment in the play, when the stage is crammed with every surviving character, each unfolding their own secret revelation. But it is secret, of course, only to those on stage: 'we' already know, hence the rich gauze of farce which threatens any encomiums about harmony. And this mingled mood of the precipitous and the belated, the sense that the play still works multiply, in terms of time-span as well as perspective, indicates the action's continuing roots in the precedent confusions. The 'Counter-change Is severally in all' well describes *Cymbeline*'s constructive principle, its mix of recriminative oppositions and consequential, paradoxical identity. The hurly-burly battle, for instance, is a furious blazon of just such undistinguishing counter-change. As Sheen notes, every

[21] Erica Sheen, ' "The Agent for His Master": Political Service and Professional Liberty In *Cymbeline*', in Gordon McMullan and Jonathan Hope, eds., *The Politics of Tragicomedy: Skakespeare and after* (London, 1992), 69–72 et al.

verb is violent.[22] Even within the reconciled royal family the moment of 'Ioy' contains intimations of its fracturing, the sense that the 'severally in all' might quickly replicate past duels. The activity offered by each is a slightly unreliable combination of self-sufficiency and renunciation. They each have stored up a potent measure of violence, which at this moment is delivered, exultantly but still a little like a dare, to their rediscovered relatives. Above all, authority is seen to cohere only in a kind of individuated opposition: the politics are oddly feudal, each tangent meeting at a centre, but held by memorial strings to a provincial point in which self-definition and assurance are grounded. The various pasts of the characters—as outlaws in the mountains, as an outsider at court, as an impatient and rebellious princess—are here drawn upon, their respective self-esteems offered up but, crucially, never quite relinquished. The prognosis is neither of autocratic control nor euphonious surcease, but rather an argumentative ruling class and a mobile body politic. Yet they are united, for a moment, in a common if paradoxical emotion: a kind of bloody peace, its motives at a recess, sublimated into romance.

Typically, this emotion is not shared by the king, who observes the lot and draws a quite singular conclusion. Somewhat like Autolicus—though unconsciously—Cymbeline parodies romantic closure; impotent in submission and petulant in decision, he undermines unfettered monarchy as irrevocably as does Leontes. Furthermore, it is he who, Jupiter's obliging agent, is stepfather to Cloten, and who gives name and protection to Posthumus (I. i. 40–2). The twin sovereigns, Cymbeline and Jupiter, are made to mirror each other's embarrassments, each as belated and otiose as the other.[23] But other allusions to Jupiter similarly render the god a servile minister or cipher of unstable political desire. Imogen's hysterical blazon culminates in the

---

[22] Ibid. 68.

[23] Cf. Patricia Parker, 'Romance and Empire: Anachronistic *Cymbeline*', in Logan and Teskey, *Unfolded Tales*, 205–6, who understands Cymbeline to represent the Jacobean 'pax', which James exploited in Hesperian terms as monarch of Third Troy, the 'Glory of Our Western World' (cf. the soothsayer's 'the radiant Cymbeline Which shines here in the West', V. v. 477–8). Parker compares the panegyrics by Dekker (a militant protestant) and Jonson upon James's accession in 1603. I would suggest, if there is any such allusion, that after six or so disappointing years it is probably sardonic.

absent 'Ioviall face'. Imogen's characteristically hapless pun collapses mythic grandeur into fairground doltishness. The godhead—leering, rapacious, lobotomized—becomes a meta-dramatic, tragi-comic fusion of Cloten and Posthumus (IV. ii. 311). Jove joins the duellers as absent, itinerant, balloon-like authority, a 'head' of affairs almost better, one might think, off than on. Preparing for such derogation is Iachimo's 'corporal sign', his trumping proof that he seduced Imogen: the oath that 'By Iupiter, I had it from her Arme'; 'Hearke you, he sweares', responds Posthumus, 'by Iupiter he sweares. 'Tis true, nay keepe the Ring; 'tis true' (II. iv. 121–3). Jupiter's name becomes a cruel criminal password, a dark joke with which to punish the gullible. In Posthumus' dream Jupiter explains his role as a benevolent overseer. But his bird and bolts seem more complicit in than solving of the prevalent chaos and bigotries. That Posthumus was married in Jupiter's temple is hardly reassuring (V. iv. 105–6). Nuptials are not normally the thunderer's function,[24] and the thought that this reigning god-cum-priest can thus calmly behold the slander and wreck of his favoured marriage seems perversely, voyeuristically negligent.[25]

The play's closing gesture of triumph is to offer oblations in Jupiter's temple; again, however, the ritual of transcendence appears to be degraded by lingering analogies. Instead of a cleansing propitiation, the sacrifice evokes the 'reek' of Cloten:

> Laud we the Gods
> And let our crooked Smoakes climbe to their Nostrils
> From our blest Altars. Publish we this Peace
> To all our Subiects.

(V. v. 477–80)

---

[24] In Beaumont's *Masque of the Inner Temple and Gray's Inn* Iris protests about Mercury's antimasque: 'But what hath he to doe with Nuptiall rights? Let him keepe state upon his starry throne, And fight poore mortals with his thunderbolts, Leaving to us the mutuall darts of eyes' (ll. 127–30). Mercury responds by claiming that Jove reserves a special right over this particular marriage (between Princess Elizabeth and Frederick), 'Whose match concernes his generall government' (ll. 131–3). Either way, the contrast with *Cymbeline* serves to reinforce Jupiter's negligence, presumptuousness, or indecorum. See *A Book of Masques*, 135.

[25] In Beaumont's *Inner Temple Masque*, Iris abuses the 'wanton' messages in Jupiter's 'thundring', arguing that Juno 'did never yet Claspe weak mortalitie in her white armes, As he hath often done' (ii. 702), 129.

Whatever is being sacrificed seems to recall, first, the steaming body of Cloten at his initial entrance, and second, the trunk in the wilderness. Further, both the quality of the sacrifice ('crooked') and its place of reception (the gods' 'Nostrils') reprise the colloquial political wisdom of Cloten ('we will nothing pay For wearing our owne Noses ... there is no mo such Caesars, other of them may haue crook'd Noses, but to owe such strait Armes, none', III. i. 12–14; 35–9). If the twinned noses are transposed, then the 'nostrils' which savour the smoke evoke either those of a decadent Rome, still in a place of eminence, or else a British hegemony which, true to Cloten's belligerent nationalism, has achieved its power through copying 'crooked' imperial precedent. Cymbeline's forgetful accommodations are defied by the enveloping, recapitulative smoke.

Jupiter's sulphur, then, evokes Cloten's 'reek'; the twin pungencies, underworld and underarm, meet in the closing 'crooked' sacrifice: Cymbeline's ambivalent 'blest Altars' becomes an apt image of the romances' ironical sense of the sacramental moment. The point is that the recapitulative text permits no genuine propitiation, no teleological cleansing. So the putative hero, Posthumus, remains similarly complicit in the lingering corruption. Preparing to die, Posthumus describes himself as a piece of 'Ouer-roasted' meat, his sinful body a 'well Cook'd' repast paying the 'shot', or all debts (V. iv. 153–7). Posthumus' constant reference to debt invokes the Lord's Prayer ('forgive us our debts, as we forgive our debtors', Matthew 6: 12), and so signals his attempt at a kind of repentance and transcendence. But just as Cymbeline's propitiatory ritual is confused with memories of Cloten, so is Posthumus' accounting of mortal trespass profaned by his grisly puns and their magnetic evocation of his rival's humiliating 'Sacrifice'. The text's mischievous imputation is that Cloten's 'reeke' consummates Posthumus' desire—silly, over-reaching, self-hating—to be overroasted. 'No bolts for the dead', says Posthumus (V. iv. 198), but he too is powerless to escape this turbid world—Cloten's, Cymbeline's, Jupiter's—of ineffectual 'bolts' and intemperate brimstone.

In not allowing old conflations to die, the play refuses to purge the ruling order of its violence. The issues expressed in the war—and these were the same issues as pursued through the cumulatively metamorphosing body—remain kinetic and unresolved. One might compare the close of *Locrine*, which withdraws admiration successively from each and every noble character, but then ends with a reconciliatory speech of flagrant spuriousness, contradicting all that has gone before, as if to lay jokily bare the mendacities of legend. Similarly, in *Cymbeline* order and decorum can be captured neither in a single king offering unilateral revisionism ('We were disswaded [from paying tribute] by our wicked Queene', V. v. 464), nor, a symbol of such absolutism, in a mollified divinity blithely missing the joke (Jupiter as a sop to King James). For above all, it is the 'Jouiall face'—a reflexive mix of terror, merriment, fecklessness, and dislocation—which remains the floating signifier of Britain's dilated, dilatory authority.

AUTHORITY AND THE MASQUE IN *THE TEMPEST*

Conventional courtly romance aestheticizes the workings of power, celebrating an effortless royal hegemony in terms of a magical surplus (of goods and good will) and natural harmony. The masque that Prospero confers upon the betrothed couple is *The Tempest*'s great attempt to publish such a golden myth, and to assert the continuing validity of an aristocratic romance ideology (IV. i. 60–138). However, the masque fails, curtailed amid Prospero's abrupt and confused recollection that the price of stately art is eternal martial vigilance. As the repeated dissonance and deceptiveness of the island's music suggests, the resident arts pursue a troubled, troubling aural humanism of which the masque's precipitous ending is a powerful emblem and crux. The necessary question can be carried over from the other plays: how much potency, in the end, is left to supernatural autocracy?

Throughout the play it is difficult to distinguish exactly where the respective agencies of Ariel and Prospero merge and separate. Clearly they are not simply 'correspondent', and Ariel's service is partially defined by an impatience for freedom. But the spirit is neither a rebel nor, finally, an amoral time-server; if Ariel is in some sense a kind of courtier, then the obedience is again defined by a wish both to escape the milieu and to make it more charitable. Even if Ariel's 'natural' element is air, such incorporealism is still determinedly inclusive; one might think of Imogen's status as 'mullis aer', wherein her role as the once lost, now returned, figure of promise depends upon her 'airing' herself in the country and rejecting the court's more severe prescriptions. Ariel's blossom and bee song may well reveal, as Eagleton suggests, a 'closet aesthete', but, as Caliban himself attests, there is nothing intrinsically courtly or exclusive about the cherishing of beauty and fructification:

> *Where the Bee Sucks, there suck I,*
> *In a Cowslips bell, I lie,*
> *There I cowch when Owles doe crie,*
> *On the Batts backe I doe flie*
> *after Sommer merrily.*
> *Merrily, merrily, shall I liue now,*
> *Vnder the blossom that hangs on the Bow.*

(V. i. 88–94)

Principally the song pictures Ariel as the busy celebrant of spring. However, it is not a simple fantasy of submersion in prettiness. The spirit's contented nightly rest is both the reward and preparation for the day's pollinating labour. Metaphors of the bee hive were, like so many 'natural' analogies, used to justify a comprehensive range of political organizations: the institutional details of Ariel's paradise are not given, but whatever they are Ariel is at one with the worker bee.[26] The crystalline distillations of the song come from an inclusiveness of both function and franchise: the song envisages Ariel enjoying an identity, consecutively, with the production, enjoyment, experience, and future promise of a flower. Again one might compare *Henry VIII*'s vision when 'Euery Man shall eate in safety, Vnder his owne Vine what he plants' (V. iv. 33–4). Ariel's aestheticism is also horticultural, even agricultural; its decorousness celebrates rather than excludes creative labour. The song works, then, in subtle contradistinction to the granted gifts of a prelapsarian pastoral. Weaving and humming within Eden's

---

[26] See Timothy Raylor, 'Samuel Hartlib and the Commonwealth of Bees', in Michael Leslie & Timothy Taylor, eds., *Culture and Cultivation in Early Modern England: Writing and the Land* (Leicester, 1992), 91–129.

twin punishments of toil and conception, Ariel vindicates the
fallen. But if this song expresses Ariel's 'freed thought', what
about the masque? Might its failure as transcendent idealism
reflect a commitment, directed by Ariel, to the very tilth and
sweat which, the fertilizer of sustainable beauty, is abjured in
the golden utopias of Gonzalo and Prospero?

The question once again is of the distribution of power, and
the unanimity or otherwise of effective agency. For the masque's
authorship is ambiguous: 'goe bring the rabble', says Prospero,
'(Ore whom I giue thee powre) . . . Incite them to quicke motion, for I must Bestow vpon the eyes of this yong couple Some
vanity of mine Art' (IV. i. 37–41). At no point does Prospero
take Ariel aside and tell him what to do; there is no suggestion
of script or rehearsal. On each previous occasion Prospero
makes clear the rigour and pedantry of his instructions: 'Hast
thou, Spirit, Performd to point, the Tempest that I bad thee?' (I.
ii. 193–4); 'My queint *Ariel*, Hearke in thine eare' (I. ii. 318–19);
'Of my Instruction, hast thou nothing bated In what thou had'st
to say' (III. iii. 85–6). Furthermore, the masque's immediate
aftermath seems to confirm at least the contingent authority of
Ariel. Prospero's 'old braine is troubled' (IV. i. 159), a weakness
confirmed by the reiteration of his forgetfulness ('Say again,
where didst thou leaue these varlots? *Ariel*: I told you Sir . . .',
IV. i. 170–1). Ariel anticipates Prospero's recollection of
Caliban's plot, and thinks about including a warning within the
masque: 'when I presented *Ceres* I thought to haue told thee of
it, but I fear'd Least I might anger thee' (IV. i. 167–9). The
crucial point to notice here is the power of choice assumed by
Ariel: understandably careful not to enrage the incendiary master, Ariel nonetheless implies how the masque works, at least in
part, as the spirit's commentary—prudent, anxious, but independent—upon the island's political moment.

Juno's messenger, Iris, calls upon Ceres (the goddess of agri-
culture) to leave her farming domain and to 'come, and sport'
on 'this grasse-plot' (IV. i. 73–4). Juno wants to offer up a free
donation to the lovers (IV. i. 84–6), but the sublime vision
requires labour: spontaneous magic alone will not achieve
'*Earths increase, foyzon plentie, Barnes, and Garners, neuer
empty* ' (IV. i. 110–11). Interestingly, Ceres, played by Ariel,
insists upon a certain independence from the queen of the sky's

authority: she seems to distinguish her own autonomy from the slavishness of Iris, she 'that nere Do'st disobey the wife of *Iupiter*' (IV. i. 76–7); and she continues to desist from obedience until assured that her foes, Venus and Cupid, will be absent from the entertainment. And indeed there is a certain tension in the incantation, between effortlessness and its hidden providers, which corresponds to the relative environments of its two singers, Ceres and Juno:

> *Honor, riches, marriage, blessing,*
> *Long continuance, and encreasing,*
> *Hourly joyes, be still vpon you,*
> *Iuno sings her blessings on you. . . .*
> *Spring come to you at the farthest,*
> *In the very end of Haruest.*
> *Scarcity and want shall shun you*
> *Ceres blessing so is on you.*
>
> (IV. i. 106–17)

To be sure, the sentiments are pre-eminently of co-operative blessing, but if one contrasts Ariel's pollinating song it may seem apparent that any blessing would be more rooted and secure if it acknowledged the engines of the gift. As it stands, the 'vanity' seems just that, a leisure-loving conceit. An ascendant courtliness is boasted of, yet lacks either context or, crucially, source. The masque remains top heavy, rhetorically unaccountable. It needs the antimasque which, along with the 'wanton' Venus, is denied entrance.

One needs here to consider contemporary debates about the decorum of the masque. Jonson's antimasques tend to be rumbustious, profane affairs, populated by rogues, witches, and foreigners whose habits evoke small empathy and whose exclusion commands still less regret. In *The Masque of Queenes*, for instance, there is barely even an adversarial relationship between the witches and the queens: the antimasque represents a negation and contradiction unamenable to any resolution within the terms of the Golden Age. Even where, as in *Oberon*, Jonson uses characters to bridge the gap between antimasque and masque, the methods remain generally authoritarian, the ideal definitively Platonic and exclusive. *Oberon*'s 'rough, & rude' satyrs, their mischief oscillating between playfulness and sadism, seek a share in the night's changeable government. The entrance of Oberon, however, embarrasses all such presumption: 'Giue place, and silence; you were too rude too late . . . He is aboue your reach; . . . Before his presence, you must fall, or flie'.[27] A contrast with serenity and majesty is evoked clearly enough, but there is little sense that the antimasque gets incorporated into any harmony.

However, Jonson's isn't the only method of constructing an antimasque, or of preparing for the vision of desire with which a masque should end. The text of *Tethys' Festival*, devised by Samuel Daniel and Inigo Jones for Prince Henry's investiture celebrations, includes a preface to the reader apparently criticizing both Jonson's self-regarding descriptions of his masques and the old galleon's ponderously annotated classicism: variant conceptions of the form were circulating and competing.[28] Accordingly, among the distinctive features of Daniel's extravaganza is a brace of antimasques at once more aristocratic and incorporable than any of Jonson's. The first antimasque presents Tethys' (Queen Anne's) messenger, Zephyrus (the young Duke of York), who with eight naiads (each the daughter of earls or barons) offers a trident to the Ocean King (James) and a sword and scarf to Meliades (Prince Henry); following this, the 'eight little Ladies' perform their intricately measured antimasque, dancing around the Duke of York, before the scene shifts to an underwater cavern where the Queen and her river nymphs (her assembled lady courtiers) are celebrating the glory of the Ocean King.[29] The actual argument of the masque—counselling for a pacific British strength and against aggressive imperialism[30]—is less relevant here than the simple fact that the antimasque is channelled almost imperceptibly into the masque. Of course such incorporation is made 'natural' by the nobility of the antimasquers: the young ladies are perfected in their mothers, the Duke of York merges into his father, and so on. But still it suggests how the form could prefer contiguity to dichotomy as a narrative and ideological principle.

[27] *Oberon*, 319–21; 336–40.
[28] *Daniel, Complete Works*, ed. Grosart, iii. 301–23 ('Preface', ll. 17–22, 66–76, pp. 305–7).
[29] For contemporary comments see Chambers, *The Elizabethan Stage*, iii. 281–3.
[30] See John Pitcher, 'In those figures which they seeme', in Lindley, *The Court Masque*, 33–46.

Beaumont's *Inner Temple Masque*, devised by Bacon to celebrate the marriage of Princess Elizabeth to the Elector Palatine, works similarly. Mercury and Iris, the messengers respectively of Jupiter and Juno, devise consecutive rival antimasques. Both antimasques confer disorder, but nonetheless contain social, aesthetic, and erotic energies which, when harnessed to the opposite which initially each eschews, combine to usher in the celebratory apotheosis. Mercury and Iris invite various figures to descend and dance, many of whom correspond to figures in *The Tempest*'s masque: Jupiter calls upon nymphs and naiads from fountains and streams, upon blind Cupid, as well as bringing from Jupiter's altar four statues of gold and silver to 'daunce for joy of these great Nuptialls'. Iris, undertaking to 'imitate Confusion', commands the entrance of 'the Rurall company', alive with May-games and country sports.[31] Iris' army is a Noah's ark of English society: a lord and lady, a servingman and chambermaid, a clown and wench, a shepherd and shepherdess, a host and a hostess, two baboons and two fools. The country jollity suggests that, throughout the land, the royal marriage is both celebrated and replicated. At the same time as Iris, scorning Mercury's 'high-flying devise', fashions a token that the match shall be blessed 'with the love of the Common People', bringing forth Flora as her Perdita-like confederate, she includes these common people in her celebration.[32] Iris and Mercury duly harness their energies and call forth the Olympian knights: court and hierarchy are thereby honoured, but the freshness and hope of the piece subsists in its political inclusiveness.

The intimacy and familiarity of Beaumont's masque to Shakespeare's dramatic processes is attested by its recurrence in *The Two Noble Kinsmen*. This play, a collaboration between Shakespeare and Fletcher, reproduces the second antimasque of the *Inner Temple Masque*. It may be that such borrowing was motivated mainly by a wish to capitalize upon the rural company's famous success before James; it was probably the King's Men who performed at the Banqueting House. None the less, an important character in the play, the lascivious, garrulous, pathetic Jailer's Daughter, is pressed into service in place of

---

[31] *Inner Temple Masque*, 141–215, 217–48.
[32] *Ibid*. 64–70.

Beaumont's 'She-fool'. The play's antimasque thereby harnesses
that voice, and its insistent chorus of desire, which invariably
emerges as the funniest and most endearing presence in the play.
Fletcher almost certainly composed the scene which includes the
morris dance, but the allusion could hardly not carry the consent of Shakespeare. The King's Men seem here to practise a
friendly, co-educative plagiarism, perhaps pursuing a political
aesthetic notable, whether at Blackfriars, the Globe, or Whitehall, for its differences from Jonson.

With these contemporary entertainments in mind, it might be
possible to get a closer sense of the options being played with by
Ariel. For *The Tempest's* masquers are adamant that the opening blessing requires supplementation: '*Juno and* Ceres *whisper,
and send Iris on employment*' (IV. i. 124–5). The subject of
which the spirits whisper is kept not only from the audience, but
also, it would seem, from Prospero: '*Juno* and *Ceres* whisper
seriously, There's something else to doe: hush, and be mute Or
else our spell is mar'd' (IV. i. 125–7). Prospero cannot hear the
two members of the 'rabble'; he can only see them, as we can.
His sudden unease suggests how a gap can exist between his
purposes and those of the show. Ariel and his 'rabble', it seems,
grasp the inventive nettle of liberty, and call forth exactly
those forces, 'merry' but 'temperate', on 'holiday' but 'graceful',
who legitimated and facilitated the Olympian hegemony in
Beaumont's masque:

> You Sun-burn'd Sicklemen of August weary,
> Come hether from the furrow, and be merry,
> Make holly day: your Rye-straw hats put on,
> And these fresh Nimphes encounter euery one
> In Country footing.
>
> (IV. i. 134–8)

Iris' call for the union of irrigation and the sickle stresses not the
product but the process. As in Ariel's song of the sucking bee,
celebration should proceed upon rather than precede the 'weary'
heat of August. The 'country' members here invited are by no
means an 'antic-masque'; the figures are not incompatible with
the most conservative aristocratic pastoral. But still they envisage something of a correction of the complacency of the
masques' first blessing. As in Drayton's *Poly-Olbion*, it is the

wider land which irrigates, dignifies, and even permits the duly
revamped court. Furthermore, with temperance joined thus
with fertility, the moment would apotheosize a semi-populist
romance optimism, centred in the figure of the princess. For
the masque's feminine agents combine to fill out Miranda's
symbolic burden: as well as the green-fingered Ceres, she is
Proserpine, innocence awaiting sustainable rebirth; Iris, like
Miranda an etymological 'wonder'; Juno, 'Queene o' th Skie'
(IV. i. 70); and the 'temperate *Nimphes*', the '*Nayades*' who
cultivate Ceres' commonwealth. That Miranda fails to enter the
dance and so assume such multiplicity signifies a characteristic
deferral of idealism's consummation.

For Prospero, suddenly remembering the conspiracy of the
'beast Caliban', banishes the '*properly habited*' country dancers.[33] The peremptoriness of the moment has often been thought
perplexing: surely, the burlesque insurrection alone could not
provoke Prospero into such violence. But there is a crucial link
between the 'rabble[s]' dance and the drunkard's plot. The
nymphs, naiads, and country fellows might suggest the tolerant
demotic of Beaumont's Iris and Mercury. Prospero, however,
prefers the more punitive, bifurcatory morality of a Jonson. He
cannot see 'Country footing' without sniffing country matters.
So, 'Make holly day', hears the mage: but instead of a holy,
processional reverence, he fears a reprise, beastly and rumbustious, of a few earlier 'rabble'-rousers: 'Freedome, high-day,
high-day freedome, freedome high-day, freedome' (II. ii. 186–7).
The 'Sicklemen' evoke Prospero's enemies, those crapulent confederates who, like a grotesque Jonsonian antimasque, must
either 'fall, or flie'. He can banish the dancers, but he cannot,
within the terms of his own preferred fiction, do anything to still
the thrummings of dissidence.[34]

Prospero's inability to confer his chosen wedding gift is both
an emblem and catalyst of a growing alienation from his own
denouement; he wanted a different, more aristocratic and stately

[33] At the end of the *Inner Temple Masque* James called for a replay of exactly
those dancers whom Prospero violently dispels (133–4).

[34] Compare the peremptory ending to Beaumont and Fletcher's *The Maid's Tragedy*'s spurious 'marriage masque' (also played by the King's Men, probably in 1611).
With its ill-fitting agents and unreconciled rebelliousness, it too is threatened by the
imperative to chain or exile any murmur of otherness, as it is startled into shabby
exit by the impatient and unsettling project of its patron (I. i–I. ii).

form of romantic ending than the one now emerging from
muddy confusions. The masque is a meta-capsule of Prospero's
world: neither genre nor future are in his gift. Instead of a
sweeping display of order, the masque ends amid the clamour
and cacophony which, throughout the play, has been the aural
sign of history's conflictory turbulence: *'to a strange hollow and
confused noyse, they heauily vanish'*.[35] Prospero's massive rhetorical project, his mission to persuade his 'subjects' into contri-
tion and reform, suffers a disquieting jolt. It is true that he
pushes things through to their necessary conclusion, but the
failure of the masque suggests an arrest of his teleological con-
fidence, a check from which he perhaps never quite recovers:

> Our Reuels now are ended; These our actors,
> (As I foretold you) were all Spirits, and
> Are melted into Ayre, into thin Ayre,
> And like the baselesse fabricke of this vision
> The Clowd-capt Towres, the gorgeous Pallaces,
> The solemne Temples, the great Globe it selfe,
> Yea, all which it inherit, shall dissolue,
> And like this insubstantiall Pageant faded
> Leaue not a racke behinde: we are such stuffe
> As dreames are made on; and our little life
> Is rounded with a sleepe: Sir, I am vext,
> Beare with my weakenesse, my old braine is troubled:
> Be not disturb'd with my infirmitie,
> If you be pleas'd, retire into my Cell,
> And there repose, a turne or two, Ile walke
> To still my beating minde.

(IV. i. 148–63)

This and his other renunciatory elegies are justly famous; that
they are so cherished suggests how sudden is the change in
Prospero from his peremptory custom. It is a private Prospero,
contingently disrobed; even when speaking publically, the tone
is distracted, as though he is dredging up long-cogitated fears or
falls which are quite beyond the moment's efficient need. But
efficiency, like anything inexorably profitable, is outside the
reach of empathy. Here, Prospero is plaintive and, significantly,
he is suddenly nostalgic. His words shimmer with an as-if lost

---

[35] Although the stage description might be Crane's, who didn't shy from interfer-
ing in such things: Wells et al., *Textual Companion*, 22.

sense of the irenic, correspondent not only to fears about the blankness of death but to the masque's meta-failure as surceasing romance. He is pitched, then, from ascendance into a kind of tender concert with the audience. It is perhaps no coincidence that, in stumbling upon a 'universally' affecting discourse, Prospero joins his slave Caliban as the folk lyricist of longing and loss.

Some such sense of Prospero as a subject is seen in an unusual inclusiveness of diction: 'Our Reuels . . . These our actors . . . we are such stuffe'. Rather than the royal plural, both possessive adjective and pronoun suggest an experiential sharing between 'master' and 'servants'. It is a crucial pointer to the promises folded into the play's ending. The wistful senescence stays as the bass tone of Prospero's being; it returns in the deepening shades of the Epilogue: 'Now my Charmes are all ore-throwne, And what strength I haue's mine owne. Which is most faint' (1–3). He comes at the play's end to a strange kind of loneliness, in which he has neither partner nor companion but those he must renounce. Those whom nominally he joins—his aristocratic peers—stay remote from any generically governing consciousness. Prospero's peculiar state of abandonment in victory comes from having to abjure all that gives him purpose; the poignancy of his isolation suggests an effective absorption into that crowd which both place and pride will never let him join. And so the presences which, almost spectrally, inhabit Prospero's horizon are his two servants. It is Ariel who figures forth a capacious, vivifying, 'feminine' popular optimism;[36] and it is Caliban, still the magnetic 'history man', who remains within Prospero as the predicate, condition, consequence, and telos of his being.

For the re-emerging Italian hegemony, the ostensible subject of Prospero's 'proiect', stays somehow parallel rather than responsible to the stakes in his would-be epiphany. Various of his crucial, and as-if long-prepared, set pieces have a strangely redundant quality. His main speech of rebuke to old enemies is spoken, unaccountably, whilst they are spell-stopped, quite beyond comprehension (V. i. 58–83). The travellers are soon

---

[36] The burden of hope placed upon Perdita and Imogen is deflected from Miranda; throughout the play somewhat prone to neoplatonic gullibility, she is already captured by her beau's politic cheating, and embraces a 'brave new world' depressing in its corrupted familiarity.

suitably dumbstruck by 'Prospero's' reappearance, but still he falls curiously short of effortless command. The sceptical Alonso remains at the play's end waiting for verification; Prospero speaks of Sebastian's guilty 'inward pinches', but Sebastian shows few signs of reform, promptly identifying Prospero with the 'Diuell', and soon rejoining Anthonio in a laconically cynical materialism; Anthonio's famous silence, his vicious and sardonic recalcitrance, adds to the sense of a helpless lacuna between Prospero's designs and his reach. The chess-playing Miranda and Ferdinand are oblivious to the master's pain, quite unperturbed by the confused and violent end to 'their' celebration. The drunks come rolling in, aching with crapulence, and blithely transcend the justiciable accountabilities of Prospero's moral ledger: '*Pro.* You'ld be king o' the Isle, Sirha? *Ste.* I should haue bin a sore one then'. His dukedom seems a belated consolation which, frozen in the past, is more than anything a euphemism for the grave.

For the fading of Prospero's 'Pageant' of power 'into Ayre' evokes not only dissolution into absence, but a passing of the 'great Globe'—world and stage—into different hands. For the spirits which Prospero sends into 'ayre' are Ariel's serviceable 'rabble'; the contemptuous noun evokes an unruly demotic energy which might at any time return from the clouds. Consequently Ariel, a figure of inheriting, immanent nascence, here absorbs a potential for turbulence equally political and metadramatic. And, coterminously, Ariel starts to take over: not so much in terms of decision—the spirit still performs to instruction—but rather in terms of possessing the moment's projective energies: 'I drinke the aire before me, and returne Or ere your pulse twice beate' (V. i. 102–3). Rushing toward a freedom which is not only personal, but communal, Ariel's rising velocity expresses a political expectation which, of necessity, requires the master's abdication. Prospero seems out of step, slower, older, heavier, than the comings to life around him. This is best encapsulated in the boatswain's report of his ship's awakening:

> Where, but euen now, with strange, and seuerall noyses
> Of roring, shreeking, howling, gingling chaines,
> And mo diuersitie of sounds, all horrible.
> We were awak'd: straight way, at liberty . . .

Ari. Was't well done?
Pros. Brauely (my diligence) thou shalt be free.

(V. i. 232–42)

As at the masque's demise, release is figured through 'roring'. The caterwauling here is Ariel's: once again, the jazzy spirit plays variations upon Prospero's line, and in doing so offers a tantalizingly charged reprise of earlier storms and captivities. For such 'horrible' boisterousness, of course, enveloped Ariel's own imprisonment in the tree. It represents the violent exhilaration, the clamour and competition, which inheres equally in tyrannical oppression as in any burst into instauration. And Ariel's situation here, serving power, smelling freedom, is poised finely between these two stations: if not sycophantic 'diligence', the howling may be a last hurrah, an ironical nod toward past misery, or, like Caliban juggling with his name, an exultant appropriation of the master's loosening voice. One thing seems clear: with the hour almost up, agency flows like sand from the mage's emptying glass.

Here is where Prospero's final two requests gather their pertinence. First, he charges Ariel to deliver 'auspicious gales' to hurry home the Italians; and second, he pleads for the audience's 'Gentle breath' to release him from his 'bands' of 'despaire' and their objective correllative, 'this bare Island'. The twin agents of deliverance fold into one another as a multi-faceted popular agency: the liberated Ariel is the revivified 'rabble' is the empowering audience. Ariel is freed into those 'Elements' which so rocked 'authoritie' in the opening tempest; Prospero now pleads for a roar of 'Gentle' acclamation rather than sulphurous dissent. However, now lacking any control over winds or waves, government depends upon popular co-operation. Beyond compulsion, it must be left to trust and good will. There's little that is sanguine or assured here, and no easy prediction of either paternal benignity or a smoothly sailing mixed estate. The Epilogue is instead tense and edgy, reflecting a political situation whose palinodal rhythms make rumbles of dissonance as present as roars of applause.

Prospero's epilogue presents a mood of bereftness, of man as naked yearning prey, which even Prospero's post-project turn toward his 'graue' does not quite account for. Many have seen a valedictory Shakespeare in Prospero's proud but weakening destitution. And certainly, one can see some sort of ambivalent farewell to the stage as Prospero hands power over text and island (here merging imperceptibly into Britain) to the 'you' who watch or, indeed, read. The ultimate meta-generic effect is thus very different from *The Winter's Tale*, in whose abundance and profligacy Shakespeare appears both to tease and celebrate his own audacious powers. In *The Tempest*, the sense of an ending is as sure as its corollary, the fearless acknowledgement that more inclusive powers—audience, populace, acting troupe, readers—must take over from where the sovereign magician leaves off. One needn't transpose a hankering for political absolutism onto the moment's sad retiring reckoning; it is quite possible to mourn the passing of something quite unsustainable, even insupportable, and furthermore it is clear that the figure of 'Prospero' is here burdened with a baggage of historical, autobiographical, and generic responsibilities which are by no means univocal or even compatible. Here, the thing that is passing is not only absolutism or the sole author, but somehow the new 'romance' genre itself, consummated in such a way as to defy emulation. As with Prospero, splendour and spectacle are suddenly reigned in, succeeded by a terse, laconic, rumbling brood.

However, the projective quality of the play's ending is not finally solipsistic. As always, and however self-reflexive, Shakespeare remains attuned to the promise of his times. For the strange contingent gloom of the Epilogue points, I think, to the presence of the play's original predicate and counterpoint to Ariel's blossom: Caliban. For it is he who lurks within Prospero's disrobing prayer. This presence is prefigured by a quietly accelerating identification of master and slave. It is thoughts of Caliban's incorrigible presence which curdles the masque's milk. 'Beare with my weakenesse, my old braine is troubled', says Prospero, wracked by his 'beating minde' (IV. i. 159–63); moments later he curses his slave in words which echo his own crabby senescence: 'as with age, his body ouglier growes, So his minde cankers' (IV. i. 191–2). The monster lurks in the mage's mental horizon, an unwanted child or half-acknowledged unconscious: 'this Thing of darkenesse, I Acknowledge mine' (V. i. 275–6). Somehow inescapable, the misshapen one waits, in the 'Cell' that is Prospero's home, brain, womb, and grave, as though a principle of origin and end, precedence and inheritance. Accordingly, Caliban's departing resolve to 'seeke for grace' finds immediate parallel in Prospero's prayer for pardon (V. i. 295; Epilogue: 15–20): having drowned his book, Prospero becomes the 'Sot' that Caliban, brutally unillusioned, sees as the base shared truth of himself and the tyrant (III. ii. 90–3).

So, it is the magnetic Caliban who, as much as the cipher Ariel, holds in poise the predictive capabilities of Shakespeare's romance. For his metaphorical plurality remains until the end, defying clear recuperation. His last words have seemed to many an abject capitulation, or an unlikely sop to generic closure, but I think that they are neither. Caliban's praise of Prospero ('How fine my Master is', V. i. 262) may well express awe at the ducal robes (although Caliban was quite unmoved by the master's 'trash' moments earlier, IV. i. 224); equally, such flattery is entirely in line with recent manipulations of Stephano. Having seen how artful, opportune and expedient—how rhetorically decorous—Caliban's language can be, it would seem naïve to understand a promise to 'seeke for grace' as anything more certain than another quiver in his proleptic bow. Furthermore, even granting his sincerity, who should one see as the proper fount of 'grace'? Perhaps Caliban, like Prospero, must depend for regenerative hopes upon that audience which, as always, is a refracted mirror of himself. Indeed, in stressing the bludgeoning familiarity of the monster's predicament, the scene confirms Caliban's achieved intimacy with the playgoers. Simply enough, he fears further tortures, and tells us so in what seem to be 'asides': 'I am afraid He will chastise me . . . I shall be pincht to death' (V. i. 262–3, 276). Indeed, his very last words—perhaps a final 'aside'?—suggest a regret for poorly chosen confederates as much as any abdication of rebelliousness; his vocabulary, at least, stays vigorous and rather ascendant : 'what a thrice double Asse Was I to take this drunkard for a god? And worship this dull foole?' (V. i. 295–7).

The point is that Caliban's future is anything but set. It is impossible to say whether he leaves or remains on the island, and quite appropriate that this should be so. For he continues to straddle new and old worlds, Europe and America, the

unknown and unconscious. To the end he embodies the tension
and asymmetry of unfinished history: it is then apt that his
environment should continue to interpret and appropriate his
strangeness in ways that can only double up and compete with
one another. Ceres' topography—the 'Sea-marge stirrile', the
'boskie acres' and 'vnshrubd downe'—together evoke Caliban's
aboriginal habitat and his potential presence, along with Ariel,
in Ceres' 'proud earth' (IV. i. 69–82). By way of contrast, the
moon-calf's roaring latencies might, as the masque foretells,
uproot all georgic health. Or again, the adjective describing the
harvest dance was 'gracefull' (IV. i. 138–9), not 'deuouring' like
Prospero's supernatural peep-shows (III. iii. 84): Caliban's
search for 'grace' may dream upon just such inclusion with the
'rabble'. Less hopefully, his descent into the 'Cell' sends aspiration back to where it began: mooching sloth, just off stage,
dwelling on a history of false promise, transgressive desire, and
echoing vituperation. No prophecy or judgement can quite possess him. He is and is not 'marketable', as Anthonio avers: there
is much 'in' Caliban that shall be enslaved, sold, commodified,
but equally much beyond price or objectification. Similarly,
when Prospero calls him 'as disproportioned in his Manners As
in his shape', one recalls again the pejorative decorums of a
Jonson, and the concomitant disdain both for unbridled art and
headstrong politics: again, Caliban is the meta-figure for all such
fantastical innovation. He is an archetype of the subject, as
much as of subjection. Waxing and waning with violence,
memory, and desire, Caliban projects as much as he bears.
Hence his status as an agitated talisman of historical anticipation; he bubbles with waiting futures. Monstrously anachronistic, littered uncomprehendingly from a world long ago or far
ahead, Caliban is riddled with the pain, and the bewilderment,
of both posthumousness and precipitousness. Like the Janus-
minded author, he looks at once forward and backward, a figure
whose symbiotic nostalgia and radicalism render him an unstable analogy of both history and romance. In the 'Islander', mind
is body, just as metaphor is enacted and genre is personified. In
Caliban—protean, amoeboid, photochromic, the organ, co-
ordinator, and interpreter of a chaos of stimuli—romance's
engagement with history locates its largely undiscovered country of a brain.

POSTSCRIPT

So: one ends with an image of incipience, an almost Yeatsian sense of the beast stirring into life, uncertain whether into grace or vice, brutal or dignifying community. For this is the fearlessness of Shakespeare's last works. Their strange intensity comes, I think, from some such sense of coiled potential, desire barely reigned in, precariously decorous at best, and always tempted by the wildness which, in each play, threatens both authority and innovation. There's a sense of tumescence, equally linguistic as political, even amid the apparent quiet of closure. It comes about partly because the plays do not finally separate royalty from populace; the words and longings of one inhabit the other. For Shakespeare's basic method is one of surrogacy and projection. A semantic over-determination gives the language part of its pregnancy. Equally mnemonic and anticipatory, his words echo back and forth; the result is not so much 'richness' as dissonance, a kinetic pulse of conflict, winding, unwinding, flushing out then returning, like blood though an anxious body. And this linguistic ebb and flow in turn reflects a society flushed, nervous, palpitating, excited.

The romances explore what it means to be a subject: an agent of the self, within the state, seeking for satisfaction. And so the epitomic figures are the ones denied their place at the centre: not only the rogues, slaves, fishers, and vagabonds, but the itinerant princes and, crucially, the exiled women. In so far as Shakespearian romance is a prophetic mode, it is to these characters that one must look, for it is from their burgeoning, invariably frustrated, desires that the plays derive their momentum and tension. But the political impulsions are not ultimately defined by these characters' self-definitions or expressed wills. Rather, they depend upon the interrelationship of such self-reflection with a supra-characterological energy, located in the sleepless metaphorical patterns into which these characters dip and out of whose processes they emerge. So the plays are doubly and definitively decentred: both character and civil society find their engine in things diffuse, accelerating, polysemous. The romances offer simulacrums of closure which, though they can garner the affect and poignancy of achieved nostalgia, do little to harness the nascent politics which is romance's subject-matter. There is always, then, a doubleness of ending: the putative plot looks backward, as if to before the play begins, finding a sweet forgetful unity which is almost entirely fictive and factitious; at the same time, an in-dwelling proleptic power looks back to the play itself, and identifies the battles of the future.

And so to see Shakespeare's apprehension of imminence, one need only identify what his frustrated subjects desire and suffer. It is not an entirely comforting vision; it is an uncertain one, and above all, as I have been stressing throughout this book, an unfinished one. The plays seem surely enough to sound a kind of death-knell for monarchical absolutism, but there is no clear prediction of liberal ascendancy, or even a sanguine path of humanist civic accretion. Both Whig and Marxist traditions can find seeds for themselves in Shakespeare's plenty, but the plays don't finally endorse the teleology of either. Nor do the plays directly dramatize militancy, apocalypse, or other contemporary fundamentalisms. But in the razings of their storms, and in the sometime audacity and independence of Shakespeare's wildernesses, they offer presentments of change as radical or alarming as anything granted by subsequent history. Rampant commodification, ochlocratic riot, varieties of tyranny and enslavement, each are sketched as surely as are benign paternalism, a widening franchise, the vigour and delight of public argument. Shakespeare's age was, famously, on a kind of historical cusp. The way things might fall remained open to question.

Bibliography

SELECTED PRIMARY REFERENCES

AESOP, *Fables of Aesop*, ed. S. A. Hanford (1954; repr. London, 1964).

ARISTOTLE, *The Politics*, trans. T. A. Sinclair (1962; repr. Harmondsworth, 1982).

ASCHAM, ROGER, *The Scholemaster* (1570; repr. Menston, 1967).

BACON, FRANCIS, *Essays* (London, 1879).

——*The Advancement of Learning and New Atlantis*, ed. Arthur Johnston (1974; repr. Oxford, 1988).

BEAUMONT, FRANCIS, and FLETCHER, JOHN, *The Maid's Tragedy*, ed. T. W. Craik (Manchester, 1988).

———*Philaster, or, Love Lies A-bleeding*, ed. Andrew Gurr (London, 1969).

———*The Dramatic Works in the Beaumont and Fletcher Canon*, ed. Fredson Bowers, 11 vols. (Cambridge, 1966).

A Book of Masques in Honour of Allardyce Nicoll (London, 1967).

BOWYER, ROBERT, *The Parliamentary Diary of Robert Bowyer 1606–1607*, ed. D. H. Willson (Minneapolis, 1931).

BROOKE, TUCKER, ed., *The Shakespeare Apocrypha* (Oxford, 1908).

BROWNE, WILLIAM, *The Poems of William Browne of Taristock*, ed. Gordon Gooodwin, 2 vols. (London, 1893).

BURTON, ROBERT, *The Anatomy of Melancholy*, ed. Holbrook Jackson, 3 vols. (London, 1932).

CAMPION, THOMAS, *The Works of Thomas Campion: Complete Songs, Masques, and Treatises with a Selection of the Latin Verse*, ed. Walter R. Davis (London, 1969).

CASTIGLIONE, BALDASSARE, *The Book of the Courtier*, trans. Sir Thomas Hoby from the 1558 edition (1928; repr. London and New York, 1944).

CERVANTES, MIGUEL DE, *The History of Don Quixote of the Mancha*, 4 vols., trans. Thomas Shelton (1612; repr. London, 1896).

CHAMBERLAIN, JOHN, *The Letters of John Chamberlain*, ed. N. E. McClure, 2 vols. (Philadelphia, 1939).

CHAUCER, GEOFFREY, *The Canterbury Tales*, ed. A. C. Cawley (1958; repr. London, 1989).

CICERO, *On Moral Obligation: A New Translation of Cicero's 'De Officiis'*, by John Higginbotham (Berkeley and Los Angeles, 1967).

——*Clyomon and Clamydes*, ed. W. W. Greg (1599; repr. Oxford 1913).

——*Clyomon and Clamydes: A Critical Edition*, ed. Betty T. Lyttleton (The Haghe, 1968).

DANIEL, SAMUEL, *The Complete Works in Verse and Prose of Samuel Daniel*, ed. Alexander B. Grosart, 4 vols. (London, 1885).

——'Samuel Daniel's Occasional and Dedicatory Verse: A Critical Edition', ed. John Pitcher, 2 vols. (Oxford D. Phil. Thesis, 1978).

DANTE ALIGHIERI, *The Divine Comedy: 1. Hell (L'Inferno)*, trans. Dorothy L. Sayers (1949; repr. Harmondsworth, 1982).

DEKKER, THOMAS, *The Belman of London* (London, 1608).

DONNE, JOHN, *John Donne Dean of St. Paul's: Complete Poetry and Selected Prose* (1929; repr. London, 1936).

——*The Complete English Poems of John Donne* (1985, repr. London, 1988).

DRAYTON, MICHAEL, *The Works of Michael Drayton*, ed. William J. Hebel, 5 vols. (1956; repr. Oxford, 1961).

DRYDEN, JOHN, *Essays of John Dryden*, ed. W. P. Kerr, 2 vols. (London, 1900).

ELYOT, THOMAS, *A Critical Edition of Sir Thomas Elyot's The Boke Named the Governour*, ed. Donald W. Rude (New York, 1992).

EURIPIDES, *The Bacchae and Other Plays*, trans. Philip Vellacott (1954; repr. London, 1973).

FLORIO, JOHN, *Queen Anna's New World of Words* (1611; repr. Menston, 1968).

FORMAN, SIMON, *The Bocke of Plaies* (1611).

FORSET, EDWARD, *A Comparative Discourse of the Bodies Natural and Politique* (London, 1606).

GREEN, MARY ANNE EVERETT, ed., *Calendar of State Papers: Domestic Series, James I 1611–1618* (London, 1858).

GUICCIARDINI, *The Historie of Guicciardin*, trans. Geoffrey Fenton (London, 1579).

HEYWOOD, SIR JOHN, *Proverbs and Epigrams* (1562; Spenser Society, 1867).

HEYWOOD, THOMAS, *An Apology for Actors* (1612), ed. Richard H. Perkinson (New York, 1941).

——*The Escapes of Jupiter*, ed. G. R. Proudfoot (Oxford, 1978).

——*The Fair Maid of the West Parts I and II*, ed. Robert K. Turner (London, 1968).

——*The Four Prentices of London: A Critical Old-Spelling Edition*, ed. Mary Ann Weber Gasior (New York, 1980).

——*The Golden and Silver Ages*, ed. J. Payne Collier (London, 1851).

HESIOD, *The Homeric Hymns and Homerica*, ed. and trans. Hugh Evelyn-White (1936; 2nd edn. London, 1948).

HOBBES, THOMAS, *Leviathan* (1651), ed. C. B. Macpherson (1968; repr. Harmondsworth, 1976).

JAMES I, *The Workes of the most high and mighty prince Iames* (London, 1616).

——*The Political Works of James I*, ed. Charles McIlwain (Cambridge, Mass.; 1918).

JONES, EDMUND, D., ed., *English Critical Essays (Sixteenth, Seventeenth and Eighteenth Centuries)* (1922; repr. London, 1952).

JONSON, BEN, *Ben Jonson*, ed. C. H. Herford and Percy and Evelyn Simpson, 7 vols. (Oxford, 1925–63).

KENYON, J. P., *The Stuart Constitution 1603–1688* (2nd edn. Cambridge, 1986).

KINNEY, ARTHUR F., ed., *Rogues, Vagabonds, and Sturdy Beggars* (Massachusetts, 1973).

——*The Lamentable Tragedy of Locrine: A Critical Edition*, ed. Jane Lytton Gooch (New York, 1981).

LARKIN, JAMES F. and HUGHES, PAUL L., eds., *Stuart Royal Proclamations*, 2 vols. (Oxford, 1973).

LYLY, JOHN, *The Complete Works of John Lyly*, ed. Warwick P. Bond, 3 vols. (1902; repr. Oxford, 1967).

MCPEAK, JAMES A. S., *The Black Book of Knaves and Unthrifts in Shakespeare and other Renaissance Authors* (Connecticut, 1969).

MACHIAVELLI, NICCOLÒ, *The Prince*, ed. George Bull (London, 1961).

——*Machiavels Discourses*, trans. Edward Dacres (London, 1636).

MARLOWE, CHRISTOPHER, *Plays and Poems*, ed. M. R. Ridley (1909; repr. London, 1958).

——*The Complete Plays*, ed. J. B. Steane (1969; repr. Harmondsworth, 1984).

MARSTON, JOHN, *The Works of John Marston*, ed. A. H. Bullen, 3 vols. (London, 1887).

——*The Selected Plays of John Marston*, ed. Macdonald P. Jackson and Michael Neill (Cambridge, 1986).

MIDDLETON, THOMAS, *A Chaste Maid in Cheapside*, ed. Alan Brissenden (London, 1968).

——*A Game at Chess*, ed. J. W. Harper (London, 1966).

——*The Works of Thomas Middleton*, ed. A. H. Bullen, 8 vols. (London, 1885).

MONTAIGNE, MICHEL, *The Essayes of Michael Lord of Montaigne*, trans. John Florio, 3 vols. (1603; repr. London, 1904).

MORE, THOMAS, *Utopia*, trans. Paul Turner (Harmondsworth, 1965).

NASHE, THOMAS, *The Works of Thomas Nashe*, ed. R. B. McKerrow, 5 vols. (Oxford, 1958; repr. with corrections by F. P. Wilson, Oxford, 1966).

OVID, *Metamorphoses*, trans. A. D. Melville (1986; repr. Oxford, 1988).

——*Shakespeare's Ovid Being Arthur Golding's Translation of the Metamorphoses*, ed. W. H. D. Rouse (London, 1961).

PEACHAM, HENRY, *The Garden of Eloquence* (1577; repr. Menston, 1971).

PLATO, *The Republic*, trans. H. D. P. Lee (Harmondsworth, 1955).

Plutarch's Lives of the Noble Grecians and Romans, trans. Sir Thomas North, 6 vols. (1579; repr. London, 1895).

PUTTENHAM, GEORGE, *The Arte of English Poesie*, ed. Gladys Doidge Willcock and Alice Walker (Cambridge, 1936).

The Rare Triumphs of Love and Fortune, ed. W. W. Greg (1589; repr. Oxford, 1913).

——*An Edition of the Rare Triumphs of Love and Fortune*, ed. John Isaac Owen (New York, 1979).

RELF, F. H., ed., *Notes of the Debates in the House of Lords Officially Taken by Robert Bowyer and Henry Elsing* (London, 1929).

ROLLINS, HYDE EDWARD, ed., *The Pepys Ballads*, i: 1535–1625 (Cambridge, Mass., 1929).

ROSS, ALEXANDER, *Mystagogus, or The Muses Interpreter* (London, 1648).

SHAKESPEARE, WILLIAM, *The Complete Works: Original Spelling Edition*, ed. Stanley Wells, Gary Taylor, John Jowelt, and William Montgomery (Oxford, 1986).

——and FLETCHER, JOHN, *The Two Noble Kinsmen*, ed. N. W. Bawcutt (Harmondsworth, 1977; repr. 1981).

SIDNEY, SIR PHILIP, *A Defence of Poetry*, ed. J. A. Van Dorsten (London, 1966).

——*Miscellaneous Prose of Sir Philip Sidney*, ed. Katherine Duncan-Jones and Jan Van Dorsten (Oxford, 1973).

——*The Countess of Pembroke's Arcadia 1590*, ed. Albert Feuillerat (1912; repr. Cambridge, 1939).

——*The Complete Works of Sir Philip Sidney*, ed. Albert Feuillerat, 4 vols. (Cambridge, 1912–26).

SMITH, G. GREGORY, *Elizabethan Critical Essays*, 2 vols. (1904; repr. London, 1950).

SOPHOCLES, *The Theban Plays*, trans. E. F. Watling (1947; repr. London, 1974).

SPEED, JOHN, *The History of Great Britaine* (London, 1611).

SPENSER, EDMUND, *A View of the Present State of Ireland*, ed. W. L.

Renwick (Oxford, 1970).

——*The Faerie Queene*, ed. A. C. Hamilton (1977; repr. 1989).

STARKEY, THOMAS, *A Dialogue between Pole and Lupset*, ed. T. F. Mayer (London, 1989).

STUBBES, PHILIP, *Anatomy of the Abuses in England in Shakespeare's Youth A.D. 1583*, ed. Frederick J. Furnival (London, 1877).

The Thracian Wonder: A Comical History (London, 1661).

THUCYDIDES, *Eight Books of the Peloponnesian Warre*, trans. Thomas Hobbes (London, 1629).

——*The Hystory Writtone by Thucidides*, trans. Thomas Nicolls (London, 1550).

——*The Peloponnesian War: The Complete Hobbes Translation*, ed. David Grene (1959; repr. Chicago, 1989).

TILLEY, M. P., *A Dictionary of the Proverbs in England in the Sixteenth and Seventeenth Centuries: A Collection of the Proverbs Found in English Literature and the Dictionaries of the Period* (Ann Arbor, 1950).

WEBSTER, JOHN, *The Complete Works of John Webster*, ed. F. L. Lucas, 4 vols. (London, 1927).

WILSON, THOMAS, *A Discourse upon Usury*, ed. R. H. Tawney (1572; repr. 1925).

SELECTED SECONDARY REFERENCES

ABBOTT, EVELYN, *Pericles and the Golden Age of Athens* (London, 1891).

ADELMAN, JANET, *Suffocating Mothers: Fantasies and Maternal Origin in Shakespeare's Plays: Hamlet to The Tempest* (New York, 1992).

ADKINS, M. G. M., 'The Citizens in *Philaster*: Their Function and Significance', *Studies in Philology*, 63 (1946).

AERS, DAVID, HODGE, BOB, and KRESS, GUNTHER, eds., *Literature, Language and Society in England 1580–1680* (Dublin, 1981).

AGNEW, JEAN-CHRISTOPHE, *Worlds Apart: The Market and the Theater in Anglo-American Thought* (Cambridge, 1986).

ALTHUSSER, LOUIS, *Lenin and Philosophy and Other Essays* (New York, 1971).

ANDREWS, K. R., CANNY, N. P., and HAIR, P. E., eds., *The Westward Enterprise: English Activities in Ireland, the Atlantic, and America 1480–1650* (Liverpool, 1978).

ANGLO, SYDNEY, ed., *Chivalry in the Renaissance* (Woodbridge, 1990).

ARENDT, HANNAH, *On Revolution* (Harmondsworth, 1973).

AUDEN, W. H., *Selected Poems*, ed. Edward Mendelson (1979; repr. London, 1989).

——*The Dyer's Hand and Other Essays* (1963; repr. London, 1987).

——*The Enchafèd Flood; or, the Romantic Iconography of the Sea* (1951; repr. London, 1985).

AXTON, MARIE, *The Queen's Two Bodies: Drama and the Elizabethan Succession* (London, 1977).

BADCOCK, BARBARA, *The Reversible World: Symbolic Inversion in Art and Society* (Ithaca, NY, 1978).

BAKER-SMITH, DOMINIC, and BARFOOT, C. C., eds., *Between Dream and Nature: Essays on Utopia and Dystopia* (Amsterdam, 1987).

BAKHTIN, MIKHAIL M., *Rabelais and His World*, trans. Hélène Iswolsky (Bloomington, Ind., 1984).

——*The Dialogic Imagination: Four Essays*, trans. Caryl Emerson and Michael Holquist (Austin, Tex., 1981).

BAMBER, LINDA, *Comic Women, Tragic Men: A Study of Gender and Genre in Shakespeare* (Stanford, Calif., 1982).

BARBER, C. L., *Shakespeare's Festive Comedy* (Princeton, 1959).

——' "Thou that beget'st him that did thee beget": Transformation in *Pericles* and *The Winter's Tale*', *Sh. S* 22 (1969), 59–67.

——'*The Winter's Tale* and Jacobean Society', in Arnold Kettle, ed., *Shakespeare in a Changing World* (London, 1964), 233–52.

BARKER, FRANCIS, *The Tremulous Private Body: Essays on Subjection* (London, 1984).

BARROLL, J. LEEDS, *Politics, Plague, and Shakespeare's Theater: The Stuart Years* (Ithaca, NY, 1991).

——'A New History for Shakespeare and his Time', *SQ* 39 (1988), 441–64.

BARTHES, ROLAND, *Barthes: Selected Writings*, ed. Susan Sontag (1983; repr. Glasgow, 1989).

BARTHOLOMEUSZ, DENNIS, *The Winter's Tale in Performance in England and America 1611–1976* (Cambridge, 1982).

BARTON, ANNE, 'Perils of Historicism', *NYRB* 6 March 1991, pp. 51–4.

——'Shakespeare and the Limits of Language', *Sh. S* 24 (1971), 19–30.

——'Livy, Machiavelli, and Shakespeare's *Coriolanus*', *Sh. S.* 38 (1985), 115–29.

——*Ben Jonson, Dramatist* (Cambridge, 1984).

BATE, JONATHAN, *Shakespeare and Ovid* (Oxford, 1993).

——*Shakespeare and the English Romantic Imagination* (1986; repr. Oxford, 1989).

—— *The Romantics on Shakespeare* (Oxford, 1992).

BEER, GILLIAN, *The Romance* (1970; repr. London, 1977).

BELSEY, CATHERINE, 'Towards Cultural History—in Theory and Practice', *Textual Practice*, 3 (1989), 159–77.

—— *The Subject of Tragedy: Identity and Difference in Renaissance Drama* (London, 1985).

BENTLEY, G. E., 'Shakespeare and the Blackfriars Theatre', *Sh. S* 1 (1948), 38–50.

BERGER, HARRY JR., *Second World and Green World: Studies in Renaissance Fiction-Making* (Berkeley, 1988).

BERGERON, DAVID M., ed., *Pageantry in the Shakespearean Theater* (Athens, Ga., 1985).

—— *Shakespeare's Romances and the Royal Family* (Lawrence, Kans., 1985).

BERNHEIMER, RICHARD, *Wild Men in the Middle Ages: A Study in Art, Sentiment, and Demonology* (Cambridge, 1952).

BINDOFF, S. T., 'The Stuarts and Their Style', *EHR* 60 (1945), 192–216.

—— *Tudor England* (1950; repr. Harmondsworth, 1955).

BLACK, JAMES, 'The Latter End of Prospero's Commonwealth', *Sh. S* 43 (1990), 29–41.

BLISS, LEE, 'The Wheel of Fortune and the Maiden Phoenix of Shakespeare's *King Henry The Eighth*', *ELH* 42 (1975), 1–25.

BOAS, FREDERICK S., *Thomas Heywood* (London, 1950).

BOLD, ALAN, *The Ballad* (London, 1979).

BOOTH, STEPHEN, *King Lear, Macbeth, Indefinition and Tragedy* (New Haven, Conn., 1983).

BOWERS, FREDSON, *Elizabethan Revenge Tragedy 1587–1642* (Gloucester, Mass., 1959).

BRADLEY, A. C., *Shakespearean Tragedy* (1905; repr. Basingstoke, 1985).

BRANT, CLARE, and PURKISS, DIANE, eds., *Women, Texts and Histories 1575–1760* (London, 1992).

BRAUNMULLER, A. R., and BULMAN, J. C., eds., *Comedy from Shakespeare to Sheridan: Change and Continuity in the English and European Dramatic Tradition* (Newark, NJ, 1986).

BRAY, ALAN, *Homosexuality in Renaissance England* (London, 1982).

BRINK, JEAN R., *Michael Drayton Revisited* (Boston, 1990).

BRISTOL, MICHAEL, *Carnival and Theater: Plebeian Culture and the Structure of Authority in Renaissance England* (London, 1985).

BROCKBANK, PHILIP, *On Shakespeare, Jesus, Shakespeare and Karl Marx, and Other Essays* (Oxford, 1989).

BROOKS, KEITH, and SHARPE, KEVIN, 'History, English Law and the Renaissance', *P&P* 72 (1976), 134–42.

BROOKS-DAVIES, DOUGLAS, *The Mercurian Monarch: Magical Politics from Spenser to Pope* (Manchester, 1983).

BULLOUGH, GEOFFREY, ed., *Narrative and Dramatic Sources of Shakespeare*, 8 vols. (1966; repr. London, 1977).

BURFORD, E. J., *Bawds and Lodgings: A History of the London Bankside Brothels c.100–1675* (London, 1976).

BURKE, PETER, *Popular Culture in Early Modern Europe* (London, 1978).

BURT, RICHARD, *Licensed by Authority: Ben Jonson and the Discourses of Censorship* (Ithaca, NY, 1993).

BUTLER, MARTIN, *Theatre and Crisis 1632–1642* (Cambridge, 1984).

CALDERWOOD, JAMES L., *Shakespearean Metadrama* (Minneapolis, 1971).

CALLAGHAN, DYMPNA C., HELMS, LORRAINE, and SINGH, JYOTSNA, *The Weyward Sisters: Shakespeare and Feminist Politics* (Oxford, 1994).

CANNY, NICHOLAS, 'Spenser's Irish Crisis: Humanism and Experience in the 1590s', *P&P* 120 (1988), 201–9.

—— *The Elizabethan Conquest of Ireland: A Pattern Established 1565–76* (Brighton, 1976).

—— and PAGDEN, ANTHONY, eds., *Colonial Identity in the Atlantic World 1500–1800* (Princeton, 1987).

CAREY, JOHN, ed., *English Renaissance Studies: Presented to Dame Helen Gardner in Honour of Her Seventieth Birthday* (Oxford, 1980).

—— *John Donne: Life, Mind And Art* (1981; repr. London, 1985).

CAVE, TERENCE, *Recognitions: A Study in Poetics* (Oxford, 1988).

CESPEDES, FRANK V., ' "We are one in fortunes": The Sense of History in *Henry VIII*', *ELR* 10 (1980), 413–38.

CHAMBERS, E. K., *The Elizabethan Stage*, 4 vols. (Oxford, 1923).

—— *William Shakespeare: A Study of Facts and Problems*, 2 vols. (Oxford, 1930).

CHRIMES, S. B., 'The Constitutional Views of Dr. John Cowell', *EHR* 64 (1949), 461–75.

CLARE, JANET, *'Art made tongue-tied by authority': Elizabethan and Jacobean Dramatic Censorship* (Manchester, 1990).

CLAY, CHRISTOPHER, ed., *Rural Society: Landowners, Peasants and Labourers 1500–1750* (Cambridge, 1990).

CLEMEN, WOLFGANG, *English Tragedy before Shakespeare: The Development of Dramatic Speech*, trans. T. S. Dorsch (London, 1961).

COHEN, DEREK 'Patriarchy and Jealousy in *Othello* and *The Winter's Tale*', *MLQ* 48 (1987), 207–23.

COHEN, WALTER, *Drama of a Nation: Public Theater in Renaissance England and Spain* (Ithaca, NY, 1985).

COLIE, ROSALIE, *Shakespeare's Living Art* (Princeton, 1974).

COLLINSON, PATRICK, *The Religion of Protestants: The Church in English Society 1559–1625* (1982; repr. Oxford, 1985).

——*The Compact Edition of the Oxford English Dictionary*, 2 vols. (1971; repr. Oxford, 1980).

COOK, ANN JENNALIE, *The Privileged Playgoers of Shakespeare's London 1576–1642* (Princeton, 1981).

COOPER, HELEN, *Pastoral: Mediaeval into Renaissance* (Ipswich, 1977).

COX, LEE SHERIDAN, 'The Role of Autolycus in *The Winter's Tale*', *SEL* 9 (1969), 283–301.

CULLER, JONATHAN, ed., *On Puns: The Foundation of Letters* (Oxford, 1988).

DALY, JAMES, 'Cosmic Harmony and Political Thinking in Early Stuart England', *Transactions of the American Philosophical Society*, 69, part 7 (1979).

DANBY, JOHN F., *Poets on Fortune's Hill* (London, 1952).

DAVIES, STEVIE, *The Idea of Woman in Renaissance Literature: The Feminine Reclaimed* (Brighton, 1986).

DAVIS, J. C., *Utopia and the Ideal Society: A Study of English Utopian Writing 1516–1700* (Cambridge, 1981).

DAVISON, PETER, 'The Serious Concerns of *Philaster*', *ELH* 30 (1963), 1–16.

DE GRAZIA, MARGRETA, 'Shakespeare's View of Language: An Historical Perspective', *SQ* 29 (1978), 374–83.

——'*The Tempest*: Gratuitous Movement or Action without Kibes and Pinches', *Sh. Studies* 14 (1986), 249–70.

——*Shakespeare Verbatim: The Reproduction of Authenticity and the 1790 Apparatus* (Oxford, 1991).

DERRIDA, JACQUES, *Dissemination*, trans. Barbara Johnson (London, 1981).

——*Positions*, trans. Alan Bass (Chicago, 1981).

——*Writing and Difference*, trans. Alan Bass (London, 1978).

DICKEY, STEPHEN, 'Language and Role in *Pericles*', *ELR* 16 (1986), 550–66.

DIEFENDORF, BARBARA B., 'Family Culture, Renaissance Culture', *RQ* (1987), 661–81.

DOLLIMORE, JONATHAN, 'Shakespeare, Cultural Materialism, Feminism and Marxist Humanism', *NLH* 21 (1989–90), 471–93.

DOLLIMORE, JONATHAN, *Radical Tragedy: Religion, Ideology and Power in the Drama of Shakespeare and his Contemporaries* (1984; 2nd edn., New York, 1989).

DONALDSON, IAN, ed., *Jonson and Shakespeare* (Canberra, 1983).

DOVER, K. J., *Perceptions of the Ancient Greeks* (Oxford, 1992).

DRAKAKIS, JOHN, ed., *Alternative Shakespeares* (London, 1985).

DREHER, DIANE ELIZABETH, *Domination and Defiance: Fathers and Daughters in Shakespeare* (Lexington, Mass., 1986).

DUBROW, HEATHER, and STRIER, RICHARD, eds., *The Historical Renaissance: New Essays on Tudor and Stuart Literature and Culture* (Chicago, 1988).

DUTTON, RICHARD, *Ben Jonson* (Cambridge, 1983).

EAGLETON, TERRY, *William Shakespeare* (Oxford, 1986).

EDWARDS, PHILIP, 'An Approach to the Problem of *Pericles*', *Sh. S* (1952), 25–49.

——EWBANK, INGA-STINA, HUNTER, G. K., eds., *Shakespeare's Style: Essays in Honour of Kenneth Muir* (Cambridge, 1980).

EISENSTEIN, ELIZABETH, *The Printing Press as an Agent of Change: Communications and Cultural Transformations in Early Modern Europe* (Cambridge, 1985).

ELIAR-FELDON, MIRIAM, *Realistic Utopias: The Ideal Imaginary Societies of the Renaissance* (Oxford, 1982).

EMPSON, WILLIAM, *Essays on Shakespeare* (1986; repr. Cambridge, 1988).

——*Some Versions of Pastoral* (1935; repr. London, 1986).

——*The Structure of Complex Words* (1951; repr. London, 1985).

ERICKSON, PETER, *Patriarchal Structures in Shakespeare's Drama* (Berkeley, 1985).

EVANS, BERTRAND, *Shakespeare's Comedies* (Oxford, 1960).

EVANS, MALCOLM, *Signifying Nothing: Truth's True Contents in Shakespeare's Text* (1986; new edn. Brighton, 1990).

EWBANK, INGA-STINA, 'The Triumph of Time in The Winter's Tale', *A Review of English Literature*, 5 (1964), 83–100.

FARRELL, KIRBY, *Shakespeare's Creation* (Amherst, 1975).

FELPERIN, HOWARD, *Beyond Deconstructionism: The Uses and Abuses of Literary Theory* (Oxford, 1985).

——*The Uses of the Canon: Elizabethan Literature and Contemporary Theory* (Oxford, 1990).

FERGUSON, MARGARET W., QUILLIGAN, MAUREEN, and VICKERS, NANCY J., eds., *Rewriting the Renaissance: The Discourses of Sexual Difference in Early Modern Europe* (Chicago, 1986).

FINKELPEARL, PHILIP J., *Court and Country Politics in the Plays of Beaumont and Fletcher* (Princeton, 1990).

FIRTH, KATHARINE R. *The Apocalyptic Tradition in Reformation Britain 1530–1645* (Oxford, 1979).

FLETCHER, ANTHONY, ed., *Order and Disorder in Early-Modern England* (Cambridge, 1985).

FOAKES, R. A., *Shakespeare, the Dark Comedies to the Last Plays* (Charlottesville, Va., 1971).

FOUCAULT, MICHEL, 'The Subject and Power', *Critical Inquiry* 8 (1982), 777–90.

FREUD, SIGMUND, *Jokes And Their Relation to the Unconscious*, trans. and ed. James Strachey (1905; London, 1976).

——*Art and Literature*, trans. and ed. James Strachey (1985; repr. London, 1988).

FREY, CHARLES H., ed., *Shakespeare, Fletcher, and The Two Noble Kinsmen* (Columbia, 1989).

FROST, DAVID L., ' "Mouldy Tales": The Context of Shakespeare's *Cymbeline*', *Essays and Studies* (1986), 23–37.

FRYE, NORTHROP, *A Natural Perspective: The Development of Shakespearean Comedy and Romance* (New York, 1965).

——*Anatomy of Criticism: Four Essays* (Princeton, 1957).

——*The Secular Scripture: A Study of Romance* (Cambridge, Mass., 1976).

FULTON, R. C., *Shakespeare and the Masque* (New York, 1988).

GASPER, JULIA, *The Dragon and the Dove: The Plays of Thomas Dekker* (Oxford, 1990).

GAYLEY, CHARLES MILLS, *Shakespeare and the Founders of Liberty in America* (New York, 1917).

GESNER, CAROL, *Shakespeare and the Greek Romance: A Study of Origins* (Lexington, Ky., 1970).

GIBBONS, BRIAN, *Shakespeare and Multiplicity* (Cambridge, 1993).

GILLIES, JOHN, 'Shakespeare's Virginian Masque', *ELH* 53 (1986), 673–708.

——*Shakespeare and the Geography of Difference* (Cambridge, 1994).

GOLDSTONE, JACK A., *Revolution and Rebellion in the Early Modern World* (Berkeley, 1991).

GRANVILLE-BARKER, H., *Prefaces to Shakespeare, Second Series* (London, 1930).

GREEN, ANDRÉ, *The Tragic Effect: The Oedipus Complex in Tragedy*, trans. A. Sheridan (Cambridge, 1977).

GREENBLATT, STEPHEN J., *Learning to Curse: Essays in Early Modern Culture* (New York, 1990).

——*Renaissance Self-Fashioning: From More to Shakespeare* (Chicago, 1980).

——*Shakespearean Negotiations: The Circulation of Social Energy in Renaissance England* (1988; repr. Oxford, 1990).

GREENE, GAYLE, and KAHN, COPPÉLIA, eds., *Making a Difference: Feminist Literary Criticism* (1985; repr. London, 1988).

GREENE, THOMAS M., *The Vulnerable Text: Essays on Renaissance Literature* (New York, 1986).

GREG, W. W., *The Shakespeare First Folio: Its Bibliographical and Textual History* (Oxford, 1955).

GRUNDY, JOAN, *The Spenserian Poets: A Study in Elizabethan and Jacobean Poetry* (London, 1969).

GUILLEN, CLAUDIO, *Literature as System: Essays toward the Theory of Literary History* (Princeton, 1971).

GURR, ANDREW, 'The Bear, the Statue, and Hysteria in *The Winter's Tale*', *SQ* 34 (1983), 420–5.

——*Playgoing in Shakespeare's London* (Cambridge, 1987).

HALPERIN, RICHARD, *The Poetics of Primitive Accumulation: English Renaissance Culture and the Genealogy of Capital* (Ithaca, NY, 1991).

HAMILTON, DONNA B., *Shakespeare and the Politics of Protestant England* (London, 1992).

——*Virgil and The Tempest: The Politics of Imitation* (Columbus, Oh., 1990).

——'*The Winter's Tale* and the Language of Union, 1604–1610', *Sh. Studies*, 21 (1993), 228–50.

HARARI, JOSUÉ V., ed., *Textual Strategies: Perspective in Post-Structuralist Criticism* (Ithaca, NY, 1979).

HARDMAN, C. B., 'Theory, Form, and Meaning in Shakespeare's *The Winter's Tale*', *RES* 36 (1985), 228–35.

HARTWIG, JOAN, *Shakespeare's Analogical Scene: Parody as Structural Syntax* (Lincoln, Neb., 1983).

——*Shakespeare's Tragicomic Vision* (Baton Rouge, La., 1972).

HARVEY, ELIZABETH D., *Ventriloquized Voices: Feminist Theory and English Renaissance Texts* (London, 1992).

HEALY, THOMAS, and SAWDAY, JONATHAN, eds., *Literature and the English Civil War* (Cambridge, 1990).

HELMS, LORRAINE, 'The Saint in the Brothel: Or, Eloquence Rewarded', *SQ* 41 (1990), 319–32.

HEXTER, J. H., *Parliament and Liberty from the Reign of Elizabeth to the English Civil War* (Stanford, Calif., 1992).

HILL, CHRISTOPHER, *Change and Continuity in Seventeenth Century England* (London, 1974).

——*Intellectual Origins of the English Revolution* (Oxford, 1965).

HILLMAN, RICHARD, 'Shakespeare's Gower and Gower's Shakespeare: The Larger Debt of *Pericles*', *SQ* 36 (1985), 427–37.

HILLMAN, RICHARD, *Shakespearean Subversions: The Trickster and the Play-text* (London, 1992).

HOENIGER, F. D., 'Gower and Shakespeare in *Pericles*', *SQ* 33 (1982), 461–80.

HOLDERNESS, GRAHAM, *Shakespeare Recycled: The Making of Historical Drama* (Hemel Hempstead, 1992).

——POTTER, NICK, and TURNER, JOHN, *Out of Court: Dramatizations of Court Society* (Baringstoke, 1990).

————*Shakespeare: The Play of History* (Iowa City, 1987).

HOLLANDER, JOHN, *The Untuning of the Sky: Ideas of Music in English Poetry 1500–1700* (Princeton, 1961).

HOWARD, JEAN E., 'Crossdressing, the Theatre, and Gender Struggle', *SQ* 39 (1988), 418–40.

HULME, PETER, *Colonialist Encounters: Europe and the Native Caribbean 1492–1797* (New York, 1986).

HUNT, MAURICE, *Shakespeare's Romance of the Word* (Lewisburg, Pa., 1990).

HUNTER, G. K., *Dramatic Identities and Cultural Tradition: Studies in Shakespeare and his Contemporaries* (Liverpool, 1978).

HUTSON, LORNA, *Thomas Nashe in Context* (Oxford, 1989).

JAFRI, S. NAQI HUSAIN, *Aspects of Drayton's Poetry* (Delhi, 1988).

JAMES, MERVYN, *Society, Politics, and Culture: Studies in Early Modern England* (Cambridge, 1986).

JAMESON, FREDRIC, *The Political Unconscious: Narrative as a Socially Symbolic Act* (1981; repr. London, 1986).

JARDINE, ALICE, *Gynesis: Configurations of Woman and Modernity* (Ithaca, NY, 1985).

JEFFERSON, D. W., ed., *The Morality of Art: Essays Presented to G. Wilson Knight* (London, 1969).

JOHNSON, SAMUEL, *Johnson on Shakespeare*, ed. Walter Raleigh (Oxford, 1908; repr. 1959).

JONES, EMRYS, 'Stuart *Cymbeline*', *Essays in Criticism*, 11 (1961), 84–99.

——*The Origins of Shakespeare* (Oxford, 1977).

——*Scenic Form in Shakespeare* (Oxford, 1971).

JONES, JOHN, *Shakespeare at Work* (Oxford, 1995).

JUNG, C. G., and KERENYI, K., *Science of Mythology: Essays on the Myth of the Divine Child and the Mysteries of Eleusis* (1949; repr. London, 1985).

KAHN, COPPÉLIA, *Man's Estate: Masculine Identity in Shakespeare* (Berkeley, 1981).

KAHN, VICTORIA, *Machiavellian Rhetoric: From the Counter-Reformation to Milton* (Princeton, 1994).

——*Rhetoric, Prudence, and Skepticism in the Renaissance* (Ithaca, NY, 1985).

KAY, CAROL MCGINNIS, and JACOBS, HENRY E., eds., *Shakespeare's Romances Reconsidered* (Lincoln, Neb., 1978).

KEHLER, DOROTHEA, and BAKER, SUSAN, eds., *In Another Country: Feminist Perspectives on Renaissance Drama* (Metuchen, NJ, 1991).

KETTLE, ARNOLD ed., *Shakespeare in a Changing World: Essays* (London, 1964).

KINNEY, ARTHUR F., and editors of *ELR*, *Sidney in Retrospect: Selections from 'English Literary Renaissance'* (Amherst, 1988).

KNAPP, ROBERT S., *Shakespeare: The Theater and the Book* (Princeton, 1989).

KNIGHT, G. WILSON, *The Crown of Life: Essays in Interpretation of Shakespeare's Final Plays* (London, 1947).

KNIGHTS, L. C., *Drama & Society in the Age of Jonson* (1937; repr. London, 1962).

KNOWLES, RICHARD P., ' "Wishes Fall out as They're Will'd": Artist, Audience, and *Pericles*' Gower', *English Studies in Canada*, 9 (1983), 14–24.

KNOWLSON, JAMES, *Universal Language Schemes in England and France 1600–1800* (Toronto, 1975).

KRISTEVA, JULIA, *Revolution and Poetic Language*, trans. Margaret Waller (New York, 1984).

KURLAND, STUART M. ' "We need no more of your advice": Political Realism in *The Winter's Tale*', *SEL* 31 (1991), 365–86.

LACAN, JACQUES, *Écrits: A Selection*, trans. Alan Sheridan (1977; repr. London, 1989).

LANDRY, D. E., 'Dreams as History: The Strange Unity of *Cymbeline*', *SQ* 33 (1982), 69–77.

LANHAM, RICHARD A., *A Handbook of Rhetorical Terms* (Berkeley, 1968).

LAROQUE, FRANÇOIS, *Shakespeare's Festive World: Elizabethan Seasonal Entertainment and the Professional Stage*, trans. Janet Lloyd (Cambridge, 1991).

LAWRY, J. S., ' "Perishing Root and Increasing Vine" in *Cymbeline*', *Sh. Studies*, 12 (1984), 179–93.

LEGGATT, ALEXANDER, '*Henry VIII* and the Ideal England', *Sh. S* 38 (1985), 131–43.

——*Jacobean Public Theatre* (London, 1992).

LENTRICCHIA, FRANK, *Criticism and Social Change* (Chicago, 1983).

LEVAO, RONALD, *Renaissance Minds and their Fictions* (Berkeley, 1985).

LEVIN, HARRY, *The Myth of the Golden Age in the Renaissance* (London, 1970).

LEWALSKI, BARBARA KIEFER, *Writing Women in Jacobean England* (Cambridge, Mass., 1993).

——ed., *Renaissance Genres: Essays on Theory, History, and Interpretation* (Cambridge, Mass., 1986).

LEWIS, CYNTHIA, ' "With Simular Proof": Modes of Misperception in *Cymbeline*', *SEL* 31 (1991).

LIEF, MADELON, and RADEL, NICHOLAS F., 'Linguistic Subversion and the Artifice of Rhetoric in *The Two Noble Kinsmen*', *SQ* 38 (1987), 405–25.

LINDENBAUM, PETER, *Changing Landscapes: Anti-Pastoral Sentiment in the English Renaissance* (Athens, Ga., 1986).

LINDLEY, DAVID, ed., *The Court Masque* (Manchester, 1984).

LIVINGSTONE, MARY L., 'The Natural Art of *The Winter's Tale*', *MLQ* 30 (1969), 340–55.

LOCKYER, ROGER, *The Early Stuarts: A Political History of England 1603–1642* (London, 1989).

LOEWENSTEIN, DAVID, *Milton and the Drama of History: Historical Vision, Iconoclasm, and the Literary Imagination* (Cambridge, 1990).

——and TURNER, JAMES GRANTHAM, *Politics, Poetics, and Hermeneutics in Milton's Prose* (Cambridge, 1990).

LOGAN, GEORGE M., and TESKEY, GORDON, eds., *Unfolded Tales: Essays on Renaissance Romance* (Ithaca, NY, 1989).

LOUGHREY, BRYAN, ed., *The Pastoral Mode* (London, 1984).

LOW, ANTHONY, *The Georgic Revolution* (Princeton, 1985).

MCALINDON, T. A., *Shakespeare and Decorum* (London, 1973).

MCCOY, RICHARD C., *Sir Philip Sidney: Rebellion in Arcadia* (Brighton, 1979).

——*The Rites of Knighthood: The Literature and Politics of Elizabethan Chivalry* (Berkeley, 1989).

MCDONALD, RUSS, 'Reading *The Tempest*', *Sh. S* 43 (1990), 15–28.

MACHEREY, PIERRE, *A Theory of Literary Production*, trans. Geoffrey Wall (London, 1978).

MACK, PETER, ed., *Renaissance Rhetoric* (Basingstoke, 1994).

MCLUHAN, MARSHALL, *The Gutenberg Galaxy: The Making of Typographic Man* (London, 1962).

MCLUSKIE, KATHLEEN, *Renaissance Dramatists* (Hemel Hempstead, 1989).

MCMULLAN, GORDON, and HOPE, JONATHAN, eds., *The Politics of Tragicomedy: Shakespeare and after* (London, 1992).

MAGUIRE, NANCY KLEIN, *Renaissance Tragicomedy: Explorations in Genre and Politics* (New York, 1987).

MAHOOD, M. M., *Shakespeare's Word Play* (London, 1957).

MANNING, ROGER B., *Village Revolts: Social Protest and Popular Disturbances in England 1509–1640* (Oxford, 1988).

MARCUS, LEAH S., *The Politics of Mirth: Jonson, Herrick, Milton, Marvell and the Defense of Old Holiday Pastimes* (Chicago, 1986).

——*Puzzling Shakespeare: Local Reading and Its Discontents* (Berkeley, 1988).

MARSHALL, CYNTHIA, *Last Things and Last Plays: Shakespearean Echatology* (Carbondale, 1991).

MARTINDALE, CHARLES, and MARTINDALE, MICHELLE, *Shakespeare and the Uses of Antiquity: An Introductory Essay* (London, 1990).

MIKO, STEPHEN J., 'Winter's Tale' *SEL* 29 (1989), 259–76.

MILES, GEOFFREY, *Shakespeare and the Constant Romans* (Oxford, 1996).

MILLER, DAVID LEE, *The Poem's Two Bodies: The Poetics of the 1590 Faerie Queene* (Princeton, 1988).

MIOLA, ROBERT S., *Shakespeare's Rome* (Cambridge, 1983).

MOI, TORIL, ed., *Sexual/Textual Politics: Feminist Literary Theory* (1985; repr. London, 1988).

——ed., *The Kristeva Reader* (Oxford, 1986).

MONTROSE, LOUIS, ' "Eliza, Queene of shepheardes" and the Pastoral of Power', *ELR* 10 (1980), 113–82.

MORETTI, FRANCO, *Signs Taken for Wonders: Essays in the Sociology of Literary Forms*, trans. Susan Fischer et al. (London, 1983).

MORGAN, EDMUND S., *American Slavery: American Freedom: The Ordeal of Colonial Virginia* (New York, 1975).

MUIR, KENNETH, ed., *The Winter's Tale: Casebook* (Glasgow, 1968).

MULLANEY, STEPHEN, *The Place of the Stage: License, Play, and Power in Renaissance England* (Chicago, 1988).

MURRAY, TIMOTHY, *Theatrical Legitimation: Allegories of Genius in Seventeenth-Century England and France* (New York, 1987).

MUSGROVE, STEPHEN, 'The First Quarts of *Pericles* Reconsidered', *SQ* 29 (1978), 389–406.

NEELY, CAROL THOMAS, 'Constructing the Subject: Feminist Practice and the New Renaissance Discourses', *ELR* 18 (1988), 5–18.

——*Broken Nuptials in Shakespeare's Plays* (New Haven, 1985).

NEVO, RUTH, *Shakespeare's Other Language* (New York, 1987).

NEWEY, VINCENT, and THOMPSON, ANN, eds., *Literature and Nationalism* (Liverpool, 1990).

NEWTON, JUDITH, and ROSENFELT, DEBORAH, eds., *Feminist Criticism and Social Change: Sex, Class and Race in Literature and Culture* (New York, 1985).

NIETZSCHE, FRIEDRICH, *On the Geneology of Morals/Ecce Homo*, trans. Walter Kaufman (New York, 1969).

——*The Birth of Tragedy and the Case of Wagner*, trans. Walter Kaufmann (New York, 1967).

NORBROOK, DAVID, *Poetry and Politics in the English Renaissance* (London, 1984).

NORRIS, CHRISTOPHER, *Derrida* (London, 1987).

NOVY, MARIANNE, *Love's Argument: Gender Relations in Shakespeare* (Chapel Hill, NC, 1984).

ORGEL, STEPHEN, *The Jonsonian Masque* (Cambridge, Mass., 1965).

OVERTON, BILL, *The Winter's Tale* (London, 1989).

——*The Oxford Classical Dictionary* (Oxford, 1949).

PAGDEN, ANTHONY, *Spanish Imperialism and the Political Imagination: Studies in European and Spanish-American Social and Political Theory 1513–1830* (New Haven, 1990).

——*The Fall of Natural Man: The American Indian and the Origins of Comparative Ethnology* (Cambridge, 1982).

PARKER, G. F., *Johnson's Shakespeare* (Oxford, 1989).

PARKER, PATRICIA, and QUINT, DAVID, eds., *Literary Theory/Renaissance Texts* (Baltimore, 1986).

——*Inescapable Romance: Studies in the Poetics of a Mode* (Princeton, 1979).

PARKER, PATRICA, *Literary Fat Ladies: Rhetoric, Gender, Property* (New York, 1987).

——*Shakespeare from the Margins: Language, Culture, Context* (Chicago, 1996).

PARRY, GRAHAM, *The Golden Age Restor'd: The Culture of the Stuart Court 1603–42* (Manchester, 1981).

PARTRIDGE, ERIC, *Shakespeare's Bawdy: A Literary and Psychological Essay and a Comprehensive Glossary* (1947; rev. edn. London, 1968).

PATRIDES, C. A., and WITTREICH, JOSEPH, eds., *The Apocalypse in English Renaissance Thought and Literature: Patterns, Antecedents and Repercussions* (Manchester, 1984).

PATTERSON, ANNABEL, *Censorship and Interpretation: The Conditions of Writing and Reading in Early Modern England* (Madison, 1984).

——*Fables of Power: Aesopian Writing and Political History* (Durham, 1991).

——*Pastoral and Ideology: From Virgil to Valéry* (Oxford, 1988).

PATTERSON, ANNABEL, *Shakespeare and the Popular Voice* (Oxford, 1989).

PEARSON, D'ORSAY W., 'Witchcraft in *The Winter's Tale*: Paulina as "Alcahueta y vn Poquito Hechizera"', *Sh. Studies* 15 (1982), 195–213.

PENNINGTON, DONALD, and THOMAS, KEITH, eds., *Puritans and Revolutionaries: Essays in Seventeenth Century History Presented to Christopher Hill* (Oxford, 1978).

PETTET, E. C., *Shakespeare and the Romance Tradition* (London, 1970).

PHILLIPS, MARGARET MANN, *The 'Adages' of Erasmus: A Study with Translations* (Cambridge, 1964).

PIGGOTT, STUART, *Ancient Britons and the Antiquarian Imagination: Ideas from the Renaissance to the Regency* (London, 1989).

PITCHER, JOHN, 'A Theatre of the Future: *The Aeneid* and *The Tempest*', *Essays in Criticism*, 34 (1984), 193–215.

——'The Poet and Taboo: The Riddle of Shakespeare's *Pericles*', *Essays and Studies* (1982), 14–29.

POCOCK, J. G. A., *Politics, Language and Time: Essays on Political Thought and History* (London, 1972).

——*The Machiavellian Moment: Florentine Political Thought and the Atlantic Republican Tradition* (Princeton, 1975).

POOLE, ADRIAN, *Tragedy: Shakespeare and the Greek Example* (Oxford, 1987).

PORTER, CAROLYN, 'Are We Being Historical Yet?', *South Atlantic Quarterly*, 87 (1988), 743–86.

PRIOR, MARY, ed., *Women in English Society 1500–1800* (London, 1985).

QUAIFE, G. R., *Wanton Wenches and Wayward Wives: Peasants and Illicit Sex in Early Seventeenth Century England* (London, 1979).

RAAB, FELIX, *The English Face of Machiavelli: A Changing Interpretation 1500–1700* (London, 1964).

RABKIN, NORMAN, *Shakespeare and the Problem of Meaning* (Chicago, 1981).

REAY, BARRY, ed., *Popular Culture in Seventeenth-Century England* (London, 1985).

REDFERN, WALTER, *Puns* (Oxford, 1984).

REISS, TIMOTHY, *The Discourse of Modernism* (Ithaca, NY, 1982).

ROBERTS, JEANNE ADDISON, *The Shakespearean Wild: Geography, Genus, and Gender* (Lincoln, 1991).

RODGERS, C. P., 'Humanism, History and the Common Law', *JLH* 6 (1985), 129–57.

ROMANY, FRANK, 'Shakespeare and the New Historicism', *Essays in Criticism*, 39 (1989), 271–88.

ROSE MARY BETH, ed., *Women in the Middle Ages and Renaissance* (Syracuse, 1986).

ROWSE, A. L., *Simon Forman: Sex and Society in Shakespeare's Age* (London, 1974).

RUBINSTEIN, FRANKIE, *A Dictionary of Shakespeare's Sexual Puns and their Significance* (1984; 2nd edn. Basingstoke, 1989).

RUDNYTSKY, PETER L., 'Henry VIII and the Deconstruction of History', *Sh. S* 43 (1992), 43–58.

RUSSELL, CONRAD, *The Crisis of Parliaments: English History 1509–1660* (Oxford, 1971).

RUSSELL, D. A., and WINTERBOTTOM, M. eds., *Classical Literary Criticism*, trans. D. A. Russell (1972; rev. edn. Oxford, 1989).

RUTH NEVO, *Shakespeare's Other Language* (New York, 1987).

RUTHVEN, K. K., *Feminist Literary Studies: An Introduction* (Cambridge, 1984).

RYAN, KIERNAN, *Shakespeare* (New York, 1989).

SACKS, DAVID HARRIS, 'Searching for "Culture" in the English Renaissance', *SQ* 39 (1988), 465–88.

SAID, EDWARD, *Literature and Society: Selected Papers from the English Institute, 1978* (Baltimore, 1980).

SALGADO, GAMINI, ed., *The Elizabethan Underworld* (London, 1977).

SALMON, J. H. M., 'Stoicism and the Roman Example: Seneca and Tacitus in Jacobean England', *Journal of the History of Ideas*, 50 (1989), 199–226.

SALUSINSKY, IMRE, *Criticism in Society* (New York, 1987).

SALZMAN, PAUL, *English Prose Fiction 1558–1700: A Critical History* (Oxford, 1985).

SAMAHA, JOEL, 'Gleamings from Local Criminal-Court Records: Sedition amongst the 'Inarticulate' in Elizabethan Essex', *Journal of Social History*, 8 (1974–75), 61–80.

SCAGLIONE, ALDO, *Knights at Court: Courtliness, Chivalry, and Courtesy from Ottoman Germany to the Italian Renaissance* (Berkeley, 1991).

SCHANZER, ERNEST, 'Heywood's *Ages* and Shakespeare', *RES* 11 (1960), 18–28.

SCHOENBAUM, S., *William Shakespeare: A Compact Documentary Life* (1977; new edn. Oxford, 1987).

SCHWARTZ, MURRAY M., and KAHN, COPPÉLIA, eds., *Representing Shakespeare: New Psychoanalytic Essays* (Baltimore, 1980).

SCOTT-KILVERT, IAN, *The Rise and Fall of Athens* (Bristol, 1987).

SHARPE, KEVIN, *Politics and Ideas in Early Stuart England: Essays and Studies* (London, 1989).

——and ZWICKER, STEPHEN N., eds., *Politics of Discourse: The*

Literature and History of Seventeenth-Century England (Berkeley, 1987).

SHEEHAN, BERNARD W., *Savagism and Civility: Indians and Englishmen in Colonial Virginia* (Cambridge, 1980).

SHEPHERD, SIMON, *Amazons and Warrior Women: Varieties of Feminism in Seventeenth Century Drama* (Brighton, 1981).

SHERIDAN, ALAN, *Michel Foucault: The Will To Truth* (London, 1980).

SHIRLEY, F. J., *Richard Hooker and Contemporary Political Ideas* (London, 1949).

SHIRLEY, FRANCES A., *Swearing and Perjury in Shakespeare's Plays* (London, 1979).

SHUGG, WALLACE, 'Prostitution in Shakespeare's London', *Sh. S* 10 (1977), 291–313.

SIEMON, JAMES EDWARD, 'Noble Virtue in *Cymbeline*', *Sh. S* 29 (1976).

SIMONDS, PEGGY MUNÔZ, 'The Marriage Topos in *Cymbeline*: Shakespeare's Variations on a Classical Theme', *ELR* 19 (1989), 94–117.

SINFIELD, ALAN, *Faultlines: Cultural Materialism and the Politics of Dissident Reading* (Oxford, 1992).

SINGER, THOMAS C., 'Hieroglyphs in the Seventeenth Century', *Journal of the History of Ideas*, 50 (1989), 50–60.

SKURA, MEREDITH ANNE, 'Discourse and the Individual: The Case of Colonialism in *The Tempest*', *SQ* 40 (1989), 42–69.

SMITH, HALLETT, *Shakespeare's Romances. A Study of Some Ways of the Imagination* (San Marino, Calif., 1972).

SMITH, IRWIN, *Shakespeare's Blackfriars Playhouse: Its History and Design* (New York, 1964).

SMITH, NIGEL, 'The Two Economies of *Measure for Measure*', *English*, 36 (1987).

SMUTS, R. MALCOLM, *Court Culture and the Origins of a Royalist Tradition in Early Stuart England* (Philadelphia, 1987).

SOMMERVILLE, J. P., *Politics and Ideology in England 1603–1640* (London, 1986).

SPEVACK, MARTIN, *The Harvard Concordance to Shakespeare* (Hildeshein, 1973).

STALLYBRASS, PETER and WHITE, ALLON, *The Politics and Poetics of Transgression* (London, 1986).

STARNES, D. T. and TALBERT, E. W., *Classical Myth and Legend in Renaissance Dictionaries* (Chapel Hill, NC, 1955).

STEINER, GEORGE, *Language and Silence* (1967; repr. London, 1990).
——*Real Presences* (1989; repr. London, 1991).

STOCKTON, DAVID, *The Classical Athenian Democracy* (Oxford, 1990).

STONE, LAWRENCE, *The Family, Sex and Marriage in England 1500–1800* (London, 1977).

STRONG, ROY, *Art and Power: Renaissance Festivals 1450–1650* (Woodbridge, 1984).

—— *Henry, Prince of Wales and England's Lost Renaissance* (London, 1986).

TANNER, J. R., *Constitutional Documents of the Reign of James I 1603–1625* (Cambridge, 1930).

TAYLOR, GARY, 'The Transmission of *Pericles*', *Papers of the Bibliographical Sociely of America* (1986), 193–217.

TAYLOR, MICHAEL, 'The Pastoral Reckoning in *Cymbeline*', *Sh. S* 36 (1983).

—— '"Here is a thing too young for such a place": Innocence in *Pericles*', *Ariel*, 13 (1982), 3–19.

TAYLOR, RUPERT, *The Political Prophecy in England* (1911; repr. New York, 1967).

TERRILL, R. J., 'Humanism and Rhetoric in Legal Education: The Contribution of Sir John Dodderidge (1555–1628)', *JLH* 2 (1981), 30–44.

THIRSK, JOAN, *Economic Policy and Projects: The Development of a Consumer Society in Early Modern England* (1978; repr. Oxford, 1988).

THOMAS, KEITH, 'Age and Authority in Early Modern England', *From the Proceedings of the British Academy*, 62 (London, 1976).

—— 'The Perception of the Past in Early Modern England', the Creighton Trust Lecture, 1983.

—— 'The Place of Laughter in Tudor and Stuart England', *TLS* (1977), 77–80.

—— *Man and the Natural World: Changing Attitudes in England 1500–1800* (London, 1983).

—— *Religion and the Decline of Magic* (1971; repr. Harmondsworth, 1984).

THOMAS, SIDNEY, 'The Problem of *Pericles*, *SQ* 34 (1983), 448–50.

THOMPSON, E. P., 'The Moral Economy of the English Crowd in the Eighteenth Century', *P&P* 50 (1971), 76–136.

TILLYARD, E. M. W., *Shakespeare's Last Plays* (1938; repr. London, 1968).

—— *The Elizabethan World Picture* (1943; repr. Harmondsworth, 1970).

TOMPKINS, J. M. S., 'Why *Pericles*?', *RES* 3 (1952), 315–24.

TRAUB, VALERIE, *Desire and Anxiety: Circulations of Sexuality in Shakespearean Drama* (London, 1992).

TRAVERSI, DEREK, *Shakespeare: The Last Phase* (1954; repr. London, 1965).

TREVOR-ROPER, HUGH, *Catholics, Anglicans and Puritans: Seventeenth-Century Essays* (London, 1987).

——*Renaissance Essays* (London, 1986).

TRIPP, EDWARD, *Dictionary of Classical Mythology* (London, 1988).

TURNER, FREDERICK, *Shakespeare and the Nature Of Time* (Oxford, 1971).

UNDERDOWN, DAVID, *Revel, Riot, and Rebellion: Popular Politics and Culture in England 1603–1660* (Oxford, 1985).

VAUGHAN, ALDEN T., and VAUGHAN, VIRGINIA MASON, *Shakespeare's Caliban: A Cultural History* (Cambridge, 1991).

VEESER, H. ARAM, ed., *The New Historicism* (New York, 1989).

VICKERS, BRIAN, *The Artistry of Shakespeare's Prose* (London, 1968).

——ed., *Shakespeare: The Critical Heritage*, ii: *1693–1753* (London, 1974).

VINAVER, EUGENE, *The Rise of Romance* (1971; repr. Cambridge, 1984).

VON ROASADER, KURT TETZELI, 'The Power of Magic: From Endimion to *The Tempest*', *Sh. S* 43 (1990), 1–13.

WALKER, D. P., *Music, Spirit and Language in the Renaissance*, ed. Penelope Gouk (London, 1985).

WARNER, REX, *Pericles the Athenian* (London, 1963).

WARREN, ROGER, *Cymbeline* (Manchester, 1989).

WAYNE, VALERIE, ed., *The Matter of Difference: Materialist Feminist Criticism of Shakespeare* (New York, 1991).

WEIMANN, ROBERT, *Shakespeare and the Popular Tradition in the Theater*, ed. R. Schwartz (Baltimore, 1978).

WELLS, STANLEY, TAYLOR, GARY, JOWETT, JOHN, and MONTGOMERY, WILLIAM, eds., *William Shakespeare: A Textual Companion* (Oxford, 1986).

WELSFORD, ENID, *The Fool: His Social and Literary History* (London, 1935).

WHITNEY, CHARLES, 'Francis Bacon's Instauratio: Dominion of and over Humanity', *JHI* 50 (1989), 371–90.

WICKHAM, GLYNNE, 'Shakespeare's Investiture Play: The Occasion and Subject of *The Winter's Tale*', *TLS* 18 Dec. (1969), 1456.

——'From Tragedy to Tragi-comedy: *King Lear* as Prologue', *Sh. S* 26 (1973), 33–48.

WILLIAMS, RAYMOND, *Keywords: A Vocabulary of Culture and Soci-*

ety (1976; repr. London, 1988).

WILLIAMSON, ARTHUR H., *Scottish National Consciousness in the Age of James VI: The Apocalypse, the Union and the Shaping of Scotland's Public Culture* (Edinburgh, 1979).

WILLIAMSON, MARILYN L., *The Patriarchy of Shakespeare's Comedies* (Detroit, 1986).

WILSON, F. P., *Shakespeare and other Studies*, ed. Helen Gardner (Oxford, 1969).

WIMSATT, W. K., *Dr. Johnson on Shakespeare* (Harmondsworth, 1960).

WOOD, JAMES O., 'Shakespeare and the Belching Whale', *English Language Notes*, 11 (1973), 40–4.

WOODBRIDGE, LINDA, *Women and the English Renaissance: Literature and the Nature of Womanhood 1540–1620* (Urbana, IU., 1984).

WOOLF, D. R., 'Erudition and the Idea of History in Renaissance England', *RQ* 40 (1987), 11–49.

——'The "Common Voice": History, Folklore and Oral Tradition in Early Modern England', *P&P* 120 (1988), 26–53.

——*The Idea of History in Early Stuart England: Erudition, Ideology and 'The Light of Truth' from the Accession of James I to the Civil War* (Toronto, 1990).

WORDEN, BLAIR, ed., *Stuart England* (Oxford, 1986).

WRIGHT, ELIZABETH, *Psychoanalytic Criticism: Theory in Practice* (1984; repr. London, 1987).

WRIGHT, LOUIS. B., *Middle Class Culture in Elizabethan England* (1935; repr. Ithaca, NY, 1958).

YATES, FRANCES A., *Ideas And Ideals in the North European Renaissance: Collected Essays*, 3 vols. (London, 1984).

——*Astraea: The Imperial Theme in the Sixteenth Century* (London, 1975).

——*Shakespeare's Last Plays: A New Approach* (London, 1975).

YEATS, W. B., *Essays and Introductions* (1961; repr. London, 1989).

ZAGORIN, PEREZ, *The Court and the Country: The Beginning of the English Revolution* (London, 1969).

Index